Creationism, Curriculum, and the Constitution

Effects of the Scopes Trial

Was it a victory for evolutionists?

Creationism in Many Illinois Schools

Scholarship

Pervasive Belief in 'Creation Science' Dismays and Perplexes Researchers

They reject arguments that it deserves equal time with evolution in the classroom

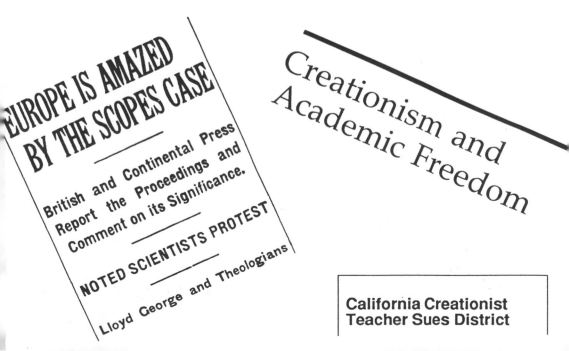

EUROPE IS AMAZED BY THE SCOPES CASE

British and Continental Press Report the Proceedings and Comment on its Significance.

NOTED SCIENTISTS PROTEST

Lloyd George and Theologians

Creationism and Academic Freedom

California Creationist Teacher Sues District

THE
EVOLUTION
CONTROVERSY
IN AMERICA

THE
EVOLUTION
CONTROVERSY
IN AMERICA

George E. Webb

THE UNIVERSITY PRESS OF KENTUCKY

Library of Congress Cataloging-in-Publication Data
Webb, George Ernest.
    The evolution controversy in America / George E. Webb.
        p.   cm.
    Includes bibliographical references (p.   ) and index.
    ISBN 0-8131-1864-6 (acid-free)
        1. Evolution (Biology)—Religious aspects—Christianity—History.
2. Religion and science—United States—History.   3. Creationism—
United States—History.   4. Evolution (Biology)—History
I. Title.
BT712.W43   1994
231.7′65—dc20   93-45410

APR. O 3 1995

For Mark

Contents

Preface

The doorbell rang shortly after five o'clock. I had just returned from campus, where my teaching duties included a lecture course in the history of American science. As it was late in the quarter, topics had focused on the place of science in contemporary American life. One of the issues I had covered that day, in what I thought was a prudent and dispassionate fashion, was the ongoing opposition to the teaching of evolution in the public schools. In an attempt to show how the American public's erroneous view of science led to widespread support for such opposition, my lecture had stressed the scientific weaknesses in "creation science" explanations. Pointing out creationists' questionable use of such concepts as entropy and their insistence on defining science as little more than a collection of "facts," I concluded that creation science did not represent science as it was practiced in the late twentieth century. Instead, as had been emphasized by recent court decisions, it represented a specific religious view.

Imagine my surprise when, upon answering the door, I found that one of the students who had been in class that day had followed me home. While I attempted to regain my composure, he announced that he wanted to talk to me about the day's lecture in an effort to show me how wrong I was in my "atheistic" ways. "You're obviously not a Christian," he told me, "so what gives you the right to criticize my beliefs?" By this time my brain and my voice had become reacquainted, so I was able to suggest that my apartment was hardly the place for such a discussion. He agreed to come by my office during scheduled hours to discuss the matter.

A few days later he appeared in my office. Although the student remained short of abusive, it was clear that his beliefs would not tolerate any ideas that challenged his view of the literal truth of the Bible, including a six-day creation that took place some six thousand years ago. My rejection of that view, obvious from my lecture on creationism, branded me as an atheist. "Wait a minute," I said, after listening to the traditional creationist litany for some five minutes. "Do you really think you have the right to judge someone else as an atheist?" "Of course I do," he retorted. "Christ gave me that right." The conversation ended shortly thereafter.

Quite apart from this young man's questionable theology, his devotion to the creationist cause troubled me greatly. It was not the first time that a creationist student had attempted to challenge discussions in my history of science course that provided a favorable reading of the Darwinian revolution. A few years before, in fact, two students who were secondary education-biology majors made it quite clear that when they began teaching in the public schools they would not present anything other than creationist orthodoxy. What troubled me was that the controversy surrounding the theory of evolution remained a contentious one, even in the supposedly intellectual confines of an American university. What was it about the theory that precipitated such vituperative and long-lasting opposition? Admittedly, in the few years after publication of *Origin of Species,* coming to terms with the new idea proved difficult. Darwin had, after all, fundamentally changed the way we looked at nature and our place in it. But that was more than a century ago. Similarly, I had always assumed, the antievolution crusade of the 1920s, associated with the figure of William Jennings Bryan, represented a historical artifact of a disappearing rural America. But that was half a century ago, and the United States was no longer rural. Why, in the 1980s, after decades of scientific research that confirmed and expanded Darwin's original hypothesis, did large numbers of Americans embrace a worldview that rejected the results of that research?

It soon became clear that understanding the creationist phenomenon could involve a number of different approaches. In *God's Own Scientists* (1994), anthropologist Christopher Toumey examined creation science as a social phenomenon, providing significant insight concerning the movement's role in the religious conservatism of the 1970s and 1980s. Similar analysis by sociologist Raymond A. Eve and anthropologist Francis B. Harrold can be found in *The Creationist Movement in Modern America* (1990). Emphasizing the various factions within the movement, this volume nonetheless describes common themes and characteristics of creation science. Edward J. Larson's *Trial and Error: The American Controversy Over Creation and Evolution* (1985) describes the clash as it relates to public education and the legal confrontations which have attracted significant public attention. In *The Creationists* (1992), historian of science Ronald L. Numbers provides an intellectual history of creationism that stresses the discontinuity between earlier antievolutionists and contemporary creationists. The resurrection of flood geology and "young earth" concepts by Henry M. Morris and others provided a more specific definition of creationism and led to the emergence of creation science.

Although the internal divisions within creationism and the differences between contemporary and earlier antievolution sentiment are important, a historical survey of the American controversy over evolution provides an equally valuable perspective. By focusing on the public campaigns of antievolutionists, one sees the emergence of common themes. From my earliest perusal of the existing literature, it became obvious that significant continuity existed from the initial opponents of Darwin through the antievolutionists of the 1920s to the "scientific creationists" of the 1970s and 1980s. The continuity appeared to embrace a specific view of science that defined the scientific pursuit as the collection and organization of data. From this perspective, any theory that attempted to extrapolate from the data to answer larger questions represented nothing more than a guess. Antievolutionists also appeared to be unwilling to assimilate the post-Darwinian discoveries that provided confirmation of basic evolutionary concepts. The pioneering genetics work of Thomas Hunt Morgan in the early twentieth century and the multidisciplinary investigations that led to the Modern Synthesis of the 1940s were either ignored or misinterpreted by antievolutionists. They thus continued to make the same arguments in the 1970s as their predecessors had made in the 1870s and the 1920s. Indeed, many of the phrases that appear in the writings of scientific creationists can be found in the earlier works of Louis Agassiz or William Jennings Bryan.

Tracing the evolution controversy in America leads the historian down intriguing pathways that converge on an important message for the present. The nation's continued difficulty in accepting this fundamental explanation of the biological world represents a forceful indictment of our educational system, especially in science. Our reluctance to include the topic of evolution in our textbooks and our biology classes is part of a larger problem. As a nation, we have failed to provide the education necessary for the increasingly technical world of the late twentieth century. While government and business leaders decry our lack of "competitiveness" in science and technology, schools remain afraid to teach modern science, including evolution, lest they arouse controversy in their communities. The lack of knowledge about the "facts" and the methods of science not only condemns large numbers of American citizens to scientific illiteracy but also provides pseudoscience with a nourishing growth medium. This account of the evolution controversy in America provides a sobering vision of a culture that has repeatedly faltered in its attempt to understand modern science.

The writing of any historical work is a collaborative enterprise. The notes in this volume provide a clear indication of my intellectual debt to the many scholars who have examined America's evolution debate. A few individuals have contributed more specifically. My examination of this topic was first suggested many years ago by Paul A. Carter at the University of Arizona. More recently, John Lankford and Ferenc M. Szasz have provided encouragement and valuable suggestions. Others who have contributed support and ideas include Herman E. Bateman, Roger L. Nichols, Christopher Toumey, Ronald L. Numbers, Bryant Bannister, Edward J. Larson, and Gerald Thompson. As have all historians, I benefited greatly from interlibrary loan, and I wish to express my sincere thanks to Linda Mulder at Tennessee Technological University. Chapters 3 and 4 were largely completed under the terms of a Non-Instructional Assignment grant from Tennessee Tech during the 1988-89 academic year. To colleagues in the history department, I offer my appreciation for their support. Acknowledgment is also owed to the Arizona Historical Society for permission to reprint material from the *Journal of Arizona History* and to *Journal of the Southwest* for similar courtesy. Finally, special thanks are due to William Jerome Crouch and the University Press of Kentucky for their faith in and enthusiasm for this project.

This book has taken more than a decade to complete, during which time my energies were also absorbed by progressive kidney failure that led to a renal transplant in October 1991. I humbly acknowledge my debt and gratitude to the many individuals who shared this ordeal with me: to physicians and other medical personnel in Tucson and Cookeville who aided me throughout this experience, to family and friends who provided unselfish support, and to the renal transplant team at Vanderbilt University Medical Center, for reasons they well know.

Prologue

Few ideas in the development of modern thought have been more controversial than the theory of organic evolution through natural selection. From its development in the mid-nineteenth century to the present, the concept of biological change through natural processes has presented formidable challenges to deeply held intellectual, social, and religious views. The work of Charles Darwin and his followers provided explanations of nature with few of the comforting assurances of earlier accounts based on religious or social conventions. The increasing importance of science in the century following Darwin's efforts failed to ease the discomfort many felt toward the new explanations; indeed, the growing presence and power of science in society may well have exacerbated this discomfort. Because views toward evolution remain inextricably tied to political, social, and religious perspectives, the controversy surrounding the theory is unlikely to disappear.

Darwin's work is equally important for the positive contribution it made. The theory of evolution through natural selection accomplished something few ideas ever do. It fundamentally changed the way humans viewed nature. In time, Darwinian thought also altered humanity's view of its own place in nature, an experience with far-reaching consequences. No longer could humans see in nature a stable, comforting organization of life forms leading to man. No longer would clerics use the evidences from nature to support a literal reading of the Old Testament. No longer could individuals accept religious explanations of the progression of life on earth as part of modern science; such explanations had become part of religious faith only.

Within the scientific world as well, the Darwinian revolution overturned former ways of viewing nature. Greek naturalists such as Aristotle had observed plant and animal life, eventually developing a hierarchical organization of life forms. More than fifteen centuries later, this hierarchical perspective had taken on added significance because of the growing power of the Church. The gradual merger of existing scientific and theological views, particularly evident in the work of St. Thomas Aquinas in the thirteenth century, led to the concept of the Great Chain of Being. In this scheme, terrestrial life led inexorably from the simpler organisms such as plants through increasingly complex animals to humans and ultimately to the angels and to God. Proponents of this view made clear, however, that the Great Chain represented a static hierarchy, with no movement possible from one link to another.

By the eighteenth century, however, the chain had begun to weaken. Social, political, and religious upheavals over the past two hundred years challenged the static hierarchy that underlay the Great Chain of Being. Similarly, this organizational scheme proved unable to absorb the large numbers of new plant and animal species that had come to the attention of naturalists through voyages of discovery. By the 1700s species from the New World that exhibited dramatic similarities to those of the Old World presented naturalists with a perplexing problem. Where did these animals fit in the Great Chain? More important, what did the differences, as well as the similarities, between the Old and New World species indicate? If differences existed, could not the possibility of change be part of the explanation?

The concept of change increasingly guided naturalists during the century preceding the development of Darwin's evolutionary theory. The investigations of George Louis Leclerc, Comte Buffon, led to a concept of developmental change on earth, with creation stretched over time. Buffon eventually accepted the idea of extinction of species through changes that took place in earlier times, but he stressed that such changes were degenerative ones. Equally important, Buffon argued that such changes no longer took place. By the early decades of the nineteenth century, other attempts to explain the diversity of animal life, especially the variety of fossil forms, had emerged. Georges Cuvier, author of the twelve-volume *Researches on Fossil Bones,* argued for a catastrophist view of geology and biological change. The fossil record could best be explained by a series of destructive catastrophes followed by the appearance of new life forms. Between these episodes of cataclysmic destruction, represented by gaps in the geological record, life existed unchanged. An alternative explanation was offered by Jean-Baptiste de Lamarck. In his *Zoological Philosophy,* Lamarck attempted to answer the question of how changes took place over time. Organisms changed, he wrote, because of needs imposed by environmental changes. In order to survive in a new environment, organisms developed new habits or physical traits. These acquired characteristics could be passed on to later generations.

Although Charles Darwin was the intellectual heir to these developmental views, his own theory owed at least as much to the work of geologists. Challenging the idea of sudden creation, James Hutton, Charles Lyell, and other geologists developed the explanation that current processes of change in the earth's structure, such as wind and water erosion, were also responsible for earlier changes. This concept of uniformitarianism—which Lyell had developed into a workable theory by 1830—sought to explain geological diversity by those processes currently visible. The slow workings of such processes led to another dramatic change in geologists' views of the earth. Long periods of time would be necessary for such processes as erosion to create deep valleys. Calculations based on biblical chronology, suggesting that the earth was only some six thousand years old, proved insufficient to encompass the changes that were so clearly visible on earth.

Lyell's discussion of uniformitarianism began to appear in print during Darwin's famous voyage in HMS *Beagle*. Darwin's geological and biological observations during this voyage were all interpreted by him in relation to Lyell's uniformitarian concepts. Darwin's recognition that the unique species of the Galápagos Islands were similar to those on the South American mainland struck him immediately. Upon closer examination, he also found variations among species on the different islands of the Galápagos chain. His examination of finches on the various islands, for example, uncovered differences in beak structure, which Darwin thought might be the result of different food supplies. He had already developed a tentative, though imperfectly formed, evolutionary idea, which he would spend the rest of his life investigating.

Shortly after his return from the *Beagle* voyage in 1836, Darwin began collecting and organizing his material, starting a notebook specifically on evolution the next year. Constantly attempting to explain how variations occurred and how they became cumulative, Darwin discovered a missing element in Thomas Malthus's *Essay on Population* (1798), a classic in British political economy that Darwin read in 1838 "for pleasure." Malthus's essay was designed to show that suffering and misery were part of the natural order and that plagues and famines were merely nature's way of keeping the population in check. If nature behaved in this fashion within the human population, Darwin reasoned, could not the same process take place throughout the rest of the organic world? This concept of natural selection proved to be the crucial aspect of Darwin's theory of evolution. Whatever changes took place in an organism were judged in terms of natural selection. If the change gave the organism a benefit in the world, the organism would survive. If not, the organism would perish, taking the change with it. In either case, nature enforced natural selection relentlessly.

For the next twenty years Darwin worked slowly and deliberately on his study of the "species question." By the late 1850s his theory was largely complete, and he began discussing it with a few of the world's leading naturalists. Unknown to Darwin and his colleagues, however, an English naturalist working in Malaya was developing a similar evolutionary theory. Alfred Russel Wallace, who began corresponding with Darwin in 1856, had developed his own version of evolution through natural selection by mid-1858, when he sent Darwin a manuscript essay on the topic. Through the work of Darwin's friends in the English scientific community, papers by Darwin and Wallace were read at the July meeting of the Linnean Society, the leading British biological organization. It was not until the completion of Darwin's "abstract" and its publication as *Origin of Species* in late November 1859, however, that the theory of evolution attracted serious attention.[1]

Darwin's explanation of organic change represented an elegant synthesis of several concepts. Given that population exceeded food supply, competition for survival characterized the natural world. Those individuals or species that could compete most successfully would survive, providing the breeding stock for the next generation. In addition to recognizing natural selection as the guiding force in this process, Darwin also perceived that variations in organisms could confer an advantage in the struggle for existence. Such changes would be passed on to succeeding generations, leading to the eventual replacement of unmodified individuals. In this fashion, new species emerged. Darwin made no claim to know the origins of these variations, which he believed to be random. Indeed, the source of the random variations upon which natural selection acted remained unclear for more than a century after *Origin of Species* appeared. Yet Darwin's insight that advantageous variations could be preserved and transmitted through natural selection provided naturalists with an explanation of organic change that ultimately led to a more profound understanding of nature.

Acting as it did on random variables, Darwin's concept of natural selection seemed to suggest that divine intervention was no longer essential. The elimination of the Deity from direct involvement in the natural world alienated many of Darwin's scientific colleagues, including noted British geologists Adam Sedgwick and Charles Lyell. More dramatic, however, was the reaction of the orthodox religious community, who initially saw in Darwin's theory a strong suggestion of atheism. The June 1860 meeting of the British Association for the Advancement of Science brought these two paths of the response to the new theory together, although Darwin, who made it a practice to avoid such gatherings, did not attend. The BAAS meeting provided a convenient symbol of the early controversy by scheduling the main debate for Saturday afternoon. The opposition to Darwin would be presented by the Reverend Samuel Wilberforce, bishop of Oxford, while Darwin would be defended by noted naturalist Thomas Henry Huxley. That Wilberforce attempted to present the scientific case against evolution indicated the remaining close connection between theology and science. That he failed miserably in this attempt indicated the increasingly specialized knowledge necessary to understand science. In a well-polished speech lasting thirty minutes, Wilberforce used his considerable speaking ability to make Darwin's theory appear to be nothing more than an absurd guess, establishing a tradition that would characterize the antievolution movement for decades. Yet it was clear to scientists who were beginning to understand Darwinism that Wilberforce had an inadequate grasp of modern science. This inadequacy appeared clearly in the sarcastic conclusion to his speech. "I should like to ask Professor Huxley," he exclaimed, "who is sitting by me, and is about to tear me to pieces when I have sat down, as to his belief in being descended from an ape. Is it on his grandfather's or his grandmother's side," Wilberforce queried, "that the ape ancestry comes in?"[2]

Huxley's reply to Wilberforce's comments began with a quiet, well-reasoned discussion that showed how Darwin's theory explained many unanswered questions about the natural world. He also effectively countered Wilberforce's "scientific" arguments by emphasizing the many errors in his opponent's presentation. Huxley could not, however, leave Wilberforce's snide conclusion unanswered. Uttering words that have become part of the Darwinian mythology, the naturalist concluded:

> I asserted, and I repeat, that a man has no reason to be ashamed of having an ape for his grandfather. If there were an ancestor whom I should feel shame in recalling, it would be a *man,* a man of restless and versatile intellect, who, not content with an equivocal success in his own sphere of activity, plunges into scientific questions with which he has no real acquaintance, only to obscure them by an aimless rhetoric, and distract the attention of his hearers from the real point at issue by eloquent digressions, and skilled appeals to religious prejudice.[3]

Although opposition to Darwinism would continue to be evident, acceptance of the new theory in Victorian England proved only moderately contentious.[4]

The situation would be quite different on the other side of the Atlantic. In the United States, Darwinism would have a much more difficult time gaining acceptance. Both scientists and theologians found the new theory troubling and, in fact, tended to accept a version of evolution that was distinctly unlike that proposed by Darwin. In America, the 130 years that followed the publication of *Origin of Species* were marked by endless controversy.

1

Origins

"This book is already exciting much attention," wrote Harvard botanist Asa Gray to begin his review of Charles Darwin's *Origin of Species*.[1] Despite the increasingly bitter arguments plaguing American life in the months leading to the firing on Fort Sumter, the American scientific community expressed significant interest in Darwin's discussion of evolutionary theory. Even in the midst of the carnage that followed the outbreak of war, scientists continued to examine and debate the theory in their efforts to come to terms with this new explanation of life's origins and development. During the decades that followed, few topics excited as much intellectual interest as Darwin's hypothesis of evolution through natural selection.[2]

The Initial American Reaction

America's most respected botanist, Asa Gray received his copy of *Origin of Species* shortly before Christmas 1859 and immediately began examining the volume. As acting senior editor of the *American Journal of Science and Arts*, the nation's leading science periodical, Gray decided to review *Origin* for the journal himself. He and Darwin had corresponded for several years: Gray provided his English colleague with information concerning North American botany, and Darwin returned the favor by discussing his developmental hypothesis. Far more than a summary of Darwin's work, Gray's extensive review in the March 1860 issue of the journal provided a clear discussion of evolutionary concepts.[3]

Early in his review, Gray counterpoised Darwin's theory of evolution by natural selection with Harvard geologist Louis Agassiz's concept of creation by divine will, which Gray described as "theistic to excess." It remained clear to Gray that the coming debate would largely be between those who accepted aspects of Darwin's work—such as Gray himself—and those who continued to accept the creationism of

Cuvier and Agassiz. In this debate, Agassiz's reputation as one of America's most famous scientists would undoubtedly play an important role. Gray, however, was more concerned with the potential contribution to be made by the evolutionary hypothesis. The great advantage to Darwin's theory was that it described the origin and distribution of species in natural terms. The supernatural explanations preferred by Agassiz, in contrast, actually explained very little. Carefully delineating the views of Agassiz and Darwin, Gray observed that his Harvard colleague viewed life forms and their interrelationships as "ultimate facts" that were to be interpreted theologically. Darwin, on the other hand, viewed such phenomena "as complex facts, to be analyzed and interpreted scientifically." Unlike Agassiz, who apparently assumed "the scientifically unexplained to be inexplicable," Darwin expected these phenomena to be comprehensible through explanations based on natural causes.[4]

Gray recognized that gaps existed in Darwin's theory. *Origin of Species* could not, for example, answer the important question of how organisms varied so that natural selection could act on them. Gray argued that when Darwin attempted to account for such variations, he seemed to retreat into some form of a Lamarckian concept. Gray admitted that such shortcomings, as well as the nature of the evidence available to naturalists, prevented Darwin from proving his "theory of derivation," but the Harvard botanist emphasized that the development of such a theory was far less unlikely than before Darwin's work. This situation paralleled that which held in the physical sciences, where explanatory power, rather than abstract "proof," was the key determinant in the acceptance of theories. Yet proof was at least possible for Darwin's theory, in contrast with the concepts presented by Agassiz. "From the very nature of the case," Gray explained, "substantive proof of specific creation is not attainable; but that of derivation or transmutation of species may be."[5]

Because of Gray's religious views—he sympathized with New England Calvinism rather than with the more fashionable Unitarianism— the theological implications of Darwinian evolution could not be ignored. Was evolution, as Agassiz suggested, atheistic? If so, could anyone with religious sensibilities accept evolution as the explanation of the organic world? Gray examined such questions in the latter pages of his review, stressing that Darwin's theory was not necessarily atheistic. Admittedly, Darwinian evolution could be used to support an atheistic view of the universe, but that was true of all physical theories. The nebular hypothesis, for example, the leading theory of the origin of the solar system, could be interpreted as removing God from the day-to-day control of the cosmos. The majority of scientists, however, including Agassiz himself, accepted this theory with no great crisis of religious conscience.

Asa Gray saw sufficient reason to assume that Darwin had based his theory on some concept of design and an intelligent (or divine) first cause. Gray wrote that Darwin might well view nature as a system of laws that derived from "the will of its Author" who had foreseen the entire working of the system. From that perspective, Gray could emphasize his own view of the validity of the design argument. For Gray, natural law was "the human conception of continued and orderly Divine action." Darwin's theory of evolution merely described how the divine plan was proceeding.[6]

Yet Darwin's description of the divine plan was the English naturalist's great contribution, a contribution that Gray recognized as an important step in the advance of science. The aim of *Origin of Species,* according to Gray, was not to deny divine intervention "but to maintain that Natural Selection, in explaining the facts, explains also many classes of facts which thousand-fold repeated independent acts of creation do not explain, but leave more mysterious than ever." Evolution thus presented a credible scientific alternative to the divine creation of each species because of its explanatory ability and its greater efficacy in answering a multitude of important questions. This theory's success in answering such questions would be determined by the scientific community, which would not have to concern itself with supposed atheistic implications of evolution through natural selection.[7]

Asa Gray's review provided American scientists with a valuable insight into the new theory of evolution. His careful analysis of the book also pleased Charles Darwin, who had received an early offprint from Gray. Writing to his Harvard friend on 18 February 1860, Darwin described the review as "by far the best which I have read." Although unconvinced by Gray's comments concerning the design argument, Darwin was nonetheless pleased with Gray's work, sharing it with friends such as Sir Joseph Hooker and writing American geologist James Dwight Dana that "no one person understands my views and has defended them so well as A. Gray; though he does not by any means go all the way with me."[8]

Shortly after the publication of Gray's review, the debate over Darwin's theory of evolution focused on the meetings of the American Academy of Arts and Sciences. An amalgam of scientists, literary figures, and Boston elites, the academy called a special meeting for 27 March to discuss the new theory. Opponents of evolution were given the opportunity to present their views at this time, with a rebuttal to be scheduled for later meetings. Although Agassiz was not on the program, his allies ably defended his ideas. Francis Bowen, a philosophy professor at Harvard, presented a discussion that he had prepared for *North American Review.* Bowen was particularly concerned about the religious implications of evolution, arguing that Darwin had put forth his theory "to the entire denial of the doctrine of final causes." Similarly, the philosopher expressed outrage over Darwin's suggestion that humans were part of the animal kingdom. "Mr. Darwin boldly traces out the geneology [sic] of man," Bowen objected, "and affirms that the monkey is his brother,—and the horse his cousin, and the oyster his remote ancestor." Bowen's outrage was a product of reading far more into Darwin's *Origin* than the English naturalist intended, a trait common to many of Darwin's critics. *Origin of Species* was not about human evolution. Only at the end of his concluding chapter did Darwin pen the intriguing (but ambiguous) observation that, through future research based on evolutionary concepts, "light will be thrown on the origin of man and his history." To interpret *Origin* as Bowen did required more imagination than insight.[9]

Another Agassiz ally who spoke at the 27 March meeting was John Amory Lowell, an amateur botanist who had helped support several of Gray's field expeditions in the 1840s. Lowell, firmly wedded to Agassiz's opposition to Darwin, denied that observed variations contributed to an understanding of organisms and their development. Like Agassiz, Lowell argued that the variation observed by Darwin, whether in domesticated animals or in the wild, represented nothing more than a stage of growth or change in the individual. Variation was, indeed, visible, but it remained largely transitory or, at best, a result of hybridization. In cither case, such variation could have little impact on the development of life on earth. Lowell also examined the religious aspects of evolution, especially the idea that variations could be explained through natural events. He found it "more reverent, and more consonant to the feelings implanted in our nature," to accept the belief that adaptations were "the direct act of the Creator."[10]

The Darwinian rebuttal was scheduled for the 10 April and 1 May meetings of the academy. To present this discussion, Asa Gray was the obvious choice as the American most familiar with Darwin's theory. Although he spent the early portion of his time discussing the scientific aspects of the new theory, Gray also examined the religious implications, which were of perhaps greater importance to the many nonscientists in the audience. As he had done in his review for the *American Journal of Science and Arts,* Gray focused on the design argument to emphasize that evolution need not be atheistic. In point of fact, he argued, Darwin's work left untouched the question of ultimate cause because natural selection represented a secondary cause. The confirmation of evolution through scientific evidence, according to Gray, "would leave the doctrines of final cause, utility, special design, or whatever other teleological view, just where they were before its promulgation, in all fundamental respects." The academy debates, of course, did not end the controversy over Darwinian evolution, even within the confines of the meeting hall, but the perspectives of the two sides had more clearly emerged.[11]

It remained for Louis Agassiz, who had kept to the sidelines during these early debates, to record his views on Darwin's *Origin of Species.* Given the opportunity to write his own review for the *American Journal of Science and Arts,* however, Agassiz produced neither a review nor a comment on Gray's earlier discussion of evolution. Instead, Agassiz submitted part of a manuscript that would be published later in the year as the third volume of his *Contributions to the Natural History of the United States of America.* Nonetheless, readers of Agassiz's discussion in the July 1860 issue of the journal received a clear view of his response to Darwinian evolution. Referring to Darwinism as a collection of "mere guesses," Agassiz argued that this hypothesis was "a scientific mistake, untrue in its facts, unscientific in its methods, and mischievous in its tendency." Darwin had rejected the most basic concept that determined the legitimacy of theories about the organic world. For Agassiz, all such theories had to be based on the idea that the world was the product of original and continuous intervention by a deity. The naturalist's duty was to observe the world within this framework, a duty that Darwin had abandoned in his construction of a speculative account.[12]

Agassiz's objections to Darwin's theory followed two major paths. His characterization of evolution as "unscientific" or as "mere guesses" was based on the view, shared by many naturalists and most nonscientists, that science was the organization of "facts" into a descriptive body of knowledge. Darwin's work, according to Agassiz, violated that definition in many instances. More damaging, Darwin and his followers had failed to produce one single example to prove that individuals change in such a way as to produce different species. There existed no examples of living forms changing in this fashion, and there was no fossil evidence of intermediate forms linking two dissimilar beings. Agassiz wrote: "The geological record, even with all its imperfections exaggerated to distortion, tells now, what it has told from the beginning, that the supposed intermediate forms between the species of different geological periods are imaginary beings, called up merely in support of a fanciful theory. The origin of all the diversity among living beings remains a mystery, as totally unexplained as if the book of Darwin had never been written; for no theory, unsupported by fact, however plausible it may appear, can be admitted in science." If Darwin's hypothesis represented unsupported speculation that Agassiz rejected as unscientific, evolution was also unacceptable because it rejected the most basic feature of the natural world, the "unmistakable evidence of thought." This thought, which corresponded to human thought, could only be explained as the product of intelligence. Any theory that refused to accept the existence of an intelligence guiding the actions of nature in every respect could not claim to be a valid description of the natural world. [13]

For Agassiz, the existence of intelligence in nature explained both the variability of individual organisms and the constancy in the higher organizational divisions such as species, genera, and orders. Individuals were, in this sense, facts; the higher groups were thoughts. As Agassiz wrote near the end of his discussion, the higher levels of biological classification "exist only as categories of thought in the Supreme Intelligence, and, as such, have as truly an independent existence, and are as unvarying, as thought itself after it has once been expressed." By refusing to accept this most basic of ideas, Darwin had abandoned any claim to scientific credibility. [14]

By the summer of 1860 the Darwinian debate had attracted considerable attention among American intellectuals. Realizing the importance of an understanding of evolution by nonscientists, Asa Gray began writing an extended treatment of the Darwinian theory for publication in the *Atlantic Monthly*. Although examining many aspects of the continuing debate, he expended most of his energy to show that evolution worked best with theism, not with atheism. To Gray, the design argument was as valuable after Darwin as it had been before, since nature was filled with "unmistakable and irresistible indications of design." [15]

Gray's attempt to merge Darwinian evolution with natural theology serves as an appropriate conclusion to the initial episode in the debate over Darwinian evolution. Within the scientific community, a variety of views were represented, but one factor seemed clear. Although many scientists had misgivings about certain aspects of this new theory, the general concept of evolution continued to be of intense interest to the majority of naturalists in America. Among scientists, natural history would increasingly be defined via the Darwinian theory.

Expansion of the Debate

Quite apart from their questions concerning the details of Darwinian evolution, many scientists had philosophical qualms about the new theory. Critics frequently charged that Darwin's science was insufficiently inductive. In the mid-nineteenth century scientists tended to see themselves as disciples of Francis Bacon, who had argued more than three hundred years earlier that science could only progress through the accumulation of large amounts of data, from which theories would emerge. Many of the early critics of Darwinian evolution objected to evolution because the theory was insufficiently Baconian and, hence, unscientific. This criticism, which would be consistently cited by American antievolutionists, represented an imperfect awareness of the state of science in the nineteenth century. Although scientists accepted the Baconian ideal, many of them also accepted an increased role for deduction in science, through which a hypothesis would be deduced and then tested against nature. Among Darwin's great contributions to biology was the merger of induction and deduction, a process that had already transformed the physical sciences through the work of Newton, Laplace, and others. Darwin's application of this combination of methods in natural history was no less revolutionary than his theory of evolution through natural selection.[16]

Another objection lodged against Darwin's work was that he had failed to "prove" his hypothesis. Those who opposed evolution for other reasons, whether religious or scientific, frequently used this charge to argue that there existed no compelling reason to abandon earlier views of the organic world. In his review of *Origin of Species,* Asa Gray provided an insightful analysis of this aspect of the Darwinian debate. Gray stressed that supporters of the evolution hypothesis could travel down two paths in their attempt to prove the theory. In the first place, they could "assign real and adequate causes" that would necessarily result in the observed diversity and relations of species. Successfully pursuing this path would establish evolution as a "true physical theory." Alternatively, Gray argued, Darwin and his followers could show that the "whole body of facts" generally conformed to the evolutionary hypothesis. This tactic could perhaps convince naturalists to accept the new doctrine "through its competency to harmonize all the facts," even though the cause of variation remained unknown. Successfully completing this task would establish evolution as a "sufficient hypothesis," in Gray's view, that would also be valuable in offering a better understanding of the natural world. Gray emphasized that Darwin had not proved his theory, although he had made such a derivation less unlikely than before. Because Darwin's theory fit in nicely with the physical sciences and explained much in the organic world, however, Gray predicted that evolution "is not unlikely to be largely accepted long before it can be proved."[17]

Darwin's enthusiastic response to his Harvard friend's review extended to this discussion of theories and hypotheses, although Darwin brought a different perspective to the topic. He applauded Gray's distinction between theory and hypothesis as "very ingenious" but suggested that such a discrimination was rarely followed. Scientists discussed the wave *theory* of light, despite their inability to isolate the ether necessary to transmit waves. Similarly, the *theory* of gravitation was widely accepted, although the cause of the attractive power remained mysterious. "It seems to me," Darwin concluded, "that an hypothesis is developed into a theory solely by explaining an ample lot of facts."[18] The interrelationships among theories, hypotheses, and facts would remain a central part of the evolution debate for many decades. Darwin's reliance on deductions, based on and tested by observations, nonetheless pointed the way toward a new way of looking at natural history that would increasingly become the orthodox view during the last years of the nineteenth century.

Darwin himself maintained a flexible attitude toward *Origin of Species,* revising the volume five times between 1859 and 1872. Perhaps the most important impetus to Darwin's revisions were new estimates of the earth's age. William Thompson, later Lord Kelvin, calculated the age of the earth based on the estimated cooling rates of terrestrial rocks. From such estimates, Thompson concluded that the earth was between twenty million and four hundred million years old, with ninety-eight million the most likely figure. These estimates, far below what was needed for gradual evolution through natural selection, forced Darwin to accept the inheritance of acquired characteristics to speed up the evolutionary process. Although Darwin hoped that the physicists had underestimated the amount of time available, he nonetheless incorporated modifications of his theory based on the shorter time scale into later editions of *Origin of Species.* Darwin's modifications, however, weakened his work considerably. By the sixth edition, published in 1872, as Michael Ruse has written, Darwin "had on his hands an awkward patchwork quilt of a book rather than the forceful and elegant work he had started with."[19]

As Darwin refined and modified his ideas, American naturalists developed their own contributions to the theory of evolution. No longer simply reacting to the new theory, Americans began looking more closely at the explanatory power of evolution by natural selection.

Among the most interesting conclusions from this closer analysis was the recognition of weaknesses in Darwin's concept of natural selection. Asa Gray's continuing discussion of evolution during the early 1870s emphasized that natural selection was the method of evolution, preserving those variations that helped the species survive and eliminating those variations that were harmful. Gray stressed, however, that natural selection could in no way account for the variations themselves, the cause of which remained an open question.[20]

The evidence for evolution, however, received an important boost from American paleontologists such as Ferdinand V. Hayden and Othniel C. Marsh, who had discovered significant fossil deposits in the western United States by the early 1870s. Among the most famous of these discoveries was Marsh's retrieval of fossil birds with teeth and other reptilian characteristics. Such finds proved to be important support for the evolutionary theory, showing as they did a transitional form between two paths of evolutionary development. These discoveries played a major role in the increasingly positive reception evolution received in the United States and even led Louis Agassiz to a more moderate stance toward the new theory before his death in 1873. Although still convinced of design and meaning in nature, Agassiz had stopped arguing from metaphysics by the early 1870s and was relying more on factual problems with evolution.[21]

Despite continuing scientific debates over the details of Darwin's theory, the status of the general evolutionary concept seemed secure. Addressing the American Association for the Advancement of Science on 30 August 1877, O.C. Marsh, vice president of the organization, presented his audience with an intriguing view of the place of evolution and science in America. No argument needed to be presented for evolution, Marsh stated, "since to doubt evolution to-day is to doubt science, and science is only another name for truth."[22] Marsh's rhetorical flourish may have appealed to his audience, but others in the United States had a distinctly different view of "truth." Theologians, no less than scientists, had been challenged by the evolutionary hypothesis to review many deeply held beliefs. Their response to Darwinism represented a crucial chapter in American religious thought.

The Religious Response

From the opening rounds of the Darwinian debate, opponents of evolution claimed an important ally in Louis Agassiz. The Harvard zoologist enjoyed a popular scientific reputation at least as impressive as that of Darwin's supporters, suggesting that opposition to evolution presented a valid intellectual position. Agassiz's repeated criticism that Darwin's work remained speculative and insufficiently inductive was embraced by many theologians who had been educated in the tradition of Scottish Common Sense Realism. This tradition held that all truth, scientific or religious, must be based on observable facts. Heman Lincoln, professor of ecclesiastical history at Newton Theological Institution, wrote in *Baptist Quarterly* that Darwin's theory was supported by no facts worthy of consideration. "Not one decisive fact is found in the whole geologic record," he proclaimed. There existed no fossil evidence "of any species assuming new organs, or changing its internal structure,—no connecting links to prove that such changes were ever in progress." Another opponent of evolution, the Reverend Thomas A. Eliot, rejected fossil evidence altogether, arguing, "We must witness the process; we must see one animal turn into another."[23] The demand for such proof characterized much of the early antievolution sentiment of the Gilded Age.

The Scottish Common Sense philosophy played a particularly important role among all but the most liberal Protestant denominations. Originating in the early 1800s as a response to Enlightenment secularism, this philosophy claimed descent from the inductive (or "Baconian") method. Common Sense Realism accepted that the external world was exactly as it appeared and that facts concerning the world could be known directly. From the religious standpoint, Common Sense Realism held that God's truth represented a single and unified order and that all persons of "common sense" were capable of knowing that truth. The "facts" leading to that truth could be found in Scripture. Common Sense philosophy also defined the proper pursuit of science. The method used to determine the facts of the Bible, proponents of these ideas believed, should also be used when investigating the less dependable facts of nature. Legitimate science, in this view, was the gathering and classification of facts. Darwin's hypothesis, variously described as a "mere theory" or a "monstrous assumption," represented nothing more than speculation. Where were the facts to support evolution through natural selection? Had Darwin seen one species turning into another? With this view of the scientific pursuit, the Common Sense rejection of Darwinian evolution was based as much on philosophy as on orthodox religion.[24]

The concept of evolution through natural selection troubled many Americans because it opened the possibility of the development of life on earth through natural processes. Opponents of evolution did not, however, agonize about man's place in the natural order, as Darwin had carefully avoided the question of human evolution in the various editions of *Origin of Species*. The publication of Darwin's *Descent of Man* in 1871, however, eliminated the option of ignoring the implications of evolution for humanity. Clearly applying evolutionary concepts to the development of the human race, *Descent of Man* led to harsher arguments and positions on both sides of the debate. Many theologians attempted to distinguish between the Darwin of *Origin,* whom they could accept with reservations, and the Darwin of *Descent,* whom they could only reject. The status of humans was special, such opponents argued, if for no other reasons than the human possession of a soul and a clearly moral order in society. To suggest that humans were merely part of the animal kingdom, subject to the same laws as horses and elephants, was unacceptable.

Among the most vocal of the initial opponents of the concepts included in *The Descent of Man* was the Presbyterian editor and lecturer De Witt Talmage. Although evolution represented only one part of his concern with the growing infidelity in America, Talmage proved particularly strident in his attacks on Darwinian concepts. In a sermon preached in Brooklyn in the early 1870s, Talmage stressed that according to evolutionary theory, if one went far enough back in time, "you will find a vegetable stuff that might be called a mushroom. This mushroom by innate force develops a tadpole, the tadpole by innate force develops a polywog, the polywog develops a fish, the fish by natural force develops into a reptile, the reptile develops into a quadruped, the quadruped develops into a baboon, the baboon develops into a man."[25] Described in this way, evolution appeared not only infidel but also absurd.

More concerned with the specific religious impact of evolution, Enoch Fitch Burr focused on the encouragement Darwin's philosophy gave to an atheistic view of the universe. After several years as a Congregational minister in Connecticut, Burr was serving as lecturer on the scientific evidences of religion at Amherst College when *Descent* appeared. In a volume of lectures published in 1873, Burr recorded his opposition to evolution because it taught that "all things we perceive, including what are called spiritual phenomena, have come from the simplest beginnings, solely by means of such forces and laws as belong to matter." This materialistic philosophy was unworthy of support, as it remained self-evident that nature could best be explained as the result of an eternal being characterized by eternal power and unlimited eternal intelligence. Evolution, on the other hand, was "founded by atheism, claimed by atheism, supported by atheism, used exclusively in the interest of atheism," and attempted to suppress all evidence for the existence of God.[26]

In many respects, the leading religious opponent of Darwin during the 1870s was Charles Alexander Hodge, who guided the intellectual development of Princeton Theological Seminary from the mid-1820s to his death in 1878. The "Princeton theology," grounded in the Scottish Common Sense philosophy and biblical inerrancy, represented Hodge's intellectual legacy. Hodge focused specifically on the evolutionary concept in his most dramatic work, *What Is Darwinism?* Although Hodge praised Darwin as a careful naturalist, he emphasized that Darwin's work was flawed because it was too speculative. Darwin had not, Hodge stressed, followed the Baconian method. The Princeton divine cited Agassiz to support his view, writing that "religious men believe with Agassiz that facts are sacred." Because Darwin had failed to keep his focus firmly on facts, all conclusions derived from evolution could be ignored. Darwin's rejection of design was similarly unfounded, as "the denial of design in nature is virtually the denial of God." At root, Hodge's rejection of Darwin remained a religious one. The Princeton theologian rejected Darwin because he had failed to develop an explanation of nature based on "truth," a common failing of all evolutionary theories. "Science, so called," Hodge wrote, "when it comes in conflict with truth, is what man is when he comes in conflict with God." The answer to the question "What is Darwinism?" was simple: "It is atheism."[27]

These religious opponents of evolution embraced the same rejection of speculation in science as had many of the early scientific opponents of the Darwinian theory. Evangelical opponents also emphasized that the theory removed any role for God in the universe and brutalized the place of man in that universe. Without divine interaction, the argument continued, very little of the visible universe could be explained.[28] These opponents, however, represented only one segment of the religious reaction to evolution. Another group was working diligently to assimilate evolution into some form of religious outlook, aided by scientists who wished to reconcile the new science of Darwin with traditional religious beliefs.

The Scientific Reconcilers

In addition to representing a particularly active period in science itself, the Gilded Age witnessed significant popular interest in scientific topics. The leading periodicals of the day frequently published articles geared toward this growing audience. Of those writers, scientists and nonscientists alike, who examined evolution in a popular fashion, many tried to reconcile evolution with religion. A notable exception to this rule, of course, was Louis Agassiz, who attempted to popularize science in opposition to evolution, but the extent of Agassiz's separation from the mainstream can be determined from a short article published in *The Nation* in early January 1867. The anonymous author of "Popularizing Science" took Agassiz to task for his recent series of antievolution lectures in Boston. The essay emphasized that Agassiz had succumbed to the dangers of reckless popularization, especially by uttering such statements as "We are the children of God, and not of monkeys." Arguing that naturalists favored the developmental hypothesis, the author concluded that Agassiz was not popularizing science, but only his own views on the issue at hand.[29]

Among the most active of the early popularizers of the Darwinian hypothesis was Harvard's Asa Gray, whose theistic evolution appeared very attractive to nonscientists in the United States. In his effort to reconcile evolution and religion, Gray emphasized that Darwin was not asking the same questions as theologians. Darwin, according to the Harvard botanist, was only concerned with efficient causes, not the final causes of interest to religious thinkers. Evolution need not disprove theism, any more than it proved theism, because it represented an intermediate level of analysis. Gray argued that "God himself is the very last, irreducible causal factor and, hence, the source of all evolutionary change." That evolution appeared to be the method through which terrestrial life developed need not detract from the divine ultimate origin of that life, any more than it challenged the design argument. In fact, Gray argued, natural selection actually strengthened the design argument, as selection was the method through which diversification led to higher forms. "In this system," Gray observed, "the forms and species, in all their variety, are not mere ends in themselves, but the whole a series of means and ends, in the contemplation of which we may obtain higher and more comprehensive, and perhaps worthier, as well [as] more consistent, views of design in Nature than heretofore." If those who wrote about Darwin continued to argue that evolution represented an atheistic view of the universe, Gray countered, they must be misinterpreting Darwin's work rather badly.[30]

By the mid-1870s Asa Gray had established himself as the chief proponent of Darwinian theism. George Frederick Wright, a minister in Andover, Massachusetts, and a respected student of glacial geology, urged Gray to reprint some of his earlier essays relating to evolution to counteract both the extreme materialists and the militant antievolutionists. Gray agreed that such a volume might do some good, and he began to collect his essays and reviews that had appeared over the past fifteen years. He also added a new essay entitled "Evolutionary Teleology." When the collection was published in 1876 as *Darwiniana,* it represented a clear delineation of the middle position in the Darwinian debate.

Gray's "Evolutionary Teleology" reemphasized design in nature but also suggested that Darwin's introduction of a utilitarian explanation assisted those who wished a better understanding of the natural world. This explanation removed many difficulties usually associated with teleology. Waste in nature as well as seemingly useless organs could all be explained by natural selection, the former eliminating the unfit and the latter representing mechanisms that might have been useful in the recent past. Such a teleology, Gray argued, "has the special advantage of accounting for the imperfections and failures as well as for successes." When viewed in this fashion, the Darwinian system fitted admirably within the theistic view of nature. Not only does evolution acknowledge purpose—albeit a utilitarian one—"but builds upon it; and if purpose in this sense does not of itself imply design, it is certainly compatible with it, and suggestive of it." Although neither design nor the absence of design could be proved, Gray suggested that the latter was less satisfactory than the former.[31]

Although Gray and Darwin had parted company over the issue of design in nature, the publication of *Darwiniana* brought the Harvard botanist even more firmly into the limelight of the Darwinian debates in America. Reviews in both the scientific and religious press were generally favorable. His clear acceptance of a theistic view of the universe attracted the attention of religious thinkers who realized the value of the linkage between a respected scientist and orthodox religion. From the perspective of theology, Gray's book was a crucial contribution to the acceptance by religious groups of the general concept of evolution.[32]

As the leading American reconciler, Gray continued to present his views through public lectures and various publications.[33] Yet Gray's work suffered from a shortcoming that prevented *Darwiniana* and other contributions from becoming the final answer to the religious questions concerning evolution. Gray was, after all, a scientist. Although receptive clergy did not denigrate Gray for his choice of careers, his work remained that of an outsider. More important, however, Gray had been one of the earliest supporters of Darwin in the United States and had, indeed, contributed significantly to the scientific reception of the theory of evolution. Fortunately for those clergy who wished to reconcile their faith with the new science, Gray's collaborator on *Darwiniana*, George Frederick Wright, had impeccable religious credentials and could claim expertise in scientific pursuits.

An 1859 graduate of Oberlin College under the presidency of Charles Grandison Finney, Wright had a clear affiliation with Finney's New School Calvinism. After theological training at Oberlin, Wright became the pastor of a Congregational church in Vermont in 1862 and soon began studying the glacial geology of the region. Within a decade Wright had assumed the pulpit of the Free Christian Church in Andover, Massachusetts, which has been described as the "intellectual centre of Congregationalism." Despite Andover's increasing theological liberalism, Wright remained true to his orthodox background and eventually joined the theology faculty at Oberlin in 1881. Throughout this period he continued to conduct geological research, developing glacial theories that were later endorsed by the eminent geologists James Dwight Dana and Clarence King.

Wright's ability to reconcile evolution with his orthodox theology grew from the perception—which he shared with Gray—that God's purposes were comprehensive and interrelated. It remained impossible to know the ultimate purpose of a sovereign God, so Darwinian evolution did not present a serious challenge to his place in the universe. More specifically, Wright argued, the ultimate causes of the variations that were the foundation of evolution could not be known, providing another role for divine action. Naturalists knew too little about the details of nature to suggest that there remained no place for God. As Wright stressed in 1882, "It would seem that such an hypothesis [evolution] left God's hands as free as could be desired for contrivances of whatever sort he pleased." Variations could be useful for artificial and natural selection, while still being part of the grander, benevolent design of a creator.[34]

Wright's effort to reconcile Darwin and orthodox theology led him to publish a collection of essays in 1882 under the title *Studies in Science and Religion*. In this volume Wright attempted to provide a more sophisticated description of the inductive method and its utility in understanding nature. He emphasized the importance of hypotheses in science, arguing that hypotheses directed observation. The alternative was random data gathering, of little value in any effort to describe the visible world. Once defined in this manner, the inductive method emerged as the most appropriate path to knowledge because the universe proceeded in a divinely ordered fashion. The benevolent end of the universe came directly from God, who provided the human species with sufficient uniformity of facts, material and spiritual, to justify induction as the principal technique to understand nature.[35]

Having established that nature could be understood through observation, Wright pointed out in *Studies in Science and Religion* that naturalists accepted the Darwinian theory because it agreed with observed facts, just as did Christianity. The observation of nature led to the conclusion that Darwin had understood very well how the biological world operated. His facts were as dependable as the "facts" spoken of by Agassiz, Hodge, and other anti-Darwinists. If theologians rejected Darwin, Wright argued, they must believe that God could not be trusted to supply humans with true and accurate facts. This led to rather frightening possibilities for the relationship between God and man. Wright remained equally concerned, however, with the seeming abandonment of induction by those special creationists who argued against any form of evolution. To explain the variety and distribution of species by the argument that this was God's way "would be suicidal to all scientific thought, and would endanger the rational foundation upon which our proof of revelation rests." Wright insisted that all the observed facts of nature be accepted, as all the facts were part of the divine plan.[36]

Wright hoped to expand the concept of design to include the many observations that did not fit into the traditional design argument. The most important of these observations was the waste and apparent failure that Darwin had observed in nature. This situation was very difficult to fit into the idea of a benevolent universe unless one looked behind the surface events. Wright argued that humans could not see anything but the parts involved; only God could see the whole. Humans were thus incompetent to base their evaluation of the benevolence of the universe on the parts that could be seen. This expanded version of design, which attempted to integrate observed data into a coherent whole, provided a workable explanation of variation as well. Wright did not need to refer to variation as guided, as had earlier arguments from design, because his expanded version of design referred to the sum of all possible ends that these variations served. All variations were participating in the benevolent universe of the Divine Being, which was the only design of any meaning. Humans should not restrict God to working with human methods and ideas.[37]

The work of Gray, Wright, and other reconcilers did much to calm the fears of those American intellectuals who saw in evolutionary concepts a challenge to religious orthodoxy. The reconcilers provided arguments and perspectives that could be employed by the growing number of Protestant divines who had accepted the need to come to terms with Darwin. Historian Jon H. Roberts has cogently argued that

American Protestant intellectuals remained convinced until the mid-1870s that evolution was bad science. Wedded as they were to the traditional belief that science provided data to support the Christian worldview, these thinkers concluded that any scientific idea that appeared to challenge orthodoxy was simply wrong. As the scientific community increasingly accepted evolution, however, Protestant intellectuals reevaluated the role of science in theology. Although a minority decided to reject evolution in favor of biblical literalism, mainstream Protestant leaders began to modify their theology in order to accommodate the new science.[38] Their path to accommodation was eased by developments within the American scientific community that provided a less threatening version of the evolutionary hypothesis.

Neo-Lamarckism

At the end of the Civil War, several American naturalists began developing an alternative to natural selection as the explanation for the evolution of organic forms. During the late nineteenth century this modified evolutionary theory, called neo-Lamarckism, became the most influential explanation of organic change. Although a number of American scientists participated in the development of this theory, three stand out as the leaders of this new school of scientific thought. Two students of Louis Agassiz, Alpheus Hyatt and Alpheus S. Packard, Jr., examined zoological evidence for development, while paleontologist Edward Drinker Cope added data from the rich fossil-bearing areas of the West. These three also guided the fortunes of *American Naturalist,* the leading periodical for the neo-Lamarckian view and a respected journal in natural history.[39]

The first clear expression of American neo-Lamarckism came from Alpheus Hyatt at the Boston Society of Natural History in 1866. In preparing his paper "On the Parallelism between the Different Stages of Life in the Individual and Those in the Entire Group of the Molluscous Order Tetrabrachiata," Hyatt had examined fossil shellfish for evidence of change over time. He announced that this group of organisms had passed through stages corresponding to those of a single life. Such parallel development suggested to Hyatt a mechanism for evolution in his theory of acceleration and retardation. The characteristics of adults of a maturing species became embryonic in the next higher species. These later groups possessed the more advanced traits at an earlier age, allowing them to make yet more advances, which became hereditary. Retardation also took place, leading to degradation and, ultimately, to extinction. No matter what direction such changes took, the influence of the environment was crucial. Although stated differently from Lamarck's concept of the inheritance of acquired characteristics, Hyatt's concept was formulated in a similar fashion.[40]

Within the next year Hyatt and his fellow naturalist Alpheus S. Packard, Jr., decided that this new concept of evolution required a separate journal for the dissemination of research supporting the neo-Lamarckian perspective. In 1867 the two scholars founded *American Naturalist* to broadcast the "American" (or neo-Lamarckian) view of evolution. Far more than a narrowly specialized journal devoted to detailed analysis of zoological and paleontological evidence for neo-Lamarckism, *American Naturalist* sought to become a periodical of interest to all naturalists. In the opening statement to their first issue in March 1867, the editors wrote that the value of the journal "will depend more on its power to awaken the absorbing interest invariably excited by the contemplation of nature, and of illustrating the wisdom and goodness of the Creator, than on any adornment of style, or cunning devices of the artist."[41]

The role the Creator played in this version of evolution was uppermost in the mind of Edward Drinker Cope, who later joined the editorial board of *American Naturalist*. His extensive essay "On the Origin of Genera," published in the October 1868 issue of *Proceedings of the Philadelphia Academy of Natural Sciences,* explained the production of variant forms from common ancestral types in terms consistent with theistic evolution. For Cope, there were two distinct laws of development: natural selection and the law of acceleration and retardation, which he had developed independently of Hyatt. Cope admitted freely that natural selection was at work in the world, preserving or eliminating variations according to their environmental fitness. Yet such variations were only the superficial characteristics of species, not the fundamental ones of genera, the latter of which could not arise through natural selection. The law of acceleration and retardation, on the other hand, worked independent of fitness.

As had Hyatt, Cope focused on embryology to show how development took place. According to Cope, embryological development accelerated at certain points in history. This acceleration allowed the embryo to complete its normal development more quickly and to add another stage to this development. Later individuals also developed to this new level, effectively creating a new species. Because the later forms were more complex and more specialized, Cope rejected any rigid linear developmentalism in favor of branching evolution, with each branch leading to a modern, more specialized form. Students of evolution could find much of value in this "parallelism," because less complex forms—frequently only available as fossils—were similar to the embryonic and early forms of more complex organisms. Development could be traced throughout the evolutionary "tree" in this fashion.[42]

In his attempt to explain how this important process of acceleration took place, Cope abandoned naturalistic explanations. Changes in the environment did not produce changes in the rate of embryological growth. Rather, such changes were the result of supernatural design, placing the ultimate cause of evolution firmly in the hands of the Creator. As Cope wrote in 1868, "[O]ur present knowledge will only permit us to suppose that the resulting and now existing kingdoms and classes of animals and plants were conceived by the Creator according to a plan of his own, according to his pleasure." The development of organisms within the divine plan, however, was guided by the laws of acceleration/retardation and natural selection. The workings of evolution had been foreseen in every detail by the Creator, whose design made such changes possible.[43]

In the conclusion to his article, Cope summarized his findings along three major lines. First, he argued that species developed from existing species through their "inherent tendency to variation," the products of which were preserved or eliminated by natural selection. Here Cope followed Darwin's theory closely. Second, Cope suggested that genera were produced through the processes of acceleration and retardation. Such generic changes, however, were "limited, modified, and terminated" by natural selection. His third conclusion predicted what would be discovered through further paleontological research. The "successional metamorphoses" that were the cause of evolutionary changes would lead to "more or less abrupt transitions" in the geological record, rather than the "uniformly gradual successions" predicted by Darwin. Although admitting a role for natural selection in evolution, Cope remained convinced that it played only a subsidiary part to the law of acceleration and retardation in the Creator's ultimate plan for life on earth.[44]

Cope's commitment to theistic evolution grew less rigid over the next few years, as he and his neo-Lamarckian colleagues relied increasingly on the effects of the environment to explain new stages of growth. Cope's continued work with the fossil evidence further convinced him that evolution had no overall goal, leading him to reject earlier developmental views of a single hierarchy of living forms showing progress. Each branch of the evolutionary tree had to be considered separately. In several essays published during the early 1870s, Cope attempted to develop a more complete version of his evolutionary ideas, eventually abandoning both the concept of a divine plan and the applicability of natural selection to organic development. He suggested that all organisms were impelled by an inherent growth force, *bathmism,* which led in certain directions to further adaptation. Cope also argued that such adaptations would be reinforced if they helped an individual respond to a new environment and would appear in later generations if they continued to provide advantage.

Cope was also quite sure that natural selection could not in any way explain the origins of variations. The inherited effects of habit and environment were the most important factors in the origin of variations and, hence, of species. Resurrecting Lamarck's concept of use/disuse— although Cope was unaware of this at the time—he suggested that modifications of organic structures resulted from use and effort, guided by the intelligence of the animal and passed to later generations. By the end of the decade Cope had assigned an even larger role to intelligence, concluding that evolution was guided by the fundamental consciousness of life. He defined this consciousness as the third element in the universe, along with matter and force. Cope's theory also supplied the mechanism through which environmentally induced change became heritable. Such changes were compressed into earlier stages of development through acceleration. Natural selection was no longer necessary.[45]

As Cope developed his ideas, the neo-Lamarckians gained an important ally in noted geologist Joseph LeConte. A student of Agassiz in the early 1850s, LeConte subscribed to the view of species as products of a divine intelligence for a decade after publication of *Origin of Species.* Aware of evolutionary ideas even before *Origin* appeared, LeConte had argued in the *Southern Presbyterian Review* that the "transmutation of species was as impossible as the transmutation of metals" and suggested that the "development theorists" were no more scientific than the medieval alchemists. Over the next decade, however, especially after he moved from South Carolina to the University of California, LeConte slowly embraced the neo-Lamarckian view of evolution. This conversion paralleled his growing interest in "natural religion" and his increasing belief in the allegorical nature of some of the Bible.[46]

LeConte's religious views and his distrust of such materialistic explanations as natural selection merged nicely into the growing neo-Lamarckism of the 1870s. Addressing the American Association for the Advancement of Science as its retiring president in 1875, LeConte reiterated the design argument as part of neo-Lamarckism. Stressing that nature displayed the same techniques as man would develop, he argued that a "creative or directive power" was at work behind the observed phenomena of the natural world. Throughout the rest of his long career, LeConte continued to apply neo-Lamarckian concepts to virtually every topic he considered.[47]

By the late 1870s neo-Lamarckian ideas had attracted significant interest and acceptance among American naturalists. The neo-Lamarckians' reliance on the inheritance of acquired characteristics minimized the impact of the shorter time scale developed by physicists, an advantage confirmed by Darwin's adoption of Lamarckian inheritance in later editions of *Origin of Species*. Similarly, American neo-Lamarckians tended to advocate saltatory evolution, by which gaps in the fossil record could be explained and through which the limited time scale could be ignored. At the time neo-Lamarckism seemed to represent the most complete version of evolution available.

As neo-Lamarckism gained in acceptance during the early 1880s, its adherents continued to develop their arguments in an attempt to increase the explanatory power of their theory. Few contributed as much to this effort as Cope, who by the middle years of the decade had completed the abandonment of his earlier reliance on the active intervention of a creator. He continued to argue that consciousness and the growth force were both of supernatural origin but produced adaptations through purely natural forces. Cope's continuous, utilitarian concept of evolution thus avoided the problem of explaining design in a universe governed by natural law.[48]

Cope also continued to investigate the origin of variations. Writing for *American Naturalist* in 1882, Cope addressed the Darwinians' lack of success in explaining variations. "On this point the Darwinian is on the same footing as the old-time Creationist," he wrote. "The latter says God made the variations, and the Darwinian says that they came by chance. Between these positions science can perceive nothing to choose." During the early 1880s Cope developed more completely his ideas of variation based on use/disuse and the effort of the organism. Announced at the Philadelphia meeting of the American Association for the Advancement of Science in the fall of 1884, Cope's explanation of variation proceeded along two paths. His doctrine of *kinetogenesis* argued that animal structures were produced by "animal movements." Such movements tended to strengthen certain structures by adding mass, as in the development of the horse's hoof from separate toes. Cope also announced his doctrine of *archaesthetism* to explain the important role consciousness played in evolution. Animal movements, he argued, "are primitively determined by sensibility, or consciousness." This idea led Cope to conclude that consciousness represented "one of the primary factors in the evolution of animal forms." Despite the metaphysical quality of this latter concept, Cope's neo-Lamarckism allowed him to reject the philosophical materialism that he and his colleagues associated with Darwinian natural selection. In his 1887 essay *Theology of Evolution,* Cope specifically stated that neo-Lamarckism was "entirely subversive of atheism," because the primitive conscious energy that permeated his system could only have come from a supernatural force.[49]

By the mid-1880s American neo-Lamarckism appeared to be in a superior position over the more traditional Darwinian evolution through natural selection. In addition to their reliance on environmental influences and the inheritance of acquired characteristics, neo-Lamarckians had developed an internal component in the belief that organisms possessed an innate predisposition to vary in certain ways. This concept of orthogenesis, in fact, became increasingly central to American neo-Lamarckians and provided important support for their views of the interrelationship between nature and the supernatural. Convinced that the evolution of life could not be a product of blind chance—as they interpreted Darwinian evolution—Cope and his colleagues argued that orthogenesis offered a superior explanation. This theory could also provide a basis for stressing the progressive nature of evolution, as the internal drive for greater adaptation resulted in an improved species. When combined with the older Lamarckian concept of the environment's direct impact on organisms, orthogenesis gave American neo-Lamarckians the ability, in Peter J. Bowler's insightful phrase, "to believe what one could no longer prove: that the whole system was set up by a benevolent God."[50] The ability of the American neo-Lamarckians to explain the development of life on earth, without abandoning all orthodox religious concepts, proved to be one of the major reasons for their success in the late nineteenth century.

The supposed theological advantages of neo-Lamarckism were not lost on Protestant intellectual leaders of the Gilded Age. Continuing their efforts to integrate the new biology into religious orthodoxy, many clerics found in neo-Lamarckism a scientific perspective that paralleled certain aspects of their religion. The inherent progress in the organic world suggested that a benevolent God had, at a minimum, initiated the entire process. Equally important, organic progress paralleled the human spiritual progress that represented the goal of organized religion. No longer willing to reject the developmental hypothesis as "bad science," Protestant leaders increasingly embraced the neo-Lamarckian view of evolution as an important element in their theology.

2

Toward the New Century

Religious leaders of the Gilded Age generally gained their knowledge of evolution through the various popularizations that appeared throughout the period. The theistic evolution that underlay many of these discussions provided a developmental perspective that left room for divine intervention, if only as the ultimate cause of variation or the guiding force behind the cosmos. Protestant intellectuals who accepted this idea need not reject natural selection, because a sovereign God directed the process. Another group of Gilded Age theologians, however, remained unable to incorporate the underlying principle of Darwinian evolution into their explanation of the world. The "struggle for existence" that Darwin described struck these clerics as unnecessarily cruel, wasteful, and utterly repugnant to the idea of a beneficent deity. In order to bring the new science into their theology, these religious leaders embraced neo-Lamarckian concepts to create a version of evolution based on the idea of inevitable progress in the material, social, and spiritual realms. As this concept grew during the late nineteenth century, nature began to emerge as a series of self-guiding events that could explain the observed world without the distinct, active intervention of God.[1] Quite different from the theistic evolution proposed by Gray, Wright, and their colleagues, this theology proved to be a potent force in gaining the acceptance of evolution during the Gilded Age.

Many writers of the late nineteenth century attempted to examine the relationship of nature, man, and God by focusing on nature as the bridge between the latter two. Among the earliest Protestant leaders in America to examine the evolution question from this perspective was Princeton president James McCosh, who had arrived from Scotland in 1868. A leading proponent of the Scottish Common Sense tradition, McCosh increased the science offerings at the college and had come to terms with the new developmental hypothesis by the early 1870s. His *Christianity and Positivism*, published in 1871, put forth a view of evolution that enabled like-minded religious thinkers to accept Darwin's work as at least a partial explanation of nature. McCosh emphasized that Darwinian evolution was based on an impressive amount of evidence and had to be dealt with by all who attempted to explain the natural world. Darwin had provided a scientific law that churchmen must integrate into their own philosophy.

Evolution through natural selection, however, represented only part of the story. Other forces clearly were at work, and many questions, such as the nature of the mechanism that guided natural selection, remained unanswered. Further, McCosh rejected the application of natural selection to human development, observing that this would result in the law of the jungle. Human life could only be explained by a "profounder set of facts." The uniqueness of man, based on the existence of a soul, was a result of divine intervention. Nonetheless, McCosh saw no difficulty with evolution and design working in a complementary fashion to guide nature. The clash between science and religion need not take place. As McCosh wrote several years later, "We give to science the things that belong to science, and to God the things that are God's." When evaluating a scientific theory, "our first inquiry is not whether it is consistent with religion, but whether it is true."[2]

If McCosh could assimilate evolution in this fashion, the task proved far easier for members of the theological left wing. Unitarian minister Francis Ellingwood Abbot had put forth his own version of evolutionary theology as early as 1868 in a review of *Principles of Biology,* written by British philosopher Herbert Spencer. Writing in the *North American Review,* Abbot agreed with Spencer that the special creation hypothesis was vastly inferior to the developmental theory, a conclusion that all "disciplined minds" would eventually accept. He rejected, however, the idea that evolution was irreconcilable with theism. On the contrary, Abbot argued, evolution supported the existence of an "omnipotent reason" behind nature. As the developmental theory explained more of nature, "so much the more does the entire system of Nature become admirably intelligible, and so much the greater becomes the probability of its origination in intelligence." Once convinced of the presence of "Infinite Intelligence," the enlightened theist need no longer be troubled by the discoveries of science.[3]

Among the liberal Protestant clergy who attempted to create a new theology that would include a role for evolution, the figure of Henry Ward Beecher assumed a leading position. A highly regarded preacher, Beecher aimed his theological and political liberalism at the middle class through popular sermons and a doctrine based on love, individualism, and the joy of life. Careful never to stray too far from the forms of orthodoxy, he was able to present new ideas more effectively than the more intellectually consistent members of the theological Left. Historian Paul A. Carter captured the essence of Beecher's philosophical outlook by stressing that the New York pastor was content to achieve "charity at the price of clarity" and by describing him as a "broker of ideas."[4]

Beecher's conversion to the new scientific theory began during the winter of 1870, when he led a group of twenty-five Brooklyn ministers in a series of weekly meetings with science popularizer E. L. Youmans. Held in secret, these meetings convinced Beecher and some of his colleagues that evolution had a major role to play in Gilded Age thought. By the summer of 1882, when he composed "Progress of Thought in the Church" for the *North American Review,* Beecher had incorporated evolution into his new theology. Rejecting the suggestion that the United States was less religious than in the past, Beecher argued that religion had only become less narrow. "There is a strong and growing tendency," he wrote, "to enlarge the sphere of Divine Revelation by adding to the Bible the revelation of Nature, and of man's reason and moral consciousness, which are a chief part of Nature." The great scientific developments of the late nineteenth century, evolution and the conservation of mass and energy, had to be dealt with by the old theology, which had erroneously described God as vengeful and punishing. By merging evolution and the fundamentals of Christianity, Beecher wrote, American religion could frame "a theology consistent with the life and teachings of Jesus Christ."[5]

Beecher's essay attracted much attention, not the least of which came from *Popular Science Monthly.* In a two-page summary of his essay, the magazine applauded Beecher's work as a "large and hearty recognition of science as an agency for the purification of religion." Over the next three years Beecher further developed his thoughts, and in May 1885 he began a series of sermons on evolution at Brooklyn's Plymouth Church. These sermons proved so popular that hundreds were turned away for lack of space. Later in the year Beecher published his sermons in a two-volume collection entitled *Evolution and Religion.* Emphasizing that the natural world showed the "sublime history of God as an engineer and architect and as a master-builder," he went on to describe the progress in science and morality as nothing less than the coming of God's kingdom. Such progress was the "record of the unfolding of *man* and of the race under the inspiration of God's nature."[6]

Progressive evolution merged easily with Beecher's positive theological outlook. Equally important, however, was his exposure to the concepts of innate progressive development, which he gleaned from his scientific mentor, E. L. Youmans. Neo-Lamarckism, largely accepted by American naturalists, suggested to Beecher that the unguided, random evolution proposed by the Darwinians need not be considered too favorably. The idea of progress thus emerged as the cornerstone of Beecher's religious liberalism. The kingdom of God was increasingly identified with the progress of civilization, especially the advances in science and morality.[7]

As Henry Ward Beecher developed his own theology of evolution, he realized that a scientific examination of the evolution/religion topic would also be valuable. Beginning in 1883, therefore, Beecher urged Joseph LeConte, well known as a theologically minded naturalist, to write a book on the subject of evolution and religion. Although wary of doing this, LeConte eventually began the manuscript in 1885, completing it three years later and titling it *Evolution and Its Relation to Religious Thought*. Favorably reviewed, LeConte's volume soon attracted the attention of American clergy who desired a cogent discussion of the topic. LeConte's analysis of evolution merged his neo-Lamarckian perspective with the traditional design argument. He could thus define the law of evolution as the technique of the "divine energy in originating and developing the cosmos." Writing that science was nothing more than "a rational system of natural theology," LeConte showed the necessity of a divine being by stressing, "There is no real efficient force but spirit, and no real *independent* existence but God."[8]

LeConte also examined various details of evolution in light of his theology. The tension between the "external progressive force"—use-inheritance and the direct action of the environment—and the "internal conservative force" of like producing like—heredity—was relieved periodically by mutations that accelerated evolutionary change. Rejecting explanations based on Darwinian natural selection, however, LeConte wrote that these phenomena were merely "objectified modes of divine thought" and that the forces involved in such phenomena were nothing more than "different forms of one omnipresent divine energy."[9] LeConte's evolution was thus much more than "God's way of doing things." For the California naturalist, the Divine Being remained intimately involved in terrestrial life, unlike the "master clockmaker" described by other evolutionists.

By the late 1880s the impact of the religious acceptance of some form of evolution was quite visible, with a number of American theologians putting forth various ideas concerning the role of evolution in the natural and theological worlds.[10] Thoughtful Christians in late nineteenth-century America could thus reconcile evolution and religion without abandoning important beliefs that had identified pre-evolutionary theology. Whether arguing that man was in important respects beyond evolution—at least where the soul was concerned—or that a "divine immanence" guided all aspects of nature, American theologians constructed a new view of religion that left many doctrines largely intact. The new theology, however, was not accepted by all. During the same period of theological liberalism that led to the acceptance of developmentalism, other religious thinkers constructed barriers to the acceptance of evolution that would have far-reaching effects.

Continuing Controversy

The reconciliation of evolution and theology remained primarily a northern phenomenon. The lack of a southern attempt to assimilate Darwinism resulted from social, political, and religious characteristics of the region that had been well established before the firing on Fort Sumter. Antebellum southern Protestantism emerged from Puritan and Scottish Common Sense influences and served as one of the institutional foundations for the conservative southern character. The Civil War itself merely intensified the resistance to change that had long characterized the region. New ideas of any kind, according to historian Sydney E. Ahlstrom, were identified with the North and thus rejected by southern thinkers, who transferred the military engagements of the past from the battlefield to the pulpit and lecture room.[11]

By the mid-1870s debates concerning evolution had precipitated several controversies involving higher education in the South. Geologist Alexander Winchell accepted a visiting professorship at Vanderbilt University in 1876, agreeing to teach courses in geology, zoology, and botany. Founded three years earlier over the objections of a majority of both bishops and members of the Southern Methodist Church, Vanderbilt made no claims to be anything other than a training school for Methodist clergy. Winchell, who had been a moderate evolutionist for several years, undoubtedly caused some raised eyebrows in his classes, but his position on campus was not threatened until 1878, when he published *Adamites and Pre-Adamites*. Although not primarily an evolution text, Winchell's volume argued for the existence of humans before Adam and stressed the long time scale that geologists had proposed in contrast to a literal reading of Genesis. Winchell's support of such ideas, which the conservatives on Vanderbilt's Board of Trustees regarded as evolutionary, led to his dismissal from the school in May 1878, an action that Methodists in the region enthusiastically endorsed.

Methodist newspapers emphasized that Vanderbilt was primarily a theological school and thus had a duty to prevent the teaching of scientific theories that could confuse ministerial students.[12]

Vanderbilt's decision was not applauded by everyone. The Nashville *Banner* referred to Vanderbilt University as "a choice fossil specimen of an era that has passed away to come no more." *Popular Science Monthly* exhibited rage over the Winchell dismissal. Emphasizing that most mainstream theologians had accepted the antiquity of the earth, editor E. L. Youmans wrote, "The stupid Southern Methodists that control the university, it seems, can learn nothing. . . . The theologians battled long and fiercely against the geologists on this question, but have been so utterly routed that hardly a man of them can now be found who holds to the old belief."[13]

During the 1880s the southern opposition to evolution received more attention through increased media coverage. Among the most dramatic of the decade's controversies, which focused the attention of a wide segment of public opinion toward the status of evolution among southern clergy, was the case of James Woodrow in South Carolina. Appointed the first Perkins Professor of Natural Sciences in Connexion with Revelation at the Columbia Theological Seminary, Woodrow brought impeccable scientific and theological credentials to his post. A doctoral graduate of the University of Heidelberg, Woodrow had earlier studied with Louis Agassiz. He became an ordained Presbyterian minister in 1859 and soon began editing the quarterly *Southern Presbyterian Review.* Later adding the weekly *Southern Presbyterian* to his editorial duties, Woodrow was an important part of the religious establishment of Southern Presbyterianism. His articles and lectures gave no evidence of any unorthodox views concerning science and Scripture.

By the early 1880s Woodrow had become more sympathetic toward evolutionary concepts. In 1882, at the fall meeting of the seminary's board of directors, suspicions were voiced over his new ideas. Aware that Woodrow was not openly hostile to the new theory, the board feared that the scientist had departed from the faith on this issue. The board took no action until the following May, when it passed a resolution requesting that Woodrow publish an article in *Southern Presbyterian Review* detailing his perspective on evolution. Working on this essay for a year, Woodrow presented his views in a speech to the alumni and board of directors of the seminary in May 1884. In this discussion, published in the July *Review,* Woodrow argued that Adam's body had probably been created through evolution but that the soul had been immediately created by God. Emphasizing that nothing in science contradicted the literal truth of Scripture, Woodrow stressed that his study of nature made him even more impressed with God's plan of creation.

Woodrow's exposition satisfied board members, but opponents insisted that the case be brought before the Synod of South Carolina. Despite an impassioned five-hour speech by Woodrow and five days of debate, the synod passed a resolution that disapproved of the teaching of evolution, "except in a purely expository manner, without intention of inculcating its truth." Other synods in the area opposed the teaching of evolution more forcefully, directing the seminary's board of directors to prohibit such teaching at the school. Faced with this opposition, the seminary's board asked Woodrow to resign, which he refused to do. The board then dismissed Woodrow. Over the next four years the Woodrow case coursed its way through the tortuous channels of Presbyterian government, ultimately reaching the General Assembly meeting in Baltimore in May 1888. There, despite national attention over the years from such periodicals as *Popular Science Monthly, The Nation*, and *American Naturalist*, the assembly voted to uphold Woodrow's dismissal by a vote of 139 to 31. Church doctrine was declared to be that Adam had been formed from the dust of the ground, "without any natural animal parentage of any kind."[14]

Although the publicity surrounding the Woodrow case led many Americans to believe that heresy trials and dismissals were the exclusive province of conservative southern churchmen, religious unorthodoxy led to similar actions in other parts of the country.[15] The Reverend Thomas Howard MacQuery, an Episcopal priest in Canton, Ohio, had been greatly influenced by LeConte's discussion of the reconciliation of science and religion. LeConte's work served as the basis for his own book, *The Evolution of Man and Christianity,* published in 1890, which attempted to carry the reconciliation even further. Although praised by *Popular Science Monthly* as "an earnest and honest attempt to reflect the light of science and modern research on the most difficult points of Christian doctrine," the book outraged the Episcopal Church and led to the first heresy trial in the history of that denomination. MacQuery was tried and removed from the ministry in 1891. In California, a group of San Francisco Bay clergy began criticizing Joseph LeConte over the evolution issue. Led by the Reverend C. H. Hobart of Oakland's First Baptist Church, these clerics accused the Berkeley professor of leading youth astray through the teaching of evolution. Although Hobart's attacks led to much public support for LeConte and an increase in speaking engagements for the naturalist, it was clear that large segments of the religious community throughout the United States were still unwilling to accept evolution as part of the theological foundation of their faith.[16]

Evolution and Society

Although the theological implications of organic evolution provided the basis for many of the most dramatic debates of the Gilded Age, the new theory also attracted the attention of individuals searching for a better understanding of human society. The developmental hypothesis emerged as an important element in the analysis of contemporary America, ultimately supporting a number of different ideas concerning the proper direction of American life. Historians have largely discredited the earlier view of "social Darwinism" as the guiding force behind the economic and political developments of the period, but the assimilation of evolutionary views in American social thought represents an important chapter in the nation's attempt to come to terms with Darwinism.[17]

The philosophy that attracted much attention from American social theorists came from the pen of British philosopher Herbert Spencer, whose ideas antedated *Origin of Species* by a decade. Progressive social evolution was a given, in Spencer's view, but it could only be fully realized through the appropriate role of government. Because society advanced through "the stern discipline of Nature," a concept later defined as survival of the fittest, social policy must allow nature to take its course. Spencer thus called for minimum government interference, as government intervention would artificially preserve the less fit at the expense of society as a whole. Only through such laissez-faire policies could society progress.[18]

Spencer later merged Darwinian concepts of natural selection with his own ideas of the effects of habit and environment. Neither Darwinian nor neo-Lamarckian, Spencer attempted to create a social philosophy to guide the progress that his optimism determined was the natural order. His optimism, further, led to a less harsh view of survival of the fittest than that embraced by those who attempted a more intellectually consistent philosophy. For Spencer, laissez-faire represented a policy that would threaten those individuals in society who did not act appropriately. If such individuals failed to labor diligently and save in a thrifty fashion, their lives would be filled with misery. Such misery would not necessarily eliminate these unfit individuals; rather, a laissez-faire policy would force individuals to become fit, for the greater good of society at large.[19]

Spencer's attempt to formulate a philosophical system to guide society did not please everyone. Despite criticism of his work as excessively speculative, however, Spencer's ideas struck a responsive chord in Gilded Age America. For the most part, Spencer's philosophical writings were not too difficult for the lay public to digest, at least at the superficial level. These writings presented a comprehensive social philosophy that appeared to be based on the science that Americans embraced enthusiastically following the Civil War. Equally important, laissez-faire proved attractive to a nation in which business success was increasingly evident and applauded. Spencer's philosophy also proved compatible with religion, as shown by the work of Henry Ward Beecher and others, as it all but guaranteed human progress while still allowing an important role for "The Unknowable." At the time of Spencer's death in 1903, American sales of authorized editions were approaching 370,000 volumes. Clearly, his optimistic theory of social evolution had caught the nation's attention, and in a way Darwin's more scientific views could not.[20]

The individual most responsible for Spencer's great success in the United States was E. L. Youmans. Largely self-educated and untrained in science, Youmans began reading Spencer's work in the mid-1850s, attracted like many Americans of the period to the Englishman's supposed cosmic philosophy. After meeting Spencer in England in 1862, Youmans served as Spencer's "literary agent" in the United States, promoting the philosopher's ideas through numerous public speaking engagements and arranging for the publication of his essays and books. Of special importance to the spread of Spencerism in America was the periodical *Popular Science Monthly,* founded by Youmans in 1872 as a general magazine of science and current affairs. From the beginning, he sought to popularize Spencer's ideas through the new periodical. Youmans emphasized that the English writer's work was more valuable than the limited evolutionism of Darwin, as Spencer was attempting to create a complete evolutionary system.[21]

Despite Youmans's campaign to make Spencer the philosopher of Gilded Age America, a campaign that was not completely unsuccessful, challenges to Spencerism were prevalent. As historian Robert C. Bannister has demonstrated, neither the business, religious, nor academic communities were composed of devout Spencerians. Even less sympathetic to Spencer's philosophy were American scientists. As the editors of *American Naturalist* emphasized in early 1883, Spencerism was really only accepted by philosophers and metaphysicians. Naturalists, on the other hand, spoke about Darwinism, whether or not they accepted natural selection as the guiding force of evolution. Editors Alpheus S.

Packard, Jr., and Edward Drinker Cope rejected Spencer's multivolume *Biology* (1866-71) as "a collection of general principles in very general and often vague language, with a few facts gleaned from the writings of naturalists." How different was Darwin's work, they argued, which was based on the careful observation of nature. The scientific world accepted evolution because of the careful analyses of Charles Darwin, not because of the rampant speculation of Herbert Spencer.[22]

Challenges to Spencer's evolutionary philosophy, however, must not be interpreted as challenges to developmentalism. Through the writings of various intellectuals and popularizers, evolution percolated through American thought of the Gilded Age. The concept of evolution touched most segments of American life, including the social and economic developments that characterized the United States of the late nineteenth century. During the post-Civil War period, such views attracted much notice, appealing as they did to the growing interest in and awe of science, as well as to the belief that progress was part of the natural order. Spencerian evolution, popularized and disseminated by a number of writers, also suggested to some that worldly success was a measure of fitness in human society. It is now well established that business leaders of the Gilded Age only rarely defined their success as "survival of the fittest," arguing instead that success came through a combination of hard work and Christian stewardship. The concepts generally referred to as social Darwinism, however, remained an important part of American thought in the late nineteenth century.[23]

The archetypal figure in the development of social Darwinism was the clergyman turned sociologist William Graham Sumner. As a minister in New York and New Jersey during the 1860s, Sumner became increasingly interested in science. As it did for many Americans, science provided Sumner with a concept of truth that could be empirically confirmed. This view of empirical truth, however, proved jarring to Sumner's religious faith, which he found increasingly difficult to reconcile with modern science. In an oft-quoted statement, Sumner later wrote, "I never consciously gave up a religious belief. It was as if I had put my beliefs into a drawer, and when I opened it there was nothing there at all." Appointed to the Yale faculty in 1872, Sumner focused his career on efforts to develop a logical defense of social Darwinism based on the Protestant ethic, classical economics, and, most important, the concept of evolutionary change.[24]

Sumner's view of society focused on economic criteria as the essence of societal virtues. For him, capital represented the primary index of social improvement, which, in turn, was the foundation of civilization. The individuals who accumulated capital were thus serving society by bolstering the civilization that guaranteed liberty and rights. This natural order should be allowed to proceed unimpeded. In contrast, government had proved itself unequal to the task of securing these goals. Without a decision-making meritocracy, made impossible by the American belief in political equality, government decisions were increasingly made on the basis of effective lobbying and shifting coalitions of interests. These inherent weaknesses of government made the state incompetent to deal with the vast and complex society of the late nineteenth century. It would be better to leave the many and interrelated parts free to operate according to natural laws. In what may be his most famous utterance, Sumner told the Free Trade Club in 1879 that "the law of the survival of the fittest was not made by man. . . . We can only, by interfering with it, produce the survival of the unfittest."[25]

Gilded Age America provided Sumner with more than enough evidence to support his ideas concerning the need for a new philosophy of government and society based on what he perceived as the purifying influence of Spencerism. His English colleague's advocacy of limited government would rid America of the danger of misguided egalitarianism leading to the economic deprivation of the able by the less able. If the government were modified to support the ill-equipped at the expense of the successful, both groups would lose. The successful would be deprived of their means, while the unsuccessful would abandon their efforts at self-improvement. By denying the unsuccessful the chance to attempt to fend for themselves, the state arbitrarily limited the possibility of societal improvement through the natural developmental process associated with social Darwinism.[26]

Evolutionary concepts, as defined by Sumner and other social theorists, pointed toward the improvement of society. As these philosophers advocated a laissez-faire policy, however, others began to question the applicability of biological theories to human society. Stressing the importance of intellect and culture in human evolution, these "reform Darwinists" called for greater, not less, government regulation and some form of social welfare. As Robert Bannister persuasively argued, these reformers were the true Darwinians of the late nineteenth century. Supporters of the Spencerian/Sumnerian laissez-faire concept, whether they realized it or not, based their philosophy on the existence of a beneficent natural order. Reform Darwinists, in contrast, recognized and accepted the disorderly nature of the struggle for existence. For humanity to progress, society must transcend nature, not meekly surrender to it. To suggest that humans struggled in the same fashion as the lower orders of animal life denigrated human society and trivialized human thought and culture.[27]

Among the most famous of the reform Darwinists was Lester Frank Ward, who served variously as a government geologist, a paleontologist, and later as professor of sociology at Brown University. Beginning in the mid-1870s Ward stressed that nature, operating as it did through natural selection, was an inherently wasteful system. Especially in human society, positive or "integrative" forces were necessary to counter the negative or "disintegrative" forces symbolized by the struggle for existence. The contrast between integrative and disintegrative processes suggested that schemes of cosmic evolution, such as those of Spencer and Sumner, were inherently flawed. The evolution of the physical world was a process of disintegration, while organic evolution accounted for an integrative progression.

Ward's best-known analysis of social evolution appeared in 1883 in his book *Dynamic Sociology*. Rejecting Spencer's ideas—compare the title of Ward's volume with *Social Statics*—Ward argued that evolution had brought humanity to the point of escape from natural selection. The emergence of the human mind through the physical processes of evolution had introduced a new and powerful variable that had changed the rules of the game. Spencer had erred when he postulated a society that did not allow for the improvement of the quality of life. "We are told to let things alone, and allow nature to take its course," Ward argued. "But has intelligent man ever done this? Is not civilization, with all it has accomplished, the result of man's *not* letting things alone, and of his *not* letting nature take its course?" For human society to progress, social forces had to be harnessed through Ward's version of scientific government. Such a government was to be an instrument of "amelioration" to provide positive benefits to its citizens. In a feat of civil engineering, scientific government would use knowledge for the benefit of society.[28]

As Ward and other secular reformers attempted to establish an intellectual foundation for a new view of society, clerical reformers focused on the specific problems facing America in the Gilded Age. Increasingly visible labor unrest and the growing realization that American Protestantism was largely a middle- and upper-class phenomenon led many concerned clerics to embrace a new philosophy usually referred to as the Social Gospel. Although in clear contrast to the general Gilded Age Protestant view that the "gospel of Christ was . . . in full harmony with the Gospel of Wealth," the Social Gospel was similarly based on evolutionary concepts of development and progress.[29]

The best-known figure in the Social Gospel movement was Congregational minister and popularizer of higher criticism Washington Gladden. In his pioneering work, *Applied Christianity* (1887), Gladden repeated the arguments of Lester Frank Ward and others that competition and survival of the fittest were the laws of plants and animals, not of civilized society. As society progressed, the struggle for existence disappeared, to be replaced by the higher principles of goodwill and mutual assistance. Such progress, from Gladden's perspective, was completely compatible with the concept of evolution, which he described as "a most impressive demonstration of the presence of God in the world." By replacing the laissez-faire competitive order with a new social order based on Christian ethics and Christian conscience, the interests of employers and employees could be merged for the good of society.[30]

To believe that such a change in American thought was possible in the days of the Homestead and Pullman strikes, the growth of the Standard Oil Trust, and the development of the United States Senate into one of the most exclusive businessmen's clubs in the world required a rare degree of optimism. Gladden's 1893 book, *Tools and Man: Property and Industry under the Christian Law,* is a testament to the spirit of optimistic reform. Gladden believed "that industry and trade can be so transformed by humane motives that they shall be serviceable to all the higher interests of men." All would benefit from the new society, which would establish social justice in a way hitherto unknown. Through acceptance of the Social Gospel, Gladden proclaimed, he could see the day when business emerged as the "high calling of God" and unscrupulous capitalists became "almost as fabulous as the dragons and vampires of mythologic lore."[31]

While it is true that Social Gospelers failed to progress beyond a general concern with social problems and lacked an overriding philosophy or theology, Gladden and his followers nonetheless provided religious Americans with a new focus in dealing with the changes of the Gilded Age. If the traditional Protestant concern with individual salvation had been tarnished by contact with the economic individualism of Henry Ward Beecher's theology, the Social Gospel could at least provide a concept of "Christian" work that had relevance to the closing decades of the nineteenth century. Feeding the hungry, clothing the poor, and housing the unemployed represented the proper Christian life and were as much a part of the New Testament message as personal salvation. By the early twentieth century even the evangelical conservatives were considering social reconstruction as a worthwhile goal of organized religion.

Equally important, however, the proponents of the Social Gospel were successful in accommodating their reformist views to evolutionary concepts, in much the same fashion as the reform Darwinists. The message from Gladden was essentially that of *Dynamic Sociology:* Nature must be overcome, not fatalistically submitted to. Only by overcoming nature could man become truly human. Gladden wrote in 1899: "We know that we have the power to choose the better life and to struggle toward it. . . . Even if we are crippled by heredity and borne down by a hostile environment, we can turn our faces upstream and swim against the current." Evolutionary concepts, whether Darwinian or neo-Lamarckian, need not doom humanity to a social parody of natural selection. Whether as a result of mental, moral, ethical, or religious development, humans were different from the rest of the natural world. As Lester Frank Ward and Washington Gladden both emphasized, that difference created a new set of rules, allowing man to transcend nature and to improve human society in the process.[32]

The Return of Natural Selection

As Gilded Age theologians and philosophers assimilated evolutionary concepts, the scientific community continued to explore and refine the developmental hypothesis. Despite the general acceptance of neo-Lamarckism by American naturalists, Darwin's evolutionary theory based on natural selection continued to enjoy support in the late nineteenth century. At least part of this support emerged from the philosophical preference for the primacy of law as the guiding force in explanations of nature. Although there existed uncertainties in Darwin's explanation of the origin and progress of life on earth, his theory of evolution did have a strong "legalistic" focus. Those theories based on the inheritance of acquired characteristics, growth force, and the organism's internally directed progress all seemed to suggest an extralegal guiding principle. American naturalists who were uncomfortable with this latter version of evolutionary theory thus sought to explain observed phenomena in terms more compatible with Darwin's original formulation of evolution, despite the minority status of their outlook.[33]

The leader of these American Darwinists was the Yale paleontologist Othniel C. Marsh, who unearthed much of the fossil evidence used to support evolutionary theories. Examining the fossil horse sequence and the fossilized remains of birds with teeth and other reptilian characteristics, Marsh provided crucial evidence of the dramatic change over time in various organic forms. The increasing complexity shown by these developmental sequences also provided a better delineation of geologic chronology, which allowed fossils and geological structures to be dated in more precise terms.

As great as Marsh's field contributions were, however, his adherence to natural selection established him as part of the continuity from Darwin's original formulations to the later perspective generally identified as neo-Darwinism. In a survey of fossil forms from North America published in *Popular Science Monthly* in early 1878, Marsh emphasized the increasing complexity of fossilized organisms over time, as well as the extinction of various species. Focusing more specifically on mammalian forms, he argued that certain structural changes could best be explained through natural selection, which Marsh defined as a Malthusian struggle among animals and also a struggle with the environment. Changes in brain size, teeth, limbs, and feet all could be explained better by the natural struggle in the world, rather than by the organism's inherent desire to progress or the guidance of an external (supernatural) agency.[34] For Marsh, as for his Darwinian colleagues, natural selection offered a superior law to explain evolution.

The development that ultimately led to greater credibility for the selectionist position proved to be the work of German zoologist August Weismann of the University of Freiburg. During the 1880s Weismann developed his "germ plasm" theory through his observation of cellular division and other aspects of the reproductive process. From these investigations, he developed the concept that the germ cells of the body remained entirely different from the somatic cells. If the germ cells were, indeed, separate from the somatic cells throughout the life of the organism, no changes produced by the action of the environment on the organism could be transmitted through heredity. The inheritance of acquired characteristics was an impossibility. In an attempt to gain experimental confirmation of his theory, Weismann severed the tails of several generations of mice, finding that these mutilated mice never transmitted their tailless condition to their offspring. If correct, Weismann's theory allowed only two possibilities for evolution. Either changes took place as sudden and large-scale saltations, or minor variations were acted upon by natural selection over time, creating the changes that were the foundation of evolution. For Weismann, the latter explanation provided a more naturalistic account of the observed phenomena.[35]

Weismann identified the germ plasm with the chromosomes in the cell nucleus. He was thus able to define chromosomal recombination as the source of the required genetic variability upon which natural selection acted. This recognition of the importance of sexual recombination in the generation of genetic variability later proved to be one of Weismann's most important contributions to the debate over evolution. During the 1880s, however, more attention was paid to the impact of his new germ plasm theory on the continuing debate between natural selection and the inheritance of acquired characteristics. For Weismann and his followers, the separation of the germ cells from the body, making impossible the transmission of any environmentally induced changes, invalidated the basis of neo-Lamarckism. Natural selection alone could explain the process of evolution. Later known as neo-Darwinism, this evolutionary theory purged Darwinism of the Lamarckian taint visible in the later editions of *Origin of Species.*

The translation of Weismann's work in the late 1880s and early 1890s encouraged those American naturalists who had continued to focus on natural selection as the key factor in evolution. Showing, as it seemed to do, that the inheritance of acquired characteristics was an impossibility, the germ plasm theory left only natural selection as the basis for evolutionary change. Yet Weismann's reliance on many experimentally unconfirmed concepts limited his theory. The assumption of particulate inheritance, for example, seemed remarkably imaginative in the late nineteenth century, but little more.[36] Although Weismann's theory appears intriguingly modern in some ways and certainly stimulated the investigations that led to the development of a workable hereditarian theory, it is unlikely that the germ plasm concept converted any but those already sympathetic to natural selection as the primary force in evolution.

As the central tenet in Weismann's selectionist arguments, the germ plasm concept became the focus of the neo-Lamarckian challenge to neo-Darwinism. The concept of a separate germ plasm seemed to be at odds with the traditional view of an organism as an integrated, self-regulating system. The germ cells, as part of the body, must be subject to the same external forces. If the somatic cells could change as a result of environmental impact, so could the germ cells. Further, opponents of Weismann's ideas stressed, growth was an open-ended process at every stage, from the formation of the egg through fertilization and embryological development. To place the germ cells outside this process appeared both arbitrary and unsupported by evidence, leading some to argue that this scheme dramatized the weakness of evolution through natural selection.[37]

The most prolific of the neo-Lamarckians, Edward Drinker Cope proved to be the most vocal American opponent of Weismann's theories. A recent addition to the faculty at the University of Pennsylvania, Cope examined the new ideas in an article for *American Naturalist* in

December 1889. He dismissed Weismann's evidence from mice as irrelevant, arguing that all naturalists knew that such mutilations could not be inherited and were thus not part of the natural order. Cope was willing to admit the existence, and perhaps even the inheritability, of what he called "promiscuous variations," but he stressed that such variations would likely last no more than a generation. He found it "highly improbable" that a succession of such random variations would lead to a structure or other change that would be beneficial to the organism and, thus, ultimately to the species. In short, Cope argued, if acquired characteristics were not inherited, evolution could not work for the benefit of the individual or the species.[38]

Seven years later Cope contributed the most complete argument in favor of neo-Lamarckism and against neo-Darwinism in his imposing volume *The Primary Factors of Organic Evolution.* Although he reiterated criticisms that Darwinian theories remained flawed because they could not explain the origins of variation, Cope stressed that his purpose was to show the impressive evidence that supported neo-Lamarckian ideas. For Cope, the paleontological record showed development not in random fashion but in a clear progressive line from less to more advanced organisms. The succession of fossil forms showed clearly a direction in evolution.[39] Having rejected random variations as the cause of evolution, Cope developed his own argument to account for the development of organic life through external influences. Assuming the inheritance of acquired characteristics, he discussed two classes of influences that led to evolution. The first Cope described as a physico-chemical influence, to which he attached the name *physiogenesis.* Physiogenesis was the impact of climate and other environmental causes on an organism. More important in Cope's arguments was the second influence, which was the mechanical influence he had earlier called kinetogenesis. Cope based this theory on extensive studies of muscles, bones, horns, teeth, and the size and strength of limbs, as evidenced in the fossil record. Impact and strain were directly responsible for the lengthening of limb bones in heavy animals, for example, as well as for other skeletal changes. Such mechanical explanations could be illustrated by analogy, which Cope did dramatically in his discussion of the ankle joint of the horse. Calling this structure a "treble tongue-and-groove joint," Cope concluded that the structure of the joint was "exactly what would happen if two pieces of plastic dead material, similarly placed, should be subjected to a continual pounding in the direction of their length."[40]

The changes Cope cited to explain his kinetogenetic theory could clearly be seen as useful to the organism involved. These modifications would equally be useful to later generations, a fact that Cope used to challenge natural selection as the primary cause of evolution. He admitted that minute variations took place, but he questioned whether such changes could result in cumulative variations of evolutionary significance. "That minute advantageous differences will secure survival no one can doubt," Cope wrote in *Primary Factors,* "but it must be remembered that the variations which constitute evolution have been in a vast number of cases too minute to be useful." Developed and preserved through kinetogenesis, however, variations could follow the progressive development that was the heart of evolution.[41]

The debate between the neo-Darwinists and the neo-Lamarckians characterized much of the discussion of evolution during the last decade of the nineteenth century. In 1898 Alpheus S. Packard, Jr., one of the founding fathers of American neo-Lamarckism, devoted his address before the zoology section of the American Association for the Advancement of Science to a discussion of the development of evolution. Packard characterized the second half of the nineteenth century by the acceptance of "epigenetic evolution," as opposed to the pre-Darwinian acceptance of preformation. This advance was crucial to a better understanding of organic change. Packard thus found it "not a little strange" that the supporters of Weismann's germ plasm theory seemed to be returning to a preformationist concept. Far better, in Packard's view, was the current neo-Lamarckian explanation, combining as it did Lamarck's concepts of the inheritance of acquired characteristics and the Darwinian concepts of competition and natural selection.

Packard also stressed another important factor in the history of evolution that discredited the Weismann theory. Rather than displaying the randomness that was a part of neo-Darwinism, evolutionary changes over time had developed in an "orderly and progressive way." Not only did this directional component of evolution undermine neo-Darwinism, but it also provided an entry for theistic evolution. Packard informed his audience that evolutionary changes appeared to be "purposive rather than fortuitous" and to have emerged from natural laws that were "impressed on matter by an intelligence and force outside of, yet immanent in, all things material." The existing natural order had not evolved on its own but was a product of "an infinite Intelligence and Will."[42] Packard's discussion displayed the acceptance of theistic evolution that frequently appeared in neo-Lamarckian arguments. The randomness of Weismann's concept of variations seemed to challenge such beliefs and was often the aspect of neo-Darwinism that most troubled neo-Lamarckians.

By the late 1890s, however, naturalists were beginning to ask questions that challenged many assumptions of the debate. Henry S. Williams of Yale argued in the *American Naturalist* that the orthodox view of evolution, whether neo-Darwinian or neo-Lamarckian, was "inconsistent" in its attempt to explain the relation of variation and heredity to evolution. The orthodox view accepted the mutability of organic species, while rejecting the mutability of the "fundamental units of biology," such as the cell, the individual, and the "protoplasmic states of matter."[43] The accuracy of Williams's definition of the "orthodox" view of evolution remains a debatable point. Yet his emphasis on those aspects of growth that could be studied best in the laboratory pointed to an important change in the outlook of the scientific community by the end of the nineteenth century. Despite Packard's argument for a guiding Intelligence and Will, such supernatural concepts were increasingly viewed as irrelevant to scientific explanations. Although many scientists embraced religious orthodoxy in their personal lives, their goals as scientists focused on naturalistic explanations.[44]

At the turn of the twentieth century, the concept of evolution, broadly defined, was largely integrated into the American scientific community. Although naturalists differed greatly in their specific views of what evolution was and how it progressed, such debates were waged within the context of an accepted theory of organic development over time. The debates that involved American scientists in the years surrounding 1900 provided clear evidence of the vitality of the evolutionary concept and its value as a stimulus to further investigation. Whether neo-Darwinist or neo-Lamarckian, evolutionary scientists were engaged in the development of a theory that represented a crucial contribution to the understanding of life on earth. This development would continue throughout the next century.

The Religious Impact of Evolution

As scientists refined the evolutionary concept in the late nineteenth century, the American religious community continued its efforts to integrate the new biological worldview into theology. By the 1890s many American theologians had accepted evolutionary ideas, as they had accepted such developments as the study of comparative religions and biblical criticism. Although reaction against such views remained visible, this liberal response appeared to be a growing movement that represented the future of American religion.[45] Yet American religion included a wide variety of viewpoints, some of which remained hostile to the new orthodoxy built on evolution and biblical criticism. The late nineteenth century witnessed the emergence of "liberal" and "conservative" wings in almost all Protestant denominations. Such internal divisions proved far more important than denominational differences in shaping the American religious community of the twentieth century. In almost every case, the divisive topics focused on scriptural authority and the scientific accuracy of the Bible. Those who rejected challenges to these concepts would be identified with the fundamentalists of the twentieth century.[46]

In the late nineteenth century, however, a growing number of proto-fundamentalists expressed their displeasure with the new orthodoxy embraced by theological liberals. Two of the most effective spokesmen for this conservative view were evangelist Dwight L. Moody and popular Presbyterian preacher De Witt Talmage, both of whom emphasized biblical infallibility as the foundation of meaningful religion. Talmage referred to those scholars who attempted to apply the new techniques of historical criticism to the Bible as "hybrid theologians" and "mongrel ecclesiastics." Moody dismissed the movement toward biblical criticism with the intriguing statement "The Bible was not made to understand!" In one of Moody's more popular sermons, he spoke of the "four great temptations that threaten us to-day," including the theater, disregard of the Sabbath, and Sunday newspapers, all of which separated man from the proper life expected by God. Particularly threatening was the fourth temptation of atheistic teachings, which Moody identified with evolution. While opposing biblical criticism and other examples of the new theology, conservatives like Talmage and Moody continued to emphasize evolution as a major obstacle on the road to salvation.[47]

The views represented by Talmage and Moody were also prevalent in the meetings of the Niagara Bible Conference. Founded in 1876, the conference had consistently condemned biblical criticism and many other aspects of the new theology. By 1895 the Niagara biblicists were ready to announce the five points deemed indispensable for the Christian faith. Offered as an alternative to the liberal theology that seemed to be in control of American Protestantism, these points included scriptural inerrancy, the divinity of Christ, the Virgin Birth, the substitutionary atonement of Christ, and the Resurrection and Second Coming. These beliefs later became the base for twentieth-century fundamentalism, but their exposition in 1895 clearly indicated the existence of a strong challenge to the liberal Protestantism of Gilded Age America.[48]

The increase in church membership in the late nineteenth century, the vitality of both the liberal and conservative wings of American Protestantism, and the active attempt to reconcile the discoveries of science with traditional religion all represent an important part of the religious history of the period. Yet the emergence of an increasingly evident disbelief also characterized the late nineteenth century. An essay published in *Popular Science Monthly* in July 1874, for example, asked the question "Who are the propagators of atheism?" Arguing that the acrimonious debate over science and religion came primarily from the religious side of the issue, the anonymous author followed the *Monthly*'s editorial policy of stressing the unreasonableness of all who challenged science. Yet he also made an insightful point when he wrote that those who connected science with atheism were actually propagating the latter by suggesting that a demonstrated truth—evolution, for example—was atheism. Defining the existence of God as dependent upon modern science, the author continued, was "rather suicidal theology" and might help to explain the increase in unbelief.[49]

A more involved discussion of the future of belief appeared in the July-August 1878 issue of *North American Review* under the title "An Advertisement for a New Religion." The author, who identified himself only as "An Evolutionist," emphasized that "advanced thinkers" agreed that all the old religions were dying and must soon disappear. He also stressed, however, that these same thinkers recognized that humans had religious instincts that would have to be satisfied in some way. A new religion was needed, the evolutionist argued, and would undoubtedly arise through natural means, including natural selection.

The author attempted to sketch the outlines of this new religion by listing the components necessary for a workable modern theology. First, God could not be living and personal. Second, there was no personal immortality of the soul. The author's third point stressed that there were no terrors to be feared from the day of judgment. "These may frighten children, and men and women weak as children," he emphasized, "but highly-developed men are beyond them." Point 4 announced that there were neither "ghostly sanctions" nor "motives" derived from supernatural power or the world to come. The author concluded that everything beyond the senses must be represented as unknown and unknowable. What, then, was the basis for this new religion? The new religion would have "humanity as its god."[50]

Although a leading periodical of the day, *North American Review* was not one of the large-circulation magazines that were growing in popularity during the late nineteenth century. It is thus unlikely that

"An Advertisement for a New Religion" attracted the same kind of attention as the statements of Dwight L. Moody or Henry Ward Beecher. Indeed, most American free thinkers were not well known, despite their organizations, such as the Free Religious Association, the National Liberal League, or the Society for Ethical Culture. Robert Green Ingersoll, however, represented the free thinkers in the public mind because of his dramatic oratory and ability to attract the interest of the press. Known to conservatives as the Devil's Ambassador, the Pagan Prophet, or Robert Godless Injuresoul, this most famous of Gilded Age agnostics commanded much attention throughout the late nineteenth century.

Characterizing the post-Darwinian concept of natural law as "the death-knell of superstition," Ingersoll rejected both conservative orthodoxy and the liberal Protestant attempt to reconcile traditional theology with Darwin. He dismissed the design argument, relying instead on Darwinism without design. From Ingersoll's perspective, Darwin had served humanity better than he knew, by providing a profounder discussion of human history. Darwin's work had shown "that man has for thousands of years steadily advanced" and that "the Garden of Eden is an ignorant myth." The doctrine of original sin had "no foundation in fact," and the atonement was "an absurdity." Darwin showed further, according to Ingersoll, "that the serpent did not tempt; and that man did not 'fall.' " Rather than rely on outmoded religious views, Ingersoll preferred to see Christ as an ethical teacher who showed man how to live an appropriate life. All else was mythology.[51]

Ingersoll's value as a symbol of the growing unbelief in America cannot be overemphasized, but unbelief in general had established itself far beyond his agnosticism. As shown by James Turner in his book *Without God, Without Creed: The Origins of Unbelief in America,* orthodox religion had defined belief in a self-defeating fashion by the late 1800s. Not only did the pre-Darwinian "proofs" of God's existence lose their impact as science explained more and more of the natural world, but the liberal Protestant attempt to reformulate ideas of God led some thinkers to the conclusion that such ideas were gratuitous, as perhaps was the very concept of God. As Turner wrote, "Having made God more and more like man—intellectually, morally, emotionally— the shapers of religion made it feasible to abandon God, to believe simply in man."[52]

Not surprisingly, it appears to have been the concept of natural selection, and its relation to the design argument, that launched many on the path to unbelief. Natural selection explained much in nature without reliance on any supernatural or metaphysical ideas. This situation reflected and reinforced the new view of science as totally focused on the physical world, no longer relying on religious views as part of the explanatory process. More important, however, natural selection as explanation led to the recognition of pain and suffering as nature's way. This recognition led many to argue against religious faith based on the goodness of God. Turner summarized the feelings of the time: "If this [natural selection] were design, its sloppiness and inefficiency suggested gross incompetence; and if this were benevolence, the designer exercised it with a paradoxical delight in suffering." Whether or not Darwin and his supporters could prove evolution by natural selection was immaterial. The likelihood that Darwinian evolution explained much of nature was enough to destroy the argument from design as proof of God's existence.[53]

The Gilded Age devotion to science as the path to knowledge and, thus, to truth also played a role in supporting the growing unbelief of the period. Orthodox religion asked humans to believe in things that they could not know were true. Such belief struck many in the Gilded Age as somehow immoral, as it would be impossible to continue progress—which, after all, was based on knowledge—with such belief. Arguing that progress was the "keystone in the arch of morality," American agnostics rejected belief without knowledge to insure that progress would continue. Progress thus became the agnostics' god. Progress, like God, gave purpose to life and could extend across generations. But it was science, not belief without knowledge, that led to this progress.[54]

Agnostics also had to propose a workable view of morality to replace the one developed through centuries of religious thought. Here, too, evolution played the crucial role. The development of human morality could be defined in evolutionary terms as another aspect of the progress of humanity. Morality was thus a natural outgrowth of evolution, which had, according to the agnostics, nothing to do with a supreme being. With this concept as a foundation, American unbelievers also challenged the ethical basis of Christianity, replacing such ethics with two principles: the "nobility of uncompromised pursuit of truth" and a "commitment to human progress." These principles led agnostics to a view of human society that could promise as much as that of the liberal Protestant orthodoxy, which appeared to command the theological field of the late nineteenth century. If the agnostics' view of society provided no afterlife for the individual, at least it provided a better life for later generations.[55]

The significance of the agnostic movement in Gilded Age America is not a function of its size, as the number of individuals involved remained much smaller than either the liberal or conservative wings of Protestantism. The significance of this group, rather, stems from its ability to abandon orthodox religion and to replace it with an intellectually defensible position of unbelief. To have succeeded in this effort during a period of vitality in American churches suggests that the agnostics viewed religious developments of the period in a different light than did the orthodox. While liberal Protestants adapted their faiths to the new science of evolution, however they defined it, agnostics questioned whether anything of value was left in religion. As James Turner cogently concluded, the changes in orthodox religion provided the impetus for unbelief. In their attempts to assimilate the new scientific outlook, church leaders put aside the transcendent quality that defined a meaningful deity. They focused much of their religion on improving the world from the human perspective, while embracing an epistemology that was only appropriate for understanding physical reality.[56] The American church hierarchy thus committed theological suicide and opened the door to both agnostics and conservatives, neither of whom could accept the new view of God.

3

Gathering at the River

As the twentieth century began, the assimilation of evolutionary concepts within the American intellectual community had been largely completed. Scientists, theologians, and philosophers had examined the new biological theory and its many implications, coming to terms with evolution in a variety of ways. During the first quarter of the century, however, the evolution controversy underwent a profound transformation, as debates and discussions involved a broader segment of the American public. Led by a number of religious and political figures, a recognizable movement emerged that attempted to spread the anti-evolution gospel across the nation. Symbolized by the passage of several laws prohibiting the teaching of evolution and by the Scopes trial of 1925, this crusade represented an important facet of the broader movement known as Protestant fundamentalism. In many respects, this broader movement may be seen as a response to events no less dramatic than those that characterized the late nineteenth century.

Quite apart from the chronological drama of the opening of a new century, the early 1900s seemed to promise major changes in the United States. Having weathered the intellectual and social upheavals of previous decades, Americans embraced a new view of society and politics, symbolized by the word *progressivism*. The political and social reforms associated with the presidencies of Theodore Roosevelt, William Howard Taft, and Woodrow Wilson represented the best-known aspects of this period, but Progressive views permeated American society from the beginning of the century through the end of World War I. Evolutionary thought, frequently defined in relation to progress and improvement, played an important role in the development of these ideas. Progressives had little doubt concerning the prospects of beneficial change in the United States.[1]

The reform mentality symbolized by the Progressives was shared by the American religious community as well. The Social Gospel outlook proved to be an important part of reform in the early twentieth century and led to clerical activism on a wide front. Although liberal reform activity was the best known, conservatives—many of whom would later become active fundamentalists—also participated in the movement.[2] If liberals and conservatives could agree on the need for social reform, however, another development in American religion would ultimately divide American Protestantism into two hostile camps. The scholarly techniques of biblical criticism had been accepted by the liberals—or modernists, as they were increasingly called—in American denominations by 1900. Although at first restricted to the centers of scholarship in seminaries and universities, "higher criticism" was seen as an important tool to improve Christianity. In addition to providing more accurate translations of religious material, biblical criticism represented another attempt to assimilate American religion into an increasingly secular community marked by a scientific outlook.

By the beginning of World War I, modernism had been well established in virtually all major American denominations, spreading from the scholars into the local churches. Theology, popular understanding of the Christian message, and denominational creeds all appeared to be changing, with liberal theology seeming to advocate the existence of God as a benevolent father, rather than as a judge, and appearing to view the Bible as a great work of literature, rather than as a sacred text.[3] These perceived changes precipitated a response on the part of American religionists who were uncomfortable with the new order. Eventually known as fundamentalists, these American Protestants represented the conservative challenge to the modernists. In part, this challenge emerged from a rejection of biblical criticism and other modernist doctrines that appeared to threaten traditional religious views. Of even greater import, as stressed by Ernest R. Sandeen in his classic 1970 study, *The Roots of Fundamentalism,* was the fundamentalists' devotion to millenarian doctrines, which emphasized the return of Christ as the beginning of the millennial process. In the decades before World War I, these millenarians established themselves as accepted members of many denominations, providing conservatives with a unifying view and raising questions concerning the observed liberal drift. Representing an internal challenge to the modernists in many denominations, the millenarians continued to speak out against the weakening of doctrines, stressed the work of evangelism, and led the way in the creation of a new kind of school known as the Bible institute.[4]

Although the Protestants who would eventually become known as fundamentalists never represented a monolithic social or political viewpoint, they were nonetheless able to define themselves through their antimodernist views. Their attempt to defend traditional theology appeared most clearly in the twelve small volumes published between 1910 and 1915 under the title *The Fundamentals.* These volumes contained ninety articles on a variety of topics, yet their continuity appeared more evident than their diversity. Safeguarding the Bible, defending orthodox doctrines and personal testimonies, attacking incorrect beliefs, and appealing for missions and evangelism characterized most of the material in the volumes. Other aspects of what would become the fundamentalist-modernist debate were of less concern, with the topic of evolution, for example, practically ignored and covered in a nonconfrontational manner. Distributed free of charge to pastors, missionaries, educators, and others, *The Fundamentals* received wide exposure, with an average press run of some 250,000 copies per volume. Despite the lack of immediate response on the part of the public or religious leaders, *The Fundamentals* became a symbolic reference point for the antimodernists of the early twentieth century.[5]

By the time the twelfth volume of the series appeared in the spring of 1915, American evangelicals had become concerned with the impact of World War I. The eruption of a world conflict had a major effect on American religious conservatives, apparently confirming the millenarians' predictions of disasters leading to Christ's return. As a result, the United States witnessed an increase in premillennial literature during the war and a parallel increase in the number of premillennial conferences. The interest in millenarian thought and biblical prophecy led to two important meetings in 1918. During late May in Philadelphia and late November in New York, prophetic conferences convened to great enthusiasm and large crowds. At the New York conference, William Bell Riley of Minneapolis proposed a third meeting in Philadelphia for the following spring, convincing his colleagues that such a conference could represent the first step in a broader campaign. In late May 1919 the Philadelphia conference witnessed the creation of a new organization, the World's Christian Fundamentals Association, which redirected the antimodernist movement toward an emphasis on the fundamentals of the faith. Riley later wrote his own view of the events by arguing that the foundation of the association would eventually be seen "as an event of more historical moment than the nailing up, at Wittenberg, of Martin Luther's ninety-five theses. The hour has struck for the rise of a new Protestantism." The association quickly launched a massive conference campaign in eighteen American and Canadian cities, including Minneapolis, Denver, Calgary, and Seattle.[6]

The concern that led to the institutionalization of fundamentalism by 1919 was only one product of the Great War. The events of 1914-18 led to a significant disillusionment among Americans who had hoped that the war would make the world a better place. As troops returned from Europe bearing the emotional and physical scars of trench warfare, not to mention the results of machine gun fire and poison gas, it became difficult to view the war as a product of a modern, progressive civilization. Although written from a much more intimate perspective than that available to most Americans, Winston Churchill's comments following the war probably reflected the disillusionment felt by many. Churchill, then the British secretary of state for war, pointed out that military and civilian rulers during the war stopped at nothing to give their countries an advantage. "When all was over," Churchill said, "Torture and Cannibalism were the only two expedients that the civilized, scientific, Christian States had been able to deny themselves: and they were of doubtful utility."[7]

Such disillusionment added to the evangelicals' feelings of despair following the war. Despite their seeming success with prophetic conferences and the like, they continued to view World War I as evidence of something very wrong in the world. How could civilized states spend four years slaughtering each other? Why had Germany behaved the way it had? The answer to this second question was relatively easy to develop for the fundamentalists, as German scholars had long been suspect because of their influence on biblical criticism.[8] Identifying the underlying philosophy behind German *Kultur* with Darwinian evolution served to revolutionize the movement into the crusade it became in the 1920s. This idea first surfaced in 1917 in a volume entitled *Headquarters Nights,* written by biologist Vernon L. Kellogg. During his service as a member of Herbert Hoover's staff in Belgium, Kellogg interviewed several German officers and concluded that German philosophy reflected a crude Darwinism ruthlessly applied to international affairs. Kellogg, despite his rejection of natural selection as the guiding force of evolution, was a sufficiently knowledgeable biologist to realize precisely how crudely Darwinism would have to be applied to justify German activity. Other biologists of the period similarly stressed the "distorted" nature of "Germanized" Darwinism.[9] Such distinctions, however, were frequently lost on less sophisticated readers, who saw in "evolution" the explanation of the war's horrors. By the summer of 1918 premillennialist Howard W. Kellogg could address the Bible Institute of Los Angeles with this statement: "Loud are the cries against German Kultur. . . . Let this now be identified with Evolution, and the truth begins to be told."[10]

Once defined as part of the problem symbolized by German culture, evolution became an important part of the fundamentalist campaign against modernism. Evangelist Amzi C. Dixon, addressing a conference of conservative Northern Baptists in 1920, discussed the deleterious role evolution had played in the collapse of civilization during the early twentieth century. Dixon stated that he had traced evolutionary ideas back to the ancient Greeks, who, he pronounced, had descended from Cain. Darwin had added the concept of survival of the fittest, which Nietzsche expanded into a social philosophy. German leaders employed this philosophy to justify their actions during the war. Having defined German culture as the cause of many of the world's problems and having further defined evolution as the ultimate basis for that culture, Dixon, Riley, and other fundamentalist leaders began to devote themselves to a campaign against evolution that would soon come to characterize the fundamentalist crusade.[11]

Toward a New Science

Although the immediate impetus to the fundamentalists' antievolution crusade focused on the supposed connection between Darwinian evolution and the First World War, significant continuities existed between the postwar reaction and the earlier antievolution controversy of the late nineteenth century. As had their precursors, fundamentalist opponents of evolution stressed what they considered to be the unscientific nature of this theory by contrasting Darwin's work with the "Baconian" ideals of induction based on facts. This devotion to inductivism—as defined by antievolutionists—not only justified the opposition to evolutionary theory but also played an important role in supporting the literal interpretation of the Bible, which was also a crucial part of the fundamentalist philosophy. When wedded to the "common sense" outlook, so important to American evangelicals because it guaranteed their ability to observe accurately both the facts of nature and the even more trustworthy facts of the Bible, the commitment to inductivism provided the fundamentalists with an intellectual defense of their antievolution viewpoint.

As had been clear during the debates of a half century earlier, however, this view of science stood in sharp contrast to that of the scientific community. Darwin and his followers had revolutionized science by doing far more than collecting data and organizing it into descriptive volumes. Attempting to explain rather than simply to classify, modern scientists needed to interpret as well as to record their data. Two entirely different scientific worldviews were thus represented, making it increasingly difficult for any coherent exchange to pass between them. At the heart of this gap was the evangelicals' belief that evolution represented the most obvious example of the unscientific, speculative hypotheses that characterized much of contemporary science.[12] As the editor of the *Presbyterian* wrote in 1911, "To jumble opinion, hypothesis and facts together in thinking is pernicious to intelligence and morals. . . . [W]ith true science, there is no admittance for anything but facts." Similarly, when Canadian theologian Dyson Hague contributed his essay "The History of Higher Criticism" to *The Fundamentals,* he also emphasized the danger of speculative thinking. In "philosophical and scientific enquiries," he announced, "no regard whatever should be paid to the conjectures or hypotheses of thinkers."[13]

The explanations that fundamentalists dismissed as speculation, however, had undergone significant modification in the early twentieth century and represented a more complete theory than antievolutionists acknowledged. Scientists investigating inheritance, for example, combined sophisticated research concerning cellular phenomena with observations of variations to explain both change and continuity in the organic world. Dutch botanist Hugo de Vries was particularly active in this experimental work and, by the fall of 1899, had discovered simple mathematical laws of inheritance. Several observed characteristics segregated themselves into a 3:1 ratio in the second filial generation, referred to as F2. By this time de Vries had also discovered the neglected 1866 work of Gregor Mendel, who had determined the same ratios during extensive research in the mid-nineteenth century.[14] The rediscovery of Mendel's laws in 1900 stimulated several American biologists to search for the explanation of Mendelian segregation. Embryologists Edmund B. Wilson and Walter S. Sutton examined chromosome behavior and, by 1903, concluded that the pairing of chromosomes from the male and female represented the basic mechanism of heredity. The chromosomes, further, showed segregation and independent assortment, following the same rules as the genetic characters studied by Mendel and his followers.[15]

Wilson also greatly expanded the details of chromosome activity through his examination of sex determination. Although details differed from species to species, Wilson discovered that clear chromosome differences existed in different sexes. Referring to the sex-determining element as an accessory chromosome, Wilson worked out the chromosome theory of sex determination in a series of eight papers published between 1905 and 1912. In addition to providing an essentially modern view of this phenomenon, Wilson's work for the first time identified a specific phenotypic character (sex) with a definite chromosome, thus linking chromosomes with Mendelian concepts. Although Wilson's theory met with opposition, his study of sex determination heightened the interest in chromosomes as the hereditary material.[16]

Among the early students of heredity in the United States, Thomas Hunt Morgan of Columbia University assumed the major role. By the time of the rediscovery of Mendel's work, Morgan had established a reputation as a leader in experimental biology, especially in the field of embryology. Morgan's experimental emphasis, however, led him to distrust large-scale hypotheses and to remain skeptical of both Darwinian and Mendelian theories in the early 1900s.[17] As had other critics since the first edition of *Origin of Species*, Morgan stressed that natural selection could only serve as a negative factor in evolution. Although the process could eliminate the unfit, it could not create the variations that would determine fitness. Also repeating earlier arguments, Morgan emphasized that selection could not explain the incipient stages of highly adaptive organs. The eye, for example, possessed too many parts to be explained by individual variations.

For these and other reasons, Morgan felt more at ease with large-scale mutations as the origin of species. By 1906 he had begun a series of genetic experiments designed to induce such saltations in laboratory animals—rats, mice, and insects—by exposing them to various substances. He soon switched his experiments to the fruit fly *Drosophila melanogaster,* which had become increasingly popular for laboratory use because of its short generation period, ease of cultivation, and, crucial for Morgan's later work, four pairs of chromosomes. Morgan's *Drosophila* investigations led to a rapid increase in the knowledge of transmission genetics through his focus on phylogenetic characters that could be examined empirically. By examining the genetics of transmission rather than development, Morgan and his coworkers were ultimately able to merge chromosome theory and Mendelism into a workable theory of heredity.[18]

Despite his broad-scale research program, Morgan was unable to produce macromutations in *Drosophila.* In early 1910, however, Morgan discovered a single white-eyed male in a culture of normal "wild type" flies. Although a discrete and apparently random change, this was hardly the major modification he had hoped to find. Morgan focused his attention on this rare individual, breeding him with his red-eyed sisters. The first generation (F1) of offspring from this cross were all red-eyed; they were then crossed with each other to produce the major finding associated with the early development of the chromosome theory of inheritance. The F2 progeny displayed a 3:1 red-white ratio, in perfect agreement with Mendelian rules of inheritance. Equally important, however, all white-eyed flies were males. The white-eye condition was thus clearly a Mendelian recessive and a sex-linked character. Because sex determination was largely accepted as a function of the chromosomes, Morgan was able to combine Mendelism and chromosome theory in his paper published in *Science* on 22 July 1910. He explained his experimental results by invoking "factors" that followed Mendelian rules.[19]

During the two years following Morgan's initial *Drosophila* publication, he and his assistants at Columbia found more sex-linked traits that helped to convince him that the factors (later called genes) were structural parts of the chromosomes. The Morgan group developed this idea into their famous beads-on-a-string model, in which the "beads" represented genes and the "string" represented the chromosome. Yet the linkages of characters in *Drosophila* were not stable. The Columbia group found a wide range of broken linkages in their fly cultures that nonetheless displayed a regular pattern. Certain linkages were frequently broken, while others were rarely broken. Morgan had begun to consider that the variation in strength of linkages was a result of the factors' spatial separation on the chromosomes, but it was one of his assistants who took the next important step. Discussing the problem with Morgan in late 1911, Alfred H. Sturtevant realized that linkage variation could be used to determine the relative sequence of genes on the chromosomes. Genes far apart on the chromosome would be more likely to separate than those close together. By focusing on the degree of incomplete linkage, Sturtevant could calculate the position and sequence of genes, producing a "map" of the chromosome. Cytologists studying the behavior of chromosomes during meiosis had previously found that the loops of chromosome material occasionally crossed over each other. If the chromosomes broke at that point, linkage would be broken as well. Although the details of "crossing over" were not worked out until the 1940s, the physical explanation for the linkage phenomenon was yet another important step in connecting heredity with the structure and behavior of the chromosomes.[20]

The concepts of linkage and mapping guided much of the work of the Morgan group. By 1915 the Columbia researchers had studied more than one hundred mutant genes, which fell into four linkage groups corresponding to the chromosomes in *Drosophila*. The 1915 publication of *The Mechanism of Mendelian Heredity* played a crucial role in the dissemination of the Morgan group's discoveries. Jointly authored by Morgan and his principal assistants Alfred H. Sturtevant, Calvin B. Bridges, and Hermann J. Muller, *Mechanism* provided a complete discussion of the new theory of heredity. The volume relied heavily on data from the *Drosophila* work but also showed the applicability of Mendelian theory to other species for which hereditary data were avaiable. *Mechanism* explained many of the old problems of heredity, including sex determination, variations of expected Mendelian ratios, and the distinction between continuous and discontinuous variation. Morgan's work also opened new areas of research that would determine the agenda of geneticists for several decades.[21]

The publication of *Mechanism* paralleled Morgan's gradual acceptance of the role of his genetic theory in evolution. He stressed discontinuous variations as the material of evolution but emphasized that these variations were of the type visible in the *Drosophila* research: mutations that occurred in single genes to introduce new characters into species, rather than to create new species. The random nature of such variations also led Morgan to a greater appreciation of natural selection, in which he joined Muller and Sturtevant, who had long argued that Mendelian genetics and natural selection formed the mechanism of evolution. Convinced that the *Drosophila* work showed that heredity could be discontinuous while still serving as the source of variability on which natural selection acted, Morgan became increasingly active in arguing for an interpretation of Darwinian theory that would encompass the new genetics.[22]

Despite the recognized achievements and potential of the new genetics, the biological community remained divided. Among scientists skeptical about the new ideas was British biologist William Bateson, who stressed the limited nature of chromosome theory and questioned its relation to the broader concept of evolution itself. In an address to the Toronto meeting of the American Association for the Advancement of Science in late December 1921, Bateson attracted much press attention through his emphasis on the incomplete nature of evolutionary theory. Throughout his address, Bateson focused on the unanswered questions of evolution. "In dim outline evolution is evident enough," he argued. "From the facts it is a conclusion which inevitably follows. But that particular and essential bit of the theory of evolution which is concerned with the origin and nature of *species* remains utterly mysterious." Bateson concluded by predicting that the "enemies of science" would pounce on his statements concerning the problems of evolution, but he urged his scientific audience to emphasize their "faith" in evolution and assure the public that the details of evolution would be disclosed in the future.[23]

If Bateson's purpose was to emphasize to the public the "faith" scientists had in evolution, he failed dramatically. Instead, reporters covering his address filed stories discussing the "collapse of Darwinism."

Bateson's comments prompted noted paleontologist Henry Fairfield Osborn to dispatch a heated rejoinder to *Science,* which had published Bateson's address. It was bad enough that some of Bateson's remarks were misleading and inaccurate, Osborn argued, but they also led to "a very regrettable impression" on the part of the public, who tended to view Bateson's comments as supporting the religious and political leaders who most vocally opposed the teaching of evolution in the public schools of the United States.[24] Despite the impressive achievements of Morgan and others, the scientific validity of evolutionary theory had ceased to be the issue of greatest concern to the antievolutionists. Indeed, the new view of biology went largely unnoticed by the opponents of evolution.

Fundamentalists and Science

After the Great War had increased the visibility of evolution as a target for the fundamentalists, the theory came under attack for many of the evils associated with the modern world. Writing in *Christian Standard* in early 1919, for example, Glenn Gates Cole argued that evolution represented the foundation of what he called "destructive criticism" of the Bible. This should come as no surprise, Cole observed, as evolution appeared to be the "sole working basis for the investigation of all knowledge" to many scientists. "Making a mere theory the final test in all thinking," he continued, "they are forced to interpret everything in its light." This devotion to such a speculative hypothesis represented an absurd course of action, especially for those who believed in religious orthodoxy. "The godly man is right in refusing to surrender his faith in God's revealed word," Cole stressed, "because it fails to agree with one of man's theories. The path of man's progress is everywhere strewn with the discarded theories of some scientist's dreaming." Such comments reinforced the idea prevalent among fundamentalists that evolution constituted rampant speculation and only gained public support through the dogmatism of scientists.[25]

In addition to their concern about evolution as an illegitimate intellectual concept, however, the fundamentalists were also disturbed by a more specific impact of evolution in the early twentieth century: its growing presence in the American public education system. Evolutionary ideas were clearly visible in the botany and zoology texts used early in the 1900s as well as in the newer biology texts that followed curricular reforms during the second decade of the twentieth century.[26] These texts showed a confidence in evolutionary theory that conflicted with the fundamentalists' rejection of it as mere speculation. *Botany for High School,* for example, written by Cornell professor George Atkinson in 1912, forcefully stated that evolution "has been accepted because it appeals to the mind of man as being more reasonable that species should be created according to natural laws rather than by an arbitrary and special creation." Three years later a zoology text coauthored by Vernon L. Kellogg and Rennie W. Doane included this statement: "Although there is much discussion of the causes of evolution there is practically none any longer of evolution itself. Organic evolution is a fact, demonstrated and accepted."[27]

Concern for the path education seemed to be taking in the United States led evangelical authors to produce several volumes indicting the educational establishment. William Bell Riley's *The Menace of Modernism* (1917) included many attacks on the intellectuals and educators who seemed to be challenging the orthodox worldview embraced by fundamentalists. University officials, liberal pastors, and teachers at various levels proved their loyalty to modernism "by their scoffs at Scripture, their rejection of Jesus, their insistence on Darwinism, their exaltation of Man!" More specifically concerned with the impact of evolutionary teaching in the schools was the 1923 diatribe *Hell and the High Schools: Christ or Evolution, Which?* written by Baptist evangelist Thomas T. Martin. Arguing forcefully that high school students in America were doomed to hell because of their acceptance of evolution, Martin placed the blame for this state of affairs jointly on the intellectuals who had changed American education and the parents who had allowed this to happen. He accused American parents of "cowering before the sneers of a lot of high brows supported by your taxes" and refusing to challenge the teaching of evolution in the public schools. Martin urged his readers to revolt against the situation in the high schools to stem the tide of infidelity that seemed to be swamping orthodox America.[28]

Martin's attack on the "high brows" who appeared to manipulate American education displayed in extreme form a more general concern of the period. To many in the United States, American life was increasingly controlled by a new elite who dictated "truth" in a fashion that challenged traditional beliefs. This new situation, symbolized by the teaching of evolution in the public schools, represented a challenge to traditional concepts of democracy as well. The new elite had achieved success through mental ability, rather than through the traditional American ethic of hard work. Martin's fulminations against the "high brows" indicated a far more complex concern than his opposition to evolution.[29]

As science became more difficult for the layman to comprehend in the early twentieth century, it came into increasing conflict with the traditional American view of "common sense" as the guiding force behind all intellectual pursuits. Modern science was no longer accessible to all. In order to acquaint the public with science, clearly a topic of great interest, reporters and science writers had to present the results of new research in a carefully packaged fashion. Although well-meant and pursued diligently, these attempts to disseminate the new science in a democratic fashion could not avoid the problem of elitism. However reported, the new science of the 1920s remained complex and difficult to understand. Vocabularies could be simplified, models and analogies could be used, details could be ignored; but the simplification of science frequently led to the conclusion that the popularizers were engaged in the same kind of propaganda as the scientists themselves. For those who saw science as challenging the traditional worldview, the arrogant expert became the symbol of the new order.[30]

The significance of science, however, could not be ignored. Fundamentalists might reject evolution and relativity as leading to an abandonment of morality, but they could not pretend that the modern world was not interested in science. Despite their lack of understanding of the realities of modern science, fundamentalist opponents of evolution accepted the need for a scientific base for their antievolution arguments. Antievolutionists continued to argue that Darwinism was not science because of its speculative nature, but they also began to develop "scientific" challenges to the theory they militantly opposed.

Antievolutionists who wished to present a scientific challenge to the theory were, of course, proceeding from a position of weakness. Despite some concern about the details of evolution, it had become clear by the 1920s that the essentials of evolution represented a trustworthy addition to biological knowledge. Religious opponents of evolution were thus forced to base many of their arguments on religious, moral, or ethical grounds, rather than on scientific alternatives. There existed, however, material that could be defined as scientific in the work of Seventh-Day Adventist geologist George McCready Price. A self-trained scientist whose formal education was restricted to two years in a Michigan denominational college and a teacher-training course in his native New Brunswick, Price based his science on the acceptance of a six-day creation and flood geology. By 1906, while serving as a handyman at an Adventist sanitarium in southern California, Price had developed his scientific views into a small volume entitled *Illogical Geology: The Weakest Point in the Evolution Theory*. Price's thesis was that the idea of the succession of life, which established the chronological record of fossil forms so important to evolutionists, had no basis in fact. Indeed, he offered a thousand dollars to anyone who could prove that one fossil was older than another, an offer he claimed never to have honored. As the succession of life was irrelevant, at best, Price concluded that the entire Darwinian theory represented "a most gigantic hoax" that should be summarily rejected.[31]

For the next few decades Price served in various academic positions in Adventist schools in California and Nebraska. He continued to publish his creationist scientific works based on a literal interpretation of the Bible, including a worldwide flood as the cause of the observed strata in the geological record. His most important books included *Fundamentals of Geology* (1913), *Q.E.D.; or, New Light on the Doctrine of Creation* (1917), and his magnum opus, *The New Geology* (1923). Arguing that the Noachian flood explained most of the observed geological phenomena, including fossil-bearing rocks, Price was applauded by fundamentalists as a true scientist who had avoided the speculative guesswork of the evolutionists. He quickly became the antievolutionists' leading scientific resource, even though few fundamentalists accepted completely his flood geology. He made little impact on the scientific establishment.[32]

Of less immediate significance during the 1920s but an important figure somewhat later was Harry Rimmer, a Presbyterian minister and evangelist who devoted his efforts jointly to evangelistic work and proving the literal truth of the Bible through scientific investigation. Rimmer's only exposure to scientific training was a brief course of study at the Hahnemann Medical College in San Francisco, a small, homeopathic school that required only a high school diploma for admission. Despite his inadequate background, he established a laboratory in his house in Los Angeles, where he conducted experiments in embryology. Of greater importance for opponents of evolution was his founding of the Research Science Bureau in the early 1920s. Selling memberships to support his work, Rimmer served as the entire staff of the bureau, issuing publications and attempting "to prove through findings in biology, paleontology, and anthropology that science and the literal Bible were not contradictory." Although more concerned with evangelistic work than Price (Rimmer became field secretary for the World's Christian Fundamentals Association in the late 1920s), he nonetheless served an important function for the antievolutionist crusade by presenting himself as a scientist in his various public presentations and debates.[33]

By 1920 the position of antievolution sentiment in the fundamentalist movement had been fairly well established. An obvious part of the modernist drift, evolution symbolized many of the things that seemed to be going wrong in the United States after World War I. As such, this scientific theory represented a challenge to orthodoxy that could not be ignored. Yet antievolution sentiment had not yet assumed the monumental importance in the fundamentalist crusade that is usually associated with the 1920s. The movement still required a focal point to generate the national interest that would propel antievolution sentiment into its most active phase. That focal point proved to be William Jennings Bryan, three times presidential candidate, populist reformer, and active Presbyterian layman, whose interest in the antievolution crusade established it as a national issue.[34]

William Jennings Bryan and the Antievolution Crusade

Although Bryan was a relatively late convert to the antievolution cause, he brought with him the same zeal that had characterized his political career since the 1890s. Long a supporter of such reforms as women's suffrage, the income tax, and the popular election of United States senators, the Nebraska populist based his reformist view of America on an optimism that stemmed from his own orthodox religiosity, his faith in humanity's reason and goodness, and a devout belief in his own and his country's divine destiny. A civilization based on the teachings of Christ, for Bryan, represented the highest order possible; it was the duty of the United States to establish such teachings as the foundation for a new world order. Small wonder that Bryan was increasingly troubled by the path of American thought that appeared to be separating Christianity and American culture.[35]

Despite his concern with the modernist drift in American society, Bryan did not focus on the evolution issue until World War I. In 1915 Amzi C. Dixon discussed with Bryan the vague idea that German militarism was based on Darwinism. Over the next few years, especially after American entry into the global conflict, Bryan's interest in this topic increased, leading him to read such volumes as Vernon L. Kellogg's *Headquarters Nights* and Benjamin Kidd's *The Science of Power* (1918). Both of these books strengthened the Great Commoner's belief that German militarists had applied evolution toward a philosophy leading away from traditional Christian virtues. By 1920, when he addressed the World Brotherhood Congress, Bryan had become convinced that Darwinism represented "the most paralyzing influence with which civilization has had to contend during the last century."[36]

Bryan's emergence as the national spokesman for the antievolution crusade had been accomplished no later than the spring of 1921, when he began a series of attacks on the theory that propelled him to the head of the antievolution fundamentalists. Through such speeches as "The Menace of Darwinism" and "The Bible and Its Enemies," Bryan redirected the perceived national focus of fundamentalism toward the antievolution crusade, a topic that proved far more easily understood among the American public than the theological disputations of the millenarians. Although Bryan's entry into the controversy and his redefinition of fundamentalism as antievolution served to attract national attention, it eliminated any possibility for fundamentalism to appear as a positive movement. Antievolution was, by definition, a negative campaign that increasingly appeared to be a last-ditch effort to secure the "old-time religion." The internal division thus precipitated among fundamentalists was at least in part responsible for Bryan's lack of success in his 1923 campaign to gain election as moderator of the General Assembly of the Presbyterian Church. His single-minded focus on the evolution question struck many as inappropriate for a leader of a major Protestant denomination.[37]

Bryan's concern with the place of evolution in American culture and society followed several paths, all of which appeared to reinforce each other, until his campaign represented an imposing edifice. His emphasis on the connection between Darwin and Nietzsche led to a clear statement of the dangers of the new philosophy, which Bryan presented in his speech "Brother or Brute?" at the World Brotherhood Congress in the fall of 1920. Arguing that Nietzsche had carried Darwinism to its ultimate conclusion, Bryan accused the German philosopher of developing a philosophy that "condemned democracy as the refuge of the weakling, denounced Christianity as a system calculated to make degenerates out of men, denied the existence of God, overturned all standards of morality, eulogized war as both necessary and desirable, praised hatred because it leads to war, denied to sympathy and pity any rightful place in a manly heart and endeavored to substitute the worship of the superman for the worship of Jehovah."[38]

Similar charges against evolution were leveled in Bryan's "The Menace of Darwinism," in which he stressed that morality and virtue depended on religion and belief in God. Anything that weakened this belief weakened humanity, making it impossible for the race to do good. Evolution did precisely that, in Bryan's view, not by denying God's existence directly, but by putting "the creative act so far away that reverence for the creator is likely to be lost." The ultimate result of the evolutionary philosophy was to place man on the level of the brute, without regard for spiritual values and in direct contradiction of the Bible. Thus, as Bryan later argued in *Seven Questions in Dispute*, "The principal objection to evolution is that it is highly harmful to those who accept it."[39]

The personal harm that Bryan perceived evolution as causing would have been bad enough, but the theory had even broader implications, which troubled him. Devoted to reform, Bryan was disconcerted about the lack of reform possibilities in his understanding of evolution. For Bryan, evolution limited social improvements to the same gradual, slow developments that characterized the changes in organic species in nature. Humans were thus unable to do anything toward reform, no matter how devoted they might be to Christian actions and principles. Frightening as this situation might have been to Bryan, it did at least provide him with an explanation of the problems facing the United States in the postwar world, problems that he identified with the lack of the reform enthusiasm that had characterized earlier decades. Because evolution was taught in the schools of America, students learned that humans were little different from brutes. Humans could not truly overcome their animal nature, therefore, which made all prospects of reform pointless. The solution to this difficulty was obvious: human evolution must be eliminated from the material taught in American schools.[40]

Having determined that evolution harmed individuals and placed severe limits on reform, Bryan nonetheless had to develop compelling arguments to eliminate the suspect doctrine from American education. Like other antievolutionists, Bryan frequently focused on the supposed speculative nature of evolution to discredit it in his speeches and writings. In "Menace of Darwinism," for example, Bryan argued that the concept of natural selection represented an unwarranted assumption, as it required "more faith in CHANCE than a Christian is required to have in God." Later in the same essay, Bryan dismissed evolution as science altogether, writing that "Darwinism is not science at all; it is a string of guesses strung together. There is more science in the twenty-fourth verse of the first chapter of Genesis . . . than in all that Darwin wrote."[41]

Early in 1922, in a letter to the Chicago *Evening Post,* Bryan expanded his views concerning the speculative nature of evolution, clearly showing his rejection of the new methods of science based on the interpretation as well as the collection of data. Darwinism, he wrote, was nothing more than a guess, "for the word 'hypothesis' is merely a scientific synonym for guess." To support his conclusion, Bryan emphasized the lack of incontrovertible evidence to prove evolution. Despite the fact that scientists had been observing millions of species and had been attempting to prove Darwinism for more than sixty years, the evolutionists had "never found a single instance in which it can be shown that one species changed into another." The speculative nature of evolution, especially as it was applied to humans, made it an illegitimate topic to be included in the public schools, as Bryan stressed: "Evolution, so far as it is applied to man, is nothing more than a guess and ought not to be taught as if it were a fact. It ought not to be taught even as a guess unless the teacher explains to his pupils that it is an unsupported guess. But why should a mere guess, without a fact in the universe to support it, be taught at all, when the effect of that teaching is to weaken faith in God and to undermine faith in the Bible as the Word of God?"[42]

Clearly, a significant change was required in the public school curriculum of the United States. In order to effect this change, Bryan forcefully challenged the idea that educators were largely free to teach what their professional judgments dictated. In his 1922 book, *In His Image*, Bryan succinctly recorded his views: "If it is contended that an instructor has a right to teach anything he likes, I reply that the parents who pay the salary have a right to decide what shall be taught. . . . A man can believe anything he pleases but he has no right to teach it against the protest of his employers." Bryan's belief in teachers as "hired servants"—as he referred to them in a 1921 article in the *Commoner*—led him to argue that the "Christian taxpayers" who supplied the money to run American schools ought to be the ones to determine what was taught, rather than the skeptics and atheists who appeared to be controlling American education. After all, he wrote in early 1923, when Christians wanted to establish a religiously based education, they built their own schools and hired their own teachers. Why not compel "those who worship brute ancestry" to do the same thing?[43]

If Bryan appeared incensed at the supposed intellectual arrogance of public school teachers who promulgated evolution, he approached apoplectic rage when he considered the scientists who provided the information used by such teachers. "A scientific soviet is attempting to dictate what shall be taught in our schools," Bryan wrote in 1924, "and, in so doing, is attempting to mould the religion of the nation. It is the smallest, the most impudent, and the most tyrannical oligarchy that ever attempted to exercise arbitrary power." Bryan's innate distrust of an intellectual elite, quite apart from their acceptance of evolution, was made complete by his continued analysis of the intellectuals' role in World War I. The war could not be blamed on ignorance, for educated men had controlled the governments of the warring nations. College graduates had designed the weapons of destruction and had trained the armies. "Scientists," Bryan continued, had "mixed the poisonous gases and manufactured liquid fire. Intellect guided the nations, and learning without heart made war so hellish that civilization itself was about to commit suicide." Bryan saw no reason to entrust the education of succeeding generations of Americans to the hands of such men as these.[44]

For William Jennings Bryan, the early 1920s represented a critical period in the history of American civilization. Atheists and skeptics, aided by a "scientific soviet," appeared to be engaged in a campaign to establish a society based on concepts and ideas alien to Bryan and his supporters. To counter such developments would require nothing less than a similarly dedicated campaign on the part of the fundamentalists. Bryan was ready to play the leading role in that campaign. He began by giving addresses attacking Darwinism in various locations, including major educational institutions, where he frequently attracted large crowds. His speeches were reprinted and distributed in great numbers, adding to the impact of his other published works.[45] Bryan's devotion to the cause and his ability to attract equally devoted followers combined to make him the leading figure in the campaign to secure legislation to prohibit the teaching of human evolution in American public schools.

The Early Years of the Antievolution Campaign

In addition to providing a national figure with which to identify the fundamentalist movement, the entry of William Jennings Bryan into the evolution controversy changed the focus of fundamentalism itself. The desire to prohibit the teaching of human evolution in the public schools not only reflected the interventionist pattern characteristic of progressive reform but also provided a broader focus to the fundamentalist movement. Seldom a major part of the debates within churches, antievolution nevertheless represented the issue of greatest interest to the interdenominational fundamentalists who represented a large and important audience for the movement. American society appeared to include a great many people who were uninterested in the doctrinal debates of fundamentalist theologians but who were vitally concerned with keeping evolution out of the public schools. By the early 1920s the topic of evolution had emerged as the prime issue in the fundamentalist-modernist clash, with the fundamentalists' chief concern focused on the passage of state laws to prohibit the teaching of evolution in the public schools. Leaders of the movement accepted this redirection of focus with little difficulty. As William Bell Riley recalled later in the decade, the movement had originally focused its attention on the challenges to orthodoxy symbolized by higher criticism, but "in the onward going affairs, we discovered that basal to the many forms of modern infidelity is the philosophy of evolution."[46] Bryan's singular concern with evolution fit nicely into the new fundamentalist outlook.

The concern with evolution as a challenge to orthodox religion was widespread in the United States throughout the decade following the end of World War I. North Carolina emerged as one of the earliest centers of the controversy that developed, as shown by the frequent attacks on President William L. Poteat of Wake Forest College. Trained in zoology at the University of Berlin after attending Wake Forest as an undergraduate, Poteat had returned to the Baptist school as a faculty member in the 1880s, stressing in his biology classes that science and religion need not conflict. Baptist evangelist Thomas T. Martin, however, charged that Poteat's acceptance of evolution and higher criticism made the scholar unfit to serve as president of a Baptist institution of higher education. Martin's charges led the national fundamentalist movement to pay increased attention to North Carolina. Beginning in the spring of 1920, the World's Christian Fundamentals Association held annual Bible conferences in the Baptist Tabernacle in Raleigh. Attended by such leading fundamentalist figures as William Bell Riley and Amzi C. Dixon, these conferences further established antievolution as an important part of North Carolina's religious and political outlook during the 1920s.[47]

The 1922 Bible conference, led by Riley, focused as no earlier one had on the evolution question. The interest generated by this conference led to a formal debate between Riley and entomologist Zeno P. Metcalf on the North Carolina State College campus in Raleigh. Before an audience of some two thousand, the two men debated the resolution "that evolution is a demonstrated fact." As was usually the case in such debates, Riley used his oratorical skills to full advantage and left Metcalf struggling to discuss the scientific evidence supporting evolution. Poteat continued to be a favorite target of North Carolina fundamentalists, who leveled various charges against the Wake Forest president. Although Poteat secured votes of confidence from the Wake Forest board of trustees and the Baptist State Convention, fundamentalists continued to view him with suspicion.[48]

Attacking supposed evolutionists on the faculty of a church-related school also proved a profitable course of action for J. Frank Norris of Fort Worth, Texas. A product of Baylor University and the Southern Baptist Theological Seminary in St. Louis, Norris had been pastor of First Baptist Church in Fort Worth since 1909, building his pastorate into one of the most successful in the denomination. In an attempt to launch his own attack on modernism and evolution in 1921, Norris examined the teachings on various Baptist campuses, finding a suitable target in the Baylor sociology department. Samuel Dow, who had authored a book tracing humanity's development from less civilized beings, appeared to Norris to be a typical modernist who embraced evolution. Norris attacked Dow's ideas concerning the institution of family life as the cause for civilization's advance. Not only did such ideas support evolution, but to Norris they also appeared ridiculous, as everyone knew that Adam and Eve were the first family. Therefore, man was never uncivilized. Although Dow vehemently denied that he was a modernist or an evolutionist, he resigned his position as a result of Norris's harassment. The high point of Norris's efforts came in May 1923, when his church hosted the annual meeting of the World's Christian Fundamentals Association. Norris and his followers arranged a "trial" of Texas colleges accused of teaching evolution, rationalism, and higher criticism. Six students testified against several Texas schools, all of which were easily "convicted" of their crimes. Norris had long offered students money to testify against their schools for teaching modernism, so he had little difficulty in arranging such a mock trial for the entertainment of the conference.[49]

The activities of Riley, Martin, and Norris encouraged antievolutionists, who increasingly viewed legislation as the best means to eliminate the teaching of evolution from the public schools. Sharing Bryan's philosophy of absolute popular control of public education, fundamentalists in many states, especially in the South and West, urged their state legislatures to enact laws that would prohibit or restrict the teaching of evolution. In 1921, for example, the South Carolina legislature considered a rider to an annual appropriations bill that would have prohibited state funds from going to any school that taught the "cult known as 'Darwinism.' " Although a joint committee removed this rider, the outlook it represented was common among many legislators of the period.[50]

The most intense early activity aimed toward a legislative solution to the perceived problems associated with teaching evolution in public schools took place in Kentucky. Agitation in this state for antievolutionist activity had been evident as early as 1917, but it was not until the spring of 1921 that concerted efforts appeared in the form of a series of twenty-two antievolution meetings organized by William Bell Riley. Such activities attracted much attention and helped to mobilize public antievolution sentiment. The Kentucky controversy grew to greater proportions during the summer, however, when University of Kentucky officials began to solicit increased funding from the legislature, which would meet early the next year. Questions concerning the place of evolution and other modernist doctrines on the Lexington campus had occasionally surfaced in the past, but efforts to increase funding for the Kentucky school precipitated an active campaign aimed toward legislative restrictions on the teaching of evolution.[51]

Although Kentucky Baptist leaders kept the issue in front of the public during late 1921, the arrival of William Jennings Bryan in January 1922 galvanized the campaign. Repeating his charges that teachers supported by public taxes should not be permitted to teach what the public did not want and that evolution represented no more than speculation, Bryan addressed local groups and a joint session of the legislature in his efforts to gain widespread support for appropriate legislation. When added to the actions of other Kentucky antievolutionists, Bryan's speeches proved quite effective.[52]

During the last week in January, antievolution bills were introduced in both the House and the Senate, calling for fines and/or imprisonment for any teacher convicted of teaching "Darwinism, Atheism, agnosticism or evolution as it pertains to the origin of man" (House Bill 191) or "any theory of evolution that derives man from the brute, or any lower form of life, or that eliminates God as the Creator of man by a direct creative act" (Senate Bill 136). The introduction of these bills led to significant action on the part of University of Kentucky president Frank L. McVey, who cooperated with state newspapers opposed to such legislation and organized a successful campaign to secure support from educational leaders throughout the United States. McVey also emphasized in public statements that the university was teaching neither atheism nor agnosticism and that the morals and spiritual ideals of students on the Lexington campus were beyond question. There existed, in McVey's mind, no reason for the current attack on the school. Further, if the University of Kentucky were restricted from teaching evolution in a scientific fashion, it would be shutting itself off from the outside world. McVey's conciliatory tone and the support he gained from national colleagues and state newspapers helped to defeat the antievolution bills in Kentucky, despite arguments by supporters of such legislation that students were returning home from the university filled with dangerous ideas.[53]

The defeat of the Kentucky legislation did little to challenge the growing interest in prohibiting the teaching of evolution in the United States. Bryan and other antievolution leaders continued to travel around the country attempting to establish support for legislative campaigns to outlaw the suspect theory. During the fall of 1922 and the spring of 1923 Bryan participated in such activities in Minnesota, West Virginia, and his recently adopted home state of Florida. Although none of these efforts resulted in antievolution statutes, the national scope of the movement had been clearly established. Events in Oklahoma provided the crusade with its first victory. As early as November 1922 the state Baptist General Session had called for legislation to ban the teaching of evolution in the public schools of the state. Evidence of support for such action was also visible in the election campaigns waged that fall, in which several candidates committed themselves to antievolution legislation. When the legislative session opened early in 1923, lawmakers added a rider to a free textbook bill that prohibited the use of any textbook that advocated "a materialistic conception of history, that is, the Darwin theory of evolution versus the Bible theory of creation." Passed overwhelmingly by the House, the rider survived the Senate by only four votes. Although disturbed by the antievolution rider, Oklahoma governor John C. Walton saw the free textbook bill as more important for the progressive reforms he had in mind for his state, and he signed the entire bill in late March.[54]

For reasons that had nothing to do with the antievolution rider, the Oklahoma bill was repealed two years later. Yet the immediate impact of this first successful antievolution legislation was evident in increased activity throughout the nation. Texas legislators considered a bill during the spring of 1923 both to prohibit the teaching of evolution and to censor texts that included discussions of the theory. During the debates on the bill, it became clear that the most convincing argument emphasized that a majority of Texans did not want evolution to be taught in the state's schools, so it was inappropriate to use tax monies to teach such a concept. As Representative J.A. Dodd argued during the debates, the state forced his children to attend schools and then showed them "the road to hell through teaching them the hellish infidelity of evolution." Despite such arguments, the Texas legislature could not agree on the antievolution legislation. The House passed it easily by a vote of seventy-one to thirty-four, but the bill died in the Senate. Similar campaigns over the next few months in Georgia, Tennessee, and Alabama proved no more successful.[55]

Although the focus of the early antievolution campaigns tended to be on states in the South, other areas of the nation, particularly the West, participated in a fashion seldom appreciated by students of the phenomenon. Concerned with the state's role in promoting the moral order but unsure of the specific impact of evolutionary teaching on that order, the Utah legislature examined public education closely in 1921 and again in 1925. An act passed in early 1921 prohibited atheistic or religious doctrines from being taught in the public schools. Four years later the legislature extended this law to include state-supported colleges and universities. Neither law specifically mentioned the teaching of evolution, at least in part because the Mormon Church had taken no official position on the topic. The concern expressed by the Utah legislature over appropriate public school teaching, however, paralleled similar concerns about the role of state-supported education throughout the nation.[56]

The evolution controversy in the West became more heated during the mid-1920s. Among the earliest public clashes was the debate that smoldered in Tucson, Arizona, in early 1924. The controversy followed an address to an Episcopal women's group on 8 January by University of Arizona astronomer A.E. Douglass. Calling for a union of science and religion, Douglass examined several biblical discussions of scientific phenomena that could not be taken literally, including Joshua's command for the sun to cease its motion. Douglass stressed the compatibility of religion and science, while emphasizing the danger of requiring young people in the church to believe things that their education showed to be false. Covered by both Tucson newspapers, Douglass's remarks precipitated a forceful response by the Reverend R.S. Beal of the city's First Baptist Church. In an open letter to university president C.H. Marvin, Beal objected to the teaching of evolution on campus. Beal stated his fondness for the University of Arizona but described himself as "grieved beyond expression with the bold materialism and gross infidelity of many of its professors." He urged the faculty to look at the other side of the question to "save from ship wreck on the rocks of infidelity the faith of many of the students."[57]

The topic of evolution proved of great interest to residents of Tucson, with various discussions appearing in the city's churches and newspapers. In March the Tucson *Citizen* began a series of articles about evolution by university faculty, who examined the theory from the perspective of their own academic specialties. The essay that precipitated the most notable response was the work of A.E. Douglass, who used the history of astronomy to challenge the literal biblical account of creation. A closer examination of evolution led to the concept of individual sacrifice for the "future of the group," which, according to Douglass, represented the "essence of every religion." Thus, in times of calm, evolution supplied "an intellectual basis for religious activity which in times of stress and danger and rapid experience comes through the heart and the emotions." Douglass's essay had little impact on the Reverend Mr. Beal, who announced from his pulpit a few weeks later that Douglass's scientific arguments were irrelevant. Joshua could have stopped the earth as reported in Scripture, Beal stressed, because the centrifugal force at the equator was practically nonexistent. Beal arrived at this conclusion by calculating that the earth rotated slightly less than seven ten-thousandths of its circumference each minute. Stopping such minimal motion would have no effect on the planet. Douglass did not reply—at least in public—to Beal's sermon.[58]

California's engagement with the evolution controversy was relatively uneventful during the early 1920s. Responding to fundamentalist objections to teaching evolution as a "fact" in the public schools, the State Board of Education in 1924 directed teachers to present evolution "as a theory only." The board also appointed a Textbook Investigation Committee composed of leading California educators, including President W.W. Campbell of the University of California and Ray L. Wilbur, president of Stanford University. This committee examined biology texts used in the state in light of the board's requirement that evolution be taught as a theory. They found that the texts adopted by the state presented evolution with "moderation and circumspection" and followed the board's guidelines. The committee also stressed that the authors of these texts frequently attempted to emphasize that no inherent conflict existed between science and religion. Keenly aware of the challenges to teaching evolution in the public schools, however, members of the committee pointed out the importance of presenting the best of modern scientific knowledge, which included discussions of evolution. The textbooks under review served that purpose, as they were "concerned with presenting scientific facts and theories of which every person with any pretense to an education in the subject or subjects treated should be informed."[59]

The actions of educators and scientists in specific clashes with antievolutionists indicated a growing awareness of the strength of the movement. Although the topic of evolution remained a relatively minor part of the presentation in biology texts and classes, its presence had precipitated a dramatic response. As the antievolutionists became more and more active, gaining the attention of the media as well as the public, their opponents slowly increased their activity as well. Writers in such newspapers and periodicals as the New York *Times, Christian Century,* and the *Christian Advocate* emphasized Bryan's inadequate scientific knowledge and his inability to view science as a process of discovery.[60]

University of Chicago faculty member T.V. Smith devoted the last part of his *Scientific Monthly* article "Bases of Bryanism" to an examination of this aspect of the crusade. The "common man," so accurately symbolized by Bryan himself, had not been sufficiently exposed to many of the modern advances in science and was thus, understandably, unwilling to support the new ideas. Despite more than sixty years of evolutionary research, "the average man remains utterly ignorant of the evidence that has convinced all who have examined it fully." As did Bryan and most of the other leading antievolution figures, the average man expressed "all he knows about evolution in his retort that *you* may claim the monkey for an ancestor if you wish, but as for him, he prefers another line of descent."[61]

Because the antievolution campaign had clearly emerged as a national phenomenon by 1924, opponents of the crusade increased their efforts. The Committee on Freedom of Teaching in Science of the American Association of University Professors issued a report that stressed the inappropriateness of relying on popular votes or legislative action to determine what science was taught. Freely admitting the tentative status of much of what science teachers presented, the committee nonetheless emphasized that experts in a field were still the best people to determine what should be taught in that field. Late in 1924 in San Francisco, the Science League of America established itself as the institutional focus of the scientific opposition to Bryan and his colleagues. The brainchild of proevolution activist Maynard Shipley, the league attracted an overflow audience at Native Sons' Hall that heard speeches by such notable figures as Luther Burbank and David Starr Jordan.[62]

Similarly, professional organizations such as the American Association for the Advancement of Science challenged the antievolution crusade. The group supported the teaching of evolution in resolutions passed at its 1922 and 1923 meetings and, in 1924, further examined the antievolution campaign and the role played by William Jennings Bryan. A particularly cogent discussion of the phenomenon came from Ohio Wesleyan zoologist Edward L. Rice, who served as vice president of the organization and as chairman of the zoology section. Rice presented as his vice presidential address "Darwin and Bryan—A Study in Method," an essay that was published in *Science* the following March. The zoologist examined many of Bryan's ideas, stressing how far removed the Great Commoner was from the scientific community and its way of looking at the world. He emphasized the illegitimacy of Bryan's merger of *hypothesis* and *guess,* attempting to show clearly the complicated nature of modern science and its commitment to explanation as well as to the collection of data. Yet the major problem with Bryan, according to Rice, remained his inability to accept the significance of the facts that scientists had discovered over the decades since Darwin wrote *Origin of Species.* Because Bryan was unaware of the scientific support for evolution, he could not accept that the evidence that "seems conclusive" to biologists had any significance. "In large part, doubt-less," Rice suggested, "this difference is due to Mr. Bryan's simple ig-norance of the facts. Ignorance of the details of biology is no disgrace to a lawyer; but a lawyer should be slow to pronounce a judicial decision upon technical evidence which he does not understand."[63]

Despite scientists' growing concern about the antievolution crusade and their initial efforts to counteract that movement, the antievolution-ists continued to hold the upper hand in the controversy. In few areas of the United States were the fundamentalist opponents of evolution more active than in the state of North Carolina. Although ultimately unsuc-cessful in their attempt to secure legislation in the state, antievolution-ists waged a well-organized campaign against the theory throughout the early 1920s. At least in part, this campaign was a response to attempts initiated by academics, journalists, politicians, and clergy in North Carolina who recognized that the state could play an important role in modernizing the region. For those who opposed such changes, the state university in Chapel Hill became the symbol of the modernism that was creeping into the Tar Heel State. Under the presidency of Massachusetts-born psychologist Harry W. Chase, the university began attracting able scholars from the Northeast and Midwest in an attempt to establish the academic credentials of the school. Equally disturbing were such visible reminders of secularization as the discontinuation of required chapel at-tendance and Chase's decision to end the practice of presenting grad-uates with Bibles at commencement. The combination of "foreign" scholars, "foreign" ideas, and a secular focus to the university troubled many of the orthodox in North Carolina.[64]

If modernism was important to those who wished to bring North Carolina into the twentieth century, it was even more important to those who wished to maintain the status quo. Fundamentalists realized that North Carolina represented an important battleground between the op-posing forces. As a result, the early 1920s witnessed a large number of free-lance evangelists and spokesmen for national fundamentalist groups entering the state to encourage the opposition to modernism. Billy Sunday, for example, attracted more than four thousand people to one of his speeches given in Wilson in 1923 and attracted even larger crowds when he initiated a campaign in Charlotte later in the year. The World's Christian Fundamentals Association realized the importance of North Carolina for its campaign, arguing that if a state attempting pro-gressive reforms could be persuaded to enact antievolution legislation. the rest of the region might follow suit. Riley and his colleagues in-vested much time and effort toward convincing North Carolinians to embrace antievolution, as did William Jennings Bryan, who gave several speeches in the state beginning in the spring of 1923. Attracting the support of various religious groups, such speakers were able to generate a great deal of interest in attempts to prohibit the teaching of evolution.[65]

In early 1924 the State Board of Education displayed its sympathy with the antievolution crusade by rejecting two of the six biology texts under consideration for adoption by state schools, despite the favorable recommendation of a subcommittee that had reviewed the texts. Governor Cameron Morrison persuaded the board to reject the two volumes as "unsafe," explaining his position later by saying, "I don't believe in any missing links. If there were any such things as missing links, why don't they keep on making them?"[66]

The success of the antievolution campaign before the State Board of Education led to increased interest in antievolution legislation. During the political campaigns of the summer and fall of 1924, many candidates included antievolution planks in their campaign platforms. Among the most active of the antievolution candidates was David Scott Poole of Raeford, whose campaign for a House seat focused almost entirely on the evolution issue. Pledging his support for an antievolution bill and making the most of his long-standing activity in the Presbyterian church, Poole was easily elected. True to his campaign promises, Poole introduced House Resolution number 10 on 8 January 1925, the second day of the legislative session. Similar to other bills around the nation, the Poole resolution declared that the North Carolina legislature believed that teaching "Darwinism or any other evolutionary hypothesis" was "injurious to the welfare" of the state's citizens.[67]

Educational leaders in the state presented a less unified front than one might have anticipated. Poteat played little role in this controversy, telling his colleagues that the opposition to the Poole bill should be led and coordinated by the state schools and their spokesmen. President Eugene C. Brooks of North Carolina State College, like many of his friends in the state's higher education system, at first underestimated the seriousness of Poole's challenge. Brooks's position was complicated by his continuing efforts to turn his agricultural and engineering school into a liberal arts college, efforts that had brought him under fire from some members of the legislature. Within a few weeks of the introduction of the Poole bill, however, President Chase had organized the opposition to the statute, despite the possibility of jeopardizing legislative appropriations for his school. Chase was far more concerned with the result if the university did not lead the fight, as many members of his faculty were already being approached by other schools with much better reputations. If the Chapel Hill institution failed to stand up against the antievolution crusade, Chase concluded, his faculty would be hard pressed to reject offers from such schools as Johns Hopkins and the University of Wisconsin.

Beginning with the Education Committee hearings on the Poole bill on 10 February, the antievolution measure kept the attention of the legislature for more than a week. Chase and a few other academics testified effectively before the committee, presented public discussions, and submitted to media interviews in their attempt to stress the disadvantages to the state of such legislation. Debate in the House chamber took nearly two full days, but by 19 February everyone was ready to vote. The House defeated the Poole measure sixty-seven to forty-six, with Wake Forest and University of North Carolina alumni for the most part voting against the bill.[68]

The defeat of the Poole bill did not, however, represent an unequivocal victory over the forces of the antievolution crusade. Local school boards began making decisions restricting the teaching of evolution within weeks after the defeat of the legislation. In March, for example, the Mecklenburg County Board of Education banned the teaching of evolution in county schools and gave the superintendent of schools the authority to remove all books discussing evolution from school libraries. Similarly, the North Carolina Education Association remained largely silent during the controversy, playing no role in the debate over the Poole bill and rarely taking a stand on the issue during the 1920s. Sharing the attitudes symbolized by the proposed legislation, local educators did not need a state law to ban evolution from the public schools.[69]

Yet the defeat of the Poole bill was a bitter disappointment to those involved in the antievolution crusade. North Carolina had been targeted as a state of crucial importance in the campaign to remove evolutionary doctrines from the public schools. The failure to secure appropriate legislation in this instance cast clouds of doubt over much of the antievolution movement. The situation, though, was not as dismal as some antievolutionists thought. A few hundred miles to the west, another state legislature was considering a measure that would provide the antievolution crusade with one of its most notable successes and would propel the movement into even greater activity during the late 1920s.

4

The Scopes Trial and Beyond

The debate over the Poole bill illustrated many aspects of the early years of the antievolution movement. Most of the issues involved in the controversy had been examined during the North Carolina debates, and the potential role of institutions of higher education had been firmly established. The activity of outside antievolution organizations, with their nationally known spokesmen, also played an important role and reinforced the orthodox religious attitudes shared by much of the state's population. Although unsuccessful in securing an antievolution statute, opponents of Darwinism frequently consolidated their position at the local level, where school boards and officials proved more than willing to prohibit or compromise the teaching of evolution in the public schools.

Led by individuals committed to bringing the state into the cultural and intellectual world of the twentieth century, North Carolina could at best respond to the antievolution crusade in an ambiguous fashion. Other states, however, proved more willing to prevent students in the public schools from learning about the supposedly dangerous doctrine of evolution. By the end of the 1920s antievolution statutes had been approved in Tennessee, Mississippi, and Arkansas, with less successful campaigns evident throughout the nation. In few states were the issues and debates more dramatically staged than in Tennessee, North Carolina's western neighbor.

Victory in Tennessee

Because the state shared many of the attitudes and characteristics usually associated with opposition to the teaching of evolution, Tennessee had long been considered a prime target for the antievolution crusade. William Bell Riley visited the state in 1923 in an unsuccessful attempt to convince the legislature to consider an antievolution bill. William Jennings Bryan added his weight to the debate the following year, presenting a speech in Nashville entitled "Is the Bible True?" This speech proved very popular among Tennessee fundamentalists, who published it as a pamphlet to support the growing antievolution campaign in the state. They distributed copies of the pamphlet to legislators shortly before the General Assembly convened in mid-January 1925.

Visible support for an antievolution law encouraged the introduction of bills in both houses of the legislature within a few days of the opening of the 1925 session. In the Senate, John A. Shelton introduced a bill prohibiting the teaching of evolution on 20 January. The next day Representative John Washington Butler introduced the bill that would become the most famous of all antievolution statutes. Butler represented several rural counties in north central Tennessee, served as clerk of the Round Lick Association of Primitive Baptists, and had campaigned for election to the state House of Representatives in 1924 on an antievolution platform. Fulfilling campaign promises, Butler's bill prohibited the teaching of "any theory that denies the story of Divine Creation of man as taught in the Bible, and to teach instead that man has descended from a lower order of animals."[1]

Butler later justified his actions by arguing that "the evolutionist who denies the Bible story of creation, as well as other biblical accounts, cannot be a Christian. . . . I regard evolution to be the greatest menace to civilization in the world today." It is important to note, however, that Butler was also concerned with protecting a traditional view of public education well established in the region in the mid-1920s. The promotion of good citizenship, based on biblical concepts of morality, represented the primary purpose of state education. Legislators and parents who had been educated in this tradition, frequently in county-supported religious academies, shared a common viewpoint that supported Butler's bill as a legitimate educational statute. The state, in their view, had an obligation to prevent the teaching of anything that challenged the biblical morality that underlay the accepted concepts of good citizenship. Once it became commonplace to accept the idea that evolution challenged the Bible, the theory's elimination from the public school curriculum could be justified as helping to fulfill the purpose of state education.[2]

Support for Butler's bill was widespread in the House. The Education Committee quickly approved the measure, with the House passing the bill seventy-one to five on 27 January. The situation in the Senate, however, proved different. The Judiciary Committee rejected the Shelton antievolution bill by one vote, arguing that it would be unwise to pass a law dealing with religious beliefs. The Butler bill met a similar fate when it reached the upper house in early February. Although the

Senate called up the Butler bill as a special order of business on the tenth, both antievolution measures were referred back to committee to clear up differences in the two pieces of legislation. The General Assembly adjourned for a four-week recess before the committee submitted its report.

During the recess, it became clear to members of the legislature that significant public support existed for an antievolution statute. Constituents stated their views from the pulpit and in the local newspapers. Although opposition to such laws emerged, the proponents of the legislation appeared to outnumber the opponents. When the legislature reconvened on 9 March, the Senate was ready to consider the Butler bill more favorably. The Judiciary Committee recommended passage by a seven-to-four vote on the tenth, with Senate debate scheduled two days later. During the more than three hours of debate on 12 March, senators were frequently applauded from the galleries for such statements as the emotional speech in support of the bill from Lew D. Hill: "If you take these young, tender children from their parents by the compulsory school law and teach them this stuff about man originating from some protoplasm or one-cell matter . . . they will never believe the Bible story of divine creation—that God created man after his own image and blew into his nostrils the breath of life." Hill and his colleagues easily passed the Butler bill by a vote of twenty-four to six and forwarded it to Governor Austin Peay for further action.[3]

The ease with which the General Assembly passed the state's antievolution bill in part resulted from the lack of any organized opposition to the proposed statute. Newspaper coverage of the legislature's deliberations proved sketchy before the passage of the bill and afterward seldom comprised more than occasional editorials, both pro and con. Of greater moment, the state's educational establishment showed no concern with the statute. In contrast to their colleagues in Kentucky and North Carolina, Tennessee's educational leaders remained quiet about the Butler bill as it coursed its way through the legislature. Harcourt A. Morgan, president of the University of Tennessee, remained silent during the consideration of the act and urged his faculty to do the same. Evidently concerned with protecting frugal legislative appropriations, Morgan also had to contend with continuing assertions that the Knoxville campus was a modernist institution. Such concerns had led to the dismissal of a half dozen faculty during the past two years.[4]

Governor Peay's action concerning the Butler bill also included diplomatic considerations; his own reform plans for the state required legislative support that might be alienated if he vetoed the measure. The governor therefore quickly signed the bill, returning it to the legislature with a long message explaining his actions. Peay stressed his opinion that the Butler Act violated neither the freedom of religion nor the "strict separation of church and state," as the act required no particular theory or interpretation of the Bible to be taught in the public schools. Yet Peay's message seemed to indicate that the governor shared many of the attitudes that had led to the passage of the new law. Arguing that the Butler Act would not be an "active statute," Peay characterized the legislation as a protest "against an irreligious tendency to exalt so-called science, and deny the Bible in some schools and quarters—a tendency fundamentally wrong and fatally mischievous in its effects on our children, our institutions and our country." "Right or wrong," he continued, "there is a deep and widespread belief that something is shaking the fundamentals of the country, both in religion and morals. It is the opinion of many that an abandonment of the old-fashioned faith and belief in the Bible is our trouble in large degree. It is my own belief." Peay also shared the attitude, often expressed by Bryan and others, that a teacher did not have absolute freedom to teach what he or she thought appropriate. The Butler Act, according to the governor, did not infringe upon the teacher's right to accept evolution, but the state constitution at no time guaranteed that a teacher could present any ideas whatsoever. "The people have the right," Peay emphasized, "and must have the right to regulate what is taught in their schools."[5]

Peay's action in signing the Butler Act pleased many in Tennessee and in the nation as a whole. William Jennings Bryan immediately forwarded a congratulatory telegram to the governor, applauding his actions and stressing that parents in Tennessee owed Peay "a debt of gratitude for saving their children from the poisonous influence of an unproven hypothesis." Bryan saw in Tennessee's action yet another example of the superiority of his recently adopted region, characterizing the South as "now leading the Nation in the defense of Bible Christianity. Other states North and South will follow the example of Tennessee."[6] In ways he could not imagine, Bryan proved remarkably accurate in his prediction.

The Scopes Trial and Its Impact

As the first statute that clearly outlawed the teaching of evolution, the Butler Act attracted a great deal of attention from both sides of the controversy. Fundamentalists applauded the action as an important step toward securing their agenda. Those concerned with combating such sentiments were no less interested in the Tennessee law. Within a few weeks of Governor Peay's approval of the Butler Act, the American Civil Liberties Union had decided that the Tennessee law represented an appropriate statute upon which to build a test case concerning the constitutionality of antievolution legislation.

Toward that end, the organization placed an advertisement in the Chattanooga *Daily Times* of 4 May 1925: "We are looking for a Tennessee teacher to accept our services in testing this law in the courts. Our lawyers think a friendly test can be arranged without costing a teacher his or her job. Distinguished counsel have volunteered their services. All we need now is a willing client." The ACLU did not have long to wait for a response. On the day following the appearance of the advertisement, several leading citizens of the small village of Dayton, forty miles north of Chattanooga, met in a local drugstore to discuss the Butler Act and the ACLU offer. Clearly interested in the prospect of attracting attention to Dayton, rather than in any constitutional or educational issues, these civic leaders were intrigued with the possibility of staging a trial based on the antievolution law. The Dayton group had asked John Thomas Scopes to attend the drugstore meeting. Scopes had been hired the previous summer as a football coach and general mathematics and science teacher at the local high school. When asked if biology could be taught without reference to evolution, Scopes not only gave his own opinion that it could not but also pointed out the appropriate passages in the officially adopted state biology textbook, George Hunter's *Civic Biology,* which had been used in the state since 1909. Scopes further provided crucial information for the eager Dayton boosters when he informed the group that in late April he had filled in for the school's principal in a biology review session, during which he had used *Civic Biology* and presumably—although Scopes could not remember this for certain—had discussed evolution. When informed of the ACLU plans, Scopes agreed to serve as the defendant in whatever case Dayton could establish.[7]

Rumors that other Tennessee towns might stage similar trials led local judge John T. Raulston to call a special meeting of the grand jury for 25 May to indict Scopes for violating the Butler Act. Although questions were later raised concerning the validity of this indictment, which would require Scopes to be reindicted before the trial began in July, Dayton had secured what would become one of the most famous court trials in American history.[8]

Forming an appropriate defense team was of great concern to the ACLU. To avoid unnecessary controversy, the union originally planned to employ respected conservative attorneys John W. Davis and Charles Evans Hughes, despite offers from Clarence Darrow and Dudley Field

Malone. Scopes and his attorney, John R. Neal of Knoxville, early believed that the trial would be more concerned with drama than legalities and informally accepted the Darrow-Malone offer without consulting ACLU officials. Beginning in early June, Scopes and Neal visited New York on several occasions for consultations with ACLU officials and legal staff. Despite lingering concern that Darrow and Malone would inject more controversy than necessary into the proceedings, Scopes continued to insist that the "gouging, roughhouse battle" the trial was sure to become required the presence of someone like Darrow. By the end of the month the basic outline of the Scopes defense had been developed, with the decision made to allow Scopes to be convicted of violating the Butler Act. The defense would, however, carefully record all possible objections to the trial proceedings for the later appeal, which could result in the law's being declared unconstitutional.[9]

The drama surrounding the Scopes trial increased visibly on the afternoon of 7 July, when William Jennings Bryan arrived from Florida to serve as special prosecutor and World's Christian Fundamentals Association attorney in the case. Honored that evening with a banquet sponsored by the Dayton Progressive Club, Bryan gave an intriguing speech in which he repeated his proposal for a constitutional amendment to prohibit evolutionary teachings and emphasized his opinion that evolutionists represented a distinct minority in the United States. He also cast the upcoming trial in apocalyptic terms, stating that "the contest between evolution and Christianity is a duel to the death. . . . If evolution wins in Dayton Christianity goes—not suddenly, of course, but gradually—for the two cannot stand together."[10]

The principal actors in the case early set the tone for the Scopes trial. Either unconcerned with or unaware of the religious aspect of the controversy, Judge Raulston insisted upon opening each day's proceedings with prayer, usually led by a local fundamentalist minister. Defense objections that such activity established a mood in the court that worked to their disadvantage were ignored. The first few days of the trial itself provided further evidence of the clash between opposing worldviews. Defense attorney Arthur Garfield Hays objected to the introduction of the Bible into evidence, arguing that the King James Version proposed represented only one of several different versions of Scripture. This news surprised many members of the audience, including John Washington Butler, who later admitted he had never known that different versions of the Bible existed.[11]

Darrow's combative nature and flair for the dramatic frequently guided the trial away from the careful examination of legal issues, but his views of the Butler Act and the evolution controversy in general were nonetheless congruent with those of the rest of the defense team. "Here we find today," Darrow remarked early in the trial, referring to the Tennessee statute, "as brazen and as bold an attempt to destroy learning as was ever made in the Middle Ages. The only difference," he argued, "is we have not provided that they shall be burned at the stake. But, there is time for that, Your Honor; we have to approach these things gradually."[12]

Despite the different worldviews represented in Dayton, the constitutionality of the Butler Act remained the central issue for the defense. By the opening of the trial, the defense had developed three main arguments supporting the contention that the statute was unconstitutional. The defense argued that the Butler Act violated the separation of church and state by attempting to establish a religion of Protestant fundamentalism in Tennessee. Both the United States and Tennessee constitutions prohibited such action. Further, the Butler Act represented an indefinite and vague statute. What did the act mean by declaring the "teaching" of evolution to be illegal? Could an instructor explain evolution without advocating its accuracy, or did Tennessee schools have to avoid even the mention of the evolutionary concept? Another aspect of the Butler Act that raised questions of vagueness concerned the provision that nothing should be taught that denied the biblical story of creation. As there were several versions of the Bible, the defense maintained, how could teachers know if they were teaching a doctrine that violated the biblical creation account? The defense counsel also raised constitutional questions based on the status of evolution among the members of the scientific community. Hays stated that evolution was as well established as the Copernican theory among scientists and that to delete such ideas from the public school curriculum represented "an unreasonable restraint on the liberty of the citizen" and was "not within the police power of the state." From a constitutional perspective, such restraint violated due process and represented further grounds for declaring the Butler Act void.[13]

The defense team also developed a specific legal objection to the Butler Act that involved the language of the statute itself. Scopes's attorneys maintained that the Butler Act defined two separate acts, both of which had to be violated for the law to come into effect. Not only did the offending teacher have to teach evolution, but he or she would also have to deny biblical creation to be guilty of violating the statute. Evolution did not necessarily contradict Genesis. To support this contention and to take advantage of a national forum to discuss evolution, the defense counsel planned to use an impressive array of expert witnesses from the scientific and theological communities. Scientists were carefully chosen as much for their status as lay leaders in various denominations as for their scientific credentials, adding weight to the contention that science and religion did not need to conflict with each other. From the prosecution's perspective, however, such expert testimony had little bearing on the case, as the central issue remained the legislature's right to control the public school curriculum and, of course, Scopes's violation of the Butler Act. Further, as historian Edward J. Larson has pointed out, court rules of the day tended to discourage expert testimony of the kind proposed by the defense. Experts could only offer their own opinions on matters beyond the ordinary understanding of the judge or jury. Testimony concerning the general acceptance of evolution was inappropriate, as that would involve others' opinions.[14]

Bryan and the prosecution argued forcefully against admitting expert testimony, leading Judge Raulston to conclude that the Butler Act made illegal the teaching that man descended from a lower order of animals. This was the only act involved, contrary to the defense's contention that two separate acts were included. Since only the teaching of human descent was at issue and this had been defined in the Butler Act in straightforward terms understandable to all, no need existed for expert witnesses to discuss the origin of man or the lack of conflict between evolution and Genesis.[15]

Raulston's decision to exclude expert testimony on Thursday, 16 July, ended the issue as far as the court was concerned, but an intriguing weekend exchange emerged in the media between Bryan and Darrow. "If a law like this were passed in New York," Bryan told reporters, "and witnesses were called from Tennessee to assure the people of New York that they were unduly alarmed and that there was nothing to fear, their testimony would be objected to as offensive as well as improper." In response, Darrow stressed the incongruity with regard to expert testimony, pointing out that debates and disagreements over the meaning of the Bible had characterized discussions of the work throughout history. As a result of Judge Raulston's decision, however, an uninformed jury "is supposed to know, first, what evolution is; secondly, what the Bible teaches in reference to the creation of man; and, third, whether these theories and the account in the Bible are in conflict. And Mr. Bryan says they should decide all this without evidence." Darrow was also unimpressed with Bryan's arguments concerning the inappropriateness of outside experts, telling reporters, "Science is the same everywhere. The Constitution does not permit the legislature to put a Chinese wall around the state of Tennessee, as Mr. Bryan seems to think should be done."[16]

Bryan and Darrow were also involved in the most dramatic moment of the trial the following Monday, when Darrow called Bryan to the stand as an expert witness on the Bible. Darrow's action was questionable, at best, as he did not have the right to call opposing counsel and expert testimony had already been ruled inadmissible. The prosecution made no objection to this grandstand play, however, even after Raulston specifically asked Bryan if he objected to testifying. During his testimony, Bryan justified his performance by suggesting that the defense had not come to Dayton to try the case of John Thomas Scopes but had come "to try revealed religion. I am here to defend it, and they can ask me any questions they please."[17]

Despite Bryan's good intentions, his testimony proved disappointing to his fundamentalist supporters. During the ninety-minute exchange between the two attorneys, Bryan's knowledge of the Bible appeared imperfect, and he admitted on several occasions that certain biblical passages could not be taken literally. Bryan's devotion to the Bible had never, to be sure, been based on absolute literalism; yet his public disavowal of that literalism troubled many of his followers and alienated some of the support that the Great Commoner had long enjoyed. Although it would have had little more impact than his own testimony, Bryan hoped to question Darrow the following day, Tuesday, 21 July, in an effort to regain lost credibility, but his colleagues in the prosecution rejected this idea. Indeed, attorney S.K. Hicks told a United Services reporter that if such activity did not end, the prosecution would move to dismiss the case against Scopes. This action would eliminate the review of the case by a higher court and would circumvent the purpose of the trial as defined by the defense counsel.[18]

When court convened on Tuesday, therefore, both prosecution and defense were ready for the proceedings to end. After a few technical exceptions were made by the defense, Darrow suggested that the jury be called in and instructed to find Scopes guilty. The defense would make no objections and would waive closing arguments, a proposal accepted by Attorney General Thomas Stewart. Darrow himself addressed the jury briefly, outlining the plans for appeal and urging the conviction of his client. Ending the trial in this fashion not only saved much time, but it also prevented Bryan from giving the long closing speech designed to summarize the philosophy of the antievolution crusade before the public. Stewart brought up the question of an appropriate fine but did not pursue the matter when Raulston explained the local custom in bootlegging cases: the jury only set the fine when they wanted to impose something other than the minimum set by law. The minimum fine for bootlegging, as for violating the Butler Act, was one hundred dollars. With such matters settled, the jury, who had been in the courtroom less than one hour during the trial—they had been excluded from hearing most of the technical debates—were given the case to decide. They returned in nine minutes with a guilty verdict, as everyone had expected. With an appeal planned from the beginning of the trial, a few technical details were all that remained to bring the Scopes trial to a conclusion in a most quiet fashion.[19]

Yet the end of the Scopes trial also served as a springboard for observations and comments. William Jennings Bryan was among the first to enter this fray with comments delivered the afternoon the trial ended. The successful conviction of Scopes apparently did little to encourage Bryan, who attempted to regain the momentum of the antievolution crusade by attacking evolutionists in general and his recent opponent Darrow in particular. Of Darrow, Bryan stated that the Chicago attorney was "the most conspicuous of the opponents of religion in the nation. He is the finished product of evolution," Bryan continued, "the most perfect that has yet developed in the United States. He embodies all that is cruel, heartless, and destructive in evolution." Of evolutionists in general, Bryan was equally vituperative, repeating charges he had made over the previous five years. He accused "a militant minority, made up of atheists, agnostics, and other dissenters from orthodox Christianity," of attempting "to use the courts to compel the majority to pay teachers to undermine the religious faith of the children of the taxpayers who employ teachers."[20]

Knoxville native Joseph Wood Krutch, covering the Scopes trial for *The Nation,* contributed a different analysis of the situation. In "Tennessee: Where Cowards Rule," Krutch attacked officials of the state for allowing the events leading to the Scopes trial to take place. At least the residents of Dayton and the surrounding rural areas were honest about their hostility to evolution and were attempting to deal with the issues. Such people as the president of the state university, however, who should know better, had done nothing to prevent the passage of the Butler Act and were conspicuously quiet during the trial itself. Emphasizing that many legislators had voted for the bill solely to gain political support from the vocal fundamentalists, Krutch lambasted the citizens of his native state. Communities as "simple-minded" as Dayton were common throughout the nation. Tennessee's recent emergence as a "laughing-stock" was not a result of the existence of "villages which are intellectually a half century behind the centers of world thought," but the product of a virtually complete absence of any leader "who has the courage to stand up for what he thinks and knows instead of flying quickly to cover lest he might have to sacrifice to his convictions some political advantage or some material gain."[21]

The role of William Jennings Bryan came in for analysis as well, with several reporters emphasizing his "weariness" and "lack of fire." In questionable health because of diabetes and related problems, Bryan died suddenly during the afternoon of 26 July, less than a week after the Scopes trial ended. The death of Bryan had a profound impact on the fundamentalist movement, as it removed a unifying force that had artificially united the disparate elements of fundamentalism. Bryan had served as an important symbol of the movement because he redefined the crusade in ways that attracted widespread support. His performance at the Scopes trial may well have disappointed many, but his ability to serve as an inclusive force had not been destroyed. With his death, that force was removed, creating the popular image of fundamentalism as little more than a rural, anti-intellectual movement.[22]

From another perspective, however, the Scopes trial proved to be beneficial for the antievolution movement and provided fundamentalism with a different unifying force that slowed the breakup of the movement following Bryan's death. If nothing else, events in Tennessee during 1925 showed that an antievolution law could be passed by a legislature and upheld in court. The state thus became a model for those who saw in evolution a convenient explanation for much that was wrong in the United States and suggested a solution to such problems in the form of antievolution legislation. Far from indicating a collapse of the rural South or of fundamentalism, the Scopes trial struck many as a positive contribution.[23]

Yet the ultimate fate of the Butler Act remained uncertain, as the ACLU appeal of Scopes's conviction would involve higher courts. Scopes himself played no role in the appeal. In fact, as he later recalled, his only knowledge of the disposition of his case came from newspaper accounts and reporters who frequently contacted him for information. The young science teacher had accepted a fellowship to the University of Chicago to pursue a doctorate in geology, but his two-year fellowship proved inadequate for completion of the degree. Beginning in the late 1920s, Scopes worked for various petroleum companies until his retirement in 1964.[24]

While Scopes embarked on his graduate education, the attorneys for the American Civil Liberties Union began to organize the appeal that they hoped would ultimately lead to a case before the United States Supreme Court and a decision concerning the constitutionality of the Butler Act. In their brief filed with the Tennessee Supreme Court in Nashville in early January 1926 and in their oral arguments five months later, Darrow and the other members of the defense argued emotionally that Scopes's individual freedom had been violated by the Butler Act and that the law represented an unreasonable restriction on teaching. The state countered by stressing that no constitutional right to employment existed and that Scopes was thus bound by state guidelines and decisions as an employee. The state also argued that the Butler Act was not unreasonable, as it represented a specific effort to protect children from evolutionary teachings, an effort that the representatives of the people could constitutionally pursue. With the arguments finished in early June, the Tennessee Supreme Court began its deliberation.[25]

Chief Justice Grafton Green announced the decision of the court on 15 January 1927, carefully answering defense contentions. He admitted that the Butler Act could have been drafted more carefully, but the meaning of the statute remained reasonably clear. *Evolution* was, indeed, a broad term, but in the context of the Butler Act it clearly meant the evolution of humans from a lower form of life. Green examined closely the construction of the statute, focusing on the second clause in the act, which the defense maintained referred to a separate action. Not so, remarked the chief justice. The clause that prohibited the teaching that man descended from a lower form was only meant to expound on the earlier clause prohibiting the teaching of any theory that denied the biblical story of creation. The Butler Act was "only intended to forbid teaching that men descended from a lower order of animals." Green also argued that Scopes was bound by state policy as a state employee and rejected the defense contention that the Butler Act violated article 11, section 12, of the Tennessee constitution. This clause stated that it was the duty of the legislature to "cherish literature and science," a directive that the defense thought had been violated by outlawing the teaching of evolution. Green saw no value in this argument, stressing that the legislature should be given wide latitude in making such decisions. If the legislature thought that "the cause of education and the study of science" would "be promoted by forbidding the teaching of evolution in the schools of the state, we can conceive of no ground to justify the court's interference." Green's decision also rejected the argument that the Butler Act represented an unconstitutional attempt to establish religion by emphasizing that no organized religious body that he knew of either denied or affirmed human evolution as part of its creed. Further, the Butler Act did not *require* the teaching of any doctrine; it only prohibited the teaching of human evolution.[26]

Despite the constitutional soundness of the Butler Act, the conviction of John Thomas Scopes could not be upheld. Following local practice, Judge Raulston had levied the minimum fine of one hundred dollars after the jury had convicted the teacher. This action, Green argued, exceeded the judge's authority, as the state constitution required all fines greater than fifty dollars to be levied by a jury. The judgment of the lower court would thus have to be reversed. Yet Chief Justice Green emphasized that he saw no reason to return the case for retrial. He urged the state to drop the matter, writing in his opinion that "we see nothing to be gained by prolonging the life of this bizarre case." As Scopes's conviction had been overturned, the defense could not appeal any further. The constitutional issues surrounding the Butler Act would not be examined at the federal level, and the act itself would remain in the Tennessee statutes. Officially, Tennessee students could not be exposed to the Darwinian doctrine.[27]

The Campaigns Continue

Following the Scopes trial, comments on the case stressed its supposed negative impact on fundamentalism in general and the antievolution crusade in particular. Symbolized by the frequently vitriolic writings of H.L. Mencken, the national press tended to emphasize the parochial, rural nature of the stereotypical fundamentalist, convincing many in the liberal camp that the issue had been laughed off the national stage. Such was clearly not the case. The Scopes trial served, instead, to fortify the antievolution crusade, convincing opponents of Darwinism that legislative and judicial activity could lead to the prohibition of evolutionary teaching in the public schools. Far from representing the culmination of the antievolution crusade in America, the Dayton proceedings marked the beginning of the most active period of the controversy.[28]

Events in Tennessee did little to interrupt the continuing campaigns for state and local action to prevent the teaching of the unpopular topic. While the Tennessee legislature considered Butler's proposed statute, Mississippi lawmakers rejected antievolution legislation early in 1925. Legislative reluctance had little effect on the antievolution crusade in Mississippi, however, as the state superintendent of schools quickly issued an official proclamation that prohibited the teaching of evolution in the public schools. Recognizing the popular support for such decisions, L. Walter Evans, a Church of God minister serving in the Mississippi House of Representatives, introduced another antievolution bill early in the 1926 session of the legislature. The Evans legislation sought to prevent teaching "the theory that man descended from a lower order of animals" but carefully avoided any comment that evolution denied or contradicted the biblical account of human creation. The bill thus bypassed the thorny issue of the interpretation of Genesis. The introduction of the Evans bill attracted much attention and brought a number of petitions supporting antievolution legislation to legislators' desks. Of even greater significance, nationally known Mississippi evangelist Thomas T. Martin, now leading the recently formed Bible Crusaders of America, entered the picture as an active lobbyist. Despite such popular support for an antievolution statute, the House Education Committee reported the Evans bill negatively by a vote of ten to four in late January. The committee minority nonetheless filed a separate report, which would bring the Evans bill before the entire House.[29]

Martin's status as one of the national spokesmen for the antievolution crusade was not lost on the Mississippi legislature, which invited him to address a joint session during the first week of February. Of particular concern to Martin in his address were comments made by various opponents of the Evans bill that passing such legislation would bring the same kind of snide criticism upon Mississippi as the Butler Act had brought upon Tennessee. Martin was unimpressed with such arguments. "It is claimed that the law will bring on Mississippi the ridicule and abuse from the North that has been heaped on Tennessee," Martin told the legislators. "Shall the legislature of Mississippi," he asked, "barter the faith of the children of Mississippi in God's word and the Savior for the fulsome praise of a paganized press?" Martin's address reinforced the lobbying of the Bible Crusaders, convincing the House that public opinion stood behind the proposed antievolution law. Ignoring the committee report, the House approved the Evans bill by a vote of seventy-six to thirty-two and forwarded it to the Senate. Although the Senate Education Committee reported the measure negatively, the Senate passed the bill twenty-nine to sixteen and sent the nation's newest antievolution statute to Governor Henry L. Whitfield for his signature.[30]

Potential opponents of the Evans bill had remained remarkably quiet during the legislative debates, partially explaining the ease of passage. Only after the bill reached the governor did Chancellor Alfred Hume of the University of Mississippi involve himself in the controversy by urging the governor to exercise his veto. Clearly aware of the support for such legislation, however, Hume assured the governor and the legislature that the university did not represent a center of modernism or suspect teachings. The university, he stressed, was a Christian institution, "shot through and through with the teachings of our Lord." The ACLU attempted to organize opposition to the proposed statute but was forced to campaign largely on its own when it could not attract significant support from scientists and educators in the state. Faced with indifferent opposition and active support, Governor Whitfield signed the bill into law on 12 March. The ACLU quickly offered to assist any Mississippi citizen who wished to contest the law, even making a specific offer to the local chapters of the American Association of University Professors, but no individual expressed interest.[31]

Although North Carolina had already dealt with its antievolution campaign before the Butler Act and other events of 1925 captured national attention, the Tar Heel State continued to debate the evolution question. Because of his actions in securing the defeat of the Poole bill, President Harry W. Chase of the University of North Carolina became one of the symbols of modernist influence and, as such, became a frequent target for fundamentalist attacks. Unsuccessful in securing antievolution legislation, fundamentalists continued their drive to eliminate infidelity in the state university, causing so much controversy that Chase seriously considered accepting the presidency of the University of Oregon in early February. A massive outpouring of support for the president convinced him to stay in Chapel Hill, but the continued opposition to modern ideas could not be ignored.

By the spring of 1926 the antievolution movement in North Carolina appeared to be making a comeback. On 4 May more than three hundred antievolutionists met in Charlotte to launch a statewide organization called the Committee of One Hundred. Embracing as their motto "Make Our Schools Safe for Our Children," the committee proposed a general campaign against public school curricula that might challenge orthodox theology. The committee arranged for a series of speakers to visit North Carolina in June, before the state primaries, in an effort to gain political support for an appropriate antievolution law in the next legislature.[32] When the new legislature convened in January 1927, Representative Poole introduced a bill drafted by a "capable Christian lawyer" hired by the North Carolina Bible League. This measure proposed to eliminate from the public school curriculum "any doctrine or theory of evolution that contradicts or denies the divine origin of man or of the universe, as taught in the Holy Bible." Perceiving less public and legislative support for such a statute than in the past, North Carolina educators chose to ignore the latest Poole effort. The House Education Committee rejected the bill by a vote of twenty-five to eleven, convincing the antievolutionists in the legislature to drop the matter. The clear memories of the Scopes trial in neighboring Tennessee did much to eliminate support for antievolution legislation in North Carolina.[33]

Florida antievolutionists continued their campaign to strengthen their state's stand against the teaching of the suspect doctrine throughout 1925 and 1926. During the first few months of 1927 it became clear that agitation for an antievolution statute had attracted significant attention among the legislators, who would convene in April for the new session. On 11 April, Representative Leo Stalnaker of Tampa introduced a bill to outlaw the teaching of evolution and to eliminate texts that discussed evolutionary concepts. Opposition to the bill surfaced immediately, with comments published in newspapers frequently emphasizing that such a bill would bring the same kind of ridicule to Florida as had recently been heaped on Tennessee. President Albert A. Murphree of the University of Florida came out forcefully against the Stalnaker bill, despite the possibility that the legislature might cause difficulties with the university budget. Rollins College faculty submitted a petition to the legislature urging lawmakers to reject the proposed statute.

Support for the bill became evident during the public hearings held by the House Education Committee on 19 April. Representatives and senators testified on both sides of the issue, but the committee voted unanimously to approve the bill and send it to the floor of the House. When the Judiciary Committee opposed the bill by a vote of nineteen to eighteen, however, antievolutionists quickly drafted a substitute measure that outlawed teaching "as a fact" any theory that denied the existence of God or the divine creation of man. The proposed statute also prohibited the teaching of atheism or infidelity and prevented the use of texts that taught any of these concepts. This bill proved acceptable to the House, which approved the new measure on 17 May by a vote of sixty-seven to twenty-four, but it died in the Senate with the closing of the legislative session.[34]

Although the focus of the antievolution crusade remained in the South, the West also witnessed notable activity. As the most populous western state, California attracted much attention as it attempted to deal with the question of teaching evolution in the public schools. In April 1925 the State Board of Education formally upheld the teaching of evolution in California but insisted that the concept be taught only as a theory. The board also announced that it would approve textbooks that presented evolution as a theory but would reject those in which evolution was presented as fact. The board's insistence that evolution be taught as a theory struck many scientists as improper. Among the most vocal of these critics was Maynard Shipley, continuing his role as one of the nation's leading opponents of the antievolution crusade. Before the board's July meeting to approve textbooks, Shipley filed a statement challenging the April decision. The validity of evolution, he urged, should be a decision for scientists, not for the state.

Antievolutionists also filed protests with the State Board of Education. The Glendale Presbyterian Church, for example, opposed all teaching of evolution in the public schools. "In view of the fact that the Bible has been ruled out of our schools," the church's protest concluded, "we demand that no other theory of the origin of man be taught our children." California fundamentalists took other actions as well, bringing in as a spokesman William Bell Riley. The Minnesota fundamentalist leader argued at the board meeting that "evolution has never been proved and never can be," an argument countered by Shipley, who assured the board that evolution *was* a fact. After much discussion, the board approved most of the texts recommended by a committee of California educators, including two books opposed by fundamentalists.[35]

Dissatisfaction with board policy increased over the next eighteen months, leading San Joaquin Valley assemblyman S.L. Heisinger to introduce an antievolution bill in early 1927. The Heisinger bill would outlaw the teaching of human evolution and would prohibit the classroom use of textbooks that discussed the topic. This proposed law would apply to all schools, colleges, and universities supported in whole or in part by state education funds. Although given little chance of passage, the Heisinger bill prompted a heated outburst from the state superintendent of public instruction, who told a New York *Times* reporter, "I am emphatically opposed to any legislation affecting the teaching of evolution in the schools. I do not think California wants to follow the example of Tennessee." The bill died in the Education Committee in May.[36]

Oregon witnessed a less contentious effort to deal with the evolution controversy during the mid-1920s, although rumors of proposed legislation continuously surfaced. Portland school officials attempted to avoid the controversy by telling their teachers not to mention creation *or* evolution. During the summer of 1925 Eugene residents were treated to one of a series of evolution debates that took place on the Pacific coast between William Bell Riley and E.A. Cantrell of the Science League of America. Although such activities brought criticism from scientists in the region, the debates kept the evolution issue before the public. As was the case in most such debates, the audience tended to be overwhelmingly in favor of the antievolution position, allowing Riley to counter the scientist's arguments with misrepresentations and snide comments. When a vote was taken at the end of the debate, Riley won easily.[37]

In Utah, Mormon scholars continued to examine the evolution question during the mid-1920s, producing a wide spectrum of opinions. University of Utah geologist Fredrick Pack published a distinctly nonliteral view in 1924 under the title *Science and Belief in God.* A 1906 doctoral graduate of Columbia University, Pack wrote that there was no doubt about the truth of evolution. The method of evolution, on the other hand, remained open to question. Pack rejected both natural selection and the Darwinian reliance on chance, because neither left sufficient room for purpose in nature. The Mormon geologist also examined the book of Genesis, characterizing it as God's explanation of the world for ancient men without modern scientific knowledge. Pack's "modernist" outlook failed to precipitate a crisis in Mormonism because of his orthodoxy in other areas and the lack of an official church teaching on the topic. Even at the time of the Scopes trial, when the LDS First Presidency released its " 'Mormon' View of Evolution," the statement skirted the issue. The members of the First Presidency merely affirmed the spiritual pedigree of man and the common descent of mankind from an ancestor named Adam, who had somehow taken on "an appropriate body."[38]

Balancing Pack's modernist view were the writings of Joseph Fielding Smith. For Smith, an apostle for many years and later president of the church, a literal Adam and a literal Fall remained necessary for orthodoxy. He frequently cited the work of fundamentalist geologist George McCready Price, who argued that evolution destroyed the concept of Adam, without which there existed no fall, no atonement, and no savior. Smith rejected the evolution of man as both untrue and destructive of faith. The suggestion that humans evolved from lower forms of life represented "the most pernicious doctrine ever entering the mind of man. . . . For its source we must go beyond the activities of men to the author of evil." Theistic evolution was no better, in Smith's view, than straightforward evolution; he characterized adherents of this concept as hypocrites. Those scholars who engaged in higher criticism were allied with evolutionists in an attempt to destroy the Bible. For these and other reasons, Smith supported campaigns to ban the teaching of evolution in the public schools. He was the only Mormon authority to advocate this in public.[39]

Another dramatic debate over evolution erupted in Tucson, Arizona, during the closing months of 1927. Baptist minister R.S. Beal opened a drive for an Arizona law similar to the Butler Act with a series of antievolution lectures in his Tucson church by the Canadian physician Arthur I. Brown. The previous year Brown had been sent by the World's Christian Fundamentals Association to North Carolina during that state's evolution debates. His Tucson appearance attracted much attention in the local press, which reported his 10 October address in detail. Making full use of his credentials, the Canadian lecturer presented himself as a scientist examining a scientific question. Brown characterized the book of Genesis as a valuable scientific work and cited Scripture as denying the possibility of species change "because God commanded that everything living must reproduce itself 'after his kind.'" Assuring his audience that this explanation was far superior to the "mythical evolutionary process," Brown asserted that "thousands of experiments have shown that this Supreme Law cannot be broken."[40]

In a letter to the editor of the *Arizona Daily Star* two days later, Brown argued even more forcefully against evolution, stressing those aspects that he and fellow fundamentalists regarded as scientific weaknesses. He rejected evolution as a science, referring to it instead as a religion that humanized God and deified humanity. Brown also held fast to the Common Sense tradition of American evangelicals, dismissing the proevolution stand of many scientists with a peroration attacking the so-called experts. "Any ordinary intelligent individual," he wrote, "is able to draw his own conclusions on this subject when the findings of science are adequately and fairly presented to him. Why should we take our opinions second-hand?"[41]

With the groundwork laid by Brown's activities, Beal's drive for an antievolution law began in earnest. He opened his campaign in mid-October, after announcing that a survey showed significant support for such a law among Arizona's ministers. For the next month the Tucson newspapers carried reports of sermons, letters to the editor, and editorials concerning the issue. Despite Beal's claim of strong support, his effort failed to gain momentum. Even in the Tucson area, an *Arizona Daily Star* poll showed that ministers tended to reject Beal's legislative proposal. Interest in the controversy had faded by mid-November, convincing Beal to abandon his campaign.[42]

The late 1920s witnessed various other attempts to secure antievolution legislation, most of them in the South. In January 1926, for example, Kentucky clergyman Andrew Johnson announced plans to combat the teaching of evolution in his state and played a key role in forming the Fundamentalists' Association toward this end. Aware of the continuing support for antievolution legislation, Representative Grover Cleveland Johnson of Hardin County soon introduced House Bill 96 to prohibit the teaching of evolution in Kentucky public schools, including colleges and universities. After the House Education Committee reported the bill negatively in February, Johnson introduced two other bills during the 1926 legislative session, one to prevent "atheistic teaching" in the public schools and the other to endorse the Mississippi antievolution action. Both of these bills failed to pass. During the next legislative session, in 1928, another antievolution bill was introduced into the House of Representatives, but this action took place too late in the session for the bill to be seriously considered. Kentucky's legislature would consider no further attempts to outlaw the teaching of evolution in the public schools.[43]

Other southern states considered similar efforts as the decade progressed. West Virginia examined antievolution bills in both the 1925 and 1927 legislative sessions, but only in 1927 did the legislature bring the issue to a vote. A resolution prohibiting the teaching of evolution failed in the House of Delegates by a vote of fifty-seven to thirty-six, and later in the session the House similarly rejected a bill "to Prevent the Teaching of Any Nefarious Matter in Our Public Schools," which included "Darwinism, Atheism, or Agnosticism." Antievolutionists in Virginia began their campaign in the late summer of 1925, but the legislature that convened in early 1926 proved unwilling to consider the matter seriously. The proposed legislation was withdrawn before a vote could be scheduled. In Louisiana, the Baptist Convention demanded that the State Board of Education abolish evolutionary teaching, while the Bible Crusaders of America spent the early months of 1926 attempting to gain support for appropriate legislation. Although the antievolution bill passed the House fifty-two to forty-three, the Senate refused to consider it in the few weeks before adjournment. Legislatures in Alabama and Oklahoma rejected similar bills early in 1927, as did the South Carolina House of Representatives a year later.[44]

The antievolution crusade tended to have less impact in the Northeast and Midwest, but even in these regions the topic of evolution attracted attention. Maine, New Hampshire, and Delaware all considered antievolution legislation during 1927, but little support developed. The Delaware House of Representatives took the matter so lightly that the proposed bill was referred to the Committee on Fish, Game and Oysters. Midwestern opponents of evolution proved somewhat more active, with local school boards in Indiana and Kansas announcing their opposition to hiring teachers who accepted evolution and removing books discussing the topic from local libraries. Fundamentalists in North Dakota, Minnesota, and Missouri persuaded legislators to introduce relevant bills during the 1927 sessions, but none of these efforts met with any success.[45]

Failure to secure legislative prohibition of evolutionary teaching rarely meant total defeat for the foes of Darwin. Antievolutionists gained great success in Texas, for example, where they were aided by Governor Miriam Ferguson and a pliant State Textbook Commission. During its mid-October 1925 meeting, the commission went along with Governor Ferguson's demands that the board only approve biology textbooks that omitted evolution. This policy would be enforced by dismissing and prosecuting any public school teacher who used nonapproved texts. Little opposition to this policy was expressed, suggesting that the governor spoke for many of her constituents when she later stated, "I am a Christian mother . . . and I am not going to let that kind of rot go into Texas textbooks." Anxious to keep their contracts with the state, publishers such as Henry Holt and Company, Allyn and Bacon, and Macmillan agreed to rewrite the objectionable passages in their biology texts to meet the Texas prohibition.[46]

The place of evolution was no more secure in Georgia education in the years following the Scopes trial, despite the legislature's refusal to enact an antievolution statute. The State Education Committee withheld a grant to the state library upon learning that the library contained books discussing evolution. In early February 1926 the Atlanta Board of Education voted to prohibit the teaching of evolution in the public schools; the board followed this action by appointing a committee to investigate the use of texts discussing evolution. When the board met in May to consider the report of this committee, legal advisers pointed out that the board had no authority to ban books within five years of their adoption. Such complications led the board to table both the committee report and its earlier prohibition of evolutionary teaching. In taking such action, however, the Board of Education made clear that its efforts in no way indicated approval of teaching evolution. The board's official explanation stressed that it did not intend to disseminate any theory that would encourage students to question the divine creation of the universe and its human inhabitants.[47]

It remained for Arkansas to contribute the final and, in some respects, most intriguing chapter to the American antievolution crusade of the 1920s. During the spring of 1926 opponents of evolution began circulating petitions to present to the legislature when it convened the following January. The popular support for antievolution legislation proved particularly gratifying to the two men who would guide the fortunes of the Arkansas antievolution bill, Representative Astor L. Rotenberry of Pulaski County and the Reverend Ben M. Bogard, pastor of the Antioch Missionary Baptist Church in Little Rock and chairman of the Antievolution Committee of the Arkansas Association of Missionary Baptist Churches. A few days before Christmas, Rotenberry released his proposed antievolution bill to the press. The Rotenberry bill contained no references to the Genesis account of creation but did make it illegal to teach evolution or to use texts that taught that man descended from a lower order of animals. The bill provided for a fine of up to one thousand dollars and revocation of the teaching license. Roten-

berry introduced House Bill 34 on 13 January.[48] Following poorly attended hearings before the House Education Committee, which resulted
in a "Do not pass" recommendation, the House brought up the measure
on 9 February as a special order of business. The Rotenberry bill passed
by a vote of fifty-one to forty-six. The Arkansas Senate considered the
bill the next day but tabled the measure by voice vote after a discussion
of only fifteen minutes. Senators also tabled an attempt to reconsider
the Rotenberry bill five days later.[49]

The defeat of the Rotenberry bill proved to be no more than a tem-
porary setback, as the bill's sponsor quickly began a campaign to allow
Arkansas voters to decide the fate of antievolution legislation in the November 1928 general election. Arkansas law required a petition signed
by the equivalent of only 8 percent of the votes cast in the 1926 guber-
natorial election to place an initiated act on the ballot, a requirement
easy to fulfill because of low turnout in general elections. Fewer than
nine thousand signatures would be needed to place the revised Rotenberry bill on the ballot. Only slight changes were made from the original bill, lowering the fine to no more than five hundred dollars and
removal from position, while prohibiting the teaching that man "as-
cended or descended" from a lower form of animal. The proposed measure also outlawed the use of texts teaching human evolution.

To assist in the initiative drive, Bogard organized the American
Antievolution Association. This group solicited membership from all
individuals except "Negroes and persons of African descent, Atheists,
Infidels, Agnostics, such persons as hold to the theory of Evolution,
habitual drunkards, gamblers, profane swearers, despoilers of the do-
mestic life of others, desecrators of the Lord's Day and those who
would depreciate feminine virtue by vulgarly discussing sex relationship." Bogard also intended to make the antievolution question an important one in Arkansas elections, announcing that every legislator who
had voted against the Rotenberry bill would be blacklisted and warning
that the evolution issue would enter every political race in the state. By
November 1927 petitions were circulating statewide. On 6 June 1928
Arkansas antievolutionists filed petitions with the secretary of state
bearing nineteen thousand signatures. The proposed antievolution law
would appear on the November ballot as Initiated Act no. 1.[50]

Despite the obvious support for antievolution legislation, significant opposition to such activity also existed. Prominent attorneys and
academic leaders formed the Committee Against Act no. 1 to oppose
the initiative. Among the best known of the committee's members was
former governor Charles H. Brough, a respected Baptist layman and
president of Central College in Conway, Arkansas. Active in Demo-

cratic politics as well as in the Baptist church, Brough risked his popularity to oppose the antievolution initiative and to campaign for Al Smith in the presidential election. To reinforce personal opposition to the act, the committee arranged for a series of newspaper advertisements to convince Arkansas voters to reject the proposed statute. These advertisements stressed the general acceptance of evolution among scientists and emphasized that evolution and religion were compatible. Their major thrust, however, rested on the frequently stated warning that Arkansas would look as ridiculous as Tennessee if the act passed.[51] Avoiding the embarrassment that had surrounded Tennessee during the Scopes trial continued to be a major concern for the opponents of the antievolution act.

Evidently aware of their own strength, supporters of the initiative advertised very little. One advertisement in the *Arkansas Gazette* appeared under the headline "The Bible or Atheism, Which?" It went on to announce that "all atheists favor evolution. If you agree with atheism, vote against Act No. 1. If you agree with the Bible, vote for Act No. 1." The advertisement concluded with an attack on those who appeared concerned with the possible embarrassment such a law might cause. "The *Gazette* said Russian Bolshevists laughed at Tennessee," blared the closing lines. "True, and that sort will laugh at Arkansas. Who cares?" Bogard made several statements during the campaign, many of which attempted to refute the charge that Arkansas would suffer with an antievolution statute. He told the *Arkansas Gazette* on 31 October that "those who make such a silly statement fail to mention that Tennessee has taken on new life since the evolution bill became law. People of the right sort want to live in a state where the faith of their children will not be attacked in the free schools." The backers of the initiative clearly had the upper hand in the contest. When the election ended, Initiated Act no. 1 had passed overwhelmingly, by a vote of 108,991 to 63,406. Only five counties failed to give the act a majority.[52]

The success of the initiative drive secured an antievolution law for Arkansas, but many questions remained concerning the impact such a law would have. Shortly after the act passed, state superintendent of public instruction J.P. Womack expressed the opinion that the act would probably have little effect on Arkansas education. He pointed out that no approved texts contained any references to evolution but added that official state approval of the *World Book Encyclopedia* had been withdrawn because certain statements in the work violated the new law. Questions also arose concerning the details of what the law prohibited, with some observers wondering if mentioning evolution was the same as "teaching" evolution. The Reverend Ben Bogard contributed his own interpretation of the question to the *Arkansas Gazette,* suggesting that discussing evolution in class would be permissible, so long as the teacher did not tell the students that evolution was true. A similar interpretation appeared in the educational journal *School and Society* the following year. The author of the article stressed the ambiguous nature of the Arkansas statute but emphasized that the most reasonable interpretation of the law would prohibit the dogmatic teaching of evolution. Such a removal of dogmatism represented a valuable educational concept and convinced the author that the Arkansas statute was "likely to do no great educational mischief, and it may even bring some educational advantages."[53] Such interpretations apparently satisfied those individuals who had questions about the statute, as the Arkansas law remained unchallenged for nearly forty years.

An Era Ends

Events in Arkansas showed the continuing support available to the antievolution crusade more than three years after the Scopes trial had captured national attention. The successful initiative campaign raised to three the number of states with antievolution statutes. In states without such legislation, local policies frequently achieved the same goal of prohibiting the teaching of evolution in the public schools. In truth, however, the situation was far less advantageous to the antievolutionists in the late 1920s than they realized. Despite their successes, the movement was losing its momentum.

Part of the reason for the collapse of the antievolution movement was the continuing opposition from the scientific and intellectual community, which increased in intensity throughout the second half of the decade. Professional organizations continued to pass resolutions and to use their meetings as forums for criticism of the attempts to prohibit the teaching of evolution. A few weeks before the Scopes trial, for example, the House of Delegates of the American Medical Association approved a resolution to support the teaching of evolution in the public schools. The AMA resolution closed with the statement that "any restriction of the proper study of scientific fact in regularly established scientific institutions [should] be considered inimical to the progress of science and to the public welfare." Less than two months after the end of the Scopes trial, the national council meeting of the prestigious honor society Phi Beta Kappa also recorded its opposition to antievolution laws and its commitment to the concept of freedom of teaching.[54]

Perceiving a threat to both science and education, the 1926 joint meeting of the American Association of University Professors and the American Association for the Advancement of Science passed resolutions that recorded the groups' opposition to antievolution laws. Press coverage of the late December conference in Philadelphia not only focused on the organizations' resolutions but also stressed that antievolution legislation was pending in seventeen states. The National Education Association recorded its opposition to antievolution laws six months later in Seattle. Supporters of the teaching of evolution also organized a publicity campaign for the spring of 1928. Scientists, educators, and clergy arranged a series of "evolution dinners" on the night of 13 April to be held in New York City, Chicago, Denver, San Francisco, and several other major cities. Those in attendance exchanged telegrams with dinner guests in other cities and listened to speakers who addressed the issues surrounding the ongoing controversy.[55]

Opponents of the antievolution crusade also attempted to counter the campaign through their contributions to various periodicals. Kirtley F. Mather, one of the expert witnesses at the Scopes trial, published "The Psychology of the Anti-Evolutionist" in the September 1926 issue of the *Harvard Graduates' Magazine*. He pointed out many of the inconsistencies in the antievolutionists' arguments, paying particular attention to their willingness to accept evolution as it applied to plants and the lower orders of animals, but not as it applied to humans. Harbor Allen, publicity director for the American Civil Liberties Union, contributed a strident essay to *Current History* at the same time, stressing that compulsory Bible reading laws and antievolution legislation showed that American fundamentalists held a strong position.[56]

From his perspective as a faculty member at Ohio Wesleyan University and one of the Scopes trial expert witnesses, zoologist Edward L. Rice contributed a more restrained essay to *Current History*. He drew an intriguing parallel between the recent Scopes trial and the problems facing Galileo in the early seventeenth century, writing that the "spirit of intolerance and persecution" remained identical. The only significant change was "a marked evolution in penal practice, a money fine and banishment from the public educational system of Tennessee taking the place of excommunication and torture popular in the seventeenth century." Rice went on to argue in quieter terms that evolutionary theory was continuing to develop, with the details of the theory still being examined. He stressed, however, that such activity had to be accomplished through the work of biologists and not through jury trials and the acts of legislatures. From Rice's perspective, the lack of knowledge concerning evolution on the part of the reasonably well educated public represented the crucial factor in explaining the continuing strength of the antievolution crusade. Those without scientific knowledge fell easy prey to the antievolutionists' arguments, many of which sounded logical upon first hearing. To solve this problem, Rice urged greater efforts in both formal education and popular education through newspapers and other media. There was nothing wrong with scientific propaganda to counter the effects of the fundamentalists' propaganda.[57]

Among the opponents of the antievolution movement, Maynard Shipley continued to be the most active throughout the late 1920s. From his position as head of the Science League of America, Shipley could command the attention of media throughout the United States. Equally important were his various published attacks on the movement, culminating in his 1927 volume, *The War on Modern Science: A Short History of the Fundamentalist Attacks on Evolution and Modernism.* No less committed to his view of the need to maintain culture and civilization in America than were his fundamentalist opponents, Shipley frequently expressed his ideas in the same apocalyptic terms as the more extreme antievolutionists. In *The War on Modern Science*, Shipley provided a clear statement of his view of the conflict. "Centering their attacks for the moment on evolution, the keystone in the arch of our modern educational edifice," he proclaimed, "the armies of ignorance are being organized, literally by the millions, for a combined political assault upon modern science. . . . For the first time in our history, organized knowledge has come into open conflict with organized ignorance." Similar comments continued to flow from Shipley's pen throughout the rest of the decade, especially after the successful Arkansas campaign, although by 1930 he appeared to be ready to accept that the movement for state legislation to outlaw the teaching of evolution had crested. He stressed in a *Current History* article, however, that legislation represented only part of the story. Shipley emphasized that the antievolutionists had merely changed their tactics, currently preferring to focus on the local level, where they could purge textbooks and convince local school boards to prohibit the teaching of the suspect biological concepts.[58]

Shipley's analysis of the continuing strength of the antievolution movement proved perceptive in many ways. In the years following the Scopes trial, proposed legislation surfaced in nearly a score of states in most regions of the nation. In 1927, the high point in the campaign, no fewer than thirteen antievolution bills were introduced into state legislatures.[59] Similar evidence of the strength of the movement was visible during the spring of 1927 at the World's Christian Fundamentals Association meeting in Atlanta. Reported in the New York *Times* under the headline "Start World Fight against Evolution," the conference focused on pushing forward the antievolution campaign throughout the United States and into Europe, China, South America, and Australia. The meeting authorized the formation of a committee to draft a uniform antievolution bill to present to all state legislatures and requested sponsors of such bills to clear their actions with the association to avoid possible clashes. Over the next few years, however, the World's Christian Fundamentals Association became less and less concerned with the evolution controversy. By the 1930 meeting, none of the scheduled speeches addressed evolution.[60]

Despite the notoriety and success of the antievolution crusade throughout much of the 1920s, its impact remained somewhat ambiguous. Even in those states with antievolution laws, no indictments took place except for that of John Thomas Scopes. Officials interpreted laws and resolutions leniently, which could explain the ACLU's inability to develop another test case during the seven years following the Scopes trial. Admittedly, attempts to repeal the existing laws proved unsuccessful, but the impact of such legislation appears less draconian than the observer would conclude from reading the comments of Maynard Shipley and his colleagues.

In addition, teachers in states with antievolution laws frequently developed various ploys to "bootleg" modern science into their classrooms. Even in Tennessee, science teachers were able to get their point across by substituting the word *development* for *evolution* in their lectures and discussions. As one faculty member at a state normal school told a journalist, "We are not going to teach a Seventeenth Century science because of a Seventeenth Century law! We are simply making an effort to be inoffensive to the existing law in our promulgation of truth." Another tactic that proved effective in states with antievolution legislation was to use "reference books" instead of "textbooks" to acquaint students with evolution. As the state laws only outlawed the use of textbooks that taught evolution, this approach was acceptable to many. Clearly, the antievolution crusade had an impact on the teaching of science in the United States, as large numbers of local school boards continued to do everything in their power to make sure teachers did not introduce even bootlegged evolution into the classroom, but opportunities did arise for students to encounter evolutionary concepts.[61]

Regardless of the ambiguity surrounding any analysis of the impact of the movement, the antievolution crusade appeared to be over by the end of the 1920s. Tennessee, Mississippi, and Arkansas all had existing statutes to prevent the teaching of evolution in the public schools, and local agencies in several other states attempted to accomplish the same end by different means. Yet the interest in such activities had clearly subsided. The evolution controversy no longer captured the public's attention, and the effect it had on Protestant fundamentalism in the United States proved to be largely a negative one. Once antievolution sentiment captured fundamentalism, at least in the public eye, the fortunes of the first dictated the fortunes of the second. From the public perspective, antievolution was fundamentalism; as the public lost interest in one, it lost interest in the other.[62]

As has frequently happened in the United States, however, the public perception of the situation represented only part of the picture. Conservative Protestantism did not die with the end of the decade, any more than opposition to the teaching of evolution disappeared. Over the next three decades the United States witnessed many developments that revolutionized religion and science in the nation. Unfortunately, these developments did little to bridge the gap between the groups that had participated in the debates of the 1920s. America's evolution controversy was far from over.

5

Decline and Revival

As the decade of the 1920s closed with the crash of the stock market and the beginning of the Great Depression, Americans continued their drift away from the topic of evolution in the public schools. Although the legal impact of the various antievolution statutes was more dramatic than meaningful, the Scopes trial and the publicity that surrounded antievolution laws had a profound effect on the teaching of biology for more than three decades. Publishers and authors of high school biology textbooks retreated from the presentation of evolution in an attempt to avoid controversy and maintain sales. Faced with inadequate source materials, classroom teachers struggled to supplement course presentations with appropriate information. They were rarely able to provide students with more than a superficial understanding of the topic. This situation was particularly ironic in light of the dramatic developments in the study of biology itself during the same period. The development and refinement of the Modern Synthesis provided biologists with a more profound understanding of nature and went far toward completing the revolution initiated by Darwin in 1859.

The Scopes Trial and Biology Education

Although the Scopes trial brought the controversy over biology education to a head, the antievolution campaign had an early impact on the material presented to American biology students. In 1924, a year after a national committee of educators had recommended evolution as one of nine major units to be covered in high school biology courses, several new texts were published that treated evolution with great reservation. As agitation to eliminate the topic from public schools increased during the next few years, successful biology texts downplayed evolution and related subjects. The word *evolution* disappeared from the indexes of these texts, and Darwin himself was frequently expunged from the historical discussion of biology. Religious statements were sometimes added as well. An interesting example of the fading status of evolution can be found in two editions of the widely used text *Biology for Beginners* by Truman Moon. The frontispiece of the 1921 edition was a portrait of Charles Darwin. The edition published five years later replaced the Darwin portrait with a cutaway drawing of the human digestive system.[1]

As pointed out by Judith V. Grabiner and Peter D. Miller in 1974, this "self-censorship exercised by the New York-based publishing industry" shaped the teaching of high school biology until the late 1950s. Commercial considerations were of paramount importance. The largest markets for text publishers were those states—mostly in the South— that had statewide adoption policies. The South's disproportionate impact was further heightened by the region's agricultural background, which led to higher biology enrollments than elsewhere in the nation. As the South remained the most militantly antievolution region throughout the 1920s, publishers geared their offerings to a market that would more than likely want evolution downplayed.

Characteristics of textbook publishing on the national level also played a role in the deterioration of biology education. For the most part, professional biologists were not involved in the writing of high school texts, leaving this task to high school teachers or professional educators. Not only did this situation make it unlikely that the most recent knowledge would be included in texts, but it also left the door open for authors to emphasize the "practical" aspects of biology. Hygiene and similar topics proved far more important than evolution. An educator writing in the journal *School Science and Mathematics* in 1928 suggested that the only topic related to evolution that had a legitimate place in a high school biology course was Mendelian inheritance. Even this topic should have a practical focus, the author argued. One of the objectives of the course should be to teach Mendelian concepts "so effectively that pupils will comprehend the principles underlying the improvement of plant, animal and human stock."[2]

Once established as a result of the antievolution campaigns of the 1920s, the new view of biology education took on a life of its own. Educators and textbook writers alike embraced the concept of meeting the needs of the students through an emphasis on health information and consumerism. Evolution and other "theoretical" concepts were largely ignored, despite occasional calls from biology educators that evolution should be part of any set of principles covered in high school biology courses. The material presented to high school students tended to focus on the "practical and interesting," emphasizing such topics as the social and economic aspects of biology. Such emphasis was quite different from that favored by university biologists surveyed by Columbia University researchers in the early 1930s. More than 80 percent of these biologists supported the teaching of the "evidences for evolution" along with the more practical topics of heredity and environment. Interestingly enough, however, these biologists were almost unanimous in their recommendation that "theories of the origin of life" should not be taught at the high school level.[3]

Although rarely involved in the writing of textbooks for high school courses, professional biologists nonetheless expressed concern with biology teaching during the 1930s. Writing from Indiana University, Alfred C. Kinsey told readers of *School Science and Mathematics* that he was well aware of the conflicting opinions concerning the subject matter of high school biology courses but remained concerned with the practical focus that seemed to be taking over the curriculum. He admitted the importance of teaching hygiene, for example, but he questioned the high school biology course as an appropriate forum for such instruction. Rather than providing future citizens with an interest in the biological world and an appreciation of the scientific method, Kinsey argued, "we are at best directing their attention to a species of toothbrush biology suspiciously fortified with the trappings of articles of personal faith." Later in the decade Kinsey would write both a text and a science methods book in which he emphasized evolution as an integral part of biology that should be taught at the high school level. Bowing to political realities, however, Kinsey stressed that evolution should be taught carefully and that human evolution should be ignored.[4]

Perhaps the most outspoken critic of the inadequate teaching of biology in America during the post-Scopes period was Oscar Riddle of the Carnegie Institution of Washington. A biologist at the Station for Experimental Evolution at Cold Spring Harbor, New York, Riddle examined the status of American biology education in an address to the American Association for the Advancement of Science on 1 January 1936. Surveying recent progress in the study of zoology as it related to evolution, Riddle emphasized that biologists had failed to disseminate the new information to the public. The antievolution movement in America thus remained vigorous, as evidenced by poor texts, the lack of public understanding of biology, and substandard teaching. In fact, he argued, secondary schools currently taught less biology than in the early years of the century, despite significant developments in the discipline. Among the cures for this dismal state of affairs, the proper training of biology teachers was high on Riddle's list. "The presumption that for making a teacher of biology there is any substitute for long-continued training under our best college biological departments is an expensive fraud," he argued, "and the extent to which that presumption is being enforced in one or another guise is now an educational disgrace."[5]

The situation had hardly improved two years later, when Riddle contributed an essay to *Science* entitled "Educational Darkness and Luminous Research." Attempting to examine the "flagrant failure of our educational program to comprehend and teach life-science," Riddle emphasized that the situation in biology was merely part of the larger problem of American education's inability or unwillingness to teach science. A citizenry aware of science was an absolute necessity in the late 1930s, he argued, and a biology course could do great good in informing that citizenry. Tragically, secondary school biology had completely ignored the scientific developments of the past three decades and, in fact, represented a far less valuable curriculum than it had earlier in the century. Riddle closed his essay by asking the dramatic question, "Shall the public that decides the fate of our democracy conceive nature and man as research discloses them, or as uninformed and essentially ignorant masses can variously imagine them?"[6]

Although Riddle's analysis of the state of science education in the late 1930s proved accurate, a few bright spots existed. One of the best biology texts was Ella T. Smith's *Exploring Biology,* published by Harcourt, Brace and Company in 1938. Smith supported evolution vigorously, arguing at one point in the text that "no one acquainted with the facts doubts that evolution, or continued change in plants and animals, has taken place. No one has discovered a single fact to disprove the theory of evolution," she went on, "and the facts that establish its truth are abundant." Later in her analysis she became even more forceful. "Evolution is a fact," she wrote. "Plants and animals do change and have always been changing."[7]

Smith's support of evolution, however, remains noteworthy because it was unusual. Most text writers and science teachers did not share the missionary zeal of Smith or Riddle, leading a later student of science education in America to conclude that "the status of science in the secondary school curriculum was never weaker" than in 1940. The 1941 report of the National Commission on Cooperative Curriculum Planning did little to improve the situation. Although listing organic evolution as one of twenty-two areas that should be included in a study of biology, the commission nonetheless continued to stress the practical value of biology by listing health, conservation, and sanitation as the focal points of biology education. Such views were shared by classroom teachers, who tended to base their decisions concerning content for science courses on such factors as the interest of students, topics' relationship to everyday living, their reference to the local community, and the practical aspects of the material to be presented.

Other factors also complicated the teaching of science in America. As suggested by *The Teaching of the Basic Sciences,* a 1943 report from the commissioner of education, at least part of the reason for the non-scientific focus of science education in the United States was the poor preparation of most science teachers. In fact, a large number of science teachers only had minors in the science area. Even had they wished to teach science legitimately, their preparation made that impossible. Yet another complication was the continuing debate over the purpose of secondary school science; professional scientists desired an emphasis on science itself, while professional educators insisted that the practical impact of science represented the only legitimate focus.[8] It is no wonder that students of the early 1940s were exposed to little of scientific value.

The criticisms of American science education typified by the comments of Riddle and others became more evident following the end of World War II. The clear importance of science to the war effort led to several examinations of the role and quality of science education in the United States. The President's Scientific Research Board published a report in 1947 entitled *Science and Public Policy,* which emphasized the serious shortage of secondary mathematics and science teachers. This report not only urged the training of more science and mathematics teachers but also stressed the need for an expanded science curriculum for these future teachers. Such expressions of concern, however, had little impact on the biology classroom—or that of any other science—in the late 1940s. Little change was evident. Textbooks continued to avoid or downplay evolution to maintain sales, as shown by the 1949 edition of *Biology in Our Lives* by George W. Hunter and F.W. Hunter. A revision of the 1941 edition, the text included a brief discussion of the origin of life on earth. "Very simple green plants probably came first," the authors argued in the 1941 edition, "and later simple forms of animal life appeared." For the 1949 edition, the authors added, "As you see, if you turn to the first chapter of Genesis, this is the order of the Creation."[9]

Despite the shortcomings in biology education, by 1950 the topic was well established as part of the secondary school curriculum in the United States. Almost all American high schools offered a general biology course of some kind, with more than 21 percent of all high school students enrolled in a biology course during the academic year. The status of evolution within the well-established biology curriculum, however, remained problematic. A study of biology teachers in Essex County, New Jersey, disclosed that nearly 30 percent of those responding failed to discuss evolution as a regular part of their classes. California educators showed similar characteristics in 1951, when a third of the state's biology teachers omitted evolution from their courses. A 1953 survey of students in biology courses taught in the Denver school system showed that they were only moderately interested in evolutionary topics, although they appeared to be quite intrigued with discussions of Mendelian inheritance and evidence of organic change over time.[10] The textbooks of the decade provided little assistance to those who might wish to improve the quality of biology education. Most of the texts published during the 1950s were revisions of prewar texts and were characterized by even less coverage of evolution than in the 1940s. Those texts that included a chapter on evolution usually placed it near the end of the volume, where it could be deleted from the course most easily.[11]

In addition to the inadequacies of textbooks, the training of biology teachers during the 1950s continued to represent a major problem, as emphasized by Oscar Riddle in an *American Biology Teacher* essay. Stressing how to teach, as was the practice in the schools of education in the United States, failed to equip people concerning what they should teach. Education in general, and especially science education, was largely failing in its responsibility to Americans. For the most part, Riddle argued, "we Americans are uninformed; worse, we are complacently drifting on or within the borders of anti-intellectualism. We are post-graduates only in gadgetry and in the hoopla and skills of production, sports and marketplace." Despite Riddle's warnings, the teaching of biology remained mired in mediocrity as the 1950s came to a close.[12]

A Hidden Revival

If the decades following the Scopes trial represented a low point in American science education, the traditional view of the fortunes of American religious conservatism suggests that fundamentalism faced a similar plight. In one sense, the accepted view that fundamentalism suffered decay and disarray following its clash with modernism offers an accurate perspective on this important phenomenon. Coalitions that had cooperated to rid America of the modernist menace began to break apart during the late 1920s, at least in part because of the negative publicity generated by the antievolution campaigns. By the end of the decade fundamentalist leaders had also become more strident, alienating much of their earlier support. As the 1930s began, however, many of the issues and concerns that had vitalized the fundamentalist movement remained visible to those troubled by perceived religious weaknesses in the United States. Manners and morals continued to change. The urban-rural split was still obvious, with the forces of urbanism apparently in control. Although fundamentalists no longer emphasized political change because of their lack of success during the 1920s, they continued to worry about the future of America as a Christian nation.[13] Their commitment to that concept guided their actions for the next three decades and eventually led the United States into a significant religious revival.

Abandoning the political activity that had earlier characterized their movement, fundamentalists refocused their energies during the 1930s toward evangelism and religious community building. Emphasizing education, summer conferences, radio broadcasts, and foreign missionary work, fundamentalists established themselves as a "growing, dynamic movement." This new state was in sharp contrast to mainline American Protestantism, which suffered a decline in support and interest during the same period. The vitality of post-1920s fundamentalism was vividly displayed in a number of areas. Bible institutes nearly tripled in number during the 1930s and 1940s. Membership in fundamentalist, Holiness, and Pentecostal groups skyrocketed during the 1930s. The Church of the Nazarene grew from fewer than 64,000 members in 1926 to more than 136,000 a decade later. Assemblies of God membership more than tripled in the same period, growing to 148,000. Within larger denominations, fundamentalism remained an important force, as shown by the 1932 organization of the General Association of Regular Baptists in response to the Northern Baptist Convention's refusal to adopt fundamentalist ideas. At the end of World War II this association claimed five hundred member churches.[14]

While building an institutional base, fundamentalists geared their campaign toward revivalism to return America to traditional Christian ideals. Economic problems and the growing difficulties in Europe led many revivalists to suggest that the beginning of the end of human history was at hand. These views tended to dissipate interest in social reform but provided adherents with comfort and assurance during a trying time in American history. Such assurance encouraged fundamentalists to continue their revivalism in the hope that this campaign would succeed where their earlier political efforts had failed. Making use of all avenues, revivalists quickly established the radio program as an important method to reach Americans. By May 1931 the *Sunday School Times* could report that seventy stations carried more than one hundred different revivalist radio programs. Perhaps the most famous of these radio evangelists was Charles E. Fuller of Orange County, California, who began full-time radio work in 1933. His "Old-Fashioned Revival Hour" soon became an important part of the Mutual Network's Sunday schedule and, by 1939, reached an estimated audience of fifteen to twenty million over 152 stations. Three years later Fuller's program was carried by more than 450 stations and represented the largest prime-time radio broadcast in the United States.[15]

Despite their activity and obvious success, fundamentalists during the 1930s found themselves struggling with two conflicting desires. They clearly wished to save American culture for God through their revivalist efforts. Yet at the same time they had defined themselves as a community of believers who, because of their faith, had become alienated from American culture as a whole. Fundamentalism thus developed a separateness that provided a clear sense of purpose and a belief that antimodernist endeavors were of crucial significance. It did not matter in the least that secular newspapers continued to describe fundamentalism as a joke. Fundamentalists were engaged in a battle for Christian civilization.

Among the most intriguing and far-reaching aspects of this separationist impulse was the growing importance placed on appropriate education. Beginning in the 1930s fundamentalists mounted a concerted effort to attract students to various evangelical colleges such as Wheaton College and the Moody Bible Institute. The goal of this educational campaign focused on counteracting modernism and, announced a Wheaton College pamphlet, teaching only "conservative social and economic views." Students were discouraged from attending secular colleges because their faculties were composed of agnostics, atheists, Communists, and others of negative influences. Far better for college-age fundamentalists to remain among their own kind at a legitimate Christian college that had not been infected by the viruses of modernism and infidelity.[16]

Fundamentalists who challenged the orthodoxy of secular colleges and universities seemed to be on firm ground in the mid-1930s, as shown by a study conducted by sociologist James H. Leuba. Examining a sample of American scientists, Leuba attempted to measure the degree of religious belief among these students of nature. His study reported several trends, all of which could be interpreted by fundamentalists as indicating the dangerous atmosphere on the secular campuses where most of these scientists pursued their crafts. Believers tended to be concentrated among the less eminent scientists and among students in the lower-level college classes. In addition, there were more believers among scientists and students in a 1914 survey than in the 1933 survey. Finally, Leuba suggested, scientists dealing with inanimate matter tended to be more orthodox believers than those dealing with life, such as biologists, sociologists, and psychologists. Leuba explained this intriguing result by arguing that because the former scientists knew less about life, society, and mind, they were more willing to believe that divine action occasionally resulted from human supplication. Although the details of Leuba's study could be challenged from various perspectives, his basic conclusion was quite clear and seemed to confirm the fundamentalists' suspicion of secular education. The sociologist argued that greater intelligence led to greater independence of mind, which made the rejection of traditional beliefs easier.[17]

Fundamentalists' desire for educational separation, however, could not justify the abandonment of all intellectual pursuits. As had been the case during the 1920s, evangelicals attempted to establish themselves as champions of legitimate science, as opposed to the speculation that they thought characterized post-Darwinian and, now, post-Einsteinian thought. Harry Rimmer became very popular during the 1930s with his "Bible and science" lectures, which he presented in churches and on college campuses throughout the nation. Despite his responsibilities as field secretary of the World's Christian Fundamentals Association and as pastor of the First Presbyterian Church of Duluth, Minnesota, Rimmer served as a leading scientific authority for those who embraced the fundamentalist worldview. The Moody Bible Institute also contributed to this effort through an illustrated lecture series entitled "Sermons from Science." The theme for fundamentalist science remained as it had been since the late nineteenth century: a commitment to a rigidly defined inductivism that tended to restrict science to the collection and classification of data. A cartoon series in the *Presbyterian Guardian* in 1935 provided a clear indication of this view of science and the position of evangelical Christians at secular universities. An earnest fundamentalist, Gary, the cartoon's main character, found himself in a science class taught by a secularist who regularly made disparaging remarks about "exploded superstitions" and "outworn dogmas." Defending the fundamentalist view of science, Gary referred to evolution in class as "merely a theory" and justified his belief by exclaiming, "I'm ready to back my statement with scientific facts!" When his roommate remarked that he had never heard of such facts, Gary responded, "And you never will—if some of these profs have anything to do with it!"[18]

As the European situation deteriorated in the late 1930s and dramatized the likelihood of a global conflict, American evangelicals found themselves in a favorable position. They had survived the depression and had, in fact, established themselves as the most vital aspect of American religion in the prewar period. The Nazi menace indicated the existence of major problems in the world, which the United States could help to solve if it pursued the revivalism that had become the central focus of the fundamentalists of the 1930s. Traditional antievolution sentiment also played a role in the development of this perspective. Writing in the *Moody Monthly* in the summer of 1940, Will Houghton, president of the Moody Bible Institute, described Nazism as a "great mechanical monster" formed from evolutionary and materialistic ideas of progress. Modernism had destroyed orthodox faith and replaced it with Darwinism and Marxism. The chief culprits in this turn of events were the universities, who owed a profound apology to the world for their "fat-headed conceit."[19]

As American involvement in the war became more and more likely in 1940 and early 1941, fundamentalists rededicated themselves to saving the nation through revivalism. Toward that end, the movement became more concerned with institutional aspects of the proposed campaign. Dissatisfied with the perceived liberalism and social focus of the Federal Council of Churches, for example, evangelicals formed such organizations as the American Council of Christian Churches and the National Association of Evangelicals. The former, under the leadership of the Reverend Carl McIntire, was an extremist group from the beginning, but the National Association of Evangelicals proved more interested in fostering cooperation among evangelical groups toward the goal of a national revival. Playing a major role in the continued evangelical resurgence during World War II, the NAE represented the moderate and progressive wing of fundamentalism, which occasionally compromised with the liberals on issues such as Darwinism and the higher criticism. Another dramatic development of the war years was the organization of the evangelistic Youth for Christ. During the last year of the war, when Youth for Christ International was formed, the organization sponsored three hundred rallies attracting more than three hundred thousand individuals. These numbers tripled during 1946, indicating that Youth for Christ had struck a responsive chord among the young people who would come to maturity in the postwar world.[20]

The end of World War II consolidated many of the trends in American evangelicalism that had begun in the early 1930s. As part of an attempt to establish a sense of national identity, a new respect for religious faith and the institutional church emerged from America's wartime experience. Evangelical Christianity became an increasingly important part of this postwar resurgence, leading religious conservatives to see themselves as part of the establishment by the late 1940s. Yet this establishment could not have been what the earlier evangelicals had in mind. Instead, the postwar period, to borrow noted church historian Sydney E. Ahlstrom's apt phrasing, was one of a "generalized kind of religiosity" characterized by "pious utilitarianism" and a "faith in faith."[21] The best-known figure in this religious revival was neither a scholarly theologian nor a revivalist evangelical, but rather Norman Vincent Peale with his message of self-worth.

The new evangelicals of the postwar period assimilated themselves into this new American religious perspective through a softening of their earlier fundamentalism. Accepting a more pluralistic view, evangelicals of the 1950s especially sought to divorce themselves from the anti-intellectual spirit that had discredited earlier fundamentalists. Although the movement continued to attack modernism, it nonetheless offered conservative theology as a *rational* choice and sought a less combative focal point for the new evangelicalism.[22]

The new focal point proved to be a young North Carolina minister who had been active in the Youth for Christ movement during the 1940s. While identifying himself with the revivalist traditions of the rural South and West, Billy Graham cast his net far wider in an attempt to establish what one scholar has called a "softened conservative gospel." Accepting support and praise from liberal Protestants, Catholics, and Jews, Graham became the focus of evangelicalism from the early 1950s through the 1960s. He used the mass media effectively, integrating television, radio, and advertising and publishing ventures to broadcast his message to as wide an audience as possible. By 1956 the Billy Graham Evangelistic Association had an annual budget of two million dollars and embodied American evangelism.[23]

By the late 1950s America's revived religious interest had led to a new sense of the importance of faith as a national characteristic. Institutional participation seemed to be the guiding force in this revival, as indicated by a 1957 Census Bureau report. When asked "What is your religion?" 96 percent of all respondents answered with the name of a specific religious denomination or other affiliation. Although virtually all denominations grew during the postwar period, conservative groups such as the Holiness and Pentecostal churches increased their membership most dramatically. Despite the success of Billy Graham and others, however, the intensity of the postwar revival seemed to be ebbing by the end of the decade. Sydney Ahlstrom later explained this phenomenon by emphasizing that the institutional focus of the revival provided little more than "a means of social identification" for an increasingly rootless population. As important as that social identification was in the postwar world, it could not serve as the basis for a lasting religious transformation of the United States.[24]

The Completion of the Darwinian Revolution

While biology education remained mired in mediocrity and American
religion seemed to be experiencing a renewal, biologists were engaged
in their own reaffirmation of faith. The collapse of the most militant
phase of the antievolution movement by the late 1920s found biologists
cautiously encouraged about the public perception of their work, but
also concerned about the many unanswered questions about that work.
College biology texts often presented several different evolutionary theories as generally equivalent, underscoring theoretical and practical divisions within biology. Geneticists, for example, tended to view the
natural world in an entirely different fashion from naturalists, who in
turn knew little about the mechanisms of heredity. Although the work
of Thomas Hunt Morgan and others had done much to revitalize Darwinism, the debate over the details of evolution remained an important
part of biology as the 1930s began.[25]

This debate involved a wide variety of biological disciplines. In the
late 1920s, paleontology remained farther away than most from Darwinian concepts, tending to reject Darwin's gradualism through natural
selection in favor of either saltationism, based on the application of de
Vriesian mutation to fossil material, or orthogenesis, based on the concept of progressive adaptation through acquired characteristics. Biologists interested in genetics also participated in the debate over the
details of evolution, proposing "mutation pressure" as the chief factor
in evolutionary development. Even after de Vries's mutation concepts
were shown to be seriously flawed, most American geneticists continued to define species as essentially pure lines that had to wait for
mutation in order to evolve. During the 1920s, however, a growing
awareness of the importance of selection emerged. Recognizing that
useful new characteristics were more likely to spread throughout a population than harmful ones and that large mutations were nearly always
harmful or fatal, a few scientists began to consider more favorably the
concept of natural selection. British geneticists R.A. Fisher and J.B.S.
Haldane provided much support for these new ideas through their dem-
onstrations that selection could act on very small character differences.
Although Fisher, Haldane, and others stopped short of embracing evolution through natural selection in the Darwinian sense, their ideas
nonetheless led to a greater acceptance of selection as a vital factor
in evolution.[26]

The emergence of a new generation of geneticists, who embraced
selectionist ideas, proved to be a crucial event in the history of evolutionary thought. These younger biologists quickly focused on diversity

and increasingly examined entire populations as the locus of evolution, emulating the outlook of the field naturalists. A merger of sorts thus took place, with each group abandoning concepts that had retarded the development of a satisfactory evolutionary theory. Naturalists gave up the belief in the inheritance of acquired characters, while geneticists abandoned typological thinking to embrace population concepts. The merger of these various ideas and concepts involved individuals from diverse backgrounds who were nonetheless united by the idea of combining the gene-frequency approach of Morgan, Fisher, and others with the population thinking of naturalists. By the early 1940s biologists were enthusiastically discussing the Modern Synthesis.[27]

The development of mathematical population genetics represented the necessary first step in the creation of the new evolutionary theory. Among the most significant early contributors to this development was the Russian geneticist Sergei S. Chetverikov, whose conclusions were reached independently by Fisher, Haldane, and Sewall Wright. Employing the sophisticated mathematical techniques that would be an increasingly important part of all genetic studies, Chetverikov examined statistical effects in various population sizes, confirming his initial idea that variability would be shown most readily in small populations. This theory contrasted with the views of Fisher and Haldane, who argued that large populations were required to maintain genetic variation. Chetverikov's work thus introduced the concept of the gene pool as a reservoir of possible genetic combinations based on the laws of probability and the interaction of genes. In its original form, the new field of population genetics remained especially abstract, relying on statistical calculations while excluding geographic factors, which naturalists knew were important. This work nonetheless contributed greatly to the emergence of a new evolutionary outlook by destroying the legacy of anti-Darwinian thought and focusing attention on new research opportunities. Few biologists made better use of these new opportunities than did Sewall Wright.[28]

A student of William E. Castle at Harvard in the early twentieth century, Wright continued his mentor's work on genetic combinations and variation. Examining the coat color characteristics of guinea pigs, Wright established the importance of interaction between genes and developed the mathematical techniques necessary to analyze the effects of inbreeding among small populations. By stressing the interaction between genes as the source of additional variability within such groups, Wright moved away from the "beanbag genetics" of Fisher and Haldane, in which selection acted on individual genes. Wright's recognition that the genetic structure of populations was complex and that small, inbreeding populations were the focus of genetic change provided a view of evolution much closer to that of the field naturalists. This latter group of biologists had long focused on small populations as the key to understanding the process of speciation through geographic isolation and the impact of natural selection. Wright's analysis of small populations ultimately led to the concept of genetic drift, favoring gene combinations that would be unlikely to appear in large populations.[29]

By the mid-1920s Wright's work had progressed sufficiently that he began to apply his ideas to the problem of evolution in nature. Combining his mathematical and biological backgrounds, Wright carefully developed his ideas into a long paper, "Evolution in Mendelian Populations," published in the March 1931 issue of *Genetics*. Although the limitations of existing quantitative methods prevented Wright from treating the interaction of genes as completely as he desired, the mathematical focus of his analysis nonetheless represented a significant step forward in the study of genetics. Applying insights gained from his guinea pig studies, Wright emphasized that in small populations inbreeding would be sufficiently intense that new interaction systems would be created through random effects. This genetic drift would not be evident in large, random breeding populations, confirming the importance of small populations in any analysis of evolutionary change. The existence of small populations also raised the issue of migration from one subpopulation to another. In Wright's view, the migration from more successful subpopulations would modify other subpopulations through crossbreeding, thus transforming an entire species over time. The combination of random drifting of gene frequencies and natural selection contributed much toward explaining how species evolved.

Wright developed another important piece of the puzzle for an invited paper delivered at the International Congress of Genetics in 1932. In a well-received presentation later published as "The Roles of Mutation, Inbreeding, Crossbreeding, and Selection in Evolution," Wright proposed the "fitness surface" concept and the "shifting balance" theory based upon it. Once again focusing on small, semi-isolated populations, Wright posited that each such group occupied a peak on the adaptive landscape. To reach a higher, unoccupied peak, the population must cross nonadaptive valleys in a two-stage process. Genetic drift would pull the population into a valley, after which natural selection might attract it to a higher peak. After its establishment on such a peak, the population would then compete with other groups on other peaks, a competition that could result in the population spreading, perhaps throughout the entire species. This second step of the process thus represented evolutionary change, which Wright characterized as an adaptive process of selection among populations that displayed variation as a result of genetic drift.[30]

Wright's emphasis on the mathematical analysis of population genetics suggested that the division between geneticists and naturalists need not be maintained. Indeed, the thinking of naturalists about populations proved crucial in the development of the new view of evolution established in the 1930s. Naturalists had shown that species were aggregates of populations that were reproductively isolated from each other. When combined with Wright's investigations, this population thinking could replace the earlier typological thinking of many biologists and lead to a better understanding of selection, adaptation, and speciation.

Among the naturalists who played a significant role in the creation of the Modern Synthesis, the Russian émigré Theodosius Dobzhansky pursued the merger of genetics and field studies in a careful manner. By the late 1920s Dobzhansky had established himself as a well-respected field naturalist after a decade of research and publication. He had reached a plateau in his understanding of evolution, however, because of his lack of background in genetics. To gain that background, Dobzhansky came to the United States in 1927 to work in Thomas Hunt Morgan's laboratory at Columbia. Here he came under the tutelage of Alfred H. Sturtevant, who guided his Russian colleague through the intricacies of *Drosophila* genetics. This work led to thirteen papers from Dobzhansky published between 1928 and 1932 and two others coauthored with Sturtevant.

Although Dobzhansky pursued genetics as genetics only, his interest in evolution remained clear. In 1936 he and Sturtevant began considering a major project on the genetics and evolution of *Drosophila pseudoobscura*. By this time it had become obvious through the work of Sewall Wright that the quantitative aspects of genetics represented a fundamental part of any such study. As neither Dobzhansky nor Sturtevant was completely comfortable with the quantitative dimension of genetics, they approached Wright as a possible collaborator on their project. The combination of Wright and Dobzhansky proved to be a particularly profitable one over the next decade, providing Wright with even greater knowledge of evolution in natural populations and providing Dobzhansky with the mathematical insight necessary for a more complete understanding of the genetic factors in evolution.[31]

Dobzhansky thus gained the perspective needed to combine naturalists' evolutionary views with the results of experimental genetics and their mathematical description. The result of this combination was Dobzhansky's 1937 book, *Genetics and the Origin of Species,* described by one historian as "perhaps the most influential single book on evolutionary biology during the period from 1937 through the 1950s." Heavily based on Wright's analyses, Dobzhansky's volume examined variation and selection from a new evolutionary perspective. His chapter "Variation in Natural Populations," for example, described variation as the result of random genetic drift in small populations, just as Wright had earlier suggested. Dobzhansky devoted an entire chapter to a treatment of natural selection as a process that could be confirmed experimentally and not solely supported as a theory. *Genetics and the Origin of Species* provided biologists with a much firmer grip on evolution, helping to reconcile the fieldwork of the naturalists with the quantitative insights of the population geneticists. It contributed greatly as well to the development of the new view of evolution by presenting Wright's work in a clear and concise fashion for those who were not as mathematically sophisticated as Wright. By making Wright's work more accessible, Dobzhansky precipitated the flurry of activity that would establish the Modern Synthesis over the next decade.[32]

Dobzhansky's book provided naturalists with important insight and led many of them toward significant contributions to the Modern Synthesis. Already thinking in population terms through his work on geographic variation and its impact on speciation, Ernst Mayr read *Genetics and the Origin of Species* and gained valuable information concerning the genetic aspect of evolution. It also provided him with the knowledge that even small selective advantages could be of evolutionary significance. Mayr combined these new insights with his own insistence on the importance of geographic isolation in his 1942 book, *Systematics and the Origin of Species.* Mayr argued that geographic factors were crucial in speciation, as the emergence of new species could only take place through an initial phase of geographic isolation. The various populations so isolated would thus develop their own unique characteristics, which could become isolating mechanisms that prevented interbreeding. The removal of geographic barriers would have no effect on such isolating mechanisms, allowing subspecies to remain distinct. Natural selection also played an important role by driving the subspecies further apart and establishing them as distinct species.[33]

Another bridge that had to be constructed for the Modern Synthesis was that between paleontology and genetics. Here again, the work of

Dobzhansky played a crucial role in the development of the ideas of George Gaylord Simpson, the paleontologist most responsible for bringing his field into the Modern Synthesis. Although trained as a geologist, Simpson realized by the 1930s that population genetics was necessary for understanding evolution. Already developing a nontraditional approach to his field, Simpson studied *Genetics and the Origin of Species,* which changed his outlook significantly. As Simpson recalled forty years later, Dobzhansky's book "started me thinking more definitely along the lines of an explanatory (causal) synthesis and less exclusively along lines more nearly traditional in paleontology."[34]

Simpson's pursuit of an "explanatory synthesis" led to the 1944 publication of *Tempo and Mode in Evolution.* Unlike traditional books in paleontology, which stressed description and chronology in discussing evolution, Simpson's volume addressed evolution from a theoretical perspective. This perspective was particularly unusual as it was based on quantitative insights gained from the work of Wright and Dobzhansky. Graphs and other mathematical illustrations were thus more important than drawings of fossils in *Tempo and Mode,* establishing this book outside the paleontological mainstream. The goal of Simpson's contribution also proved unique. Rather than the traditional proof and demonstration, Simpson offered a "consistency argument." He suggested that the macroevolutionary events displayed in the fossil record could be explained by the cumulative effects of the microevolutionary processes studied by the population geneticists. The paleontological record was thus consistent with the Modern Synthesis. Darwinian evolution, based on adaptation through natural selection, could account for the fossil data.

One aspect of the fossil record that continued to trouble paleontologists was the absence of transitional forms, a mystery that Simpson attempted to explain. Focusing on Wright's concept of genetic drift, Simpson argued that major transitions occurred within small populations, where genetic drift was most effective. The preservation of fossils, always an imperfect and rare phenomenon, would be even less likely in such small populations, making it very unlikely that transitional forms would be preserved in the paleontological record. This concept of "quantum evolution" was another part of Simpson's consistency argument, as it explained the lack of transitional forms in a more satisfying way than the traditional explanation based on the imperfection of the fossil record.[35]

By the early 1940s the new view of evolution was beginning to guide research. Later characterized by Ernst Mayr as "clearly the most decisive event in the history of evolutionary biology since the publication of the *Origin of Species* in 1859," the Modern Synthesis completed the revolution begun by Darwin. It confirmed the crucial importance of gradualism, natural selection, and hard inheritance, while emphasizing the populational structure and evolutionary role of species. The Modern Synthesis had become so well established by 1947 that an international symposium held at Princeton early in that year was marked by "universal and unanimous agreement" with the new evolutionary view. Sponsored by the National Research Council, the Princeton conference on evolution attracted the leading figures of biology, including Mayr, Dobzhansky, Simpson, Wright, Muller, and Haldane.[36]

Evolutionary biologists devoted themselves to working out the details of the Modern Synthesis for the next two decades. One of the most dramatic modifications to early views was the increasingly selectionist outlook on the part of most evolutionists. Not only did this represent a "hardening" of the synthesis to stress natural selection as the dominant force in evolution, but it also led to significant modifications in the details of the synthesis. Other developments in biology also contributed to a more complete understanding of evolution. The question of the origin of life was more profitably addressed after biologists abandoned the idea that the atmosphere of the primitive earth was the same as the modern atmosphere. Rejecting the idea of a single act of spontaneous generation, Russian biologist Alexander Oparin argued instead that life originated through chemical evolution enhanced by increasingly complex organization of preliving organisms. A type of natural selection would improve these proto-organisms, which would gradually emerge as life forms. Oparin put forth these ideas in his 1936 book, *The Origin of Life,* which was translated into English in 1938. He argued that the atmosphere of the primitive earth was composed of hydrocarbons and ammonia, in which chemical reactions produced complex organic molecules. These molecules dissolved in the primitive oceans, creating a "primordial soup" in which further combination led to organic systems with definite structures. Natural selection acted on such systems, eventually creating recognizable life. The origin of life was thus not merely a random combination of organic molecules, but rather a process in which natural selection played an important role. Oparin's basic ideas were dramatically confirmed in 1953 by the work of Stanley Miller, who passed an electric spark through a re-creation of the primitive terrestrial atmosphere as described by Oparin. This experiment produced amino acids, the basis of proteins, and greatly encouraged those biologists searching for a nonmystical explanation of the origin of life.[37]

By the 1950s as well, biologists had a much better understanding of the mechanisms of genetics and heredity through the discovery of the role of deoxyribonucleic acid. During the first half of the twentieth century, it had become increasingly clear that very complex molecules formed the basis of inheritance. Studies of the DNA molecule before the 1940s, hampered by analytical methods that broke down the molecule, led to estimates of approximately fifteen hundred for the molecular weight of DNA. The development of new techniques to analyze such molecules, however, allowed researchers to determine that the structures were very large. Much to biologists' surprise, DNA molecular weights approached one million. Given that only large molecules could carry the required genetic information, DNA seemed to be an excellent candidate for the carrier of such information. This conclusion was confirmed in 1944 by the work of Oswald T. Avery, who studied the smooth and rough strains of pneumococci to show that DNA was, indeed, responsible for hereditary transmission.

Avery's work precipitated a great deal of research concerning DNA, the best known of which was the work of James Watson and Francis Crick. Combining biology, chemistry, and physics, Watson and Crick determined the structure of the DNA molecule, describing the famous double-helix model of the molecule in *Nature* in the spring of 1953. Further research over the next few years in laboratories in Europe and the United States provided many of the details of the role of DNA in heredity, showing how the molecule replicated itself, explaining the origin of mutations, and describing the formation of polypeptides and proteins. Understanding these mechanisms of heredity and cellular differentiation thus provided biologists with a far more sophisticated grasp of life processes and enabled them to develop a more complete explanation of evolutionary change.[38]

The creation of the Modern Synthesis fundamentally changed the status of evolution among biologists. No longer did Darwinian evolution through natural selection represent only one of several competing versions of organic change. The merger of population genetics, paleontology, and naturalists' views of terrestrial life resulted in a view of evolution that only made sense when filtered through the disciplined mesh of natural selection. When combined with experimentally verified chemical explanations of life's origin and a greater understanding of the mechanisms of heredity, the Modern Synthesis by the late 1950s had emerged as the guiding force in the study of biology. Knowledge of the dramatic impact and importance of the new evolutionary view, however, remained restricted to the scientific community. Disseminating the results of the Modern Synthesis would prove nearly as difficult as developing the synthesis itself.

One Hundred Years without Darwinism Are Enough

Despite the significant achievements of biologists, the status of biology education remained at a low point. Scientists and educators concerned with the problem recognized that the shortcomings in biology education were part of a more general lack in the teaching of science in America. Describing such teaching in the 1950s as "anti-intellectual," "soft," and "behind the times," critics charged that American science education had failed in every important aspect because it did not "teach real science."

Among the most important factors influencing the poor quality of biology education in the United States was the questionable preparation of biology teachers. Various surveys and analyses indicated that many individuals who taught the topic in the secondary schools were not even biology majors, but rather individuals who had majored in science education or who had taken only enough biology courses to satisfy minimal state certification requirements. Critics also called into question the quality of biology instruction in normal schools, despite the encouraging report that only a tenth of American science teachers were products of such institutions. Throughout the decade, the institutional shortcomings in biology education were compounded by the decline in the number of science majors who wanted to teach at the secondary level. As a result, at no time during the 1950s was it possible to fill more than a fraction of teaching positions with well-qualified science graduates.

Concerned biologists and educators began to consider ways to improve the situation. Various curriculum committees examined the teaching of tenth-grade biology as the opening salvo in the battle against mediocrity in life science classes in the public schools. These reformers emphasized that a more integrated course built around an interpretive theme was crucial for any meaningful improvement. The need to improve laboratory work and the desirability of new teacher training programs were also stressed. Increasingly, research biologists participated in these considerations and integrated the most recent results from the academic community. In 1955 the American Institute of Biological Sciences formed an Education and Professional Recruitment Committee to develop a program in biology education for all levels. Biologists and public school teachers were to be involved in this program, which had as its primary goal the development of resource materials to help teachers establish an appropriate curriculum.[39]

Although the formation of curriculum committees and study groups and the organization of various teaching conferences represented an encouraging sign for American education, science education in the United States had nonetheless reached a crisis point by the second half of the 1950s. The crisis in American science education was dramatically brought to the attention of the American public and the nation's policymakers by the successful launch of the Soviet satellite *Sputnik* in October 1957 and the failure of the American *Vanguard* satellite a few weeks later. Since the end of World War II, the United States had appeared to be the world's scientific and technological leader, an assumption that seemed warranted by the rapid growth of the American scientific community and the availability of large sums for research and development. The shock of *Sputnik* called the nation's scientific preeminence into question and led to significant self-analysis of the American educational system. Fundamental weaknesses in this educational system, especially as they related to science, could no longer be ignored.

Recognizing the political and security implications of the situation, the Eisenhower administration led the way in making improved science education a national priority. Beginning in the fall of 1957 the National Science Foundation became an active partner in the campaign to revitalize the teaching of science in American public schools. Its first effort focused on the study of physics, clearly a vital topic in the newly inaugurated space age. The Physical Science Study Committee initiated a national reexamination of the teaching of science that would soon spread to other disciplines, including biology. Galvanized by the *Sputnik* crisis, the nation committed itself for the first time to significant improvement in science education. The national concern was mirrored at the local level as well, as principals and science teachers attempted to change existing science programs. In biology, this change frequently involved the addition of an advanced course for those students especially interested in life science.[40]

Despite calls for educational reform, the teaching of biology continued to suffer from a particularly vexing problem. In order to present biology in an accurate fashion, teachers would have to deal with the topic of evolution, which represented the unifying theme in the discipline. Addressing the Central Association of Science and Mathematics Teachers in late November 1958, Nobel laureate Hermann J. Muller declared, "One hundred years without Darwinism are enough." In a carefully constructed essay that gained significant attention in its later published form, Muller criticized the exclusion of evolution from the public schools, as it led to a faulty view of the biological world. He disarmed the objection made by many antievolutionists that evolution was "merely a theory" by emphasizing that "nothing whatever can be or has been proved with fully 100% certainty, not even that you or I exist, nor any one except himself, since he might be dreaming the whole thing." Evolution, though, had been confirmed by so many different discoveries in the century since Darwin published *Origin of Species* that to suggest that the theory represented anything other than a fact was ludicrous. Stressing the importance of science education in the ongoing competition with the Soviet Union, Muller challenged teachers to do more in curricular revisions to establish evolution in the public school biology class, where it clearly belonged.[41]

As part of the University of Chicago's Darwin Centennial Celebration in late November 1959, sixty-three of the nation's leading secondary school biology teachers attended the National Conference of High School Biology Teachers, funded by the National Science Foundation. Despite their being among the best-qualified biology teachers, these participants were less than committed to the teaching of evolution. Not only did they have less confidence in evolution as a "fact" than did professional biologists, but these public school teachers remained concerned about local opposition to the teaching of evolution. Citing inadequate knowledge, students' immaturity, and religious opposition, the teachers seemed to want to move very carefully in teaching evolution. Despite their hesitation, however, participants in the Chicago conference were almost unanimous in their conclusion that biology texts were inadequate in their coverage of evolution. The teachers and their biologist colleagues agreed that publishers should be pressured to improve their texts to treat evolution "openly and adequately." Yet the economic realities of the business of textbook publishing indicated that such pressure would probably have only minimal effect, as market considerations guided publishers' decisions.[42] Fortunately, the solution to the problem of inadequate texts had already been discovered by the time of the Darwin centennial in the form of federal government support for the improvement of science education.

The fall of 1958 had marked a milestone in American biology education with the announcement by the National Science Foundation of a $143,000 grant to establish the Biological Sciences Curriculum Study. With contributors such as Hermann J. Muller, George Gaylord Simpson, and other noted scientists, as well as a separate headquarters at the University of Colorado, BSCS promised to revitalize the teaching of biology. By the time of the first meeting of the steering committee in February 1959, participants in the program had decided that the focus should be on the tenth-grade biology class and the rapid development of materials for teacher and student use in such classes. As this biology class frequently represented the only science course that high school students took, the class was defined as a general education biology course for the average citizen. In addition to emphasizing science as a process of knowledge, rather than as an accumulation of facts, members of the steering committee agreed on the importance of evolution. Not only must evolution be an important part of the reformed biology classes, but it should also be one of nine themes that ran through the entire course. Indeed, the status of evolution in any biology course was never questioned.

Over the next few months plans for the creation of a new biology curriculum developed rapidly. Reflecting the intricacies of biology, planners proposed three separate texts, each with a slightly different focus. Although all three were designed for a general biology course, one text would stress an ecological perspective, another would examine the molecular and biochemical foundations of biology, and the third, the most traditional of the three, would examine biology from the perspective of cells, development, and evolution. Rather than describe these texts by such topical foci, however, the BSCS leaders decided to refer to them only by color—green, blue, and yellow, respectively—so as not to leave the impression that the texts were specialized books for advanced biology courses. Another reason for three separate editions stemmed from the criticism that BSCS was attempting to establish a national curriculum for biology. Three separate texts would provide for a great deal of flexibility, especially in laboratory work, thus countering such criticism.[43] In addition to including much more material concerning evolution and human reproduction, the BSCS experimental texts also represented a significant departure from traditional biology texts in their greater emphasis on laboratory work.

With the general outline of the texts established, the writing teams to produce the first manuscripts converged on the University of Colorado campus in the early summer of 1960. Equal numbers of high school biology teachers and university biologists made up the conference of some seventy members, with the understanding that fifteen of each group would later be members of testing centers to coordinate the initial use of the new material during the 1960-61 academic year. The writing teams worked diligently during the six weeks of the conference, completing the manuscript drafts of the texts with little difficulty. The only significant problem that arose concerned the opinions of many of the high school teachers that the reading level of the experimental texts was too advanced for American high school students. University biologists and a few of the high school teachers challenged this opinion by arguing that BSCS represented an experiment in American biology education. For that reason, it provided an opportunity to challenge students to do more than they had in the past. This argument convinced the concerned teachers that the materials should be tested before any revision of the reading level was attempted.[44]

In order to determine the effectiveness and utility of the new teaching materials, project leaders developed an extensive testing program. After an August conference in Boulder, the 105 teachers chosen to test the BSCS texts returned to their school districts to implement the testing procedures. Each of the fifteen testing centers would be composed of seven teachers within easy commuting range, a center leader from the summer writing conference, and a university consultant who would act as a resource person for the center. From the beginning the testing centers were designed to provide feedback on the BSCS material and to serve as in-service training stations for the teachers involved in the program. The results were encouraging. Teachers and students alike described the BSCS materials as stimulating and challenging. An added bonus concerned the response of school administrators, who appeared increasingly receptive to requests for new laboratory equipment to make full use of the new emphasis in the experimental material. Much to many participants' surprise, virtually no controversy over the increased coverage of evolution emerged during the first year's testing.[45]

With reports from the testing centers and evaluations by professional biologists, the writers who attended the 1961 summer writing conference began the revision of the experimental materials tested the previous year. These revised materials would be used in an expanded testing program during the 1961-62 academic year, which would triple the number of schools involved in the program. The second year's program ultimately included some five hundred schools—selected from more than a thousand applicants—enrolling approximately fifty-two thousand students in thirty-five states and the District of Columbia. Twelve testing centers were established for each BSCS version, providing even greater feedback for the final round of revisions, which were completed by January 1963. Twenty publishers submitted proposals to publish the BSCS material, all of which were reviewed by BSCS officials and individuals from the National Science Foundation and the American Institute of Biological Sciences. Despite the short time available, publishers prepared the materials for the opening of school in the fall of 1963.[46]

Although the composition and revision of the BSCS texts went relatively smoothly, difficulties arose in the campaign to revitalize biology education in the United States. Management problems and a decrease in National Science Foundation funding soon led to a cutback in staff as well as the discontinuation of programs. Such difficulties, however, failed to diminish the program's status as a successful innovation in science education. Early results indicated that BSCS students did significantly better on various tests than did non-BSCS students. Within a few years of their introduction, BSCS materials were being used in nearly half of all high school biology courses in the United States. Increasingly, too, non-BSCS texts began to resemble the new texts, even including evolution in their discussions and involving increasing numbers of professional biologists in the composition and review of such texts.[47]

Despite the success of the BSCS programs, the status of evolution in American public education failed to change overnight. A 1961 questionnaire sent to a thousand high school science teachers revealed the startling statistic that two-thirds of the teachers surveyed believed that a teacher could teach biology effectively without accepting evolution. Education officials in Texas, while accepting BSCS material, insisted on changes in the Blue Version text. The clause "To biologists there is no longer any reasonable doubt that evolution occurs" would be deleted. They also wanted the statement "Biologists are convinced that the human species evolved from nonhuman forms" replaced by "Many biologists assume that the human species evolved from nonhuman forms." Both of these changes were accepted by the publishers and appeared in all editions of the Blue Version. Later in the decade, a survey of Indiana high school biology teachers indicated that BSCS materials did not always have an immediate impact. More than 60 percent of those surveyed agreed with the statement that evolution was a theory and therefore could not be said to have definitely taken place.[48]

The BSCS program nonetheless had a noticeable effect on the teaching of biology in the United States, even if evolution remained a controversial issue in some areas. In light of the improvements in secondary biology education, many colleges by the mid-1960s had reorganized their introductory biology courses, offering one course for those students who had studied BSCS materials and a less sophisticated course for those who had not. By the end of the 1960s, the ten million dollars provided BSCS by the National Science Foundation and other agencies appeared to have contributed significantly to the improvement of biology education in the United States. Writing a memoir of the first decade of the BSCS program, project director Arnold B. Grobman prophesied in 1969, "It appears now that the major storms are over. There is every indication that the teaching of evolution is generally accepted in America and will become far more commonplace than it ever was before."[49]

He could not have been more wrong.

6

The Passing of the Old Order

The optimism that characterized many biology teachers in the early 1960s was a result of the great improvement in education symbolized by the Biological Sciences Curriculum Study. After decades of mediocrity, biology education had been revitalized to include the significant contributions of recent research. Central to this improved curriculum was the topic of evolution, which had long represented the fundamental concept in the biological sciences. The integration of this concept into high school biology courses promised to raise the scientific literacy of American students, providing them with the knowledge necessary to function in the increasingly technical world of the late twentieth century.

Optimism, however, proved only partly justified. Although the new educational materials accomplished their goal admirably within biology classrooms, they had no similar impact on the wider community. Evolution remained a contentious issue. Legislators and judges responded to the new scientific outlook by eliminating the three existing antievolution statutes by the end of the decade, but the impact such decisions would have on the public perception of evolution's place in education remained unclear.

The Conservative Challenge

Among the developments that led to the ambiguous status of evolution during the 1960s was the growth of political conservatism. Beginning in the mid-1950s, especially within the Republican party, a growing number of political activists expressed their disenchantment with the "me too" policies of the Eisenhower administration. The emergence of Arizona senator Barry M. Goldwater as the most visible leader of this movement did much to institutionalize the rightward shift. Goldwater's nomination as the GOP presidential candidate in 1964 showed the strength of the conservative revolt, although his dismal showing in the

November election raised questions about the depth of conservative support at the time.[1]

Quite apart from political interests, conservatives in the early 1960s were troubled by the secularization that they perceived overwhelming American society. The role of science in this process came in for much abuse. Conservatives found evidence for their concern in such studies as a published survey that examined the religious outlook of American scientists. Although conservatives despaired at the 20 percent classified as "nonreligious," they were probably equally dismayed with the large number of "neo-orthodox" or "liberal" responses to the survey. This situation was particularly troublesome because it showed a rejection by scientists of their parents' orthodox views. Further, respondents at major universities tended to be significantly less orthodox than those at smaller schools or in government service.[2]

The role of the federal government in the perceived secularization also became clear to conservatives through the actions of the United States Supreme Court. In June 1962 the Court announced its decision in *Engle v. Vitale,* outlawing New York's state-sponsored school prayer. The majority opinion, written by Justice Hugo Black, argued that such prayers represented a clear violation of the separation of church and state and could not be sustained. A year later the Court overturned mandated Bible reading and the recitation of the Lord's Prayer in public schools as similar attempts to establish religion, in violation of the First Amendment. Emphasizing that such laws could only avoid conflict with the establishment clause by having a clear secular purpose, the majority opinion also stressed that the primary effect of such laws must be neither to advance nor to inhibit religion.[3] These decisions convinced conservatives that secular teachings and values had not only taken over the public schools but had also been endorsed by the Supreme Court. As one of the perceived bases of this secularization, the teaching of evolutionary concepts in the public schools was again defined as an important cause of the moral and spiritual decline of the United States.

Opponents of the secular drift in American life soon focused on the efforts to reform the teaching of biology. As the BSCS textbooks and other material began to appear in public schools, the presence of evolution in the biology curriculum precipitated a dramatic increase in antievolution activity. Complaints about the inclusion of Darwin's theory in biology classes surfaced throughout the nation, although the most heated controversies tended to emerge in the Sunbelt states of the South and West. Representing the strongholds of political conservatism in the nation, these states responded to the new evolutionary focus in predictable ways.[4]

One of the first significant controversies surrounding the new biology material erupted in Phoenix, Arizona. During the 1960-61 school year, Phoenix served as one of the testing centers for the BSCS Blue Version materials. Although a few protests surfaced from local ministers and parents, the more serious objections did not appear until January 1962, midway through the second year of BSCS testing in the Phoenix schools. Three prominent Mormon lay leaders sent a letter denouncing these materials to the superintendent of the Phoenix High Schools and College System, characterizing the BSCS materials as atheistic and demanding their removal from the public schools. These critics sent a copy of their letter to the *Arizona Republic,* which gave it front-page coverage in the Sunday edition on 28 January. Objections to the evolutionary materials followed traditional paths. The Mormon leaders attempted to justify their position by arguing that "in view of the fact that the theory [of evolution] has not been established as fact," it should not be taught in the public schools. Stressing their belief that evolution was "in direct opposition" to Christian teachings, the leaders concluded that the BSCS approach to teaching biology "comes as close to teaching atheism as one can at the secondary school level."[5]

The response of the Phoenix system's superintendent, Dr. Howard C. Seymour, hardly encouraged those who hoped to improve the teaching of biology. Attempting to disarm the objections stated in the letter, Seymour emphasized that no student was required to take the course under criticism. The BSCS testing program represented an accelerated course offered as an experiment. The superintendent went further, however, stating that "students are not expected to believe this [instruction in evolution]. The instruction is only one of several attempts to explain the origin of life and no attempt is being made to supercede [*sic*] any family or religious instruction." Seymour's response apparently satisfied all but the most militant antievolutionists, as the controversy evaporated almost at once.[6]

Although Phoenix radio station KRUX broadcast a series of strong anti-BSCS editorials in the spring of 1963, no further uproar over evolution appeared in the area until the following fall. At a meeting of the school board, Harold Bates asked if teachers could be compelled to excuse his children from discussions of evolution. The board's attorney reported during the 6 November meeting that such action was in the province of the individual districts, as shown by the local decision to allow Bates's children to leave the classroom at appropriate times. This announcement struck opponents of evolution as an evasion of the issue and led Phoenix Baptist pastor Aubrey L. Moore to criticize the board for not taking a stand on the issue. Arguing that evolution should be eliminated from the curriculum, Moore told the school officials, "If you won't do it, we're going to get people together who will do something about it."[7]

A Southern Baptist and pastor of the West Van Buren Baptist Church in Phoenix, Moore had moved from Mississippi in 1955. Earlier in 1963 he led a successful campaign to repeal the Phoenix housing code, arguing that urban renewal programs based on that code violated the rights of property owners. Although the major Phoenix newspapers forcefully opposed his efforts, Moore obtained sufficient signatures on a petition to force a special election in which voters repealed the code by a ten-thousand-vote margin. Phoenix was thus prevented from implementing the urban renewal programs the city clearly needed. Fresh from this victory, Moore believed that he would be equally successful in eliminating evolution from the public school curriculum.[8]

Although criticized in some Arizona newspapers as "a publicity stunt" that threatened to bring about another Scopes trial, Moore's campaign moved forward swiftly. In public statements, he called the teaching of evolution "the first step in communism," as both doctrines were based on atheism. He also appeared before the State Board of Education on 17 December to observe the discussion of a request to ban textbooks that included evolutionary concepts. During the meeting, the board refused to ban such texts and also reported the opinion of the attorney general that the body had only limited power to prevent the teaching of evolution. Even this power, however, should be exercised only after a court case, rather than as an administrative decision. The board also endorsed the statement of superintendent Howard Seymour, in which the superintendent appeared to have abandoned his earlier fears of the evolution controversy. "I pray that the day will never come," he stated, "when all controversial material is removed from our educational program, when we are prevented by pressure groups from helping young people become self-reliant, self-activating and constructively critical—equipped with the tools to question and decide for themselves. This is a part of our heritage of freedom."[9] For the moment, at least, the place of the new evolutionary materials in the public schools of Phoenix appeared safe.

Moore was predictably upset over the board's decision. He announced the following day that he would initiate a petition drive to secure a place on next November's ballot for a proposition to outlaw the teaching of evolution in any required course. As Moore organized his drive, Phoenix area representative James F. E. Young introduced House Bill 301 in the state legislature to require "equal time" for the "Doctrine of Divine Creation" in all public school classes in which evolution was taught. When the House chose not to take any action, Moore's petition drive became the only opportunity to remove evolution from the public schools. By May 1964 he had developed an initiative measure for a constitutional amendment that defined itself as "an act defining atheism as a sectarian doctrine and prohibiting the teaching thereof in the common schools in Arizona." The next paragraph, however, provided the true meaning of the proposed amendment by defining atheism as the "teaching of any theory that denies the existence of God and the Divine creation of man in God's image" and teaching instead "that man evolved from a lower order of animals." Any teacher violating the amendment would be subject to a fine of one hundred to five hundred dollars for a first offense and revocation of teaching credentials for further violations. To have his amendment included on the November ballot, Moore would need fifty-five thousand signatures by 2 July.[10]

To attract as much attention as possible to his campaign, Moore took advantage of every opportunity for publicity. He visited a social science class at Camelback High School and told reporters that such students were being "brainwashed" in favor of Darwin and against the Bible. He belittled those who rejected his rigid fundamentalist views by stating, "The people who call themselves theistic evolutionists don't know what they're talking about. There's nothing in the Bible about a fish turning into a man." Religious leaders in the state generally opposed Moore's campaign, as did the Arizona Academy of Sciences and other professional groups. Moore remained unimpressed with such opposition. When forty-three Methodist ministers and the president of the Phoenix Rabbinical Council issued a joint statement urging Arizonans not to sign Moore's petition, the Phoenix Baptist responded, "It was the Jews who crucified Christ. Jews don't believe in the Bible. And neither do those hypocritical Methodist ministers."[11]

Despite Moore's efforts, he proved unable to secure the required number of signatures. Undaunted, he announced in early July that he would take his antievolution cause to the courts in the fall and would begin another initiative drive in 1966. Neither campaign materialized. At least in part as a response to the controversy, a bill worded exactly the same as House Bill 301 was introduced into the Arizona Senate in February 1965. The Senate bill died in the Education Committee.[12]

Although slightly less dramatic than the situation in Arizona, California's involvement with the evolution controversy proved to be of more lasting significance. Unable to convince the Orange County Board of Education to eliminate the teaching of evolution, Nell Segraves and Jean Sumrall petitioned the California Board of Education for relief in May 1963. The two homemakers stressed in their petition that teaching evolution promoted atheism and was thus unfair to Christian children. They based this argument on the decision in the recent case *School District of Abington Township v. Schempp,* in which the United States Supreme Court announced that mandated Bible reading in public schools was not religiously neutral because it violated the rights of unbelievers. Segraves and Sumrall adapted this decision to their own purposes, stressing that teaching the atheistic doctrine of evolution violated the rights of believers. If it was unconstitutional "to teach God in the school," they argued, surely it was unconstitutional "to teach the absence of God." Their solution to this problem was to require all texts used in the state's public schools to refer clearly to evolution as a "theory," thus removing much of the doctrine's credibility. [13]

When the California Board of Education met in San Francisco on 9 January 1964, Segraves and Sumrall testified concerning the place of evolution in the public schools. Segraves characterized evolution as "atheistic and agnostic" and repeated her argument that teaching the absence of religion was no less unconstitutional than the teaching of religion. She criticized existing biology texts for giving a "narrow, bigoted presentation of science," despite the recommendation of associate superintendent of public instruction Richard M. Clowes that no changes in biology texts were needed. State superintendent of public instruction Max Rafferty added his comments, stressing his belief that evolution should be referred to in texts as "an important scientific theory or hypothesis" and should be taught in classrooms "as a theory, rather than as a permanent, unchanging truth, exactly in the same manner that Einstein's theory of relativity is presented to students." The board proved unreceptive to the opponents of evolution. In a unanimous decision, board members rejected the suggestion that texts be edited to accommodate the objections of creationists. With the encouragement of Rafferty, well known for his conservative views, Segraves and Sumrall brought the issue before the board again in 1966, seeking equal time for the creationist position in texts and classes. Once again, members of the board refused to order the requested changes. The concept of equal time, however, represented an increasingly popular technique to challenge the place of evolution in the public schools. [14]

The dissemination of the new texts from BSCS also precipitated a significant response in Texas. Responding to a call for new biology texts from the Texas commissioner of education in May 1964, publishers of all three BSCS versions submitted their products for consideration. The Texas market was attractive to textbook publishers, not only because of its size but also because the new books would be adopted for a five-year period beginning in the fall of 1965. It soon became clear that virtually all of the proposed texts included discussions of evolution. By late June, lay Church of Christ evangelist Reuel Gordon Lemmons of Austin had initiated a campaign to prevent the adoption of evolutionist texts through an editorial in his widely circulated weekly newspaper, *Firm Foundation*. Stressing that evolution should only be taught as theory, he referred to BSCS publications as the "most vicious attack we have ever seen on the Christian religion." He urged his readers to write letters, circulate petitions, and make telephone calls to keep the texts from being adopted.[15]

Lemmons's campaign grew rapidly throughout the summer. More than a thousand letters descended on Governor John Connally and other state officials, protesting the inclusion of evolution in texts used in the public schools. Although most of these were form letters circulated by the Church of Christ and other fundamentalist groups in the state, opposition to the new texts could not be dismissed. Further, Lemmons's campaign was carefully orchestrated to appear as a reasonable response to questionable educational practices. The Texas crusade stressed the illegitimacy of teaching the theory of evolution as fact. The elders of the College Church of Christ in Abilene petitioned: "They [BSCS texts] violate the students [*sic*] academic right to be provided all the facts and information on any subject mentioned in such texts in order that such student may reach his own conclusions."[16]

Lemmons received valuable assistance from several individuals, including Mel and Norma Gabler of Longview, Texas, who had been examining public school texts for several years. The Gablers found in the humanistic emphasis of these texts the prime factor behind the absence of traditional morality in the public school curriculum. Antievolution groups such as the Creation Research Society also supplied material for the Texas crusade. Leading "creation scientists" Russell Artist, from David Lipscomb College in Tennessee, and Thomas G. Barnes, from Texas Western College, cooperated with Lemmons to provide a "scientific" challenge to the teaching of evolution. Although the state's scientists and educators attempted to counter such arguments, most letters and petitions directed to the State Textbook Committee expressed criticism of the new texts.[17]

When the committee met on 15 October 1964 to decide the fate of the proposed texts, both sides of the controversy were well represented. Opponents of the new texts argued that because evolution could not be proved, it represented a religion. As recent court cases had, in fundamentalist eyes, prohibited the teaching of traditional religion in the public schools, the religion of evolution should not be taught either. Unimpressed with such suggestions, the State Textbook Committee rejected the argument that the texts were guilty of promoting atheism and approved the five controversial texts—the three BSCS versions and two other texts that discussed evolution—a decision upheld by state education commissioner J.W. Edgar. On 9 November the State Board of Education reached the same conclusion by a vote of fourteen to six, although the board qualified its decision by insisting that evolution be referred to as a "theory" and not as a "fact" in the new texts. A qualified victory for supporters of the new educational materials, the board's acceptance of the concept of evolution as "theory" indicated that the nature of science remained imperfectly understood by policymakers.[18]

Although similar controversies erupted in other states considering adoption of the new biology texts, science educators in the mid-1960s remained cautiously optimistic that the teaching of evolution was gaining greater acceptance. They realized, however, that the topic continued to cause difficulties. Writing in the *American Biology Teacher* in 1965, Thomas K. Shotwell of Texas emphasized that local officials had still not come to terms with evolution in the public school curriculum. The fear of student and community response appeared to paralyze such officials and the teachers who served under them. The biologist accepted the argument that the situation was as much a public relations problem as a scientific one, but he stressed that "a PR problem becomes teachers and administrators much better than a cloak of ignorance becomes our young people." Editorials and essays in professional periodicals repeated the concern felt by biologists such as Shotwell and attempted to put forth strategies to present evolution in a way that would minimize clashes with the community. Although local opposition to teaching evolution continued to present an important problem, encouraging signs were visible in the nation's courts and legislatures, where challenges to existing antievolution laws became increasingly evident.[19]

The Challenges Begin

Even before the significant changes in biology education of the early 1960s, the existing antievolution laws appeared to many as quaint anachronisms. In Arkansas, the growing importance of science in the post-*Sputnik* era led many to view the state's statute as an embarrassment, prompting an unsuccessful 1965 attempt to repeal the law. The support of the *Arkansas Gazette*, the Arkansas Education Association, the Arkansas School Boards Association, and the Arkansas Congress of Parents and Teachers, however, led to further consideration of a repeal effort. Forrest Rozzell, executive secretary of the Arkansas Education Association, soon became convinced that legislative repeal would be impossible. He thus began planning with the association's attorney, Eugene R. Warren, to bring suit to eliminate the statute. The opening salvo of this new campaign appeared in mid-September 1965, when Rozzell issued a "personal position" statement at a press conference, stressing the importance of understanding nature and recommending the repeal of the 1928 law. Rozzell's statement brought favorable comments from the *Arkansas Gazette* and state commissioner of education Arch Ford, who argued that the antievolution law "was a dead issue and there was no reason for keeping it on the statute books." The timing of such statements proved particularly appropriate, as a new biology text was about to appear in the public schools of Little Rock. A committee of city biology teachers had chosen the 1965 edition of *Modern Biology* by James H. Otto and Albert Towle, which, following the lead of BSCS materials, included a discussion of human evolution. For the first time in nearly forty years, Little Rock students would be exposed to the concept of evolution.[20]

In their effort to present as strong a case as possible to both the court and the public, Rozzell and Warren agreed that the proposed suit should have a distinctly local focus. Such groups as the American Civil Liberties Union and the National Education Association would not be welcomed as cosponsors of the suit, in an effort to disarm potential objections that "outside agitators" were behind the effort. Similarly, repeal supporters wished to find a plaintiff with an appropriate Arkansas background. This search led to Susan Epperson, a native of Clarksville, Arkansas, and a graduate of the College of the Ozarks, a Presbyterian school where her father served as a biology professor. After graduate work in zoology at the University of Illinois, Epperson had begun teaching biology at Central High School in Little Rock in the fall of 1964 and had been on the committee that chose the Otto and Towle text. Rejecting the idea that there existed a necessary conflict between religious beliefs and evolution, she nonetheless taught evolution in her classes only as a theory.

Epperson was an ideal plaintiff. On 6 December 1965 she filed suit in the Pulaski County Chancery Court for a declaratory judgment that the 1928 antievolution law was unconstitutional. She argued that teaching evolution represented a constitutional right—academic freedom and freedom of speech—and that obeying the statute would lead to her neglect of "the obligations of a responsible teacher of biology." Epperson was later joined in the civil suit, which would be heard without a jury, by Hubert H. Blanchard, associate executive secretary of the Arkansas Education Association. Blanchard entered the case on behalf of his two sons, students in the North Little Rock public schools, and emphasized that the 1928 law damaged students as well as teachers.[21]

The Arkansas antievolution law would be defended by the state's attorney general, Bruce Bennett, best known for his legal battles against court-ordered desegregation. Bennett early made his personal position clear, writing to trial judge Murray O. Reed that Epperson "was the only person since the law was approved to 'clamor' in favor of teaching that man evolved from monkeys, apes, sharks, porpoises, seaweed, or any other form of animal or vegetable." Arkansas governor Orval Faubus, equally famous as a segregationist, shared his attorney general's view, arguing that the 1928 law should be kept intact "as a safeguard to keep way out teachers in line." Bennett's pretrial pleading followed two different paths. He emphasized that the public had every right to determine the subjects taught in the state's schools and that this right far outweighed Epperson's freedom of speech. He also defined evolution as an atheistic and thus dangerous doctrine whose validity was important to the case. Epperson's arguments for academic freedom were thus invalid, as Bennett explained: "She wants to teach the Darwin Theory only when in fact there are dozens of other off-beat theories that other teachers might want to explain to their students. Someone has to administer the schools." The 1928 antievolution law represented a "reasonable regulation" of a state employee and the public school curriculum.[22]

The trial lasted slightly more than two hours on 1 April 1966. Reed ruled early that the validity of evolution was not an issue, thus preventing Bennett from introducing evidence that he maintained challenged the theory. Bennett nonetheless provided what limited drama the trial exhibited when he relentlessly cross-examined Epperson concerning scientists' disagreements about the details of evolution. Such disagreements, in Bennett's view, indicated that there existed no proof of evolution and justified the state's prohibition on teaching such speculation. In contrast, Epperson's attorney, Eugene R. Warren, emphasized that the contested statute represented an infringement on freedom of speech, a violation of church-state separation, and an illegitimate law because of its vagueness. Reed accepted Warren's arguments in a nine-page opinion dated 27 May. Repeating his earlier decision that the validity of a scientific theory was not an actionable issue, Reed found the Arkansas antievolution statute unconstitutional because it violated free speech and tended to "hinder the quest for knowledge, restrict the freedom to learn, and restrain the freedom to teach." Upholding the law would have denied several constitutional freedoms unjustifiably. Teaching evolution was not so dangerous as to justify such action.[23]

Less than a month after Reed's judgment, the state appealed the decision to the Arkansas Supreme Court. Arguments concerning the reasonableness of the statute, the danger of evolution, and the employee status of public school teachers were again raised in the state's brief filed in October. Epperson's attorney filed a more involved brief that focused on five points. Taking advantage of court decisions of the past forty years, Warren stressed that public school teachers were entitled to all guarantees of the state and federal constitutions, including due process. The Epperson brief further argued that the law violated free speech and the equal protection clause of the Fourteenth Amendment, as it applied only to public schools and not to private ones. Warren raised the vagueness issue again, stressing that the law remained unclear as to what "teaching" meant and thus violated the due process clause. The brief also argued that the 1928 statute violated guarantees of religious freedom by involving the state in aid to religion.[24]

As the Arkansas Supreme Court attempted to deal with the contentious issues involved in the Epperson case, the nation's attention focused again on Tennessee's efforts to come to terms with evolution. Previous attempts to repeal the Butler Act, either through legislation or court cases, had failed to progress beyond the discussion stage, but the opening weeks of 1967 seemed to suggest that the state's outlook might be changing. Court-ordered reapportionment had corrected the long-standing overrepresentation of rural areas in the legislature, raising the possibility that support for the Butler Act would be less apparent. The courts also quickly became involved in the controversy. On 13 January Knoxville attorney Martin Southern filed suit in Knox County Chancery Court to test the validity of the nation's most famous antievolution law. Filing in the name of his fourteen-year-old son, Thomas, Southern argued that his son's education was being severely "limited" by the state's antievolution law and sought a declaratory judgment to overturn the statute.[25]

Although the Southern suit dropped out of the public eye as Chancellor Len G. Broughton took the matter under advisement, the Knoxville case marked only the first hint of a change in Tennessee's role in the evolution controversy. On 1 March a coalition of Memphis and Nashville legislators introduced House Bill 48 to repeal the Butler Act. Referred the next day to the Judiciary Committee, whose chairman,

Charles Galbreath, had cosponsored the bill, the repeal effort was recommended for passage on 5 April and scheduled for House debate a week later.[26]

House consideration of the repeal effort on 12 April was described by a New York *Times* reporter as "marked by emotion and comedy." When Representative D.J. Smith, the Memphis Democrat who had cosponsored the bill, asked for the repealer to be brought before the House, the chamber's sergeant at arms brought a caged monkey to Smith's desk. As the debate progressed, however, emotion replaced comedy. Chattanooga Republican LaMar Baker opposed repeal and declaimed, "The Genesis account is very important to me. God did breathe life into man. I have no hope of life after death if I accept this theory. I must cling to faith." Democrat W.A. Richardson of Columbia predicted dire consequences if the repeal effort passed: "We will bring chaos to the hearts and minds of the young if they believe they are just another type of animal. The word of God Almighty and the teachings of Jesus Christ have left the world more than the teachings of Darwin. I don't believe in fables, but I do believe in the Bible. They [proponents of evolution] said that prottoplasms [*sic*] made a wiggle-tail. It [the repeal bill] is the go-ahead word to teach as a fact that you came from a wiggle-tailed something." Despite the emotional pleas of the opponents of the repeal measure, the Tennessee House accepted House Bill 48 by a vote of fifty-nine to thirty and sent it to the Senate. Even those who supported the legislation, however, frequently expressed reservations. Representative Curtis Person, Jr., explained to his colleagues that he voted for repeal because he thought the Butler Act was an antiquated law, but he expressed concern "for the lack of religious education that our young children are receiving today." He also stated his fear that evolution would be taught in the state's schools without "any regard or thought toward requiring the study of religious creation. I pray that teachers will use discretion and care in teaching Darwin's Theory so as not to mislead young minds in their formative stages."[27]

Attention now shifted to the Tennessee Senate, whose acquiescence in the repeal effort would remove the Butler Act. The Senate Committee on Education had earlier returned a similar Senate bill to the floor "without recommendation" and was about to make the same recommendation concerning Senate Bill 536, which would amend the Butler Act to prohibit the teaching of evolution as "fact." On 20 April the Senate began debate on the House repeal measure. Sensing a story of great interest, local and national media invaded the Senate chamber with television cameras and other equipment to broadcast the debate's highlights. Memphis senator Clayton P. Elam, chief sponsor of the repeal effort, admitted during debate that he personally did not believe in evolution but thought that the state's students should have the opportunity to learn about the topic. More important, he argued, "I am tired of Tennessee being held up to ridicule to the nation and to the entire world." During the nearly two-hour debate on the bill, however, opponents of the repeal measure argued their case more dramatically. Senator Ernest Crouch, a Democrat from McMinnville, told his colleagues: "We know the greatest book ever written, the Bible, tells us where life came from and how God created man. Senator Elam says we are being ridiculed in Europe. That doesn't bother me a bit. If those countries over there would pay us what they owe us, we could retire our national debt." Opponents of the repeal effort successfully retained the spirit of the Butler Act. Voting ended in a sixteen-to-sixteen tie, which defeated the measure. Although the repeal measure could be reconsidered later in the session, senators quickly approved Senate Bill 536, to amend the Butler Act, by a vote of twenty-three to ten. The House refused to accept the proposed amendment, leaving the fate of the Butler Act uncertain.[28]

As senators attempted to come to terms with the issue of evolution before their scheduled debate, the situation became more complex through the actions of a local school board in rural east Tennessee. From a front-page story in the New York *Times* on 15 April, observers of the evolution controversy learned that Gary Lindle Scott, a twenty-four-year-old science teacher at Jacksboro High School, had been dismissed for allegedly teaching evolution. Scott had been given his notice of dismissal the previous day, at which time he also learned of the formal complaint made by Archie Cotton, a local coal mine operator and member of the Campbell County Board of Education. Cotton had charged Scott with neglect of duty, unprofessional conduct, and violation of the Butler Act. In a closed meeting of the board on 13 April, Cotton had convinced his colleagues to accept unanimously the dismissal of the young science teacher.

Over the next few days details of Scott's difficulties slowly emerged. Cotton's wife told reporters that a group of local fundamentalist ministers had approached her husband to complain about the teaching of evolution in Scott's classes. These ministers expressed outrage with Scott's reference to the Bible as "a bunch of fairy tales," the phrase used by students in reporting the incident to their parents. Scott's explanation of his comments relating to evolution were quite different. He told his superintendent, principal, and teaching supervisors that, in response to students' questions, he had given a brief summary of the theory of evolution while explaining the Tennessee law. His only comment concerning the Bible was that much scriptural material appeared in the form of parables, some of which could not be taken literally. Local support for Scott's position was difficult to find. As he told a New York *Times* reporter, many of his fellow teachers shared the fundamentalist outlook of Cotton and the local ministers. A few science teachers in the area, however, suggested that a conspiracy of sorts was behind Scott's difficulties, with local ministers orchestrating students' actions. One of these science teachers found it an interesting coincidence that he had been asked leading questions about evolution at the same time that Scott's students had initiated the controversy.[29]

Although Scott and his Knoxville attorney had originally hoped to settle the controversy as quietly as possible, it soon became clear that a court fight would be the only method to regain his position or, at the very least, recover the salary due Scott under his contract. By the end of April he had gained the support of the American Civil Liberties Union and the National Education Association, who had arranged for Scott to be represented by famed attorney William Kunstler. The NEA agreed to pay Kunstler's fees and to provide Scott and his wife with living expenses while the young teacher remained unemployed. In addition to suing the Jacksboro school system for breach of contract and damages, Scott would challenge the constitutionality of the Butler Act, unless the act were repealed before the trial began.[30]

While Scott and his attorneys prepared their suit, the Campbell County Board of Education changed its mind. In a seven-to-one vote on Thursday, 11 May 1967, the board voted to reinstate Scott and pay him his salary for the entire year. Even Archie Cotton agreed with this decision, which resulted partly from the notoriety that Scott's case had brought to the community. The large sum of money required for defense in a court case also played a prominent role in the board's decision. Scott's reinstatement removed the Campbell County Board of Education as a defendant in the case, but the issue of the Butler Act's constitutionality remained.

Scott's attorneys filed suit in federal district court in Nashville on 15 May. Filed as a class action suit, the complaint included the names of Scott, two of his students, and fifty-nine faculty members from Tennessee colleges and universities, as well as the National Science Teachers Association. The complaint charged that the Butler Act violated constitutional liberties and sought a permanent injunction to restrain state and local officials from enforcing the antievolution statute. By this time, however, Scott's suit had a nebulous existence. As one of his attorneys admitted to a reporter, no need for the suit would remain if the Senate decided to repeal the Butler Act. If that happened, the suit would be withdrawn immediately. Senator Clayton Elam had already announced that Scott's suit would probably prove unnecessary, as the Senate would reconsider the repeal measure on the sixteenth. Elam told a New York *Times* reporter that he was reasonably sure that the repeal effort would be successful.[31]

The prospect of another "monkey trial," with its attendant negative publicity, apparently convinced senators to reconsider their earlier views on the Butler Act. Senate Bill 536, which attempted to modify the Butler Act only to prohibit the teaching of evolution as "fact," no longer represented a sufficient change. House Bill 48, to repeal the Butler Act, was placed on the calendar for 16 May. With a pending court case and earlier debates on record, senators saw no need to prolong the discussion and took less than three minutes to repeal the nation's most famous antievolution statute by a vote of twenty to thirteen. Two days later Governor Buford Ellington affixed his signature to the measure, ending Tennessee's forty-two-year commitment to keeping Darwin out of the public schools. Scott and Southern quickly withdrew their lawsuits.[32]

The Last of the Monkey Laws

As the Tennessee legislature examined the Butler Act in the spring of 1967, the Arkansas Supreme Court focused its attention on the case of Susan Epperson. An elected body, the court was faced with many of the same political pressures that had delayed Tennessee's repeal of its antievolution law. On 5 June, therefore, with one judge dissenting, the Arkansas Supreme Court overturned the lower court decision and upheld the 1928 antievolution law as "a valid exercise of the state's power to specify the curriculum in its public schools." The one-paragraph opinion made no attempt to address larger issues or to comment on the validity of evolution itself, suggesting that the court remained as concerned with local politics as any legislature. Epperson and her attorney quickly appealed the decision to the United States Supreme Court, which agreed on 4 March 1968 to hear the case and scheduled oral arguments for 16 October.[33]

One of the most significant issues raised by the Epperson case— and other cases involving antievolution laws—was a question concerning the First Amendment establishment clause. As early as the Scopes trial, opponents of antievolution laws had argued that attempts to enact such laws represented an effort to establish a specific religion in the states, namely Protestant fundamentalism. Because antievolution laws were clearly based on views of a specific religious character, such laws would artificially aid those groups who shared such views. In the two decades before the Epperson case reached it, the United States Supreme Court had developed a relatively rigid outlook on such issues that promised to work to the advantage of those wishing to challenge antievolution statutes. The Court invalidated public transportation for parochial school students in the famous 1947 case *Everson v. Board of Education,* arguing that states could not legitimately aid religion in any form. Hugo Black's majority opinion both reaffirmed the concept of a "wall of separation" between church and state and clearly applied First Amendment restrictions to the states through the incorporation doctrine of the Fourteenth Amendment.[34]

Over the next fifteen years the religion clauses of the First Amendment came under frequent scrutiny by legal scholars, many of whom stressed the prohibition of government action concerning religion. The amendment's establishment clause—"Congress shall make no law respecting an establishment of religion"—meant a hands-off policy with regard to religion at the national and, applying the Fourteenth Amendment, state levels. Two cases from the early 1960s clarified this viewpoint. In June 1962 the Court outlawed compulsory state-sponsored school prayer in *Engle v. Vitale.* The relatively innocuous Regent's Prayer of New York was invalidated because its clear purpose was to further religious beliefs. The state-sponsored prayer thus represented a violation of the establishment clause. A year later, in *School District of Abington Township v. Schempp,* the Court similarly outlawed the conducting of Bible reading and the recitation of the Lord's Prayer in public schools for the same reason. Such actions represented an attempt by the state to aid religion. Although attacked by many as a judicial attempt to "outlaw God," the Court's decisions could be defended as an effort to prevent the interference of the state in religion and vice versa. The "wall of separation" between church and state would benefit both.[35]

There had also been a change in the situation in Arkansas by the time the Supreme Court heard oral arguments in the Epperson case. The 1966 state elections had been characterized by an urban, progressive revolt that had ousted Attorney General Bennett and other segregationists. In addition to opposing segregation, the new administration was less than supportive of the outdated antievolution law, sending an assistant attorney general to argue the case in Washington. The state repeated its earlier arguments that the law represented a legitimate exercise of the state's right to set the curriculum in the public schools and stressed that the act established true religious neutrality. The state's lack of enthusiasm for the statute, however, appeared clear during oral arguments. The assistant attorney general, Don Langston, admitted to the Court that, in his opinion, the law prohibited even the mention of evolution in the public schools, an admission that clearly damaged the state's case.

Epperson's attorney, Eugene Warren, repeated the arguments made in state courts, stressing First Amendment concepts such as freedom of speech. In his arguments to the Court, however, he also emphasized the vagueness concept from the Fourteenth Amendment. As it was not clear from the statute what teaching evolution meant, Arkansas teachers could not know what they were being prohibited from doing. Did the statute mean that teachers could not even mention evolution, as the state's attorney suggested during the trial, or did it merely mean that they could not state that human evolution was the only "true" explanation? Could the law also mean that teachers could not use texts discussing evolution? If Arkansas teachers were, indeed, faced with such a vague law, could any of them know when they had violated it? Such a situation clearly violated the due process clause and represented yet another reason to invalidate the law.[36]

Supporting briefs from the National Education Association, the National Science Teachers Association, the American Civil Liberties Union, and the American Jewish Congress strengthened Epperson's case. Armed with the various briefs and the results of the oral arguments, the justices retired to their conference to decide the fate of the Arkansas antievolution law. Like most educated people in America, the justices assumed that the validity of evolution was no longer in doubt. The Arkansas statute would undoubtedly be overturned. Yet the justices were deeply divided on the best issue to use to invalidate the statute, making Chief Justice Earl Warren's assignment of the opinion more difficult.[37] He ultimately chose Abe Fortas to draft the document.

In his written opinion, Fortas admitted that the Arkansas law was vague and uncertain, as shown by the Arkansas Supreme Court's refusal to state whether the act prohibited the explanation of evolution or the teaching that evolution is true. Vagueness did not represent the key issue, however. No matter how the statute was interpreted, it remained unconstitutional because it conflicted with the constitutional prohibition against state laws establishing religion. "The overriding fact is," Fortas wrote, "that Arkansas' law selects from the body of knowledge a particular segment which it proscribes for the sole reason that it is deemed to conflict with a particular religious doctrine; that is, with a particular interpretation of the Book of Genesis by a particular religious group." Fortas emphasized the various precedents that had held that federal and state governments could not pass laws that aided one religion, or aided all religions, or gave preference to one religion over another. If the Arkansas law violated the establishment clause, no other issue could balance that fact. Fortas acknowledged that a state had an "undoubted right" to establish the public school curriculum, but that right did not include the freedom to prohibit "the teaching of a scientific theory or doctrine where that prohibition is based upon reasons that violate the First Amendment."[38]

In Fortas's view, the motivation of the Arkansas law presented one of the key factors in determining the statute's constitutionality. Although the Arkansas law was less explicit about its purpose than Tennessee's Butler Act, Fortas stressed that it similarly attempted to prevent the teaching of any concept that supposedly denied the divine creation of man. Such an analysis led Fortas to conclude that religious purposes were behind the Arkansas law. There was no doubt, he wrote, "that Arkansas has sought to prevent its teachers from discussing the theory of evolution because it is contrary to the belief of some that the Book of Genesis must be the exclusive source of doctrine as to the origin of man. No suggestion has been made that Arkansas' law may be justified by considerations of state policy other than the religious views of some of its citizens. It is clear that fundamentalist sectarian conviction was and is the law's reason for existence." The state's contention that the law represented religious neutrality could not be upheld either. The law did not prohibit all discussions of the origin of man, but only a particular theory that supposedly conflicted with Genesis. Fortas viewed this as yet another indication of the fundamentally religious purpose of the statute.[39]

Although they agreed that the Arkansas law should be overturned, justices Hugo Black, John M. Harlan, and Potter Stewart disagreed with the majority's reasoning and wrote separate concurring opinions. Harlan and Stewart suggested that the vagueness issue should have been addressed more adequately, but it was Black's opinion that raised a number of interesting issues. Black's age—he was eighty-two at the time of the Epperson case—his rural Alabama background, his political alliance with the populist wing of the Democratic party in the early 1900s, and his Baptist family heritage all combined to give him a more sympathetic view of antievolution sentiment than his colleagues possessed. Vagueness, in Black's view, represented a sufficient reason for overturning the statute. He criticized his colleagues for making a more sweeping decision than necessary and opposed the tactic of examining the motives behind the Arkansas law. Black also suggested that the Court's decision might infringe on the religious freedom of those who believed that evolution was an antireligious doctrine and hinted that since Arkansas had made no attempt to include the literal Genesis account in the curriculum, removing evolution might well represent true religious neutrality. By focusing on the establishment clause, the Court may have involved itself in a more difficult situation than it realized. "Unless this Court is prepared simply to write off as pure nonsense the views of those who consider evolution an anti-religious doctrine," Black observed, "then this issue presents problems under the Establishment Clause far more troublesome than are discussed in the Court's opinion."[40]

Despite Black's discomfort with the *Epperson* decision, the Court had overturned one of two remaining antievolution statutes as an unconstitutional attempt to establish religion. Only Mississippi retained a law designed to prevent the teaching of evolution in the public schools. In late 1969 Mrs. Arthur G. Smith of Jackson filed suit in state court on behalf of her daughter Frances, a student in the state's public school system. Because Mississippi had no declaratory judgment law, the Smith suit could only ask for an injunction against the enforcement of the law, rather than for a declaration of its unconstitutionality. In her suit, Smith argued that her daughter was being deprived of a proper scientific education, which put her at a disadvantage in the competition with students elsewhere in the nation for admission to leading colleges and universities. In addition, Smith submitted that the Mississippi law violated the establishment clause, a breach that the recent *Epperson* case had shown to be unconstitutional.[41]

As the Smith case began working its way through the state courts, the Mississippi legislature found itself examining a repeal measure to eliminate the antievolution law from the statute books. Debating the repeal bill on 21 January 1970, Mississippi legislators appeared unimpressed with Supreme Court decisions and the actions of other state legislatures. One opponent of repeal argued, "Since it is against the law to teach religion, it should be against the law to teach atheism." Another opponent in the House of Representatives expressed pride in Mississippi's antievolution law. "Let's hold the line as a Christian state," he argued. "This is another attempt to chip away at religion." The Mississippi House remained dominated by rural lawmakers, many of whom were angry with the desegregation decisions of the federal courts. The repeal failed by a vote of forty-two to seventy.[42] The state's courts would have to decide the issue.

Shortly after the defeat of the repeal legislation, the lower court dismissed Smith's case. Because the state made no attempt to enforce the law, Smith's request for an injunction against enforcement did not represent a legitimate case. The court also upheld the state's contention that the law was constitutional, despite the *Epperson* decision, which suggested quite the opposite. Smith appealed this decision to the Mississippi Supreme Court, which, in late December, announced its ruling. The court unanimously overturned the lower court's judgment, stressing the *Epperson* case as precedent. After summarizing the Court's opinion, the Mississippi judges concluded that there could be' "little doubt, if any, that the court would make the same finding relative to our statute."[43] The law was void. The state did not appeal.

The decision in *Smith v. State* eliminated the last antievolution statute in the United States. Within the short span of three years, legislatures and courts had reviewed such laws and found them unsupportable. Observers of the evolution controversy undoubtedly viewed such actions as indicative of a greater respect for science and a recognition of the anachronistic nature of attempts to banish evolution from the public schools. The antievolution crusade had ended.

This view was correct, as far as it went. The optimistic observers who celebrated the repeal of the Butler Act and the decisions in *Epperson v. Arkansas* and *Smith v. State*, however, only glimpsed part of the picture. Attempts to outlaw directly the teaching of evolution could no longer be supported, but the opposition to that teaching remained strong. While legislators and judges examined the last of the old laws, new forces consolidated their strength in a movement that displayed significant similarities to the antievolution crusade of the 1920s. Calling themselves creation scientists or scientific creationists, these opponents of evolution sought to establish their belief in the literal truth of the Genesis account of creation as a *scientific* alternative to the Darwinian account. Another battle was about to erupt.

7

New Directions

Observers of American science could gaze backward from 1970 with some degree of enthusiasm. Not only had the anachronistic antievolution laws been disposed of, but positive achievements of science and technology appeared evident. Symbolized by the successful *Apollo* program, American technical accomplishments had once again claimed global preeminence. Science education had improved considerably since the 1950s, with innovative programs in biology, physics, and chemistry firmly established in the public schools. Despite a growing challenge to the importance of science and technology from those who identified with the so-called counterculture of the 1960s, the United States appeared to have regained its status as a "scientific" nation. At the very least, Americans viewed science and technology as important elements of the modern world.

The perceived importance of science, however, was not accompanied by a heightened scientific literacy. While taking for granted such conveniences as the internal combustion engine and the electric light, most Americans had little knowledge of how these devices worked. In general, Americans looked with wonder on *Saturn V* launches and communication satellites, yet few sought even the most cursory understanding of the science behind these symbols of national achievement. The existence of a supposedly scientific nation with inadequate scientific understanding provided the foundation for the next phase of the evolution controversy in America.

The Origins of Creation Science

Although most antievolutionists in the post-Scopes period based their objections on traditional religious grounds, an identifiable group existed that attempted to develop scientific explanations to support a literal reading of Genesis. These creationists also attacked evolution for its "scientific" shortcomings, conveniently ignoring contemporary developments in biology that supported the suspect theory. Following the lead of George McCready Price, a small number of antievolutionists continued to search for scientific proofs of Genesis.

Among the most prolific of creationist writers during the 1930s and 1940s were Harry Rimmer and Arthur I. Brown. Both these men remained active in evangelical work and public lecturing, but their greatest contribution to the creationist cause came through books published in the 1940s. Rimmer's attempt to provide a scientific basis for his belief in Genesis resulted in such volumes as *Modern Science and the Genesis Record* (1940), *The Theory of Evolution and the Facts of Science* (1941), and *Lot's Wife and the Science of Physics* (1947). Brown's contributions to creationist literature included *Footprints of God* (1943), *Miracles of Science* (1945), and *God's Masterpiece— Man's Body* (1946).[1]

Although frequently identified with the literalists, Rimmer and Brown accepted a great age for the earth and believed that the Noachian flood was a regional phenomenon only. They thus accepted the "gap theory" of creation, which argued that Genesis actually referred to two separate creations. The first, which could have occurred millions of years ago, was the source of most of the fossils discovered by paleontologists. God destroyed this creation approximately 4000 B.C., before the Adamic restoration which encompassed six twenty-four-hour days. The "gap theory" had gained influential support in 1909, when the *Scofield Reference Bible* embraced the concept, but it clearly represented an accommodation to secular knowledge. The "day-age theory" offered another accommodation, which argued that the days of creation mentioned in Genesis represented ages or eras. Supporters of this view were likely to accept evolutionary development of some type. Clearly, *creationism* could have a wide variety of meanings.[2]

Those individuals who believed that scientific evidence existed to support a literal reading of Genesis early realized that their work would be advanced by an organization modeled on scientific associations. During the summer of 1935 Price and others formed the Religion and Science Association on the basis of opposition to evolution. Many founding members adhered to the six-day creation and the formation of geological phenomena by the Noachian flood. Another group within the new association, however, embraced the gap theory. The leader of this "liberal" influence was L. Allen Higley, chairman of the Department of Chemistry and Geology at Wheaton College, who was chosen president of the new organization because of his scientific credentials. A similarly moderate perspective was reflected in the statement of philosophy adopted by the Religion and Science Association, which asserted that "the various phenomena of nature are only the objectified ways in which the God of nature conducts the affairs of His universe" and emphasized that God need not follow the so-called laws of nature.[3]

The presence of large numbers of Wheaton College faculty, most of whom rejected flood geology, alienated Price and his more literalistic supporters. As a result, the Religion and Science Association disintegrated after its first meeting in March 1936. Price organized another group in late 1938 from adherents of the recent earth-flood geology perspective, many of whom were fellow Seventh-Day Adventists. The Deluge Geology Society lasted for seven years and published twenty issues of the *Bulletin of Deluge Geology and Related Sciences.* During the fall of 1945, however, the group came under the influence of an old-earth minority who abandoned the literalism of the Price faction. As had been the case with the Religion and Science Association, a more liberal attitude precipitated a rapid decline in the Deluge Geology Society.[4]

Perhaps the most successful of the early creationist science organizations was the American Scientific Affiliation. After several informal meetings and much correspondence, the affiliation began with an organizational meeting in Chicago in early September 1941. Those in attendance proved most concerned with the apparent growth of materialism and secularism at state colleges and universities and the effect such changes had on Christian students who attended these institutions. Wishing to show that one could be a Christian and a scientist, the ASA early attracted both to its fold. Less concerned with doctrinal purity than with the impact of science on religion, the affiliation prided itself on embracing various views in its attempt to "correlate the facts of science and the Holy Scriptures."[5]

World War II interrupted the affiliation's immediate plans and postponed the first formal ASA meeting until 1946. The group decided that its first priority should be the publication of a science reference book based on the creationist perspective. This volume appeared in 1948 as *Modern Science and Christian Faith.* The next year ASA began publishing a periodical that soon became the *Journal of the American Scientific Affiliation.* From the beginning the periodical included divergent views. Bernard Ramm, professor of apologetics at the Bible Institute of Los Angeles, told readers of the first issue that logical weaknesses in the theory of evolution existed, resurrecting the "guess" argument long used by antievolutionists. "At best it is an effort at reconstruction as to how things might have happened," he wrote, "not how they must have happened. It is the best guess to date that an unregenerate mind can make that rejects Biblical revelation, and without revelation might never shift its position."[6]

Fifteen months later two articles in the journal attempted to integrate modern astronomy with Genesis. Focusing on George Gamow's recent "big bang" theory, P.W. Stoner, chairman of the mathematics department at Pasadena City College, and Delbert N. Eggenberger, of the Illinois Institute of Technology, each contributed essays arguing that no conflict existed between this theory and Genesis. Stoner stressed that red-shift studies that showed the expansion of the universe and, by implication, its beginning at a common starting point billions of years ago closely paralleled the first verse of Genesis. Eggenberger found a similar parallel by describing the big bang as a "sudden appearance of mass a finite length of time back."[7]

The nondoctrinal focus of the American Scientific Affiliation appeared even more clearly in the editorial objectives published in December 1950. The journal hoped to "promote a vigorous Christian Apologetic by demonstrating the essential agreement of historical Christianity and the facts of modern science" and to "provide scholarly, conservative enlightenment for all readers on Christian-scientific matters." Rejecting the concept that there existed only one "creationist" view, however, the editorial policy was designed to "permit, within the framework of conservative theology, a discussion of both sides of scientific questions on which many true Christians are known to differ."[8]

By the mid-1950s the American Scientific Affiliation had emerged as a group more concerned with science than with a literalistic interpretation of Genesis. ASA members increasingly had advanced science degrees, which led them to reject the suspect geology of George McCready Price and others. Wheaton College zoologist Russell L. Mixter precipitated a spirited debate when he argued at the 1957 affiliation meeting that evolution represented God's method in much of creation. Despite the year-long controversy that followed his address, the American Scientific Affiliation published Mixter's *Evolution and Christian Thought Today* in 1959. This collection of essays marked a clear break with the young earth, universal flood, fixity of species view, which in the public mind had characterized opponents of evolution.[9]

The concept of theistic evolution, however, did not appeal to everyone who rejected evolution. Among those who continued to accept flood geology and a young earth was an individual who would become a leading figure in the creation science movement, Henry M. Morris. As he recalled many years later, Morris had been a lukewarm theistic evolutionist during the 1930s while studying hydraulic engineering at Rice University. Working in El Paso after his 1939 graduation, Morris heard one of Irwin Moon's "Sermons from Science," which helped to convince the young engineer of the scientific validity of the Bible. His skepticism concerning evolution was compounded by his teaching experience at Rice during World War II, where he became aware of the lack of religious fervor among his students. By 1943 he had become convinced that evolution was based on "ridiculously trivial" evidence and that no biblical justification existed for the tenets of theistic evolution. Realizing the harm such concepts could do to students, Morris began writing an evangelistic book, which appeared in the spring of 1946 as *That You Might Believe.*[10]

Shortly thereafter Morris decided to pursue graduate studies in hydraulics at the University of Minnesota. "I had chosen to major in hydraulics," he later explained, "with a minor in geology, primarily because of my conviction that this was the best combination with which to develop a sound system of deluge geology, and that this, in turn, had to be the key in a genuinely Biblical doctrine of creationism." While teaching and completing his dissertation, Morris began work on a book discussing flood geology and also found time to revise *That You Might Believe.* These revisions led to a longer volume published in 1951 under the new title *The Bible and Modern Science.*[11]

During the mid-1950s, while pursuing his engineering career, Morris began corresponding with John C. Whitcomb, Jr., professor of theology and Old Testament at Grace Theological Seminary in Indiana. Whitcomb had been teaching creationism for several years and had recently decided to write his dissertation on the worldwide flood and its effects. After this project reached completion in the spring of 1957, Whitcomb and Morris decided to collaborate on a book discussing flood geology. Soon to assume the chairmanship of the department of civil engineering at Virginia Polytechnic Institute, Morris nonetheless welcomed the opportunity to put his creationist ideas into appropriate form. Beginning in December, the two writers invested most of their spare time in the preparation of a manuscript that took nearly two years to complete. Friends and colleagues who accepted flood geology and a recent earth reviewed the manuscript, beginning a fellowship that would ultimately result in the formation of the Creation Research Society. Revisions took another year, and then the manuscript was turned over to the Presbyterian and Reformed Publishing Company of Philadelphia. Morris and Whitcomb received their copies of the finished book in March 1961.[12]

Titled *The Genesis Flood,* the volume attempted to accomplish two complementary tasks. Challenging the nonliteralists, the book demonstrated that biblical teachings required both a young earth and a worldwide flood. Once that concept was established to their satisfaction, the authors reported the scientific evidence that supported their contention, arguing that the data clearly showed a recent creation. Scientists who rejected these concepts were accused of distorting the evidence to fit their own humanistic and uniformitarian prejudices. Based on a devotion to "facts" as the hallmark of science and rejecting all else as speculation, Morris and Whitcomb emphasized that humans could not possibly know and should not guess about the details of creation. They wrote:

> But during the period of Creation, God was introducing order and organization and energization into the universe in a very high degree, even to life itself! *It is thus quite plain that the processes used by God in creation were utterly different from the processes which now operate in the universe!* The Creation was a unique period, entirely incommensurate with this present world. This is plainly emphasized and reemphasized in the divine revelation which God has given us concerning Creation. . . . In view of these strong and repeated assertions, is it not the height of presumption for man to attempt to study Creation in terms of present processes?[13]

The Genesis Flood, combining as it did the form of science with the literalistic view of Genesis, proved to be the early focal point of a new challenge to all forms of biological evolution.

Although *The Genesis Flood* attracted little attention from the educational and scientific communities, those who shared Morris's view of biblical literalism found the volume of great interest. Morris was soon deluged with invitations to give speeches and write articles for Christian magazines. More important, two colleagues who had reviewed the manuscript, Walter Lammerts and William J. Tinkle, began corresponding with a small group of scientists dedicated to the concepts of recent creation and global catastrophe. This Team of Ten, as it would be called later, viewed *The Genesis Flood* as an important step toward a true creationist perspective that would challenge the theistic evolution that increasingly characterized the American Scientific Affiliation.[14]

The "liberal" drift of the ASA appeared most clearly in editorial comments in issues of the *Journal* in the early 1960s. Editor David O. Moberg, for example, in late 1962 responded to attacks against theistic evolution by emphasizing that the American Scientific Affiliation had no official position on evolution. He expressed his own view, however, by questioning whether it was not possible for God to have worked through natural processes that scientists were beginning to understand more fully. Less than a year later a similarly moderate editorial position emerged in response to criticisms that evolution remained unproven. "We may conclude that because some scientific theories have later been proven false," the editors wrote, "science must always be untrustworthy. Such a conclusion is just as incorrect as the related error of those opponents of Christianity who assume that, because some Christian interpretations have later been recognized as incorrect, no Christian perspectives are worthy of confidence."[15]

Such moderate statements proved unacceptable to literalists who believed that Genesis could be supported by proper scientific research. By the summer of 1963 the Team of Ten had nearly doubled in size and organized itself as the Creation Research Society. The eighteen founding members hoped to publish the first issue of a quarterly research journal within a year. Fearing professional difficulties, they also decided not to publish a directory in an attempt to keep membership confidential. Although a few members suggested that the society should be open to those of all faiths that accepted the creationist perspective, a majority decided that the Creation Research Society should be a Christian association only.

Despite the scientific focus of this new group, the overriding religious nature of the Creation Research Society was clear from the beginning. Members of the society were required to subscribe to a "doctrinal commitment" statement that also stressed religious perspectives. This statement defined the Bible as the "written word of God" whose "assertions are historically and scientifically true in all of the original autographs." The Genesis account of origins, further, was "a factual presentation of simple historical truths." The second two statements of doctrinal commitment provided specific details concerning biblical creation. "All basic types of living things, including man," members avowed, "were made by direct creative acts of God during Creation Week as described in Genesis. Whatever biological changes have occurred since Creation have accomplished only changes within the original created kinds." In addition, the Noachian flood was "an historic event, worldwide in its extent and effect." The underlying purpose of the Creation Research Society appeared clearly in the fourth and final statement of the doctrinal commitment: "Finally, we are an organization of Christian men of science, who accept Jesus Christ as our Lord and Savior. The account of the special creation of Adam and Eve as one man and one woman, and their subsequent Fall into sin, is the basis for our belief in the necessity of a Savior for all mankind. Therefore, salvation can come only through accepting Jesus Christ as our Savior." Because of their organizational endeavors, Lammerts and Tinkle were elected president and secretary of the new association.[16]

The Creation Research Society grew steadily over the next few years, attracting much attention from those who sought scientific proof of the literal truth of Genesis. Voting membership, restricted to those with postgraduate degrees in science, quadrupled to more than two hundred by 1967, with a total membership of more than eight hundred. A key element in the growing creation science movement, the Creation Research Society served as a source of information and speakers, as well as the research arm of the movement. The society also took steps to prevent the dilution of its commitment to a young earth and universal flood concept by reaching an agreement in early 1965 that no Creation Research Society publications would advocate old-earth concepts. This agreement was largely the work of Henry Morris, who later provided a succinct statement of the rigid creationist outlook in his 1966 book, *Studies in the Bible and Science.* If humans desired to know anything about creation, the "sole source of true information is that of divine revelation. God was there when it happened." As humans were not witnesses to creation, "we are completely limited to what God has seen fit to tell us, and this information is in His written Word. This is our textbook on the science of Creation!"[17]

Committed to many of the same goals as the Morris group, the Bible-Science Association also emerged from the discomfort with theistic evolution in the mid-1960s. The Reverend Walter Lang, a conservative Lutheran minister in Caldwell, Idaho, had long been concerned with the perceived loss of faith among students exposed to evolution at the College of Idaho. Impressed with Morris's *Genesis Flood,* Lang viewed the Creation Research Society as an important step away from the dominance of evolution in education. He quickly began editing the mimeographed *Bible-Science Newsletter,* which led to the formation of the Bible-Science Association. Southern California became the focus of the new association, through the efforts of Nell Segraves and Jean Sumrall. Segraves later recalled, "What got me involved was when my son came home from high school and started asking me questions. Both of my sons did it. Between the two of them I was forced to find answers or they would have lost their faith." Over the next five years media attention and rapid membership growth gave the Bible-Science Association a leading role in the expanding creationist movement. The *Bible-Science Newsletter* had a subscription list of fifteen thousand by the end of the decade. Lectures, debates, a large publication effort, and a radio program completed the campaign to attract national attention.[18]

The rapid growth of the creationist movement and the accompanying media interest had a profound impact on Henry Morris. His publications and addresses around the country attracted significant attention from reporters, who usually identified him as a faculty member at Virginia Polytechnic Institute. Because the Virginia school was attempting to improve its reputation by stressing its scientific work, Morris's anti-evolution stance represented something of an embarrassment, as pointed out by other faculty members. By the late 1960s Morris had become convinced that the university wished to remove him from his chairmanship. He arranged a sabbatical for the 1969-70 academic year, after which he planned to return as a faculty member but would no longer serve as department chair.[19]

During his sabbatical, which occurred in the middle of his term as Creation Research Society president, Morris continued to speak widely to various creationist groups. At the Torrey Memorial Bible Conference in Los Angeles in January 1970, he met Baptist minister Tim LaHaye, who shared with Morris his dream of establishing a Bible college in San Diego. Over the next few months the two corresponded frequently, leading Morris to resign his Virginia position and move to California to help establish Christian Heritage College. Morris would serve as academic vice president of the new school, and LaHaye would be president. Classes began in September 1970, with degree programs in Bible, education, missions, and liberal arts. Regardless of their majors, all students were required to take six semester hours of "practical Christian evidences" during the first year and six semester hours of "scientific creationism" during the second. Nell Segraves also persuaded Morris to merge her Bible-Science Association branch with the research division of the college to create a broader publishing and research organization. The Creation Science Research Center, directed by Morris, thus became the activist arm of the creationist movement and focused its energies on supplying a "scientific" alternative to evolution.[20]

Creation science, as it was increasingly called, also benefited from the liberal editorial policies of *American Biology Teacher,* the leading journal for biology educators. Biochemist Duane T. Gish, who had contributed essays to the American Scientific Affiliation, published "A Challenge to Neo-Darwinism" in the journal in late 1970. Repeating charges that would become a central theme for creationists, Gish emphasized the large number of scientists who questioned certain aspects of evolution. Taking these questions as indicating fundamental weaknesses in the theory, Gish argued that the continued support of evolution among scientists was based on something other than good scientific principles. "In all of the history of science," he wrote, "never has dogmatism had such a firm grip on science as it does today with reference to evolutionary theory. Evolutionists control our schools, the universities, and the means of publication. . . . We [creationists] believe it is possible, however, for those who fail to be swayed by the latest fashions in science, to reject the general theory of evolution after a rational assessment of the scientific evidence." Gish admitted that limited variation had taken place but emphasized the lack of intermediate forms in the fossil record. Such forms would provide evidence for the large-scale variation that he defined as the basic tenet of evolution. The transition between reptile and bird, for example, remained suspect, according to Gish, because "no one has ever found a single fossil with half-way wings and vestigial forelimbs or with half-way feathers." *Archaeopteryx,* long accepted by scientists as an excellent transitional form, "had certain alleged reptilelike features," according to Gish, "but it had fully developed wings and feathers, and it flew. It was undoubtedly a bird."[21]

Gish cited other evidence to challenge evolution, such as the sudden appearance of life at the beginning of the Cambrian period, but the underlying purpose of his article was to secure a fair hearing for creationism in the science classrooms. Stressing that special creation represented a "viable alternative" to evolution, Gish pleaded for "a *balanced* presentation in our schools, with a full disclosure of the evidence, regardless of which theory it favors." He dismissed the "dogmatic" teaching of evolution as "indoctrination" and described this practice as "as much the teaching of religion as if the theory of origins were restricted to the Book of Genesis."[22] The calls for fairness and equal time would become the rallying cry for the new antievolution crusade.

The creationist goal of equal access to the biology curriculum required educational materials appropriate to the task. Shortly after the appearance of Gish's article, creationists produced a textbook to provide students with an alternative explanation of the origin and development of life. In preparation since 1965, when the Creation Research Society committed itself to the publication of a biology text, *Biology: A Search for Order in Complexity* was published in 1970 by Zondervan, a Christian publishing house. Standard high school text publishers were not interested in the book, a situation explained later by Morris in conspiratorial terms. "In spite of the fact that most students and parents (and even teachers)," he wrote in 1984, "would have found the book more than satisfactory, the evolutionary *establishment* in science and education was too powerful for it even to be considered."[23]

Edited by John N. Moore and Harold S. Slusher, the text drew from a large number of creationist writers. The underlying theme of the book repeated many of the antievolutionist charges against science expressed in the late nineteenth and early twentieth centuries. In the preface, the editors stressed that "discussion of origins is not, strictly speaking, *science.* This is because origins are not subject to experimental verification. No scientific observers were present when life began or when different kinds of organisms first came into existence, and these events are not taking place in the present world; therefore, the solution of the problem of origins is simply impossible by scientific means." The first chapter of the text included an extended discussion of the scientific pursuit, based on the creationist view of science as a collection of facts that were later organized and classified. Ignoring more than a century of the history of science, the authors downplayed the importance of theories and minimized the importance of the uniformity of nature. While admitting the propriety of the scientific assumption of uniformity and its value in allowing science to proceed, they also stressed that "it is logical to maintain that exceptions could occur, especially in the distant past or distant future. The regular course of nature is not a 'god' to be worshipped." The text also attempted to disarm the objection to teleological explanations, frequently cited against creationism. In fact, the authors argued, teleology was widespread in biology. Biologists referred to plants growing toward the sun, flowers closing to protect their pollen, and roots growing toward water. Repeating the traditional argument from design, the authors pointed out that "flowers and roots do not have a mind to have purpose of their own; therefore, this planning must have been done for them by the Creator."[24]

Most of the rest of the textbook examined evolutionary explanations of terrestrial life and attempted to show the superiority of creationist explanations. Weaknesses or lack of information in certain aspects of evolution were presented as fundamental flaws in the theory that justified its rejection. If evolution was not completely accurate in every respect, then the only alternative explanation was creationism as defined by Morris and his followers. The investigation of existing knowledge was organized around this contrived dichotomy. Evidence from genetics, built up during the preceding half century, was dismissed as proof of evolution because genetic changes had never produced the significant alterations necessary to change one species into another:

> It is seldom claimed that any mutation confers an advantage upon the plant or animal that has it except under changed conditions of the environment, and usually examples of such advantage are hypothetical. No one has observed mutations taking place that would change one class of animal into a *more complex* type of organism: for instance the beginning of a milk gland upon the breast of a reptile, changing it into a mammal; or a feather starting instead of a scale, changing it into a bird. On the other hand those changes that have been observed are harmful and often involve *loss* of some physical trait.

In the light of the discoveries of the twentieth century, if a person still believes that mutations have changed amoeba to man it is because he has faith that at one time mutations occurred that were different from those known to occur now. He merely has an intellectual preference for that system of belief. And such a person violates belief in the uniformity of nature.[25]

Creationism and evolution, therefore, were nothing more than alternative belief systems, equally based on "scientific" evidence, which the student could equally well accept.

The development of creation science during the 1960s opened the next chapter in America's evolution controversy. Although rejecting evolution for the same reasons as their fundamentalist forebears, Morris, Gish, Lammerts, and others focused their considerable energies on a campaign to convince the public of the scientific validity of a literal reading of Genesis. Their belief that such a reading represented the only alternative to evolution enabled them to advance their own view by attacking evolution. From this perspective, any weaknesses in evolution supported creationism. Any scientist who questioned any aspect of evolution was, by definition, an ally of creationism who helped to weaken the evolutionary edifice. Biblical literalism also provided the foundation for the creationists' claim that their works represented a scientific explanation. For them, the Bible was religion. Removing references to the Bible and to God thus eliminated any religious overtones, in their minds, and established their perspective as science. References to a creator and creation did not imply "religion." Convinced of the legitimacy of their demands for equal time and balanced treatment, the creationists launched a public campaign for the inclusion of their "science" in the nation's classrooms.

The California Controversy

The public campaign initiated by the creationists to challenge evolution was aided by a growing disenchantment with science in the late 1960s. Virtually every aspect of science activity and policy aroused hostility. The "best-science" elite, who had coordinated the nation's science for decades, was criticized for its supposed lack of public accountability. Critics attacked the peer-review system as cliquish and argued that the emphasis on pure research, as opposed to investigations of immediate social benefit, represented a waste of resources. By the end of the decade the federal government had capitulated to the growing chorus of criticism, refocusing its policies toward applied research. Federal science policy also responded to demands for better geographic distribution of research grants and contracts, especially when such demands emanated from the office of President Lyndon B. Johnson. Compounding these concerns was the growing environmental awareness of the decade, which frequently led to public condemnation of science as the root of the various technological problems causing pollution. When combined with the conservative Protestant complaint that scientific knowledge threatened traditional values, the public's waning support for science paved the way for the creationist challenge.[26]

Yet science could not be ignored, least of all by those responsible for the nation's educational systems. Beginning in 1965 the California State Advisory Committee on Science Education began drafting new curriculum guidelines for public school science programs. Including such members as Jacob Bronowski of the Salk Institute and Paul DeHart Hurd of Stanford University, the committee formulated these guidelines to reinforce California's commitment to academic excellence. The guidelines eventually emerged in the fall of 1969 as *Science Framework for California Public Schools, Kindergarten—Grades One through Twelve* and represented the proposed model for science curriculum development in the state.

Science Framework examined many aspects of science, but the section that precipitated a major clash with advocates of creationism concerned evolutionary concepts. One of the chief conceptual schemes that the guidelines suggested was the idea that "units of matter interact" and that "interdependence and interaction with the environment are universal relationships." An excellent example of such interrelationships, the guidelines suggested, was the evolution of both living and nonliving phenomena: "From the origin of the first living particle, the evolution of living organisms was probably directed by environmental conditions and the changes occurring in them. A soup of amino acid-like molecules, formed in pools some 3 billion years ago, interacted with oxygen and other elemental constituents of the earth, probably giving rise to the first organization of matter which possesses the properties of life." The *Science Framework*'s next paragraph included a discussion that emphasized evolution through natural selection as the explanation for diversity among species and discussed evolution from mutations and genetic recombinations in organisms.[27]

Although innocuous from the scientific perspective, such statements troubled several members of the State Board of Education when they examined the draft at their October 1969 meeting in Los Angeles. Seven members of the board had been appointed by Governor Ronald

Reagan and predictably held very conservative views. Five of them found the two paragraphs concerning evolution objectionable enough to register their strong protest, citing creation science arguments discussed in the media. Dr. John Ford, a Seventh-Day Adventist physician from San Diego, argued, "Evolution should not be accepted as a fact without alluding to creationism, which is felt to be sound by many scientists." Dr. Thomas Harward, a Mormon from Needles who served as personal physician to state superintendent of education Max Rafferty, chided the authors of the *Science Framework:* "I believe in the creation theory, not evolution. You people should try to find out more of a scientific background of creation. A lot of evolution theory is shot through with holes and there are many discrepancies. You don't include the negative aspects of evolution." After a heated discussion, the board forwarded the guidelines to the State Department of Education for further study and revision. Superintendent Rafferty soon announced that the guidelines would be rewritten to include creationist concepts but would not include specific references to God or the Bible.[28]

Perceiving an opportunity to state their case in a visible forum, California creationists swiftly organized for the 13 November board meeting. Presented through petitions and testimony, their objections to the *Science Framework* focused on three issues. Teaching evolution alone was scientifically invalid, as shown by the evidence supporting divine creation put forth by Creation Research Society scientists and others. In addition, creationist opponents argued that the framework was philosophically unbalanced, promoting atheistic or agnostic humanism to the detriment of Christianity. Finally, creationists resurrected another argument from earlier evolution disputes when they asserted that Christian children have equal rights with atheist or agnostic children. If it was unconstitutional to teach religion in the public schools to protect the rights of nonbelievers, they argued, it was similarly unconstitutional to teach the absence of religion to protect the rights of believers.

Such arguments found many supporters among board members, who were ready to change the *Science Framework* accordingly. The key to the change came from consulting aerospace engineer Vernon L. Grose, a member of the Assemblies of God and the American Scientific Affiliation. He filed a thirteen-page memorandum with the board, in which he argued for the inclusion of creation theory in texts and classrooms. To this end, Grose proposed the deletion of the *Framework*'s paragraphs discussing evolution and their replacement by paragraphs emphasizing the need for at least two theories to explain the origin of life. All such theories were nonreligious, Grose stressed, and equally good from a scientific standpoint. The State Board of Education unanimously accepted these changes, despite Harward's objection that the new guidelines were "not strong enough."[29]

Although California scientists generally ignored these debates, members of the advisory committee who had drafted the *Science Framework* were outraged. Adamantly opposed to the Grose revisions, the committee issued a long statement on 4 December recording their "strong exception" to the changes. Drafted by Paul DeHart Hurd, the response characterized the changes as "entirely undercutting the thrust of the 205 page document" to the detriment of science. "The Board," the response continued, "by pitting a scientific fact (and theory as to its mechanism) against a particular religious belief as if they are commensurate, has thus offended the very essence of science, if not also that of religion." The advisory committee suggested options for the board to consider in an effort to maintain the scientific integrity of the document, ranging from restoring the original language to adding a committee statement repudiating the changes. The board chose the least drastic option, leaving the Grose revisions intact but adding a committee disclaimer. In this form, the *Science Framework* became the official state policy on science education and would be used to screen textbooks considered for purchase by the state. As California purchased 10 percent of the nation's texts, the impact of this new policy would be immense.[30]

The distribution of the guidelines troubled many educators, some of whom considered legal action to block implementation of the new policy. By 1971, however, the situation in California education began to brighten with the arrival of liberal Wilson Riles as the new superintendent of public instruction. One of Riles's first acts was to appoint a new Curriculum Commission, whose members were not at all sympathetic to creation science. This commission chose science texts for the public schools in late 1971 and early 1972, rejecting creationist publications. At its May meeting, however, the State Board of Education ignored the commission's recommendations and restored the creationist texts to the approved list that would be sent to local school districts for adoption. Shortly after this meeting, the board dissolved the Curriculum Commission, replacing this body with the Curriculum Development and Supplemental Materials Commission. Among the members of this commission were a large number of creationists, including Vernon L. Grose, but only one scientist. Junji Kumamoto, a chemist at the Riverside campus of the University of California, headed the science subcommittee of this body, which was charged with preparing a list of acceptable elementary science texts for submission to the new commission and the board.[31]

Despite the board's heavy-handed tactics in support of creationism, Kumamoto's subcommittee refused to recommend creationist texts. When the State Board of Education met in San Diego in September 1972, vice president John Ford and others expressed strong dissatisfaction with the recommended texts. Ford told the board, "Children are taught only one idea today: that the universe, life, and man are simply 'accidents' that occurred by fortuitous chance without cause, purpose or reason." Defending creation science, he went on to say that existing scientific data supported equally well the concept of a divine design behind the universe. A month later, after receiving a legal opinion that the State Board of Education could adopt texts whether or not they had been recommended by the curriculum commission, Ford urged his fellow board members to adopt creationist texts, arguing that "the origin of life and universe and man by evolutionary theory presupposes supernatural beginnings regardless of the cause." Given that perspective, Ford continued, special creation theory "is the only theory that can explain certain changes and lack of changes that have taken place in various orders of the universe."[32]

The continued hostility toward evolution expressed by the California Board of Education and the likelihood that text publishers would begin to include creationist ideas to maintain their share of the California market led scientists throughout the United States to record their concern. William Bevan, publisher of *Science,* expressed the fear that creationist successes would politicize the nation's classrooms to a frightening extent. It was clear, he wrote, that "if the state can dictate the content of a science, it makes little difference that its motivation is religious rather than political. The consequences will be the same. Many will recall the condition of Russian genetics during the heyday of Lysenko when Russian biologists defended an erroneous theory on the grounds that it must be true because it was Marxist." National organizations sent resolutions to the California Board of Education opposing the teaching of creationism. The National Academy of Sciences, for example, protested against the lobbying tactics of the creationists by stating: "The result of including creationism in otherwise nonreligious textbooks would be to impair the proper segregation of the teaching and understanding of science and religion. The foundations of science must exclude appeal to supernatural causes not susceptible to validation by objective criteria. Science and religion being mutually exclusive realms of human thought, their presentation in the same context is likely to lead to misunderstanding of both scientific theory and religious belief." Such statements had minimal impact on creationist board members, as evidenced by Ford's comment that the academy's resolution was "not only shortsighted but extremely biased and showing a lack of true scientific thinking."[33]

Having determined that they would choose textbooks, the State Board of Education, under the prodding of John Ford, scheduled public hearings for 9 November 1972 to examine creation science. The Sacramento meeting attracted an audience of some three hundred observers, with more than fifty speakers addressing aspects of the controversy. Duane T. Gish assured the board that "special creation not only offers credible explanation of the evidence related to origin, but thousands of scientists believe that it offers a much more credible explanation than evolution." Vernon L. Grose continued his antievolution campaign by arguing that either both creation and evolution should be taught or neither should be taught. "For the first time in the history of teaching science in the public school in areas where speculation rather than observation has often prevailed," he observed, "we have confronted speculative scientism with a balancing speculation that there may have been the participation of a designer in various origins." Nell Segraves testified that "Christian children are losing their faith because an increasingly unrelenting flood of anti-Biblical teaching in the public schools disguises historical fact and scientific truth."[34]

Creationists were not the only concerned citizens testifying at the November hearing. A number of scientists and religious leaders attempted to convince the board that the debate was not between religion and science, but only between a rigid fundamentalism and science. The Reverend Robert Bulkley, representing Catholic, Protestant, and Jewish groups, told the board that the inclusion of creationism in science texts was based on a "profound misunderstanding" of the different roles of science and religion and violated the constitutional separation of church and state. Scientists attempted to show that creationist claims of weaknesses in the theory of evolution were overstated. Berkeley geneticist Thomas Jukes told the board that "scientists argue about some of the details of evolution but the vast majority, including all biologists whose opinions are widely accepted, do not agree with any proposal that existing characteristics were part of an original special creation." Stanford biochemist David Hogness focused on educational problems by testifying, "To consider the story of creation as a scientific alternative to evolutionary theory would not only sow the confusion of intellectual dishonesty in our students, it would also create real difficulties in preparing youths to contribute to the solution of many problems." Although such testimony could not be expected to convert creationists into evolutionists, scientists' statements and resolutions at least convinced some members of the California Board of Education that professional scientists rarely rejected the validity of evolution.[35]

The November hearings reinforced the divided nature of the board. The nine members—one vacancy existed in late 1972—tended to split into a group of five creationists and another group of four noncreationists. Because board policy required six votes for a motion to pass, the board remained deadlocked. A motion to require creationism in texts failed by one vote; a motion to prohibit the teaching of creationism failed by two votes. The curriculum commission thus drew up a compromise plan that would leave out all mention of God and Genesis but would emphasize the speculative nature of Darwinian evolution. Such a compromise apparently satisfied no one. Vernon Grose told an interviewer that science had been "oversold in Western culture as the sole repository of objective truth," repeating his call for presenting both evolution and creationism. The November state convention of Southern Baptists unanimously passed a resolution calling for the State Board of Education to implement its original decision requiring the inclusion of creation science in texts. Other conservative religious groups registered their support, while an organization called Creation Evolution Equality was formed to pressure the state legislature to require equal time in the public schools for creationism.[36]

After the November meeting, creationist board members began to moderate their demands. Failing again to gain enough votes to require the inclusion of creationism in texts, creationists on the California Board of Education accepted texts recommended by the curriculum commission at their December meeting in Sacramento. The Reverend David Hubbard of Pasadena, however, continued to stress his opposition to teaching evolution. Such teaching, he told his board colleagues, "may put students in conflict between what they think they are learning in science and what they learn spiritually, morally and even politically." Protestations from the scientific community merely confirmed Hubbard's suspicions concerning scientists. "There is a notable absence of humility and repentance," he chided, "in the remonstrances coming to us from the scientific community. They have refused to recognize their complicity in the problem." He continued his call for action by stating, "The problem has not been Christians trying to sneak creation in, but over-dogmatism of text writers and the fact that the borderline between science that can be checked in the laboratory and philosophy has been violated."[37]

The charge of dogmatism apparently struck a nerve among board members, who had before them a statement from the curriculum commission calling for neutrality in texts. After discussion and some political maneuvering, the board accepted by a vote of seven to one a statement calling for the removal of dogmatism in explanations of origins in textbooks. The board appointed a four-member committee to oversee the new policy, choosing two members of the American Scientific Affiliation and board members John Ford and David Hubbard. All four identified themselves as creationists; none were biologists.[38]

For the next few months the antidogmatism concept guided decisions of the California Board of Education. Although continued attempts to include specific creationist references were made, the board decided that references to religious theories of origins were only appropriate in social studies texts. Science texts should include clear statements that stressed the conditional nature of scientific knowledge concerning origins. The committee charged with implementing the antidogmatism policy proposed a large number of textbook revisions, which the board of education accepted by a vote of seven to three at its March 1973 meeting in Los Angeles. Such changes significantly weakened the presentation of evolutionary concepts. The statement "Some fish began to change" emerged from the committee as "Some fish began to change although we don't know why." "Paleontologists have been able to date the geological history of North America" was rewritten as "Paleontologists have assembled a tentative outline of the geological history of North America." To avoid stating evolutionary assumptions, the sentence "As reptiles evolved from fishlike ancestors, they developed a thicker scaly surface" became "If reptiles evolved from fishlike ancestors, as proposed in the theory of evolution, they must have developed a thick scaly surface." Textbooks were also required to include an official introductory statement that ultimate questions of origin lay beyond science in the realm of philosophy and theology. Relieved that the proposed changes did not include specific creationist concepts, scientists raised few objections to the revisions. Compromise seemed to be the order of the day.[39]

A New Focus

Despite their inability to establish creation science in the public school curriculum, the creationists had achieved an important goal by the early 1970s. They had attracted significant attention among the public and in the media, providing an important base for their continuing efforts. Creationist organizations expanded in size and scope, beginning with the addition of two scientists to the staff of the Creation Science Research Center. Biochemist Duane T. Gish and physicist Harold S. Slusher left their positions at Upjohn and the University of Texas at El Paso, respectively, to join the San Diego center, where they would also assist in establishing the science curriculum at Christian Heritage College.

The visible success of the San Diego creationists masked an important internal division. Nell Segraves and her son, Kelly, believed that the thrust of creationist efforts should be directed toward political and promotional work. Morris, Gish, and Slusher believed that educational and scientific efforts would be more profitable in the long term. In an effort to make an early impact in California, the Segraves faction attempted to rush creationist material into print to meet the September 1971 deadline for new science texts in California. Morris had argued against this course of action, believing that the movement would better be served through the production of high-quality texts and other educational materials. By April 1972 the divisions had become too serious to ignore. The research center board decided to separate from Christian Heritage College, with the Segraves faction taking control of the Creation Science Research Center and Morris, Gish, Slusher, and most of the rest of the staff remaining with the college. This latter group soon reorganized as the Institute for Creation Research, functioning as a division of the college, which supplied most of the institute's budget.[40]

The Morris faction vigorously pursued its campaign to convince the public of the scientific legitimacy of creationism. Soon after the establishment of the Institute for Creation Research, Morris published *The Remarkable Birth of Planet Earth,* which provided "scientific" evidence of divine creation of the earth and all life forms. As had been true with earlier creationist writings, however, much of Morris's attention was devoted to challenging evolution. He described the origin of the earth as a "marvelous and fascinating story" that had been revealed in the Bible "and now strikingly confirmed by modern science." Despite the superiority of biblical explanations, the theory of evolution had dominated society and education for nearly a century, with disturbing results. The influence of the theory, Morris argued, was "largely responsible for our present-day social, political, and moral problems." Providing a succinct summary of the creationist perspective, Morris informed his readers that many people, including scientists, now believed that "evolution is merely an unreasonable theory, containing many scientific fallacies. Creation, on the other hand, is a scientific theory which does fit all the facts of true science, as well as God's revelation in the Holy Scriptures."[41]

The creationist position was made clear to the science education establishment through the pages of *American Biology Teacher,* which published two extensive articles in early 1973. Although prefaced by editorial statements emphasizing that biologists rejected such positions, the articles by John N. Moore, coeditor of *Biology: A Search for Order in Complexity,* and Duane T. Gish provided biology educators with a clear statement of creationist views. A professor of natural science at Michigan State University, where he had received a master of science degree in botany and plant pathology and a doctorate of education, Moore developed typical creationist arguments that focused on the unscientific nature of evolution theory. The predictions of evolution could not be tested, he stressed, concluding that the theory was based on little more than "circumstantial evidence." This evidence, he continued, involved "extrapolations quite beyond the realm of genuine scientific investigation; that is, experimental analysis." Equally untestable were the "hypotheses of relationships of a general evolutionary nature," which were "purely conjectural and speculative" and "doomed forever to remain a part of the untestable dogma used to support the general evolution model."[42]

Gish repeated many of the same arguments in his essay, "Creation, Evolution, and the Historical Evidence," but also focused on the suspected philosophical agenda behind the evolutionists' theories. He suggested that "the dogmatic acceptance of evolution is not due, primarily, to the nature of the evidence but to the philosophic bias peculiar to our times." Defending his "two model" concept of teaching evolution and creation, Gish maintained that materialism and humanism were the philosophical biases that required the belief in evolution. He concluded his article with a clear statement of this increasingly popular view among creationists: "The majority in the scientific community and educational circles are using the cloak of 'science' to force the teaching of their view of life upon all. The authoritarianism of the medieval church has been replaced by the authoritarianism of rationalistic materialism. Constitutional guarantees are violated and free scientific inquiry is stifled under this blanket of dogmatism. It is time for a change."[43] The change required was, of course, equal time for creationism in the public schools of the United States.

Although American scientists were only beginning to recognize the strength of the creationist movement in the early 1970s, examples of their opposition to the latest incarnation of antievolutionism nonetheless appeared. Despite significant internal dissent, part of which came from creationists, the National Association of Biology Teachers began to oppose creationist attempts to modify the biology curriculum.

The association established a Fund for Freedom in Science-Teaching and also began to cooperate with other teachers' groups that opposed creationist initiatives. Leading biologists, some of whom had been quoted out of context by creationists eager to show scientists' supposed rejection of evolution, expressed their concern with the revived anti-evolutionism. Ernst Mayr challenged creationist writers by informing readers of *American Biology Teacher* that biologists had no doubt that evolution had taken place. The situation was, to be sure, different among nonbiologists, but scientists' statements that evidence for evolution was incomplete merely referred to filling in details of the theory. George Gaylord Simpson, for example, had commented in 1944 that there was a "regular absence of transitional forms" in the fossil record. Creationists seized on this statement to discredit the theory of evolution. In 1972, however, Simpson pointed out that paleontological research over the past quarter century had uncovered "literally thousands of transitional forms," with more discovered each year. "Anyone who cites me or my work in opposition [to evolution]," he stated, "is either woefully ignorant or willfully misrepresenting the facts."[44]

Reviews of the creationist text *Biology: A Search for Order in Complexity* also provided evidence of the weaknesses of the creationist cause. A science educator from Indiana University stressed the pedagogical lapses in the volume and was especially disturbed with the authors' presentation of science as a finished product, rather than as an ongoing process. A high school teacher from Colorado reviewed the text for readers of *American Biology Teacher*. Stressing the text's questionable statements and the authors' apparent lack of knowledge concerning modern evolutionary theory, the teacher referred to the section "Theories of Biological Change" as "little more than a first-class hatchet job on evolutionary theory." Historian Richard P. Aulie, who had earned a zoology degree from Wheaton College, characterized the text as an "*apologia* for a 19th-century view" and accused the authors of attempting to return biology to the early years of that century. "Undaunted by more than a century of scholarship in geology and paleontology and a half-century in genetics," he stressed, "they argue that no evolutionary change has occurred in time—for the major groups of organisms were created fully formed, *ex nihilo,* at the beginning." Reviewers for *Science Teacher* focused on the large amount of material that was either wrong or out of date, concluding that "twentieth-century 'facts' and nineteenth-century concepts still add up to nineteenth-century biology."[45]

Despite the growing opposition among scientists to the creationist campaigns, the concept of equal time proved attractive to many Americans. If the creationist contention was true that scientific "facts" existed to support a literal reading of Genesis, then it seemed only "fair" and "democratic" to present both versions of the origin and development of terrestrial life in the classroom and allow the students to choose whichever one they wanted to "believe." The equal time concept early gained the attention of the nation's courts. In November 1970 Leona Wilson of Houston, Texas, filed suit in federal district court on behalf of her daughter, Rita Wright, and other students. Wilson charged that the Houston schools were illegitimately teaching evolution as fact, "without critical analysis and without reference to other theories which purport to explain the origin of the human species." Various difficulties delayed the case until June 1972, at which time plaintiffs argued that teaching evolution inhibited the free exercise of religion. By teaching evolution, the state was attempting to discourage them in the exercise of their religion by holding that religion up to contempt and scorn. Repeating an increasingly common theme among antievolutionists, plaintiffs also argued that the state was trying to establish the "religion of secularism" through the teaching of evolution.[46]

In an effort to justify their demands for the teaching of both creation and evolution—or neither—the plaintiffs attempted to draw an analogy to the Supreme Court's decision in *Epperson v. Arkansas.* They argued that the Arkansas prohibition against teaching evolution was little different from the Houston school district's attempt to avoid teaching creation. Neither practice was strictly neutral; both were establishments of religion. From this perspective, all their case was attempting to achieve was the true religious neutrality demanded by *Epperson.* Judge Woodrow B. Seals rejected this claim, writing that the plaintiffs had "wholly failed to establish the analogy" and stressing that the school board was not following any stated policy to further secularism as a religion. "All that can be said is that certain textbooks selected by school officials present what Plaintiffs deem a biased view in support of the theory [of evolution]," he wrote. "This Court has been cited to no case in which so nebulous an intrusion upon the principle of religious neutrality has been condemned by the Supreme Court." No evidence existed that the school system attempted to discourage free discussion in the classroom, leading Seals to conclude that the Houston "policy" was totally different from the censorship imposed by Arkansas before *Epperson.*[47]

It remained for the issue of equal time, however, to precipitate the focus of the district court's and later courts' decisions in the *Wright* case. The plaintiffs' proposal that the difficulties involved in teaching evolution could be rectified by teaching other theories of origins appeared reasonable at first glance, the judge observed, but the large number of alternative theories made the proposal unworkable. "This Court is hardly qualified to select from among the available theories those which merit attention in a public school biology class," Judge Seals concluded. "Nor have Plaintiffs suggested to the Court what standards might be applied in making such a selection." In short, he stressed, the case of the plaintiffs "must ultimately fail, then, because the proposed solutions are more onerous than the problem they purport to alleviate." Slightly more than a year later, the Fifth Circuit Court of Appeals upheld the dismissal of the *Wright* case, characterizing the proposed equal time solution as "an unwarranted intrusion into the authority of public school systems to control the academic curriculum." The following June the United States Supreme Court refused to review the case.[48]

The new creationist tactic of "balanced treatment" led to other initiatives as well. In much the same fashion as the antievolution drive in the 1920s, proposals for equal time appeared throughout the United States in the early 1970s at both the state and local levels. The board of education in Columbus, Ohio, passed a resolution in 1971 encouraging teachers to present special creation along with evolution. The Michigan legislature considered several equal time bills in 1971 and 1973. Although most such bills died in committee, the state's House of Representatives approved a later version of the 1971 legislation after amending the bill to remove specific mention of the Bible. The amended bill reached the Senate too late in the session to be considered. Early 1973 also witnessed a Wisconsin attempt to provide "balanced instruction in all major theories of the origin of life, including that of creation" in a House bill that died in committee. Later that year the Oregon School Board required school libraries to include creationist materials and informed teachers that they must urge their students to "weigh the information and arrive at their own conclusions."[49]

One of the most contentious campaigns to establish equal time for creationist ideas occurred in Colorado, despite the presence of the Biological Sciences Curriculum Study headquarters in Boulder. Fundamentalists persuaded six state senators and an equal number of representatives to introduce House Concurrent Resolution 1011 in late February 1972 as an amendment to the state constitution. Applying to any public school or state-supported institution of higher education, the proposed amendment would require that evolution and creationism be treated equally in all discussions about the origin of life, humans, or the universe. The resolution's purpose was described as "allowing all students and teachers academic freedom of choice as to which of these two theories, creation or evolution, they wish to choose." Violating the proposed amendment would result in a maximum fine of five thousand dollars or six months in jail. Referred to the Judiciary Committee, the resolution was opposed forcefully by Colorado scientists organized by BSCS director William V. Mayer. Scientists' testimony and perceived constitutional weaknesses convinced the committee to kill the legislation. Supporters of the resolution enjoyed no more success in their effort to place the amendment on the November ballot through the referendum process.[50]

Creationists' failure to secure equal time legislation was anything but a disaster. They had, after all, garnered much publicity in the media and had made significant inroads at the local level in their campaign to balance the teaching of evolution with creation science. More important, the concept of equal time had gained allies among the large number of Americans who were more concerned with "fairness" and "freedom of choice" than with the details of biological science in the 1970s. Among these sympathizers were state and local politicians who were well aware of the growing strength of conservative religions in the United States. Creationists were little discouraged by events in Michigan, Wisconsin, and Colorado. They merely needed to find a state more receptive to their particular brand of theology. Once again, Tennessee provided antievolutionists with an important, although short-lived, victory.

8

A Remedy to a Bad Act

Russell Artist, professor of biology at David Lipscomb College in Nashville, had been among the leaders of the creation science movement for more than a decade. He had served as one of the expert witnesses during the antievolutionists' Texas campaign in the mid-1960s and had taught the errors of evolution and the scientific accuracy of Genesis in his biology classes for years. Displeased with the 1967 repeal of the Butler Act, Artist encouraged his students at the Church of Christ-affiliated school to write to the Tennessee Department of Education in an effort to restore "balance" in public education. This activity had no effect, so Artist began to lobby education officials to adopt the creationist text *Biology: A Search for Order in Complexity.* Although the state textbook commission approved the volume as a supplementary text after Artist's testimony in 1970, no public school system in the state purchased the book.[1]

Realizing that Tennessee education officials remained insufficiently sympathetic to his ideas, Artist resolved to pursue legislative action. In early 1973 he approached Senator Milton Hamilton, a Methodist Democrat from rural Union City. The senator easily convinced four of his colleagues to cosponsor a bill for the "balanced treatment" of creationism and evolution. Senate Bill 394, soon to be popularly known as the Genesis Act, was introduced into the Tennessee Senate on 26 March 1973. The proposed legislation focused on public school textbooks that examined the issue of the origin of humans and the world. A clear expansion of the Butler Act, which had concerned itself only with the evolution of humans, the Genesis Act represented the broader attack on evolutionary concepts that increasingly characterized the creationist campaigns. The Hamilton bill required that all texts specifically state that discussions of origins were theories and not scientific facts. Further, the bill mandated that equal numbers of words, space, and emphasis be provided for "other theories, including, but not limited to, the Genesis account in the Bible." Easily passing the required first two readings, the legislation was referred to the Committee on Education the day after its introduction. All five sponsors were members of the eleven-man committee.[2]

The House of Representatives quickly followed the Senate's lead. On 3 April a coalition of seven representatives, including Speaker of the House Ned Ray McWherter, introduced a similar equal time bill. The Senate and House bills moved rapidly through the appropriate committees and were scheduled for floor debate on 18 and 26 April, respectively. Although the attorney general's office provided informal opinions that such legislation was probably unconstitutional, Tennessee's latest attempt to restrict the teaching of evolution appeared destined for easy passage. Among the groups urging legislators to support the bill was the fundamentalist Church of Christ, a major force in Tennessee politics.[3]

Shortly before the floor debate, Senator Hamilton told a Nashville reporter that he knew of no opposition to the bill among his colleagues. Nonetheless, the bill attracted much attention. Network television cameras would be on the Senate floor when debate began on 18 April. An editorial in that day's *Tennessean* criticized the legislature for "wasting itself on insignificant issues" while ignoring more important problems. University of Tennessee professors formed an ad hoc Committee to Prevent Anti-Evolution Law in Tennessee, releasing a statement that the proposed Genesis Act was "utterly repugnant to the American idea of democracy." This statement had little effect on legislative supporters of the bill. Senator Hamilton responded to such criticism by stating, "This is not a Ph.D. Bill. It is a people's bill."[4]

Consideration of Senate Bill 394 failed to result in the emotional debate hoped for by the media. As Hamilton had predicted, there existed virtually no opposition to the bill or to two minor amendments. The vote on the amended bill was an overwhelming twenty-nine to one, with only Memphis senator James H. White opposing the bill as a waste of the legislature's time. After the vote, Senator Avon Williams defended his yes vote by characterizing the Genesis Act as a promotion of fairness and balance. He described the bill as one "which seeks to make available to school children all theories regarding the particular subject" and explained that he favored this legislation just as he had endorsed an earlier bill mandating the teaching of black history in the public schools. Senator Hamilton explained the lack of emotion on the floor to a Nashville reporter by stating, "The reason there wasn't any debate is that the national TV came down here with the idea they would make us look like a bunch of nitpickers. You know, like barefoot Tennesseans."[5]

The Senate forwarded its bill to the House of Representatives, where members accepted the legislation in lieu of their own version of the equal time law. Public support for the proposed legislation was ev- ident to House members, as shown by more than five hundred letters to Speaker McWherter, only one of which opposed the act. During the hour-long debate on 26 April, House members added four amendments to the Senate version to make the bill's purpose even more specific. One amendment limited the restrictions in the bill to biology texts, while an- other allowed teachers to use any supplementary materials they thought appropriate to meet the bill's requirements. The two most important amendments, however, emphasized the hitherto unstated goal of includ- ing a literal reading of Genesis in the state's biology classrooms. Rep- resentatives approved the amendment "The teaching of all occult or satanical beliefs of human origin is expressly excluded from this act" and also addressed the problem of the equal time requirement as it re- lated to the Bible. House members solved this difficult problem by amending the legislation to include the passage: "Provided however that the Holy Bible shall not be defined as a textbook but is hereby de- clared to be a reference work, and shall not be required to carry the disclaimer above provided for textbooks." The amended Genesis Act passed easily, by a vote of sixty-nine to fifteen.[6]

After the vote had been tallied, several opponents took time to ex- plain their no votes to their colleagues and to the press. Knoxville Re- publican Victor Ashe expressed discomfort with defining the Genesis account as a "theory" but was equally concerned because the financial impact of the bill remained unclear. "I cannot help but think," he said from the floor, "that passage of this measure imposed a real hardship upon those who purchase textbooks since there is a paucity of books which comply with the provisions of this act. Are we being tricked into passing a bill to guarantee a market for some unknown writer who could not otherwise sell his book?" The implied definition of Genesis as a "theory" troubled several other legislators. Herbert Denton, Jr., for ex- ample, told his colleagues that he had voted against the Genesis Act because "I do not feel that the Genesis account of man's creation should be treated as a theory when I accept it as fact, and I feel it could do great harm to any child to be taught the Genesis account of man's creation by a person who could be a non-believer." Despite such con- cerns, most legislators approved of the bill. Representative W.C. Carter of Rhea County, home of the Scopes trial nearly a half century before, had voted against the Butler Act repeal and called the current House action "a remedy to a bad act."[7]

The Tennessee Senate acted quickly to approve the four House amendments on 30 April, after which the amended bill was forwarded to Republican governor Winfield Dunn. Under the Tennessee constitution, he had five days to sign the bill or veto it, or it would become law without his signature. Dunn chose the latter course, returning the legislation to the secretary of state without his signature and with no explanation for his actions. Tennessee had a new antievolution law.[8]

The Genesis Act precipitated a predictable response from those concerned with the intellectual integrity of science education in the state. By the end of the year suits had been filed in both state and federal courts to challenge the new law. A group of biology teachers, students, parents, and the Nashville chapter of Americans United for Separation of Church and State challenged the statute in Davidson County Chancery Court as an establishment of religion. Relying on the recently promulgated "three-pronged test" of *Lemon v. Kurtzman,* the plaintiffs in this case argued that the Genesis Act did not have a secular purpose. They asserted that it had a primary religious purpose and would cause excessive state entanglement in religious questions. All of this represented unconstitutional state action.

The brief filed with the state court stressed that the Genesis Act singled out for specific reference the Genesis account and excused the Bible from the disclaimer required for other works. These two actions clearly showed the sectarian purpose of the act. The brief added, parenthetically, that the biblical exemption also indicated the religious purpose of the legislature, because "the exemption was never necessary, in any case, since the Act required only that '*biology* textbooks' carry the disclaimer, a category clearly excluding the Bible." Similarly, the prohibition against occult or satanic beliefs showed that the legislature was not primarily interested in presenting a wide variety of theories, but only the one accepted by fundamentalists. Plaintiffs further argued that the motivation behind the 1973 law was identical with that behind the antievolution laws of the 1920s. The effect of compromising an accepted scientific explanation because it appeared to conflict with certain religious beliefs was "inevitably to advance religion." The equal time provision had the same impact. "Religious dogma" was to be elevated to a status in biology classes equal to "objectively formulated" scientific explanations of biological phenomena. Tennessee's 1973 law made no attempt to present Genesis in the literary or historical perspective approved in *Epperson.* Rather, the legislature had attempted to advance specific religious ideas as coequal with the ideas of science.[9]

Three days after Christmas the National Association of Biology Teachers and several science teachers joined forces to file a similar suit in federal district court in Nashville. Raising more issues than in the pending chancery court action, these plaintiffs argued that the 1973 law was an establishment of religion, violated their rights to the free exercise of religion, and abridged free speech guarantees. Their complaint went on to assert that the Genesis Act represented a prior restraint upon freedom of the press, violated the right of academic freedom, and also violated the rights of parents and children to acquire useful knowledge. Because the act did not define such terms as *theory* and *occult or satanical beliefs,* plaintiffs also objected to the law for its vagueness.[10] As the new year approached, the future of Tennessee's Genesis Act rested with the courts in Nashville.

The Creationist Campaign Expands

The Genesis Act represented only one aspect of the growing presence of the creation science movement. As Tennessee examined legislative remedies for the absence of biblical explanations in science classes, creationists in California continued their campaign at the local level. Although they enjoyed mixed success in their efforts to convince school boards to adopt creationist materials, they achieved the equally important goal of gaining significant public support. Public opinion polls in 1973 and 1974 indicated that, in some areas of the state at least, more than 80 percent of the respondents favored teaching both evolution and creation in the public schools. Such support encouraged creationists in their attempts to control the California curriculum.[11]

Education officials in the state, however, were becoming less sympathetic to the creationist cause. Junji Kumamoto's science subcommittee of the state curriculum committee spent late 1973 and early 1974 revising the *Science Framework* paragraphs that had caused earlier debates. Replacing the Grose statements with five new paragraphs, the subcommittee admitted the limitations of evolution while describing the evidence that supported the theory. They completed their revisions without mentioning creationism, although the last paragraph of the new statement emphasized that religious and philosophical considerations concerning the origin, meaning, and values of life were beyond the purview of science. The State Board of Education approved these changes at its 14 March meeting, leaving the antidogmatism statement as the only creationist bulwark against the teaching of evolution.[12]

Friends of creation science challenged the board's decision. Two conservative Republican legislators from southern California asked the state attorney general for an opinion concerning the board's recent action. Did the remaining antidogmatism policy, they queried, satisfy the constitutional requirement of religious neutrality? Or had the board of education violated that requirement by excluding creationist views from the *Science Framework*, thus eliminating the equal time provisions that guaranteed neutrality? In 1975 Attorney General Evelle J. Younger issued an opinion supporting the board of education. Even if teaching evolution promoted atheism, he argued, teaching religion to balance it represented an improper remedy. The only proper remedy in such a situation would be the teaching of neither evolution nor religion. Younger dismissed the assertion that atheism was being advanced, however, stating, "It is unlikely to the point of improbable that a court would find that a scientific treatment of evolution in science textbooks is, directly or indirectly, the advancement of an agnostic or atheistic belief." Further, creation science clearly had a religious basis, which prevented its inclusion in public school texts because of First Amendment prohibitions against the establishment of religion.[13]

Attorney General Younger's opinion paralleled the waning creationist influence on the California Board of Education. Liberal appointees of Governor Jerry Brown had replaced Governor Reagan's conservative board members. The new attitude of the board became clear at its July 1975 meeting, when members examined social science texts for use in the state's public schools. Having previously approved science texts that made no mention of creationism, the board followed suit by adopting no social science texts that included creationist explanations. The approved texts did, however, discuss evolution. Although board president John Ford and member Eugene Ragle both voted against the books because they did not include creationism, this view clearly represented the minority position on the board.[14]

Despite the setback in California, creationists continued their efforts to establish creation science as a legitimate alternative to the theory of evolution. Of great importance to the creationist campaign was the publication of alternative scientific works, including both texts and reports of creation science research. In 1974 Henry M. Morris and several other members of the Institute for Creation Research, Christian Heritage College, and Scott Memorial Church pooled their resources to establish a separate publishing company in San Diego. One of the first major projects undertaken by Creation-Life Publishers was the production of *Scientific Creationism*, a new textbook edited by Morris. Published in 1974, this text appeared in two editions, one for church-related schools and the other for the public school systems in the United States.

The latter edition omitted the chapter "Creation According to Scripture," leading Morris to characterize it later as "a completely non-Biblical, non-religious treatment of all the relevant scientific data." In his preface to the public school edition, Morris explained that the text was designed as a "reference handbook" to provide "the creationist alternative on every important topic related to origins." He assured his readers that the volume would examine all aspects of origins "solely on a scientific basis, with no references to the Bible or to religious doctrine."[15]

Morris undoubtedly believed that he had eliminated all religious references in his textbook, given the creationist belief that the absence of biblical exegesis qualified a work as secular. Yet the public school edition of *Scientific Creationism* was little more than the Genesis account in different phrasing. In his introduction to the creationist perspective, Morris dismissed the charges that creation science represented a supernatural explanation that negated its legitimacy as science. "The only aspect of supernaturalism that needs to be mentioned at all," he wrote, "is that the creation model does presuppose a God, or Creator, who did create things in the beginning. To insist that even *this* possibility should be excluded is to insist either that the universe must have originated without a God (which is the religion of atheism) or else that God could only work by a process of evolution (which is the religion of theistic evolutionism) and these concepts are every bit as 'religious' as is creationism!" Equally important to Morris in his effort to establish the scientific equivalence of creation science and evolution was the traditional antievolutionist argument that the theory of evolution remained insufficiently based on facts. Morris emphasized the impossibility of "proving" any theory of origins because of the inapplicability of experimental observation to the problem. "A scientific investigator," Morris stressed, "be he ever so resourceful and brilliant, can neither observe nor repeat *origins*!" Indeed, scientific examination of creation was probably pointless. Experiments to describe creation could not be devised, and it was probably equally impossible to determine whether creation could take place. "The Creator does not create at the whim of a scientist."[16]

Having defined evolution as a model that had no more scientific basis than creationism, Morris and his collaborators spent most of the rest of the volume emphasizing the supposed shortcomings of evolution. The authors of *Scientific Creationism* displayed a traditional antievolution perspective when evaluating evidence supporting the theory of evolution, such as estimates of a great age for the earth. Any estimate of terrestrial age, they stressed, would be based on indirect data that they characterized as "uncertain at best." In fact, the indirect evidence employed by evolutionists was fatally flawed. The use of index fossils, which allowed geologists to date rocks according to the fossils trapped in them, represented an illegitimate technique based on the assumption of an evolutionary sequence. Readers of the public school edition were informed, "If we really knew evolution were true—say by divine revelation or some other infallible means—then the stage-of-evolution of the fossils would definitely be the best way to date rocks." The authors rejected radiometric dating because it was based on the untestable assumption of a reasonably constant rate of radioactive decay. "Not even uranium dating is capable of experimental verification," they wrote, "since no one could actually watch uranium decaying for millions of years to see what happens." Displaying a similarly skeptical view of another dating method, *Scientific Creationism* attacked dendrochronology as at least 20 percent inaccurate. Believing that dendrochronologists based their calculations on the simple counting of tree rings, the authors of the text stressed that multiple growth rings frequently appeared in trees, leading to high age estimates. Nonetheless, the dendrochronologically derived bristlecone pine dates of more than four thousand years provided "good support for a recent date for the postulated worldwide cataclysm," because the pine was the oldest living thing known.[17]

Having dispensed with dating schemes that supported evolution, the authors of *Scientific Creationism* attempted to show the superiority of their own model. This superiority was based on the ability of the creation model to explain the observed world without recourse to speculations such as radioactive decay and natural selection. The short time scale thus made more sense, although the creation model did not require it. "Assuming the Creator had a purpose in His creation, and that purpose centered primarily on man," the authors concluded, "it does seem more appropriate that He would not waste aeons of time in essentially meaningless caretaking of an incomplete stage or stages of His intended creative work."[18] Although creationists argued that such statements did not represent a religious perspective, it remained clear that the agenda behind *Scientific Creationism* was a religious one. The text's authors came close to admitting this in a later summary of their view. "Unlike the evolution model," they concluded, "the creation model recognizes the scientific law of cause-and-effect. The Creator, the First Cause, is obviously capable of creating man as a religious being, with intelligence, purpose and ethical motivation. The creation model fits all the observed facts, directly and without embarrassment or equivocation."[19]

Biology: A Search for Order in Complexity, Scientific Creationism, and other creationist publications attracted much attention and significant support among educational boards throughout the nation. State and local agencies in Ohio, Oklahoma, Idaho, Georgia, Indiana, Oregon, Washington, Wisconsin, and Texas approved these texts in the mid-1970s, responding to pressure from such groups as the Creation Research Science Education Foundation and its local chapters, known as Boosters of True Education. The argument that students should be free to choose which explanation to accept, coupled with the creationists' polished presentations of the "science" in creation science, proved difficult for local school boards to resist. Bowing to creationist pressure, the Texas Board of Education issued a new resolution in the spring of 1974, requiring textbooks to emphasize that evolution was only one of several explanations of human origins. The resolution also required biology texts to include an introductory statement that evolution represented a theory only. Despite the protest of scientists, the board rejected all three BSCS textbooks under the new policy.[20]

Creationists remained significantly less successful at the legislative level, failing to secure equal time bills in Ohio, Indiana, and Kentucky. A more extensive campaign emerged in the state of Washington. During the third week of February 1973 Duane T. Gish appeared before several Seattle area church groups and schools to mobilize support for creationist legislation. Such activity soon led to the introduction of House Bill 1021, which attempted to establish equal time concepts in a carefully defined fashion. The bill stated that neither evolution nor creationism could be promoted to the exclusion of the other. Teachers were forbidden to teach catastrophism or uniformitarianism unless they taught both and were prohibited from teaching theistic evolution as a substitute for teaching both evolution and creationism. The Washington attorney general advised that the bill was probably an unconstitutional attempt to provide religious instruction, convincing the Education Committee to kill the measure. Thwarted on the legislative front, Washington creationists attempted to secure the same end through the initiative process in 1974. Coordinated by the Committee for the Initiative on Creation and Evolution, Initiative 47 fell far short of the 118,000 signatures required to transmit the measure to the legislature.[21]

The failure of legislative campaigns, however, was only part of the story. Opposition to the teaching of evolution and other "modernist" concepts held the potential for outbreaks of violence, as shown by events in Kanawha County, West Virginia. In April 1973 the county school board adopted the creationist text *Biology: A Search for Order in Complexity* and publications from the Science and Creation Series produced by the Segraves group in southern California. The availability of such books apparently failed to satisfy the more conservative residents of the county, who a year later began a concerted effort to remove public school texts that in any way challenged fundamentalist religious beliefs. The objectionable texts included works of literature as well as science.

Led by a first-term school board member, the campaign included a large number of residents of the coal-mining area who argued that the texts used in English and biology classes advocated sex and crime and generally violated local values. As one local activist observed, "We don't teach this at home, we don't want this at school." The protests quickly escalated. Coal miners went on strike to protest the books. Local ministers denounced the texts from their pulpits by a three-to-one majority. Threats on teachers' lives were followed by the activity of snipers who fired on school buses and state police cars escorting them. Outraged groups dynamited at least three cars, attacked school buses, and vandalized the board of education building.[22] Faced with little less than mob activity, board members attempted to respond in a reasoned fashion. They returned the books under fire to the classrooms but adopted creationist material for the entire district. More important, they announced a new policy that excused students from reading any book that their parents found objectionable on moral or religious grounds. When even these decisions failed to stem the violence, the board capitulated. They adopted new text guidelines that effectively eliminated the disputed texts and established screening committees of nonprofessionals to review future books under consideration.[23]

The state of Georgia was also attempting to come to terms with the creationist campaign. Legislative efforts to secure an equal time law led to a series of public hearings during the spring and summer of 1973. These hearings disclosed significant approval of the concept of equal time, but little support for creationist legislation. An equal time law became even less necessary, in many legislators' minds, after the State Board of Education decided in November to include *Biology: A Search for Order in Complexity* as an approved text. Recognizing fertile ground, the Institute for Creation Research presented a symposium at an Atlanta Baptist church early the following year. Featured speaker Henry M. Morris urged local creationists to organize themselves to achieve their goals. With Morris's encouragement, Atlanta area creationists formed Citizens for Another Voice in Education (CAVE). The group gained a formidable spokesman in state court of appeals judge

Braswell Deen, Jr., who later expressed his views by declaiming, "This monkey mythology of Darwin is the cause of permissiveness, promiscuity, pills, prophylactics, perversions, pregnancies, abortions, pornotherapy, pollution, poisoning and proliferation of crimes of all types."[24]

Deen and his fellow CAVE members apparently had little impact in the Atlanta area. On 17 June 1974 the Atlanta Board of Education accepted the report of its textbook committee to reject *Biology: A Search for Order in Complexity.* The report described the text as presenting "a one-sided view of the origin of life." It was, the report continued, "closer to being a religious tract than a scientific text." The committee emphasized that the text did not present both sides of the debate, as supporters of the book claimed, but only the case for divine creation. The text contained "numerous errors in terms of established biological fact" and, as one board member stated, was "poorly written and out of date."[25]

Although creationists enjoyed only mixed success in convincing education officials and legislators to adopt their materials and perspective, the increasing attention paid to their ideas indirectly advanced their cause. Paralleling the decline in the National Science Foundation programs that had led to the superior science texts of the 1960s, the creationist call for equal time alerted publishers to a potential cause of reduced sales. In an effort to keep their sales figures as high as possible, publishers in the early 1970s began to eliminate or dilute references to evolution in their biology texts. The California controversy represented the most dramatic confrontation over text phrasing, but publishers realized that people in other states had similar concerns. In Texas, one of the largest text purchasers in the nation, 80 percent of the texts used in 1975 made no mention of evolution.[26]

Decline and Fall of the Genesis Act

As the creationist campaign expanded in the mid-1970s, opponents of the teaching of evolution carefully watched events in Tennessee. Only in Tennessee had a creationist equal time bill become law. Although the legislature had attempted to modify the act in early 1974 to remove its most blatantly fundamentalist overtones, these efforts failed. The status of the law would be determined by the courts.

The passage of the Genesis Act had also aroused concern among American scientists. One of the most vocal of these scholars was John A. Moore, a biologist at the University of California, Riverside. In a lecture given at the San Francisco meeting of the American Association for the Advancement of Science in February 1974, Moore provided a succinct and reasoned response to the latest outbreak of antievolution sentiment. He argued that science teachers should probably do what the Tennessee law and the creationists demanded: Examine Genesis as a scientific hypothesis and test its accuracy based on available evidence. Despite difficulties in determining the precise meaning of the Genesis account of creation, Moore concluded that there existed several elements that could be tested. The two most important of these elements were the belief that life had always been in essentially the same form as today and that the earth and everything on it appeared less than six thousand years ago. The testable deductions from these premises were that the record of past life should show essentially the same life forms as today (which it did not) and that scientific dating methods should show that natural objects were less than six thousand years old (which they did not). The conclusions to be drawn from such an analysis were clearly not what the creationists had in mind. If one subjected Genesis to the kind of examination called for in the Tennessee law, Moore concluded, "the Genesis account is demolished from a scientific point of view."[27]

The opinions of biologists such as Moore, however, would not necessarily be the deciding factor in a court case. The three-judge panel hearing the challenge to Tennessee's law in the federal district court in Nashville knew more law than biology. Plaintiffs had argued that the act should be enjoined as unconstitutional because it violated free speech, the establishment clause, and due process. The state's attorneys rejected this view and urged the court either to dismiss the case or to abstain, pending the resolution of the similar suit in state court. On 26 February 1974 the district court accepted the state's argument for abstention, emphasizing that the state decision would be filed before the effective date of the new law. In addition, abstention did not preclude later federal review of the case. Attorneys for the plaintiffs appealed this decision to the circuit court of appeals.[28]

While the federal suit progressed toward the circuit court, Chancellor Ben H. Cantrell prepared his decision in the state court challenge to the Genesis Act. In an opinion filed 9 September 1974, the chancellor declared the act unconstitutional as an establishment of religion. Cantrell emphasized an important weakness in the bill, quite apart from constitutional problems, in the "many and varied" theories of origins. Presenting all theories of origin in a biology survey course would be "an altogether impossible task." Cantrell observed that the textbook commission would have to choose between literal compliance with the act or the exclusion of all discussions of origins from textbooks. Convinced that the commission would follow the latter option, Cantrell expressed his concern that a significant body of scientific thought would be excluded from the textbooks used in Tennessee.

From a constitutional standpoint, however, the law was even more flawed. No secular purpose could be discovered in the Genesis Act, nor had the legislature attempted to set forth such a purpose in the act itself. Singling out the Genesis account for inclusion provided even stronger evidence of the sectarian purpose behind the act. Such preference for a specific religion violated both federal and state constitutions. "The legislature is attempting to pick and choose among theories," Cantrell wrote, "excluding those which one sect deems antithetical to its religious conception of creation. The evident attempt is to serve a religious, sectarian purpose." Excluding accepted scientific explanation from the public schools could not be justified on such sectarian grounds. The Genesis Act clearly violated the separation of church and state and was little more than an attempt to establish a particular form of religion.[29]

Two months later, opponents of the Genesis Act filed their brief with the Sixth Circuit Court of Appeals in Cincinnati. Arguing that the district court abstention order should be vacated, the appellants emphasized the damage possible under the Genesis Act. Those appellants who were university faculty stressed that the act violated their right to teach future public school science teachers without teaching religion. The high school teacher who had joined the suit similarly argued that he should be able to teach biology without teaching and studying religious materials that he found repellant to his scientific discipline and to his own religious views. The National Association of Biology Teachers, also a partner in the suit, objected to the act because it would force association members to study and teach religious materials. The appellants' brief also pointed out that the law presented an "imminent" possibility of damage because selection of public school textbooks had already begun. It would be too late for relief after publishers had signed contracts to supply textbooks with equal time for creationism and evolution.[30]

The state's attorneys supported the district court abstention as their best tactic for keeping the law intact. Having appealed Cantrell's decision to the Tennessee Supreme Court, they argued that federal courts should not interfere with state policy unless it was absolutely necessary. The Genesis Act did not present such a situation. "This is a notorious case," the state's brief argued, "involving religious issues whose very decision by a federal court will create entanglement not only between church and state but between federal and state governments which is contrary to established constitutional and judicial principles."[31]

When the circuit court announced its decision on 10 April 1975, it became clear that the federal judges did not share the state's opinion. In a two-to-one decision, the court declared the Genesis Act unconstitutional as an establishment of religion. The court's opinion stressed that the 1973 law was little more than a revised version of the legislation that had led to the Scopes trial nearly a half century earlier. The law left little doubt that "the purpose of establishing the Biblical version of the creation of man is as clear in the 1973 statute as it was in the statute of 1925." The court also rejected the state's contention that abstention presented appropriate action, stressing that abstention was only justified if the state interpretation of an "ambiguous statute" might eliminate a clash with the federal Constitution. The Genesis Act was no such ambiguous statute. "We believe," the court concluded, "that in several respects the statute under consideration is unconstitutional on its face, [and] that no state court interpretation of it can save it."[32]

A closer examination of the statute itself provided significant evidence of the religious purpose of the Genesis Act. The amendment that defined the Bible as a reference work, thus excusing it from the disclaimer required of textbooks, resulted in "a clearly defined preferential position" for a specific religious explanation of creation. Attempting to enforce such preference by law represented "the very establishment of religion which the First Amendment to the Constitution of the United States squarely forbids." The section of the Tennessee law dealing with occult or satanic beliefs also presented difficulties. It would be impossible for the state textbook commission to determine what beliefs were satanic or occult without entering deeply into theological arguments of long standing. Not only would this lead to the "excessive entanglement" prohibited under the *Lemon v. Kurtzman* test, but it also represented another example of "preferential treatment of particular faiths by state law," which was "forbidden by the Establishment Clause of the First Amendment." Having dispensed with the Genesis Act as a clear attempt to establish religion, the circuit court chose not to determine the issues of vagueness, free speech, and freedom of the press.[33]

The circuit court decision in *Daniel v. Waters* proved to be the end of the Genesis Act. Refusing to appeal the decision, the state abandoned hope of maintaining the statute. On 20 August 1975 both the Tennessee Supreme Court and the United States District Court concurred in finding the law unconstitutional, using the reasoning of the circuit court.

One of the district court judges also observed that the requirement of equal time for all creation theories was "patently unreasonable."[34] At the legislative level, at least, the creationist crusade had again stalled.

The Creationists Regroup

The overt religious purpose of Tennessee's Genesis Act had been clear to the jurists who examined the law between 1973 and 1975. By giving preferential treatment to the Bible and discriminating against "occult or satanical beliefs"—whatever that phrase might have meant—Tennessee legislators had clearly attempted to achieve the same goal as their political forebears of the 1920s. Nothing less than the replacement of evolutionary concepts in public education with ideas compatible with Protestant fundamentalism would satisfy these lawmakers. The courts found this effort unconstitutional as an attempt to establish religion.

Creationists, however, remained enthusiastic about the ultimate success of their new antievolution campaign. The more perceptive of them admitted, at least in private, that the Tennessee legislative effort had been flawed from the outset. Interpreting the courts' comments about the unwarranted religious nature of the law in a unique fashion, creationists believed that more careful drafting of state statutes would eliminate the constitutional objections. Eliminating specific references to the Bible or to God would endow such legislation with a secular purpose, while more carefully written prohibitions against non-Christian creationist ideas would remove another flaw used by the courts to kill equal time laws. The courts' decisions represented little more than tactical setbacks, which could be overcome through greater care and effort.[35]

Achieving public support for their campaign also remained an important part of the creationist crusade. Creationist authors increased their efforts to convert the population to their beliefs, producing two major volumes in 1975 as well as numerous articles and pamphlets. Henry M. Morris completed another discussion of the evidences for Genesis, again devoting most of his considerable energies to supposed weaknesses in the theory of evolution. His religious ally, the Reverend Tim LaHaye, contributed a preface to Morris's *The Troubled Waters of Evolution*, praising the book for defining the theory of evolution as the basis for contemporary secular thought and "the platform from which socialism, communism, humanism, determinism, and one-worldism have been launched."[36]

Although agreeing with his colleague's view, Morris focused his attention on scientific topics, repeating many charges made earlier. He informed his readers early in the volume that an increasing number of future scientists were embracing creationism. "The evolutionary 'establishment' is becoming alarmed," he wrote, "as multitudes of disillusioned youth are recoiling from the precipice of animalistic amoralism and survival-of-the-fittest philosophy to which two generations of evolutionary indoctrination had led them." Morris repeated such creationist dogma as the irrelevance of observed change in species, emphasizing that species had not changed into dramatically new ones. He again devoted significant space to a discussion of the Second Law of Thermodynamics, arguing that the concept of entropy made evolution impossible. The primeval disorder described by evolutionists could only have been converted to the existing "infinitely-complex ordered structure of the universe" by a "program" of some description. The source of this program, for Morris, could only be "an infinitely-capable Programmer!" Attempting to deflect evolutionists' arguments that the Second Law did not apply to the terrestrial biosphere because the earth represented an open system, Morris again reverted to hyperbole to convince his readers. Referring to this argument as "exceedingly naive," Morris wrote: "It should be self-evident that the mere existence of an open system of some kind, with access to the sun's energy, does not of itself generate growth. The sun's energy may bathe the site of an automobile junk yard for a million years, but it will never cause the rusted, broken parts to grow together again into a functioning automobile."[37] Morris had not lost his ability to construct dramatic, if irrelevant, metaphors.

From the more politically oriented wing of the creationist crusade came a volume coauthored by Robert E. Kofahl and Kelly L. Segraves. The authors stated in their preface that the purpose of *The Creation Explanation: A Scientific Alternative to Evolution* was to correct the many misconceptions the public held concerning evolution and creation. Repeating the charge that neither evolution nor creation was science, the authors emphasized that they wished to provide individuals untrained in science with the "pertinent facts and concepts" concerning these topics.[38] Their underlying goal, however, emerged in the concluding paragraphs of their preface. Having characterized the theory of evolution as untrustworthy, the authors asked,

> Is there, then, any source of *absolute* knowledge? There can be only one, God Himself, disclosed in divine revelation. And this is what the Bible claims to be, divine revelation. The authors of *The Creation Explanation* accept the claim of the Bible to be the Word of God. They accept the opening chapters of Genesis, therefore, to be true to scientific fact. This is

their fundamental postulate and they make no apology for it. They do not claim to 'prove' creation by means of science, although the Bible says that the evidence to be found in nature for the real existence of a personal God is conclusive, rendering all men everywhere accountable to God (Romans 1:19,20).[39]

The "scientific" objections to the theory of evolution offered little new ammunition for the creationist arsenal. Calculations that led to estimates of a great age for the earth were dismissed as "circumstantial" and based on "evolutionary, materialistic philosophical principles." Attempting to deal with the obvious problem presented by stars that were ten billion light years away, given a ten-thousand-year age of the earth, Kofahl and Segraves offered several possible explanations, including inaccuracies in the astronomical distance scales and the possibility that the speed of light did not represent a constant. They supported this latter concept by suggesting that Einsteinian relativity had been "under strong criticism" recently. Kofahl and Segraves also repeated anti-evolution arguments based on entropy and gaps in the fossil record, dismissing all evidence for uniformitarianism and arguing for biblical catastrophism as the only logical alternative.[40]

The truly remarkable aspect of *The Creation Explanation* lay in its overt religiosity. The authors made no attempt to develop a "scientific" creationism. Instead, they integrated biblical references and quotations throughout the volume. Offering evidences of design in nature, Kofahl and Segraves described such evidence as pointing "unmistakably" to an all wise and all powerful designer and creator. The characteristics of water that made terrestrial life possible showed the "purposeful design" of the earth and solar system. The ability of ice to float guaranteed the accessibility of water to the living world by keeping liquid water available below the surface. This property of ice was easily explained. Ice floats, the authors opined, "because the Creator designed it that way, and when the snow and ice come, we can enjoy them (sometimes) because we know they will melt in the springtime."[41]

Scientific concepts used by evolutionists to support their views were similarly reinterpreted by the authors to support creationism. Molecular genetics emerged as nothing more than the "structures and designs by which the Creator carries out His purposes" in the biological world. The authors cited studies of high surface temperatures on Venus as evidence for a recent origin of the planet, as Venus had not had sufficient time to cool. Kofahl and Segraves even used subatomic physics to support their beliefs. Applauding the success of physicists in "relating the design of different atomic nuclei to their actual physical properties," the authors informed their readers that the "wisdom and plan of the Creator is discovered in the tiny nucleus at the center of the submicroscopic atom."[42]

Having spent most of their volume discrediting evolution, Kofahl and Segraves concluded their work by emphasizing that the reader had to make the choice between creation and evolution. The authors had no doubt about which "model" was superior. The "evidence for intelligent, purposeful design" permeated every aspect of the universe. Accepting this evidence would lead the reader to the "biblical faith" that produced "full confidence in the entire Bible as the Word of God, including the Genesis record of creation." Such faith would "redeem an individual or a nation from the destructive effects of the evolutionary faith" and could "give value and meaning to an otherwise meaningless universe and blessed fulfillment to an otherwise empty life."[43] In few examples from the massive creationist literature was the religious agenda more clearly stated.

Despite their many activities, creationists enjoyed only mixed success during the mid-1970s. Legislatures in Texas, Washington, Michigan, Indiana, and South Carolina considered various equal time bills, but all these efforts died in committee. State and local textbook boards, on the other hand, appeared to be sympathetic to arguments for equal time. Idaho and Indiana both approved the creationist text *Biology: A Search for Order in Complexity* for local adoption.[44] In Texas, the trustees of the Dallas Independent School District voted six to three in late January 1977 to approve the text for supplemental use. They decided to purchase sixty copies to place in biology classrooms in the district for use as a research source. The trustees also established training sessions for biology teachers during the summer, so that they would be able to use the new material appropriately. Board president Bill Hunter told a New York *Times* reporter that he personally favored using the creationist volume as the primary biology text, but it had not been included on the state list of approved materials. He supported the text because it "recognizes that both evolution and creation are philosophical concepts or theories, and that science needs to present the facts and let the people make their own conclusions."[45] The equal time concept was clearly gaining ground.

A more significant development took place in Indiana. Because the state textbook commission had placed *Biology: A Search for Order in Complexity* on the approved list, local school districts were free to use this volume as the only text in their biology classes. Although most districts rejected the creationist tome, the West Clark Community Schools adopted the text in the spring of 1976 as the sole biology book for the schools of the community. The Indiana Civil Liberties Union quickly challenged the West Clark decision and worked throughout the fall and winter to reach a compromise. By February 1977 it had become clear that no compromise was possible, leading the ICLU to file suit in an Indianapolis court. The complaint charged that state and local officials had attempted to establish religion by adopting a sectarian textbook. The court referred the complaint to the textbook commission for an administrative hearing, but despite the testimony of scientists who emphasized the invalidity of creationism, the commission upheld its original ruling. The ICLU thus went back to court, charging that the state textbook commission had violated the establishment clause and state laws requiring that texts be nonsectarian.[46]

Superior court judge Michael T. Dugan found the ICLU's arguments convincing. He announced his decision in the *Hendren v. Campbell* case in April, rejecting any use of the creationist text in public school classrooms. The text only presented the biblical view of creation, he argued, thus violating constitutional prohibitions against the advancement of a specific religious outlook. The purpose of the text was clearly "the promotion and inclusion of fundamentalist Christian doctrine in the public schools." Adopting the text also violated the separation of church and state. "The prospect of biology teachers and students alike," he wrote in his opinion, "forced to answer and respond to continued demand for correct fundamentalist Christian doctrines has no place in the public schools." Dugan's decision had an immediate effect. Although the West Clark schools kept the text in classrooms as supplementary material, the state textbook commission dropped the volume from the approved list without appealing Dugan's decision. The Indiana case also had an impact on events in Dallas. Reinforced by the election of new board members the same month, the *Hendren* decision convinced the Dallas school board to remove the creationist text from classrooms and place copies in school libraries only.[47]

A year after the *Hendren* decision, the creationist campaign broadened its target to include the Smithsonian Institution. Congress had recently appropriated nearly five hundred thousand dollars for a new exhibit at the Museum of Natural History entitled Dynamics of Evolution. Dale Crowley, Jr., a retired missionary and executive director of the conservative National Foundation for Fairness in Education, viewed this new exhibit as yet another example of the secular drift in American society and government. Filing suit in the federal district court for the District of Columbia on 11 April 1978, Crowley argued that the Smithsonian Institution was attempting to use public money to establish the religion of secular humanism. Such action, in Crowley's view, clearly violated the mandated religious neutrality of the federal government. The Smithsonian's evolution exhibit also violated the rights of fundamentalists to exercise their religion freely. Such believers had to choose between violating their religious beliefs by entering the museum or forsaking their right of access to public property. The only solution to this problem, according to Crowley's suit, was a judicial prohibition against the proposed exhibit or an order that the Smithsonian devote equal space and money to an exhibit discussing the biblical account of creation.[48]

District judge Barrington D. Parker proved unsympathetic to Crowley's ideas. In a decision announced on 11 December 1978, Parker rejected the contention that the Smithsonian should give equal time to the biblical account of creation. He stressed that the proposed exhibit was well within the Smithsonian's statutory authority, as it was "wholly secular" and directed toward people who chose to enter the Museum of Natural History. The plaintiffs' contention that an exhibit about evolution attempted to establish the religion of "secular humanism" was seriously flawed because the Smithsonian treated evolution as a subject of natural history, not religion. Similarly, Parker argued, the museum had not restricted the plaintiffs' free religious exercise. "The plaintiffs can carry their beliefs into the Museum with them," Parker wrote, "though they risk seeing science exhibits contrary to that faith." To provide the relief requested in Crowley's suit, the judge concluded, would violate the establishment clause, as shown in the *Epperson v. Arkansas* and *Daniel v. Waters* decisions.[49]

In an interview with a New York *Times* reporter shortly after the court's decision, Crowley vowed that he would appeal. "I object to the idea that my children go through this museum," he said, "and are indoctrinated in sheer speculation presented as fact." While Crowley and his attorneys drafted their appeal, the controversial exhibit nonetheless opened in mid-May 1979, bringing yet another public blast from Crowley. He told a reporter, "When millions of people go into the Smithsonian Institution and see displays on evolution, they automatically think that what they're seeing is a scientific fact. I mean, that's the psychological advantage the evolutionists have got." The United States Circuit Court for the District of Columbia proved no more sympathetic to Crowley's contention than had Judge Parker. Announcing their decision in 1980, the circuit court stressed that the case required balancing the creationists' rights to believe in creation and the public's right to receive knowledge from the government through schools and other institutions. "This balance was long ago struck," the court concluded, "in favor of diffusion of knowledge based on responsible scientific foundations, and against special constitutional protection of religious believers from the competition generated by such knowledge diffusion.'' The Supreme Court refused to review the case.[50]

The courts' decisions failed to end the controversy generated by the Smithsonian exhibit. During the fall of 1981 Republican representative William E. Dannemeyer urged Congress to review the Dynamics of Evolution exhibit and to limit funding if, as he believed, the exhibit was promoting the religion of secular humanism. Quoting such creationist figures as Duane T. Gish, Dannemeyer argued that much evidence existed to challenge the theory of evolution. Such evidence led him to conclude that evolution represented a religion and that his proposed legislation would guarantee that federal money would not be used to promote this religion.[51] Although Dannemeyer's bill did not gain significant support, the identification of evolution with the supposed religion of secular humanism proved to be a crucial part of the creationist campaign. Convinced that the secularization of American society had destroyed the foundation of the moral order, political and religious conservatives prepared for the next battle in their war to reclaim the nation.

9
The Creationist Challenge

Because they believed that the teaching of evolution underlay the humanistic trends visible throughout American society, creationists emerged as an important element of the increasingly conservative evangelical population. Committed to an activist agenda designed to rescue the nation from the secularist drift they perceived, these opponents of humanism soon became involved in virtually every arena of American public life. Political, legal, constitutional, and religious concerns merged together into a far-reaching campaign to restore traditional values to society. The creationist crusade was now part of a much larger movement.

Secular Humanism and the Establishment Clause

Secular humanism had become a convenient symbol of the dangers perceived by the growing conservatism of the late 1970s. Although religious and political conservatives defined humanism in many different ways, they generally described it as representing a philosophy that rejected traditional Christian beliefs concerning society and the individual's place in it. A typical conservative definition of secular humanism was distributed by Educational Research Analysts, the organization founded by Mel and Norma Gabler to monitor American textbooks for liberal bias. Characterizing this philosophy as "faith in man instead of faith in God," the Gablers described the tenets of humanism as situation ethics, evolution, sexual freedom, and internationalism. More disturbing to these self-appointed textbook critics was the impact of humanistic perspectives on public education. Because humanism recognized "no higher being to which man is responsible," educators focused on the self-image of students. "This eliminates coming to Christ for forgiveness of sin," the Gablers warned. "It eliminates the Christian attributes of meekness and humility."[1] Thus defined, humanism clearly challenged the traditional fundamentalist perspective embraced by most creationists.

A more detailed study of humanism appeared in a long *Texas Tech Law Review* article written by creationist attorney John W. Whitehead and Arizona congressman John Conlan. Observing that the purpose of secular humanism was the elimination of traditional theism from national life, the authors attempted to show that humanism nonetheless represented a faith that must be held to the same constitutional restrictions as any organized religion. Like many conservatives, Whitehead and Conlan blamed the American courts for increased hostility toward traditional religion during the post–World War II decades. Federal courts had diversified and broadened the definition of religion significantly, so that by the late 1960s judges viewed the "sustenance of belief—belief in and obligation owed to the 'Creator' " as less important than "the *impact* of the belief on the *life* of the person expressing and holding it." This change in the definition of religion was part of a broader shift in American life. "Society's basis of truth was shifting from traditional theism's emphasis on God-centeredness," the authors observed, "to Secular Humanism's emphasis on man-centeredness," leading to a rejection of absolutes. Focusing on a footnote to the 1961 Supreme Court decision in *Torcaso v. Watkins,* the authors supported their contention by citing the Court's definition of secular humanism as a belief system that did not adhere to traditional theism.[2]

Whitehead and Conlan rejected the concept of "belief-as-religion" inherent in various court decisions. This concept had allowed secular humanism to invade the public schools and establish a nontheistic foundation for American education. Yet the authors found in this situation a hopeful sign for conservatism in general and creationism in particular. If, indeed, secular humanism represented a religion—because it was a belief—then surely the First Amendment prohibition against establishment of religion applied to humanism as to any other religion. The authors viewed science, especially evolution, as the intellectual foundation of humanism, arguing that humanists accepted science as both a "guide to human progress" and the source of "an alternative to both religion and morals." As a result, science assumed "a religious character" and represented a dangerous "threat of totalitarianism." Evolution was the most religious aspect of science, because evolutionists obviously accepted the theory on faith owing to the lack of available "proof." Thus, any philosophy based on such concepts must represent religion. The situation in the United States constituted nothing less than an attempt to impose a state order based on the religion of secular humanism. This totalitarian drift, as defined by Whitehead and Conlan, could only be stopped by the recognition of humanism as a religion and the application of First Amendment prohibitions to that religion.[3]

The battlefield of the war against secular humanism would, of course, be the nation's public schools. If secular humanism was a new religion that had taken over the schools, the establishment clause of the First Amendment could be seen as a powerful weapon to use against the new order. Yale law student Wendell R. Bird, who would later become the nation's leading creationist attorney, devoted his prize-winning student note in the January 1978 *Yale Law Journal* to this perspective. Based heavily on creationist writings, Bird's essay attempted to provide a legal justification for a "neutral" curriculum based on the concept of equal time. He defended this solution by stressing the scientific validity of creation science and the weaknesses in the theory of evolution. Both required a degree of "faith" to accept and offered equally good "models." They should, therefore, be equally presented in the public schools.[4]

The current exclusive presentation of evolution, in contrast, represented an unwarranted violation of students' free exercise of religion. Such teaching undermined the religious convictions of creationist students and compelled them to make "unconscionable declarations of belief" in evolution or suffer the consequences of poor grades, peer pressure, and other penalties. This problem proved particularly acute in elementary and secondary classrooms, where students' beliefs and ideas were frequently changed under the influence of teachers. Exclusion of students from such classes failed to provide a suitable remedy, as peer pressure and the "coercive effects of influence from teachers" could not be overcome by absence from class during discussions of evolution. The only solution was the inclusion of creation science in the biology curriculum.[5]

Bird emphasized that including creation science would not represent an establishment of religion. Stressing that sound scientific evidence existed to support creation, as opposed to evolution, Bird dismissed as coincidental that certain religious beliefs were compatible with creation science. After all, he argued, evolutionary ideas could be found in various religions as well. Nor would such teaching violate the free exercise of religion by noncreationist students. A course presenting both "models" would infringe upon the rights of neither creationists nor noncreationists. "Each would confront alternate nonreligious viewpoints," he concluded, "rather than an exclusive state-endorsed perspective on the origin of the world and life."[6]

The legalistic perspective embraced by Bird, Whitehead, and Conlan focused on the establishment clause as protection against the exclusive instruction in organic evolution and its philosophical offspring, secular humanism. The development of this perspective required a specific interpretation of the establishment clause that stood in marked contrast to existing judicial opinion. Creationists and other opponents of secular humanism embraced the "nonpreferentialist" interpretation of the opening clause of the First Amendment. Whitehead and Conlan had argued in their 1978 essay that the framers of the Bill of Rights had not meant to establish a complete separation between church and state in America, as the "predominantly Christian orientation" of the nation made such separation impossible. Bird put forth a similar argument in a 1979 essay by stressing that the historical intent of the establishment clause "was to require governmental neutrality between religions; the intent was not to create an absolute wall of separation between church and state." The interpretation that the clause only prevented the government from instituting a preference for one religion over another, however, had been rejected by the United States Supreme Court for more than thirty years. In the 1947 case *Everson v. Board of Education*, the justices argued that the clause prohibited government aid to one religion at the expense of another or to religion generally. A law "respecting" an establishment of religion included far more than the overt act of a government creating a state church.[7]

In rejecting the "wall of separation" doctrine, nonpreferentialists ignored both history and judicial opinion. Although preferential establishments of religion had been widespread before the American Revolution, this practice disappeared during the late 1770s and early 1780s, to be replaced by the concept of multiple or nonpreferential establishments. Such establishments, however, troubled the delegates to the Constitutional Convention of 1787, who believed that Congress had no authority at all concerning religion. The accepted lack of congressional authority on religious matters also provided the foundation for debates concerning the Bill of Rights. James Madison and Roger Sherman argued during the debates in the House of Representatives that an amendment prohibiting religious establishment was unnecessary, as Congress had no constitutional authority to establish religion. Madison ultimately supported the establishment clause of the First Amendment for political reasons, as there existed significant public demand for an explicit statement outlawing establishment. Although originally proposing a nonpreferentialist version of the amendment, the Senate ultimately accepted their colleagues' arguments that Congress had no authority over religion. Congress had thus considered and specifically rejected the nonpreferentialist perspective. As constitutional scholar Leonard W.

Levy emphasized in 1986, interpreting the establishment clause as prohibiting only the preferential aid to religion leads to the illogical conclusion that the clause was designed to increase congressional power. This conclusion would contrast sharply with the limitation of congressional power inherent in the other portions of the Bill of Rights.[8]

Support for the hands-off interpretation of the establishment clause was widespread. In his famous letter to the Baptist Association of Danbury, Connecticut, in 1802, Thomas Jefferson praised the clause by writing, "I contemplate with sovereign reverence that act of the whole American people which declared that their legislature should 'make no law respecting an establishment of religion, or prohibiting the free exercise thereof,' thus building a wall of separation between church and state." Madison took the clause so seriously that, as president, he thought it also banned presidential proclamations of thanksgiving, tax exemptions for churches, and chaplains for the military and Congress. After leaving the White House, Madison observed that "religion and government will both exist in greater purity, the less they are mixed together."[9]

The impact of the establishment clause was expanded during the second quarter of the twentieth century with the development of the incorporation doctrine, which argued that the due process clause of the Fourteenth Amendment extended the Bill of Rights limitations to states. Supported by even the most conservative Supreme Court justices, this doctrine was specifically extended to the establishment clause in the *Everson* decision. The Court reaffirmed this interpretation in the *Abington* case of 1963 by overturning state laws that required daily Bible reading in public school classrooms. By a vote of eight to one, the justices stressed that any government sponsorship of religion violated the establishment clause. Eight years later, Chief Justice Warren Burger wrote for another eight-member majority that the clause meant far more than the mere prohibition of a state church. In formulating the three-part test of *Lemon v. Kurtzman,* moreover, Burger attempted to provide stronger bricks for the wall of separation.[10]

Although Supreme Court decisions concerning the establishment clause have been less than consistent—state-supplied buses and texts for parochial schools have been approved, while brief prayers have been outlawed—the Court has generally adhered to the concept of the wall of separation, with the height and strength of the wall dependent on one's philosophical perspective. At the very least, the Court has rejected the limited interpretation of the clause advocated by the nonpreferentialists. Given the historical background of the First Amendment, a broad in-

terpretation of the establishment clause remains closest to the original
intent of the framers of the Bill of Rights.

The Campaign for Equal Time

For the opponents of evolution, however, the nonpreferentialist viewpoint offered a foundation for the equal time concept. After graduation
from Yale Law School, Wendell Bird joined the Institute for Creation
Research as legal adviser. He quickly began to incorporate the main
points of his *Yale Law Journal* article into the model equal time resolution originally drafted by Henry M. Morris in the early 1970s. Repeating his charges that creationism was as scientific as evolution and
evolution was as religious as creationism, Bird's four-page resolution
appeared in the May 1979 issue of the institute's *Impact* series. The
"Resolution for Balanced Presentation of Evolution and Scientific Creationism" was introduced by an editorial that stressed that the document should only be used as a resolution for local school boards, not as
a model for legislation. The goal of the resolution was public education. Creationists desired to institutionalize the popular support that
they insisted favored balanced treatment. Bird and others found encouragement in a 1979 Gallup poll indicating that half of the American population believed in the literal divine creation of Adam and Eve to begin
the human race.[11]

Despite the insistence by Morris and other creationist leaders that
Bird's resolution was aimed at local school boards, other antievolutionists failed to accept the distinction. Among the most active of these individuals was Paul Ellwanger, later described by Henry Morris as an
"active and concerned Roman Catholic layman" from South Carolina.
In 1978 Ellwanger founded the Citizens for Fairness in Education.
Upon receiving a copy of the Bird resolution, he quickly modified the
document to serve as a draft bill to legislate the two-model approach.
The "clarifications" and "findings of fact" included in the Ellwanger
bill came almost verbatim from the *Impact* document, as did the phrasing of other parts of the proposed legislation. Although the bill failed in
the South Carolina legislature, within little more than a year similar
bills had been introduced into the legislatures of eight states.[12]

In addition to developing strategies to influence school boards and
legislatures, creationists continued to publish expositions of their scientific ideas. Among the most important of these was a public school
edition of Duane T. Gish's earlier volume *Evolution? The Fossils Say
NO!* published in 1978 by Creation-Life Publishers. In his preface,

Henry Morris applauded his colleague's work by describing the volume as "one of the most devastating critiques of the evolutionary philosophy one could find." Gish's arguments, according to Morris, led clearly to the conclusion that anyone who continued to accept evolution "must at least acknowledge that he *believes* in evolution in *spite* of the massive witness of the fossil record *against* it!"[13] Such comments fitted nicely into the creationist effort to define evolution as a religion requiring significant faith.

Gish's discussion repeated traditional creationist arguments against evolution, while insisting that creationism did not represent a religious doctrine. The public school edition of this volume, however, failed to present a nonreligious perspective. Attempting to show the secular nature of his philosophy, Gish wrote in the first chapter that creationism "postulates that all basic animal and plant types (the created kinds) were brought into existence by acts of a supernatural Creator using special processes which are not operative today." He later observed that humanity could not know the details of creation, because the "Creator" used processes that no longer operated in the universe. "We cannot discover by scientific investigations," Gish concluded, "anything about the creative processes used by the Creator."[14] Because he used "Creator" instead of "God," Gish evidently believed that he had avoided a religious concept.

Gish also attacked evolution as a belief system. Most scientists accepted evolution, he suggested, because they preferred a materialistic/naturalistic explanation for the origin of life, despite the evidence to the contrary. Such a preference did not surprise Gish, as he defined the nontheistic outlook based on evolution as "our unofficial state-sanctioned religion" taught throughout the public education system. This "faith" was clearly expressed in the scientific ideas used to support evolution. After a brief, oversimplified, and rather scoffing account of the "big bang" theory of astronomy, Gish concluded that this theory explained human life as "due solely to the properties inherent in electrons, protons, and neutrons. To believe *this*," he continued, "obviously requires a tremendous exercise of faith. Evolution theory is indeed no less religious nor more scientific than creation." Teaching only evolution represented nothing less than "indoctrination in a religious philosophy" that violated guarantees of church-state separation.[15] If scientists continued to support evolution, they did so for religious and philosophical reasons only.

Bolstered by the availability of model resolutions and legislation, as well as by the growing supply of creationist publications, antievolutionists expanded their efforts as the decade of the 1970s came to a close.

Legislatures in nearly a dozen states considered equal time laws during the 1979-80 sessions. In Florida, unsuccessful companion bills were introduced into both houses in late 1979. The author of the House of Representatives bill, Fort Lauderdale Democrat Tom Bush, defended this legislation by telling a New York *Times* reporter, "We're not trying to teach Genesis in the schools but rather an alternative theory of creation. Evolution is being taught as an unquestioned fact of science, and that's just not true." To the north, Georgia found itself involved in yet another creationist campaign when a bill virtually identical to earlier legislation appeared in 1979. Eventually reaching a special subcommittee of the House Education Committee, the bill underwent intense scrutiny. The subcommittee's report, issued in early 1980, stressed the benefits to the Institute for Creation Research should the proposed legislation pass. The Georgia Department of Education estimated that nearly five million dollars would be required to implement the law, with almost two million dollars earmarked for textbook purchases. As the ICR remained the sole supplier of such texts, the Georgia bill potentially offered a windfall for the creationist organization. Kept in committee for most of the session, the bill came to the floor too late in the session for passage. A similar equal time bill passed both the Senate and the House during the 1980 session, but conference committee members proved unable to resolve their differences before adjournment.[16]

The creationist movement targeted the Midwest in the late 1970s, precipitating a major conflict over the teaching of evolution in Iowa. Creationism claimed significant support in the state, having gained many allies on the campus of Iowa State University. Dean of Engineering David Boylan served on the advisory board of the Institute for Creation Research, while several other faculty members advocated creation science at the local level. Student interest in the topic soon led to the formation of a creationist organization called Students for Origins Research. Such developments encouraged Iowa creationists, who organized meetings throughout the state to consolidate their position.

Despite opposition to the equal time concept from the state's leading newspaper, the Des Moines *Register,* sufficient support had emerged by February 1979 to convince a dozen state senators to introduce an equal time bill. The proposed statute stated, "Whenever the origin of man or the origin of the earth is alluded to or taught in the educational program of public schools of this state, the concept of creation as supported by scientific evidence shall be taught as one theory." Republican senator John W. Jensen, a Baptist cattle grower who served as chief sponsor of the bill, emphasized in his public comments that evolutionary theory had no scientific validity. "We're raising better cattle than we used to," the *Wall Street Journal* quoted him as saying. "But when we cross cattle, we get cattle. We don't get a dog."[17]

The introduction of the equal time bill precipitated widespread opposition on several fronts. Some legislators were concerned about the cost of implementing such a law, especially when the Department of Public Instruction estimated that more than six million dollars would be necessary to put the equal time concept into practice. More damaging was the carefully coordinated opposition of scientists and science educators in Iowa, who lobbied legislators to defeat the bill. The Iowa Academy of Science, for example, adopted a statement in April 1979 that described creationism as "not science but 'religious' metaphor clothed as 'scientific' fact." Emphasizing that evolution enjoyed "overwhelming acceptance" among scientists of all disciplines, the academy's resolution concluded by stating that Iowa students deserved legitimate science instruction. "We fully respect the religious views of all persons," the academy asserted, "but we object to attempts to require any religious teachings in science." The continued opposition of the Des Moines *Register* and the statements of Governor Robert D. Ray criticizing the proposed legislative mandate to teach creationism further weakened the creationist position. After an Education Committee hearing in which anticreationist testimony carried the day, senators referred the bill to the Finance Committee, where it died.[18]

The creationists' failure to achieve success at the state level, through either legislation or judicial rulings, represented only one aspect of their campaign. At the local level in various states, creationists had achieved many of their goals by the late 1970s. Despite the legislature's rejection of creationist arguments, students in Cedar Falls, Iowa, learned about creationism in their seventh-grade science classes. In an approach approved by students and parents alike, a junior high school science teacher devoted one week to the origin of earth in his class, half of which examined evolution and half of which discussed creationism. The teacher accepted the latter as the best explanation. Another teacher at the Cedar Falls junior high school told a *Wall Street Journal* reporter, "If you're going to go by the evidence that exists, Creation is the only thing you can believe. I'm a show-me guy, and I've been shown." A similar situation existed in Lemmon, South Dakota, where the only biology teacher in the city's high school taught the Genesis account as an alternative to evolution. Repeating charges common in the antievolution crusades of the past, teacher W. Lloyd Dale, who was also a Baptist pastor, stated: "I maintain that if you teach a kid that he's an animal and that his behavior is based on his environment, then he's going to act like an animal. I'm convinced that the problems we have in America, and especially in the public schools in terms of dissonance and rebellion and disobedience and juvenile delinquency, are directly related to the concept of evolution."[19]

Opposition to creationism was also making headway at the local level. In the fall of 1979 creationists approached the Lexington, Kentucky, school board to demand the equal presentation of creation and evolution. University of Kentucky anthropologist Eugenie Scott quickly organized an opposition group that included university scientists, religious leaders, teachers, and parents to counter the creationist drive. Such organized opposition proved effective in convincing the school board to deny the creationists' request. As Scott explained a few years later, "We won, I think, because we outhustled the creationists, presented a more organized discussion, and appeared to have a large number of individuals supporting us."[20]

While Scott opposed Kentucky creationists, antievolutionists in Cobb County, Georgia, an Atlanta suburb, convinced the local school board to approve an equal time resolution supposedly written by board member John McClure. The board soon discovered that the resolution was actually one of the ICR drafts published by Henry Morris, thus removing any belief that the document represented an expression of local sentiment. The board also expressed its displeasure with the expenditure of some eight thousand dollars for creationist material, all of which came from the Institute for Creation Research. The board thus voted five to two to rescind its directive to teach creationism along with evolution. This decision proved to be only a partial victory for anticreationists; the board also voted to allow students to ignore the biology requirement for high school graduation if they had religious objections to evolution.[21]

Flood Tide of Creation Science

As the decade of the 1980s began, the creationist movement appeared on the brink of major success. Institutionally, the movement had spawned a wide variety of organizations devoted to the creationist cause. Older groups such as the Creation Research Society, the Creation Science Research Center, and the Bible-Science Association added members in significant numbers. They were soon joined by the National Educators Fellowship in Pasadena, California, and the Creation Social Science and Humanities Society of Wichita, Kansas. This latter group, patterned on the Creation Research Society, attempted to provide a creationist perspective for fields outside the natural sciences.

As Henry Morris commented in 1984, such an emphasis was crucial, "for evolutionary humanism today dominates the humanities and social sciences even more, if possible, than it does the natural sciences." Equally important, these fields would be greatly improved through the application of the creationist perspective. The society's journal, *Creation Social Science and Humanities Quarterly,* attracted much interest and claimed over six hundred subscribers within a few years.[22]

Creation science, however, still had its organizational focus in San Diego. Continuing the division marked out in the 1970s, the Creation Science Research Center emphasized political activities and the publication of such materials as *The Handy-Dandy Evolution Refuter.* The edifice surrounding the Institute for Creation Research, however, remained the intellectual center of the movement. Christian Heritage College had grown to an enrollment of nearly five hundred and represented the academic focal point of the multi-million-dollar Scott Memorial Baptist Church complex, which included two high schools and four grammar schools. The college was presided over by the Reverend Tim LaHaye, leader of Californians for a Biblical Majority and a close friend of the Reverend Jerry Falwell. An active lecturer and writer, LaHaye emphasized the infiltration of secular humanism into all areas of American life. In 1980 he had completed his book *The Battle for the Mind* and was at work on his next volume, *The Battle for the Public Schools.*[23]

The staff of the Institute for Creation Research now included several individuals with graduate degrees in engineering and science education. The ICR's leading science educators were Gary E. Parker and Richard B. Bliss, who held science education doctorates from Ball State University and the University of Sarasota, respectively. In 1980 the institute separated from Christian Heritage College to form a graduate school to supply creationist teachers at every level. Realizing that regional accreditation for a creationist graduate school was unlikely, Morris took advantage of a special state provision that allowed unaccredited schools to operate under the Office of Private Post-Secondary Education. Once approval was secured in June 1981, the ICR Graduate School quickly instituted its programs in astro-geophysics, biology, geology, and science education. Students and faculty alike were expected to adhere to the official ICR educational philosophy. The statement of this philosophy informed students that the institute "bases its educational philosophy on the foundational truth of a personal Creator-God and His authoritative and unique revelation of truth in the Bible, both Old and New Testaments." Although the statement drew a distinction between scientific and biblical creationism, it also stressed that the two were compatible, as "all genuine facts of science support the Bible." The special and supernatural creation of the universe and life by a creator represented one of the major tenets of creationism included in the philosophy statement, as did the emphasis on a recent creation of the earth and geological catastrophism. Students who enrolled in the ICR Graduate School could be confident that the "highly qualified and experienced faculty" would provide a sound education that would equip them "both for productive careers in their chosen fields and for making a significant contribution to the ongoing worldwide revival of theistic creationism."[24]

As the 1980s dawned, creationists benefited from increased media attention. Already aware of the growing conservatism in the nation, evidenced by Falwell's Moral Majority and a distinct shift to the right in American politics, national media began to investigate the creationist movement with greater interest.[25] As a result of the increased visibility of scientific creationism, the beginning of the new decade witnessed a dramatic growth in attempts to secure legislation favorable to the creationist campaign. By the spring of 1981 fourteen states had considered equal time legislation based on the Ellwanger draft bill. Although unwilling to enact such laws, legislators found it difficult to ignore the pleadings of Ellwanger's Citizens for Fairness in Education, described by the group's founder as "a citizen group, national in scope, who favor academic freedom and are opposed to suppression of information about evolution and creation." The model bill distributed to legislators around the nation required the "balanced treatment" of evolution and creation, the presentation of both models as nonreligious ideas, and the end to discrimination against students who believed in either concept. In an effort to strengthen the legislation, Ellwanger's draft bill included a section entitled "Legislative Findings of Fact," which attempted to protect creationist assumptions from later challenges. By giving these assumptions a legislative imprimatur, Ellwanger hoped to take advantage of jurists' unwillingness to delve too deeply into the agenda behind legislation. Although courts had examined the purpose behind antievolution laws in both the *Epperson v. Arkansas* and *Daniel v. Waters* cases, such examination remained an unusual activity of the judiciary.[26]

Despite the care used to draft the model bill for state legislatures, Ellwanger's balanced treatment law struck legislators and anticreationists as vague, contrary to accepted concepts of academic freedom, and tainted by many religious concepts. Ellwanger modified his draft in late 1980 to remove many of the most-cited weaknesses. He called his new proposal the "Unbiased Presentation of Creation-Science and Evolution-Science Bill," explaining to *Science* writer Roger Lewin that he had designed the new title to be "crisper and to reflect more immediately what our objective is. Liberals have objected to bias in education," he observed, "now let's see them support the removal of bias." Most references to a superior being were removed from the new draft, as were references to a worldwide flood and the creation of the universe, energy, and matter "from nothing." Ellwanger also attempted to counter the charge made by education officials that insufficient funds existed to implement creationist legislation. Calling these objections "sandbagging tactics," Ellwanger drafted his new bill to require that schools equip themselves to teach creation science from current funds. Schools could no longer claim that they did not have any extra money with which to purchase creationist materials, as they would be forced to reallocate money from other areas to buy such material. It was hardly a coincidence that the most likely source of money for this reallocation would be the existing science education budget.[27]

Ellwanger's draft bill, supposedly avoiding many of the weaknesses in previous creationist legislation, led to even greater consideration of equal time laws in 1981. More than two hundred creationist supporters in Huntsville, Alabama, packed the annual citizens' forum sponsored by the American Association of University Women. Following their forum appearance with a rally at the local courthouse, creationists convinced members of the Huntsville area legislative delegation to introduce equal time bills in both the House and the Senate. The publicity surrounding this attempt precipitated a well-organized response that ultimately resulted in three separate opposition groups in the Huntsville area. Enlisting local clergy, physicians, scientists, and educators, these groups held a meeting that attracted more than three hundred participants and most of the local media. By emphasizing the significant opposition to the proposed laws, the meeting countered creationist claims of wide support. Despite the procreationist testimony of Wendell Bird and Richard Bliss, the House Education Committee reported a much weaker bill, which was nonetheless killed by the filibuster of Huntsville representative Robert Albright, a former biology teacher.[28]

Colorado creationists convinced a state senator—later described by William V. Mayer as "scientifically naive"—to introduce a balanced treatment bill in early 1981. During hearings on the proposed act, Richard Bliss and Wendell Bird appeared before the Senate Education Committee to present a detailed, polished presentation complete with audiovisual material. Although the committee undermined creationist plans to dominate the hearing by limiting each side to thirty minutes of testimony, the two creationist leaders nonetheless offered a cogent discussion of their position. Less well organized, opponents of the bill still proved effective. William V. Mayer, for example, who had led the fight against earlier creationist efforts in Colorado, stressed in his testimony the nonscientific nature of creationism and the lack of legitimate scientific credentials of creationist witnesses. When the 24 March hearing ended, the committee voted to kill the bill with only one dissenting vote. By the end of the year nearly two dozen similar laws had been considered by state legislatures, with varying degrees of support expressed for the creationist cause.[29]

At the local level, creationists rarely had to face the organized opposition stirred by legislative efforts. They lobbied state textbook commissions, local school boards, and individual teachers to accommodate creationism in some fashion. A *Science* reporter estimated in the early fall of 1980 that nearly thirty state textbook commissions had come under "heavy pressure" to include creationist materials on their approved lists. Continued claims about the weaknesses of evolution and the scientific support for creationism had the desired effect. Edward Lalor, in charge of curriculum development for New York, told a reporter, "When someone says there are problems with the theory of evolution, we listen." Iowa school science consultant George Magrane informed a *Time* reporter in early 1981 that "teachers in Iowa are being intimidated by the controversy. Rather than teach both creationism and evolution, they teach neither one. It's almost a regression in history." Anti-creationists continued their challenges as well. University of Kentucky anthropologist Eugenie Scott again organized a quiet lobbying effort to convince the Fayette County School Board to reject a proposal to include creationist material in biology classes. Teachers in Cobb County, Georgia, threatened to strike unless the local school board rescinded an earlier order to include creation science in the curriculum.[30]

As the institutional focus of the creationist crusade, California presented an enticing target for local campaigns to remove evolution from the schools. In late 1980 a controversy erupted in Livermore, California, over the teaching of evolution in the sixth-grade science classes of Ray Baird. Although a music major at San Francisco State University, Baird had taken a few science courses that allowed him to be certified to teach elementary science. Converted to the creationist cause in the mid-1970s, Baird had been discussing creationism and using creationist material for two years before Livermore parents objected. These parents, many of whom were associated with the nearby Lawrence Livermore National Laboratory and other scientific or technical concerns, were outraged by the poor science included in the material Baird used. As one parent told a San Francisco *Chronicle* reporter, "I have no objection to God in schools, but I do object to poor science. The science in these books is wrong." Responding to the public outcry, the Livermore Board of Education decided at its 3 February 1981 meeting that the teaching of creationism was inappropriate in science classes and should only be included in social science or history classes. Although the community remained divided over the issue, those with a scientific background expressed relief at the board's decision. An employee of Lawrence Livermore observed, "Unless you're a scientist, the average parent wouldn't pick up on how bad this junk really is."[31]

School districts in other regions of the nation displayed a similarly mixed perspective on the place of creationism in the public schools. Dallas school officials recommended that teachers use texts that presented "two models" of origins. To avoid controversy, teachers in Anchorage, Alaska, were directed to ignore sections that discussed evolution in history textbooks. The attorney general's office in Oregon issued an opinion that teaching scientific creationism would be appropriate except in a course that appeared to be religious instruction. The study of creationism became mandatory for the 115,000 students in the Tampa, Florida, public schools as a result of a 1981 school board decision requiring equal time for evolution and creation. Although more than 90 percent of the local science teachers opposed the policy, the board accepted the creationist argument that the exclusive presentation of evolution represented unfair indoctrination.[32]

Another method used with great success by the creationist movement was the presentation of debates between creationists and evolutionists. Because the audience at such debates tended to be drawn from the local evangelical community, which responded well to the sarcastic and oversimplified performances of Duane T. Gish and others, evolutionists were rarely effective in making their points. A notable exception to this tendency took place in the fall of 1977, when San Diego State University biologists William M. Thwaites and Frank Awbrey debated Henry Morris and Duane Gish. Immersing themselves in the creationist literature, the biologists countered specific challenges to evolutionary theory. More frequently, however, scientists entered these debates with the belief that providing evidence that supported evolution would be sufficient. In the fall of 1981, for example, Henry Morris successfully debated evolutionist Ken Miller in Tampa, Florida. Staged after the Tampa school board had decided to include creationism, the debate attracted seventeen hundred spectators and was covered by six television and seven radio stations, as well as by local newspapers.[33]

The most dramatic debate of 1981 took place in October, when chemist Russell Doolittle, of the University of California, San Diego, agreed to debate Duane Gish at Jerry Falwell's Liberty Baptist College.

Organized by the "Old Time Gospel Hour" and moderated by Falwell himself, the debate represented part of Falwell's campaign to remove evolution from the public schools. Broadcast of the taped debate over national television broadened the impact. Although Doolittle had "great misgivings" about the debate on the terms dictated, he agreed to appear so that the evolution perspective would at least have a hearing. As expected, Doolittle's careful presentation of the voluminous data supporting the theory of evolution could not compete with Gish's clever anecdotes and polished performance, capped by amusing slides and references to evolution as the "fish-to-Gish" theory. Evolutionists would not defeat the creationist campaigns on the lecture circuit.[34]

The presence of the Reverend Jerry Falwell as moderator in the Doolittle-Gish debate was no coincidence. Throughout the 1970s the United States witnessed a resurgence of Protestant fundamentalism, led by evangelists who spread their gospel through television broadcasts. Such programs as "Cathedral of Tomorrow," "Revival Fires," and Falwell's "Old Time Gospel Hour" preached a theology that would have found a receptive audience among the earlier followers of William Bell Riley, J. Frank Norris, and Thomas T. Martin. Although focused in the South, including most urban areas, support for such televangelists could be found in all regions, with the rural north central states especially interested in the evangelical message. As had been the case in the 1920s, Falwell and his allies viewed the teaching of evolution in the public schools as one of the major evils of the modern world, leading as it did to the dreaded secular humanism.

The growing fundamentalist presence soon infiltrated American politics. The "born again" phenomenon was important in many elections throughout the 1970s, aided by the media's oversimplified definition of an evangelical as any politician who publicly expressed a belief in God that included the phrase "born again." Although local elections proved to be the most important focus for the political involvement of evangelicals, this phenomenon soon spread to the national level. Many factors explained the election of Jimmy Carter as president in 1976, but the Georgian's identification in the public mind with the beliefs of the rural South clearly attracted voters who embraced the current evangelicalism. When Carter's actions showed that his religion was more personal than political, fundamentalist leaders such as Falwell and the Reverend Pat Robertson began to organize their movement into a political force that became known as the New Right. The proposed merger of the political and religious worlds became evident to Americans by 1979, when Falwell formed the Moral Majority as a political pressure group devoted to the evangelical agenda.[35]

Although evangelicals' claims that they represented a voting bloc of some sixty million individuals who determined the outcome of the 1980 election is clearly inaccurate, they nonetheless played a visible role in that year's political activity. New Right support was especially important to Republican nominee Ronald Reagan, as shown by his appearance before a fundamentalist group in Dallas. Addressing an audience of some ten thousand, Reagan seemed to share evangelicals' opposition to secular humanism by accusing the government of becoming "morally neutral." In a press conference following his address, the candidate also embraced the creationist outlook of the New Right. Asked if he believed in the theory of evolution, he replied, "Well, it is a theory, it is a scientific theory only, and it has in recent years been challenged in the world of science and is not yet believed in the scientific community to be as infallible as it once was believed. But if it was going to be taught in the schools, then I think that also the biblical theory of creation, which is not a theory but the biblical story of creation, should also be taught." Reagan's opponents in the election, Congressman John B. Anderson and President Carter, refused to accept the Republican's view of evolution. Anderson identified himself as an evangelical Christian but divorced himself from any attempts to "politicize evangelical doctrine" or to say "what should be or should not be taught in the classrooms of America." Creationism, he said, should only be taught in churches, Sunday schools, or parochial schools. Carter issued his response through the presidential science adviser, describing the evidence for evolution as "convincing" and emphasizing the necessity to maintain the constitutional separation of church and state in the public schools.[36] Creationists had little difficulty choosing a candidate in 1980.

The Scientists' Response

Despite their growing involvement with the political and religious activities of the New Right, creationists continued to present their views as a scientific alternative to the theory of evolution. Because they defined the two "models" as the only possible explanations, creationists embraced any question concerning the details of evolution as evidence in favor of creationism. By the early 1980s developments in the scientific study of evolution provided valuable support for this perspective. Stephen Jay Gould, Niles Eldredge, and other scholars challenged the traditional view of evolution as a series of slow, gradual steps. Suggesting that the gaps in the fossil record represented an important datum, rather than the vagaries of fossilization, they developed the "punctu-ated equilibrium" concept to explain evolutionary change. Gould and Eldredge argued that organic evolution occurred fairly rapidly, from a paleontological point of view, followed by long periods in which spe-cies changed very little. Debates among scientists over this issue appeared in scientific and popular periodicals, providing creationists with "proof" that evolution represented mere speculation rather than proven science.[37]

From a scientific perspective, debates over punctuated equilibrium and other topics showed the health of evolutionary biology and con-firmed the theory of evolution as a valuable guide to further research. From the creationist perspective, however, any challenge to the existing evolutionary edifice—as the creationists defined it—provided evidence to support creation science as an alternative to evolution. Creationist writers thus quoted widely from the works of Gould, Eldredge, and many others, using their ideas to construct a portrait of an evolutionary theory whose foundations were crumbling. Quoting scientists out of context and ignoring the divisions within their own ranks, creationists defined evolution as a self-contradictory belief system supported by lit-tle more than scientists' devotion to a materialistic and humanistic phi-losophy. Gould himself attempted to explain the reality of the debates within evolution by stressing that the creationists were "confusing the methods by which evolution occurs with evolution itself. That evolution occurred is a fact," he continued. "People evolved from ape ancestors even though we can argue about how it happened. Scientists are debat-ing mechanism, not fact." When asked on another occasion to comment on the citation by creationists of much of his recent work, Gould re-sponded, "Let me put it as gently as I can: they are consciously dis-torting the truth."[38]

The growing political power of the New Right and the creationists' expanded campaign to show the scientific validity of their beliefs pre-cipitated an active response on the part of the American scientific com-munity. Largely through publications in various media, scientists and other scholars began to examine the creationist movement and to counter many of the arguments put forth by the antievolutionists of the late twentieth century. Evolutionists had realized the implications of the movement by the late 1970s, observing that creationist strength was a result of the poor quality of science education in the United States. As geneticist Russell Doolittle observed, most Americans were not equipped to evaluate creationist claims. "The tragedy of it all," he con-cluded, "is the state of science education in the country—it's simply, sadly, awful." Wayne Moyer, executive director of the National Association of Biology Teachers, put it more bluntly when he said, "We have done a botched job of teaching evolutionary theory, and we had better accept the creationist challenge to clean up our act."[39]

Before biology teachers could clean up their act, however, scientists had to show the invalidity of so-called creation science. Toward this end, a new periodical called *Creation/Evolution* appeared in the summer of 1980. Sponsored by the American Humanist Association—a connection gleefully used by creationists to discredit the entire effort—the journal disseminated information to counter antievolutionists' presentations in debates, legislative hearings, and public meetings. Equally important, scientists responded enthusiastically to a call by Wayne Moyer in the spring of 1980 to form "committees of correspondence" to challenge the well-organized and generously financed creationist campaign at the local level. Stressing that "well-meaning but misinformed" public officials had been convinced that creation science was science, Moyer emphasized the need for scientists to organize effectively. Professional organizations also became concerned about the creationist threat. The American Association for the Advancement of Science included a session discussing the creationist movement at its Toronto meeting in January 1981. Participants in the session stressed scientific weaknesses in creationist ideas and warned listeners of the threat to science education posed by the movement. Later in the year delegates to the annual meeting of the American Association of University Professors adopted a resolution calling on state governments to "reject creation-science legislation as utterly inconsistent with the principles of academic freedom." A joint October meeting of the National Academy of Sciences and the National Association of Biology Teachers emphasized the futility of public debates with creationists but insisted on the need to challenge creationists at the local level.[40]

Scientists and science educators also began to critique creationism as bad science in an effort to maintain the integrity of their disciplines. As Wayne Moyer observed in 1980, "No one is saying that religious and scientific views are incompatible. We just don't think students should be taught information that can't be supported by a shred of scientific proof." A large number of articles in *American Biology Teacher* examined weaknesses and inaccuracies in creation science from the late 1970s through the early 1980s. Writers discussed constitutional, theological, scientific, and educational reasons for not teaching creationism in the public schools and emphasized the importance of evolution as the "greatest unifying theme" in biology. Educators admitted that the classroom teacher had to proceed cautiously in discussing evolution, as it remained a topic likely to cause controversy. Emphasizing that a mid-

dle position existed between biblical literalism and atheistic materialism might ease the conflict, but the science teacher must not abandon
professional integrity to satisfy creationist demands.[41]

The folly of the creationists' equal time campaign also troubled
Sonoma State University philosopher Harvey Siegel, who had witnessed the California controversy at close range. In an article for the
education journal *Phi Delta Kappan,* Siegel emphasized that creationist
criticisms of evolution frequently displayed a confusion over experi-
mentation and testing. Apparently making no distinction between the
two, creationists rejected all evolutionary ideas, whether in the biological or the physical sciences, because they could not be experimentally
shown. Siegel correctly pointed out that testing a theory need not involve an experiment. In astronomy, for example, a scientist could not
devise an experiment to re-create the "big bang," but testing the predictions of that theory against observed phenomena could nonetheless
show the validity of the concept of an expanding universe.

Siegel's concern with the equal time concept, however, focused
more sharply on the educational implications of the doctrine. Accepting
the creationists' arguments for balanced presentation and students' freedom of choice would fundamentally alter the purpose of education. Rejecting the idea that the public education system was merely "a broker
of information," Siegel emphasized that educators had a responsibility
to provide their students "not just *any* material" from their discipline
"but the *best* available material." The state must exercise its right to
make curricular judgments to meet "its obligation to provide high quality education to its citizens." Including religious doctrine in the science
classroom would lead to the opposite result.[42]

The impact of the growing scientific opposition to the creationist
movement remained ambiguous. As Niles Eldredge observed in mid-
1981, it appeared likely that creationists' charges that evolution represented the religion of secular humanism would be rejected by American
courts. He went on to warn his readers, though, that the creationists
might well achieve their goals if they convinced the American public
"that science is just another authoritarian belief system, and that Americans, in the traditional sense of 'fair play,' should be allowed to 'hear
both sides.' " Various opinion polls confirmed Eldredge's fear. In January 1980, for example, the *American School Board Journal* conducted
a poll of its readers on the question "How should public schools handle
the teaching of the origin of man?" Nearly half the respondents favored
teaching both creation and evolution; only a quarter thought that evolution should be the only explanation presented. Nineteen percent argued that only biblical discussions should be included, while 8 percent

suggested that the topic should be completely avoided. Written comments that accompanied the questionnaires were even more chilling. A Kansas principal observed that "evolution cannot be justified by any person who has scientific knowledge." The intriguing statement "We need to teach facts—and creation is a fact" came from the superintendent of a Missouri school system. A North Carolina board member who wanted to avoid the topic wrote, "Teachers talk theories too much now—get them back to facts."[43]

Public opinion polls provided similar results. In Tampa, Florida, nearly three-quarters of the parents and teachers suggested that they would accept the teaching of creationism in the public schools. A 1981 California survey found that residents favored the teaching of evolution over creation by a six-to-one majority, but half of the respondents admitted that they would accept the equal presentation of both. An October 1981 Associated Press-NBC News poll provided the following results on the issue:

Only evolution should be taught 8%
Only creation should be taught 10%
Both creation and evolution should be taught 76%
Not sure which should be taught 6%

Despite scientists' opposition, the equal time concept appeared to have gained many adherents.[44]

Support for creationist arguments paralleled a decline in science education in the United States in the late 1970s and early 1980s. Despite studies that showed that the new science curricula of the 1960s—BSCS, for example—were "consistently more effective" than earlier programs, public support for the new science education dissipated throughout the 1970s and into the 1980s. Opponents of 1960s programs argued that BSCS and similar initiatives had abandoned the teaching of "facts" in favor of vaguely defined goals of awareness and understanding. Part of a growing "back to basics" movement in education, the opposition to science programs sponsored by the National Science Foundation showed that Americans continued to misunderstand the reality of the scientific pursuit. Like the creationists, many Americans believed that science was no more than the accumulation and classification of data.[45]

Never slow to react to public sentiment, textbook publishers began to modify their products almost immediately. To avoid alienation of local school officials, publishers decreased the coverage of evolution in their biology texts. Sales personnel came back from local school districts to inform their editors that sales would be lost unless evolution was downplayed, even to the point of removing photographs of fossils from the texts. An analysis of leading high school biology texts of the period showed that publishers pursued several options, ranging from an emphasis on nonevolutionary explanations through a balanced treatment approach to a description of all aspects of evolution, including human evolution. The authors of this study suggested that "market segmentation" was taking place, leading individual publishers to decide which share of the market to pursue. Although the existence of at least a few texts that discussed evolution provided anticreationists with hope, it remained clear that textbook coverage of evolution was far below previous levels. Individual public school teachers rarely courted hostility by openly teaching evolution in their classes, ignoring the topic altogether or stressing that evolution was "only" a theory.[46]

Scopes II?

The growing strength and impact of the creationist movement put California creationists, especially those associated with the Creation Science Research Center, in an awkward position. Although pleased with the success of their efforts to preach the antievolution gospel and encouraged by the wide circulation of their publications, they were disappointed by the removal of creationist concepts from the revised *Science Framework* guidelines drafted in 1978. Local school boards generally followed these guidelines. Equally important, the guidelines largely determined the actions of the textbook publishers who wished to supply texts to the large California market. To correct this embarrassing situation, Kelly L. Segraves and the Creation Science Research Center filed suit in 1979 to prevent the distribution of the *Science Framework*. The Segraves complaint charged that California's presentation of evolution without similar discussion of creationism violated the religious freedom of creationists. The suit also described the state's actions as an unconstitutional attempt to establish the religion of secular humanism by indoctrinating students in "evolutionary dogma." As these charges represented standard creationist arguments, so too did the proposed solution. Segraves asked the court to mandate equal time for creationism in the science classrooms of California.[47]

Unsuccessful efforts to achieve an out-of-court settlement continued until early 1981, when it became clear that the status of the *Science Framework* would be decided in a Sacramento courtroom. Scheduled to open on 2 March in superior court, the Segraves case attracted much attention and was frequently referred to as Scopes II. In interviews before the trial began, Segraves and his supporters provided the media with a clear view of their perspective. Segraves told reporters that teaching only evolution violated the religious freedom of creationists, but he denied that his suit was designed to require the teaching of creationism. Rather, Segraves only wanted to qualify dogmatic statements concerning the factual nature of evolution to leave the science classroom open to other theories. Creationist chemist Robert E. Kofahl also provided valuable insight into the creationist worldview. Aware that the state intended to call expert witnesses from the scientific community to support the teaching of evolution, Kofahl remarked, "Their witnesses will be cross-examined, and they'd better be able to prove that evolution is a fact. If they can't, they're finished." He also attempted to disarm suggestions that the science classrooms would be filled with so many religious ideas that teaching would become impossible. Native American creation myths, for example, would need to be taught only if scientific support could be found. Kofahl told the San Francisco *Chronicle* that as for the "view that the earth began as a ball of mud on the back of a turtle, well, we say, if they can adduce some scientific evidence, they can bring that in. But they won't."[48]

Pretrial statements from the opposing attorneys also helped to delineate the two sides. Deputy attorney general Robert Tyler represented the state in its attempt to maintain scientific integrity in the public schools. He commented in late February, "I'm not going to prove evolution as a fact," thus weakening one of the creationists' major points of attack, "just that there are no scientific alternatives. We will show that creationism is not scientific but religious." Tyler contrasted the state's view that evolution represented the most likely explanation with the creationists' perspective. "Creationists want absolute truth," he said on the eve of the trial. "They want guarantees, and the Bible is their guarantee. That's not science." The creationists' attorney embraced a predictably different outlook. Richard K. Turner, who had served as Governor Reagan's assistant legal affairs secretary for six years, planned to show that the teaching of evolution had created unnecessary conflicts between parents and their school-age children. Equally important, Turner wanted to define evolution as a religion, emphasizing that the debates among scientists concerning evolution showed the "faith" required to accept the theory.[49]

Turner's opening statements on 2 March in the nonjury trial before Judge Irving Perluss repeated traditional creationist arguments. Denying that his clients wanted to "sneak the Bible into the classroom or ban the teaching of evolution," Turner stressed that the state's actions were unnecessarily harmful to plaintiffs' religious freedom. Admittedly, he accepted the creationist agenda and its religious basis. "God made man," he told the court. "He didn't make a blob or a gila monster. He made man." Yet his opening statements indicated a greater concern with the implications of teaching evolution. "The state of California is essentially hostile to religion," he argued. "It in effect has deprived or burdened the plaintiffs' right to religious belief." Claiming that he sought only to protect his clients' constitutional right to believe, Turner insisted that "at the very least, we might expect that the government not affirmatively tell my clients' children in the public schools that their beliefs are wrong."[50]

It soon became clear, however, that the creationists no longer viewed the case in such monumental terms. By the second day of the trial Turner had abandoned his argument that teaching evolution represented an attempt to establish the religion of secular humanism. He had also backed away from his emphasis that state neutrality required equal time for creationist ideas in the science classrooms. This change in focus reduced the trial to an involved discussion over the meaning and phrasing of the *Science Framework* and mooted the defense plan to call scientific witnesses to discredit creationism as science. Segraves and his attorney told Judge Perluss that they would be content with the removal of "dogmatic" statements concerning evolution from the guidelines, an admission that surprised the judge. After questioning Segraves, Perluss observed that what he had originally seen as a "great and constitutional case has evolved—excuse me—has come down to semantics."[51]

Despite the narrowed focus of the case, the trial nonetheless produced a few dramatic moments. Kasey Segraves, thirteen-year-old son of the suit's instigator, testified on 3 March that his eighth-grade social studies teacher had taught that man evolved from apes. He told the court that this teaching conflicted with his own belief that "God created man as man and put him on the earth," a belief that came from his reading of the Bible and the teachings of church and family. When contacted about this testimony, the teacher denied Kasey's story. The testimony of Kelly Segraves repeated arguments that evolution was bad science because it could not be completely confirmed in the laboratory. He also objected to the dogmatic statements in the framework that appeared to provide evolution with more authority than he thought warranted.[52]

As the trial progressed, creationist objections to dogmatism lost some of their force through the actions of defense attorney Tyler. Although Judge Perluss ruled that testimony concerning the scientific validity of evolution remained irrelevant, scientists testifying for the state emphasized the open-ended nature of science that was anything but dogmatic. The state's attorney found a passage in one of the state-approved textbooks that mentioned that other theories in addition to evolution were used to explain origins. When presented with this information, Segraves grudgingly admitted that such statements would "possibly" satisfy his demands. Tyler also read a passage in the *Science Framework* that emphasized the nonscientific nature of ideas concerning the development of life from the prebiological earth. "Philosophic and religious considerations pertaining to the origin, meaning, and value of life," this passage stated, "are not within the realm of science because they cannot be analyzed or measured by present methods of science." Judge Perluss seized on this passage, observing that such statements accommodated many of the creationists' objections.[53]

The lack of dogmatism in the *Science Framework* allowed Judge Perluss to reach a rapid decision. Perluss ruled on 6 March that the published policies of the California Board of Education, in effect since December 1972, prohibited dogmatic statements on human evolution. The *Science Framework* provided "sufficient accommodation for the views of the plaintiff." He added, however, that the California Department of Education had not disseminated the policy sufficiently to ensure the elimination of dogmatic presentation from the science classrooms. He ordered wider dissemination and ruled that any future violation of the nondogmatism policy should be taken up with local school boards.[54]

Creationists applauded the Perluss ruling. Although California education officials expressed pleasure that the *Science Framework* had been upheld, Segraves and his allies claimed a major victory. After the trial, Segraves told a reporter, "I think this will stop dogmatic teaching in the schools. Dogmatic assertions can't be made in the science classroom." Interpreting the decision as requiring the accommodation of religious beliefs, Nell Segraves, Kelly's mother, told the New York *Times*, "We won. As long as they distribute those policy statements, we will get along fine." Creationists were also ecstatic about the significant media attention they received as a result of the trial. This attention would provide the movement with psychological momentum and would provide access to greater funding from supporters. The only real setback for the creationists was Perluss's finding that the California guidelines did not violate their religious rights, but this represented no more than a slight disappointment.[55]

The decision in the Segraves case precipitated an outpouring of opinions from both sides. Despite the state's expressed pleasure that the *Science Framework* had been left intact, scientists tended to be critical of Perluss's decision because it suggested that creationism represented a legitimate scientific alternative to evolution. The potential impact of such a decision was even more discouraging. Richard E. Dickerson, professor of physical chemistry at the California Institute of Technology and a defense witness in the Segraves trial, examined the situation in an article for the Los Angeles *Times* shortly after the trial ended. He stressed that so-called creation science abandoned the fundamental precept of science as a process, replacing it with a concept of science as a collection of "facts" that could be manipulated to support a number of different positions. Perluss's decision that creationism could be taught in science courses further troubled Dickerson because of its impact on the science curriculum. Including creationism in science classrooms would lead to "mis-taught" future scientists who "ultimately will be bad scientists, and will bequeath bad science to their successors." Dickerson and his colleagues thus opposed creationism, "not because it is religiously motivated but because it is rotten science."[56] The cost to future generations remained too high to justify on the nebulous grounds of fairness and equal time.

Understandably, comments from creationists were more positive. After nearly two decades of antievolution activity, Nell Segraves enthusiastically focused on the implications of the Perluss decision. Her son's case represented only the first step in the reformation of America's educational system. Commenting after the trial, the Segraves matriarch said, "We want 50 percent of the curriculum and the content back. We want 50 percent of the tax dollar used for education to our point of view. We have a lot to undo. Creation/evolution is only the beginning." She made her position even clearer a few months later. "We feel we are out to repossess our land," she told the Washington *Post*. Repeating charges from the antievolution crusades of the past, she continued: "The naturalist-atheist-humanists are running things in this country. If you teach that man is an animal the way these evolutionists do, then there is no right and wrong and people will act like animals. . . . That is what happens when you divorce your curriculum from religion. We cannot live with chaotic values."[57]

Other creationists examined different aspects of the situation in 1981. Attorney Richard K. Turner, basking in the glow of his "victory" at Sacramento, emphasized the debates within the scientific community as evidence of weaknesses in the theory of evolution. He was particularly contemptuous of scientists who supported evolution. Describing the scientists who testified in the Segraves case, Turner observed, "These scientists get up on the stand, and act as if their very lives were being attacked. They not only close ranks," he continued, "but they almost deny anybody the right to know of the internal fights that go on within the evolutionary crowd. They're pompous and arrogant, just the kind of people that the First Amendment was written to protect us against." The supposed weaknesses in evolutionary theory remained uppermost in the concerns of Robert E. Kofahl, who added an interesting interpretation of the underlying causes of those weaknesses. "Since the fall of Adam," he observed, "man's intellect, his emotions and his will have been shaken up." It was, therefore, pointless to use intellectual arguments in an attempt to convince evolutionists that creation science deserved support. "Their intellect is in bondage, you see, to the effects of the fall," Kofahl concluded, "and that prevents them from realizing what God wants them to do."[58]

Creationists' enthusiasm for their "victory" in California was moderated by the lack of state laws designed to guarantee a place for creationism in the public schools. Despite numerous attempts during the 1970s, the close of the Segraves case in early March 1981 found no state laws requiring the balanced treatment of evolution and creationism. Without such legislation, creationists believed, their victory remained incomplete. Their concern was short-lived. As the Segraves case captured attention throughout the nation, legislators in Arkansas considered yet another equal time bill. In a few weeks Arkansas would provide creationists with one of their most stunning victories, while laying the foundation for one of their most damaging defeats.

10

Somewhere in Heaven, John Scopes Is Smiling

The creationist "victory" in Judge Perluss's courtroom gained significant national publicity for the antievolution crusade. Although the ultimate impact of the trial remained ambiguous, widespread media attention provided the movement with well-prepared soil in which to plant the seeds of creation science. In few areas of the nation was the soil more fecund than in the state of Arkansas. The decade following the *Epperson v. Arkansas* decision had witnessed little change in the status of evolution among the state's residents, many of whom viewed the theory as responsible for the problems facing contemporary society. Few observers of the creationist movement were surprised when Arkansas passed legislation based on the equal time concept.

Victory and Defeat in Little Rock

As California creationists prepared for battle in Sacramento, their associates in Arkansas began an effort that led to the first "balanced treatment" law passed in the United States. The impetus for this legislative action began at the local level. In late 1980 the junior high schools in North Little Rock were reviewing science texts for adoption. Disturbed at the treatment of evolution in these texts, mathematics teacher Larry Fisher wanted the shortcomings of the theory emphasized in any adopted text. An avid creationist for nearly a decade, he forwarded the May 1979 Institute for Creation Research resolution to the superintendent of the Pulaski County Special School District in December 1980. His cover letter repeated many of the standard creationist arguments and emphasized that school districts throughout the nation were adopting similar resolutions. The Pulaski County district would harvest a public relations bonanza, Fisher wrote, "since surveys across the country indicate that about 80 percent of the patrons support it." He concluded his letter by stressing the value of the resolution in "promoting academic integrity and responsibility on this issue."[1]

The school board proved particularly receptive to such arguments, as they had recently been heavily lobbied by the Moral Majority and Family Life America under God (FLAG). These groups objected to sex education, liberal bias in texts, and, of course, the teaching of evolution in the public schools. When Fisher appeared before the board at its January 1981 meeting, he argued that convincing scientific evidence existed for the creationist perspective. He thus advocated the presentation of all information regarding origins, rather than the current censorship of nonevolutionary material. The fairness argument convinced board members to establish a creation science curriculum committee to meet on 6 January. Fisher brought a large number of creationist publications to this meeting but met with little enthusiasm. After reviewing the material, the committee reported that the publications represented little more than religious apologetics. Fisher nonetheless insisted that a curriculum be developed and submitted to the school board on 10 March.[2]

This school board meeting provided an important victory for the creationists. Fisher's supporters, who had packed the hall, were outraged by the negative committee report presented by chairman Bill Wood, a Little Rock science teacher. After heated discussion, the board informed Wood that his committee had not been asked for its opinion. As the existing committee had not discharged its responsibility to develop a curriculum, the board appointed a new two-member committee, comprising Fisher and district science coordinator Marianne Wilson. Wilson found virtually no creationist material of value to use in the curriculum. Institute for Creation Research staff member Richard B. Bliss flew in from California to assist the committee, but his material proved disappointing. As Wilson later recalled, "What he had was trash. It was just full of religious references, and the science was awful." Wilson and Fisher eventually developed a curriculum, but very little material came from standard scientific sources. The new committee's efforts were anticlimactic, however, as the creationist focus in Arkansas had already shifted to the legislature.[3]

The January actions of the school board had been widely reported in the Little Rock press, piquing the interest of the Reverend W.A. Blount of the Sylvan Hills Community Church. Blount had long been active in efforts to minimize the teaching of evolution in the public schools and had been on the mailing lists of creationist organizations for many years. At the January meeting of the Greater Little Rock Evangelical Fellowship, Blount and his colleagues initiated a campaign to secure a creationist statute from the Arkansas legislature. They contacted Paul Ellwanger in South Carolina to obtain the latest copy of his draft bill and used business connections to find a sympathetic legislator to introduce the measure. Senator James Holsted, a born-again evangelical, met with newly elected Republican governor Frank White before introducing the bill. White had been elected as the candidate of the Moral Majority, and he promised Holsted that he would sign the bill if it passed. With this assurance, Holsted evidently saw no reason to consult with the Arkansas Department of Education, the state attorney general, scientists, or science educators.[4]

The bill that Holsted introduced on 24 February was virtually identical to the Ellwanger modification of the ICR resolution. Requiring "balanced treatment" for creation and evolution, Act 590 repeated various creationist assumptions as "legislative findings of fact" and stressed the scientific nature of creation science. Holsted's bill was quickly referred to the Judiciary Committee, which was chaired by self-described born-again Christian Max Howell and included Holsted as a member. Howell eased the bill's progress, favorably reporting the bill out of committee a week later. His Senate colleagues, sympathetic to arguments stressing "fairness" and "freedom of choice," possessed insufficient scientific background to evaluate the intellectual content of the bill. On 13 March, after a fifteen-minute debate and no hearings, the Senate passed Act 590 by a vote of twenty-two to two.[5]

Once the bill reached the House of Representatives, significant lobbying took place by both the Moral Majority and FLAG. A carefully orchestrated telephone campaign convinced many representatives that opposing the bill would be politically dangerous. Representative Mike Wilson, who ultimately voted against the bill, told a *Science* writer, "When you get a mass of phone calls in favor of a bill and none against, and when it appears to be in support of motherhood, apple pie, and the American way of life, it is hard to vote against it." Most representatives accepted at face value creationist assurances that significant support existed among scientists for the equal time concept. Few of them read the bill carefully or knew its origin, and the ten-minute committee hearing that preceded passage of the bill provided few opportunities for careful analysis. On 17 March, the day before adjournment, the Arkansas House of Representatives passed the bill by a vote of sixty-nine to eighteen. Two days later Governor White paid his debt to the Moral Majority by signing the bill without reading it. "If we're going to teach evolution in the public school system," he explained, "why not teach scientific creationism? Both of them are theories."[6]

Even before Governor White signed the measure, the American Civil Liberties Union had vowed to challenge the statute as a violation of the separation of church and state. Anticipating this action, Arkansas creationists moved quickly. The state's Moral Majority leader, the Reverend Roy McLaughlin, formed a group called Arkansas Citizens for Balanced Education in Origins to promote implementation of the new law. Once the ACLU challenge became clear, a second group emerged to focus on the expected court battle. The Creation Science Legal Defense Fund was formed to raise money and secure the services of leading creationist attorneys Wendell R. Bird and John W. Whitehead to defend the statute. To deflect charges that the creationist movement represented a religious crusade, church leaders withdrew from these citizens' groups once they were established.[7]

The ACLU was aided by the New York law firm of Skadden, Arps, Slate, Meagher and Flom, best known for its work relating to corporate takeovers. With a long tradition of public service work, the firm supplied the lawyers, paralegal assistants, and staff members needed to mount an effective attack against the latest antievolution law. Beginning in May 1981 the firm examined creationism from religious, scientific, and educational perspectives. They rejected a point-by-point refutation of creation science as an unwise tactic that would give the impression that creationism represented a legitimate alternative theory. Instead, the attorneys divided the case into three parts, with a separate team of attorneys, witnesses, and support personnel assigned to each. The case would show that creation science was little more than a literal reading of Genesis, that creation science did not represent science, that Act 590 was "confused" about evolution, and that implementation of the law in the classroom would be all but impossible. From a constitutional perspective, the ACLU planned to show only that creation science advanced religion—not that it was religion—thus invalidating the law under the establishment clause.[8]

In the suit filed on 27 May in federal district court in Little Rock, the plaintiffs, who included various religious and educational groups, argued that Act 590 represented an establishment of religion. It had a religious rather than a secular purpose whose primary effect remained the advancement of a specific religious outlook. The act further would involve the state in excessive entanglement with religion by requiring state officials to monitor the material presented in classrooms to guard against religious instruction. The plaintiffs' brief also stressed that the Arkansas law violated the academic freedom of students and teachers, in conflict with the free speech clause of the First Amendment. By censoring evolution, the act attempted to override the professional judgment of teachers and scientists. The suit also charged Act 590 with vagueness, in violation of the due process clause of the Fourteenth

Amendment. Although the phrase "balanced treatment" appeared in the act, the concept was nowhere defined.

The Arkansas attorney general's office, aided by Duane T. Gish and other creationists, attempted to answer the ACLU charges in the pretrial brief. They argued that Act 590 did not establish religion because the two-model approach mandated in the statute could be taught in a "secular, completely non-religious manner." Although the concept of a creator might conceivably parallel certain religious ideas, such a concept was not inherently religious. Characterizing such a creator as "far, far away from any conception of a god or deity," the brief stressed that creation science merely required "that the entity which caused creation have power, intelligence, and a sense of design." Similarly, Act 590 failed to advance religion because its "primary effect" was to further academic freedom. This effect would counter the existing situation of censorship by "self-appointed guardians of what is 'science.' " In addition, academic freedom was far from absolute. Repeating arguments used to support the antievolution laws of the 1920s, the Arkansas brief stated, "The right of a teacher to determine the scope of classroom instruction is limited by the right of the State to prescribe curriculum." Nor was the Arkansas statute vague, as any competent professional educator could provide "balanced treatment" within the meaning of the law.[9]

As the case opened in the Little Rock courtroom of district judge William R. Overton, the state's arguments were presented by Attorney General Steve Clark and his staff. Wendell Bird's opinion that the state had a weak case—in part brought about by Clark's decision to exclude Bird from the state's team—proved prophetic. From the beginning of testimony from the plaintiffs' impressive array of witnesses, creationism suffered one setback after another. The Reverend Kenneth W. Hicks, Methodist bishop of Arkansas, objected to the law because it portrayed a belief in divine creation in terms totally different from those of his and others' denominations. Father Bruce Vawter of De Paul University employed his expertise on Genesis to show that the point of reference for Act 590 could only be the first eleven chapters of that book. Baptist theologian Langdon Gilkey placed creation science in the tradition of Christian apologetics by testifying that the purpose of apologetics was to reach religious conclusions through the use of nonreligious concepts. In the case of creation science, science became the tool to support traditional Protestant fundamentalism.[10]

Scholars from nonreligious fields provided important perspectives as well. Historian George Marsden examined the writings of creationists and showed that many of the phrases and ideas were identical to those of the antievolutionists of the 1920s. Philosopher of science Michael Ruse described the scientific pursuit, emphasizing the importance of theories and stressing the invalidity of creationists' calls for observation of every aspect of evolution. Ruse also examined creationist literature, testifying that the authors of such material frequently quoted evolutionists out of context to distort their meaning. Geneticist Francisco Ayala and paleontologist Stephen Jay Gould, although representing opposing sides in the ongoing evolution debate between gradualists and saltationists, stressed that the debate did not represent disagreement on the fact of evolution. Mechanisms to explain evolution remained imperfectly understood, they admitted, but the fact of evolution was beyond question. Geologist G. Brent Dalrymple proved to be an especially effective witness, deftly destroying all the creationist arguments for a young earth by emphasizing misquotations, outdated references, and computational errors.

Some of the most dramatic testimony came from Arkansas educators who explained that they could not teach creationism and maintain their intellectual integrity. They knew that creation science was bad science. Under cross-examination, one of these teachers provided a succinct summary of the problems involved: "Look, sir! I'm not a martyr or anything! But I just can't teach that stuff. I'm not a scientist. I'm a science educator. I'm like a traffic cop, directing ideas down from scientists to schoolchildren. My pupils respect me. All teachers are like parents in a way. How can I go into my classroom, spreading ideas that I know to be wrong? My students will despise me, and I'll not be able to live with myself." Such testimony clearly showed that the creationist crusade could have far-reaching consequences.[11]

Attorney General Clark faced monumental problems in his defense of the balanced treatment law. Although he found witnesses who questioned evolution from a scientific perspective, none of them embraced creationism. Those scientists who argued for creation science admitted that they accepted the concept for religious reasons, even as they repeated traditional creationist arguments that scientific evidence existed to support their view. The state's chief theological witness, Norman Geisler of Dallas Theological Seminary, proved to be a disastrous choice. Under cross-examination, Geisler argued that the existence of Satan was clear to him because he had known at least a dozen individuals who had been possessed by the devil. Unidentified flying objects offered similar proof, as they were "Satanic manifestations for the purposes of deception."[12]

Clark's efforts were made no easier by the actions of his supposed allies. Following the attorney general's rejection of his offer of assis-

tance, Wendell Bird accused Clark of "doing an inadequate job" and
excluding the creationist attorney from the case because he did not want
to share publicity. On the Wednesday after the trial opened, the Reverend Pat Robertson informed viewers of his "700 Club" that the Arkansas attorney general had contributed to an ACLU fund drive.
Outraged that Clark had consorted with the enemy, Robertson displayed Governor White's telephone number on the screen, urging his
viewers to call the governor to express their concern. Nearly five hundred calls and several dozen telegrams followed Robertson's appeal.
The next night Robertson toned down his comments somewhat, telling
Arkansas viewers, "You ought to look into how you're being represented and if it looks like attorneys for the state look like they're about
to take a dive, do something about it." Creationists also criticized Clark
for his tactics, complaining that he should put such experts as Duane
Gish on the stand. As it became clear that Clark had no intention of
further weakening a weak case by letting ACLU attorneys go after
someone like Gish, creationists abandoned the Arkansas trial as hope-
less. When court proceedings ended on the morning of 17 December,
the state's case had all but fallen apart.[13]

Judge William R. Overton, who had spent the months before the
trial investigating the issues involved, announced his decision in
McLean v. Arkansas on 5 January 1982. Overton found Act 590 unconstitutional as an establishment of religion, stressing the three-part test
of *Lemon v. Kurtzman*. The motives of the bill's sponsors and the phrasing of the act displayed a clear religious agenda, violating the secular
purpose prong of the test. That the act sought to advance a particular
form of religion further emphasized the clash with the establishment
clause. Overton also examined the status of creation science as science,
stressing that creationists' proof of their views represented little more
than criticisms of evolution. The act's definition of evolution appeared
similarly untrustworthy, as it was "simply a hodgepodge of limited assertions, many of which are factually inaccurate." From the testimony
of plaintiffs' witnesses, Overton concluded that creation science was
not science. It could not be falsified or, finally, tested in any meaningful
way. As creation science did not represent science, Overton judged that
the act's primary purpose was the advancement of religion, violating
the second element of the three-pronged test. Entanglement of the state
with religion was also guaranteed by the act, as the religious nature of
much of the creationist material would force state officials to make
"delicate religious judgments" with respect to texts and classroom activities. Such entanglement violated the third prong of the *Lemon* test.[14]

Judge Overton similarly rejected other aspects of the creationist case. The calls for balanced treatment had emerged from Wendell Bird's *Yale Law Journal* article, which Overton dismissed as a "student note" whose "argument has no legal merit." The creationist charge that evolution represented a religion was also dismissed. Even if evolution had been shown to be a religion—which, Overton emphasized, had not occurred—the remedy would be to stop the teaching of evolution, not to add a second religion to provide "balance." Creationists' repeated assertions that a majority of Americans favored equal time remained irrelevant. First Amendment principles must have priority over public opinion polls. "No group, no matter how large or small," Overton wrote, "may use the organs of government, of which the public schools are the most conspicuous and influential, to foist its religious beliefs on others." Although Senator Holsted stated that the publicity generated by the trial provided a victory in itself, the forceful nature of Overton's decision left little doubt that Act 590 was fundamentally flawed. Attorney General Clark described the religious overtones of the act as an "insurmountable problem" that made any appeal of the decision pointless. The nation's first balanced treatment law had lasted less than a year.[15]

The Controversy Escalates

Judge Overton's decision precipitated a predictably mixed response and attracted significant attention. The editors of *Science*, for example, published the complete opinion from *McLean v. Arkansas* in their issue of 19 February 1982. In late March *Newsweek* devoted five pages to a discussion of the "enigmas of evolution," focusing on Stephen Jay Gould and his concept of punctuated equilibrium. Although emphasizing that the scientific community remained divided over the new hypothesis, the magazine quoted Gould's explanation of the meaning of the debate. "Evolution is a fact, like apples falling out of trees," Gould observed. "Darwin proposed a theory, natural selection, to explain that fact. Newton's theory of gravitation was eventually superseded by general relativity. But apples didn't stop in midair while physicists debated the question."[16] Creationists, understandably, criticized the decision even though they had given up on the case midway through the trial. Henry M. Morris observed that "a lot of people are indignant about the unfairness of the decision," implying a commitment to more energetic efforts in the future. Public opinion seemed to support creationists' endeavors, as shown by a Gallup poll conducted during the summer of 1982. Forty-four percent of the population agreed with the statement "God created man pretty much in his present form at one time within the last 10,000 years," while 38 percent accepted the idea that humans had evolved through the guidance of God after he had created them.[17] Opponents of evolution did not need to admit defeat following Overton's decision.

Creationists also found hope in Louisiana events that had moved offstage as attention focused on Arkansas. During the spring of 1981 Senator William Keith introduced a bill based on the Ellwanger draft legislation. Hearings before the Senate Education Committee resulted in several amendments, one of which made balanced treatment a local option. Other modifications dropped the "findings of fact" and the prohibition against references to religious doctrine. The committee also authorized local school boards to develop creationist resources with the aid of seven creationists to be named by the governor. In early June the Senate passed the amended bill with little discussion or dissent. Passage of the bill in the House of Representatives proved equally simple. The Education Committee restored the statewide requirement for balanced treatment but accepted all other Senate amendments. The committee then added a requirement that both evolution and creation be taught as unproven theories and attached a section prohibiting discrimination against creationists. The bill reached the House floor on 6 July, where it precipitated an animated debate. Opponents disputed the "scientific" aspects of creation science. One representative, a civil engineer, told his colleagues, "I don't want my children to be subjected to an absolute lie. Let religion stay in the churches." Such views represented a minority opinion, however, as the House passed the bill seventy-one to nineteen after defeating several amendments that would have weakened the measure.[18]

The Senate approved the House version of the bill two days later, after Keith argued, "Evolution is no more than a fairy tale about a frog that turns into a prince. We force our children to go to school, and when they get there we teach them man came from monkeys." Republican governor David C. Treen had expressed doubts about the bill, but after eleven days he decided to sign the measure because of overwhelming political and popular support. As signed, the Louisiana law required that schools provide balanced treatment for evolution and creationism, emphasizing that both were theories and not facts. Local school boards were ordered to develop curriculum guides for teaching creation science and to supply these guides to teachers. The bill also directed the governor to appoint a seven-member panel of creation scientists to assist the local boards in developing these curricula.[19]

Although involved with preparations for the *McLean* case in Arkansas, the American Civil Liberties Union decided to challenge the Louisiana statute as yet another attempt to establish religion. Before the ACLU could begin its action, however, creationists seized the legal initiative. On 2 December Wendell Bird filed a suit in Baton Rouge federal court on behalf of Keith and fifty-four other plaintiffs. Bird sought a declaratory judgment that the Louisiana statute was constitutional and an order from the court requiring the State Department of Education to implement the law as scheduled. The next day the ACLU filed its suit in a New Orleans federal court, using many of the same arguments as in the Arkansas trial, which was about to begin. The course of these two cases proved convoluted. In the Baton Rouge court, district judge Frank Polozola dismissed the creationist suit in late June 1982 because it did not raise a federal question. New Orleans judge Adrian Duplantier, who had postponed the ACLU suit pending his Baton Rouge colleague's decision, announced that he would accept a motion for summary judgment based solely on the state constitution. This motion allowed Duplantier to issue a decision on 22 November, agreeing with the plaintiffs' contention that the law usurped the authority of the Board of Elementary and Secondary Education to determine curricula for the public schools.[20] Louisiana attorney general William Guste's appeal of this decision eventually led to a review of the case by the Louisiana Supreme Court. On 17 October 1983 the court announced its four-to-three verdict overturning Duplantier's decision, concluding that the legislature did have the right to mandate the teaching of creation science or to make other curricular decisions. Following this decision, the ACLU revived its original suit, which had challenged the law on First Amendment grounds. The courts had not seen the last of the Louisiana statute.[21]

As courts in Arkansas and Louisiana examined creationist legislation, scientists and other opponents of creation science expanded their efforts to counter the newest antievolution activity. Public debates, long an effective forum for creationist presentations, no longer offered the antievolutionists unchallenged opportunities to convert their audiences. By the time of the Louisiana trials, evolutionists had become much better prepared and were using polished audiovisual presentations, as their opponents did. Increasingly, evolutionists were refuting specific creationist claims, rather than making general comments concerning the religious nature of creation science. A February 1982 debate sponsored by the Baptist Student Union at the University of Arizona brought Henry Morris and Duane Gish to Tucson to debate two opponents. The two thousand members of the audience were disappointed in the creationists' presentations, especially as neither Gish nor Morris would commit themselves to testable statements. Morris complained that the scientists were attacking the biblical creation model rather than the scientific creation model, provoking notable criticism from the audience. Gish followed his Tucson performance with a debate in Tampa, Florida, the next month, but his audience numbered no more than three hundred.[22]

Scholars in many fields increased their efforts to counter creationist arguments that could no longer be ignored. Biologists, philosophers, sociologists, and historians recognized creationism as a threat to the scientific pursuit. Theologian Roland M. Frye argued in the American Philosophical Society's *Proceedings* that scientists and mainstream religionists had long ago reached a consensus concerning creation. The public's lack of awareness of this consensus provided creationists with fertile ground for their sowing of antievolution ideas. Historian Richard P. Aulie told readers of a later issue of the same periodical that special creation represented a "biological idea of a bygone age" that had little similarity to traditional biblical concepts. Although no creationist, historian George Marsden attempted to provide a sympathetic reading of the creationist crusade, stressing that evolutionists might bear some of the responsibility. He closed his essay in *Nature* by writing, "Dogmatic proponents of evolutionary anti-supernaturalistic mythologies have been inviting responses in kind." Geneticist Thomas Jukes, veteran of California's creationist controversies, took issue with Marsden's observations, criticizing the historian for failing to stress the unscientific nature of creation science. Creationists' inventive efforts to force nature into the literal Genesis account disqualified them as both scientists and theologians.[23]

Sociologist Dorothy Nelkin identified public ignorance of science as the root of the problem. "The issue of creationism cannot be separated from the issue of science literacy," she told a reporter for the *Chronicle of Higher Education.* "We have creationism because we have a public that doesn't know what science is about." Recognizing that the lack of public understanding concerning evolution lay at the base of the controversy, several authors produced books in an attempt to solve the problem. Niles Eldredge, curator of paleontology at the American Museum of Natural History and one of the original proponents of the punctuated equilibrium concept, breezily refuted creationist arguments in *The Monkey Business: A Scientist Looks at Creationism.* His emphasis on creationists' scientific misrepresentations was complemented by paleontologist Norman D. Newell's careful study of the development of evolutionary ideas in *Creation and Evolution: Myth or Reality?* published the same year. These volumes successfully challenged the creationist contention that the paleontological record supported their views. In 1983 evolutionary biologist Douglas J. Futuyma added a tightly reasoned defense of evolution in his *Science on Trial: The Case for Evolution.*[24]

It remained for two philosophers of science, however, to contribute the most telling indictments against the creationist effort. Philip Kitcher's *Abusing Science: The Case against Creationism* examined creationist arguments and rejected them because they were based on an erroneous view of how science operated. Describing his work as "a manual for self-defense," he also emphasized that creationism represented an attack on all science, not just biology, as developmental concepts underpinned most scientific disciplines. Michael Ruse followed his testimony in Little Rock with an equally effective refutation of creationism in *Darwinism Defended: A Guide to the Evolution Controversies.* He stressed the overt religious nature of creation science and emphasized its total lack of intellectual foundation, at one point describing it as "a grotesque parody of human thought." Ruse examined creationists' citations of evolutionists' writings, finding that widespread distortion characterized the former's methods. In short, Ruse concluded, creation science could make no legitimate claim to scientific integrity.[25]

Ruse saved his most devastating critique for specific creationist misconceptions. In few discussions was he more successful than in his analysis of creationist flood arguments. After describing their explanation of the fossil record based on a literal global flood, Ruse cleverly summarized the implications of this explanation:

> Let us be quite clear what this all means. The detailed record, from simple to more complex, from general to special, from fish to man, is entirely an artifact of the flood. There was *not one* human being, or horse, or cow, or fox, or deer, or hippopotamus, or tortoise, or monkey, who was so slow, or so stupid, or so crippled, that he/she/it, lagged behind his/her/its fellows, and thus got caught down at the bottom of the hill. *Not one!* Conversely, there was *not one* dinosaur, or trilobite, or mammoth, that was lucky enough, or clever enough, or fast enough, to climb up to the top of the hill, and thus escape the fate of its fellows. *Not one!* And this we are asked to believe as sound science?[26]

From his careful analysis of creationist arguments and concepts, Ruse could reach only one conclusion. The creationists, he wrote, had failed to make their case. "Their arguments are rotten, through and through. Further, they twist, misrepresent, and otherwise distort Darwinian evolutionary theory as they attempt to refute it. Their position is not simply inadequate: it is dishonest."[27]

The appearance of a large number of books detailing the inadequacies of creation science disturbed creationists greatly. Henry Morris characterized this publishing bonanza as part of "an all-out campaign against the Creator" and devoted much of his *History of Modern Creationism* (1984) to a more sympathetic analysis of the movement. Stressing the many creationist organizations and publications in existence, Morris attempted to encourage his fellow believers by writing that the movement was "far too widespread and varied . . . for the evolutionists ever to regain the obsequious submission of the public which they used to enjoy and abuse." Morris admitted, however, that creation science faced difficulties. Creationist research proved particularly difficult because of inadequate funds. Church funds were limited and legitimately dedicated to other activities, while "the evolutionary establishment which controls science, education, and government in this country" could hardly be expected to support research that challenged its hegemony. Although many scientists wanted to accept creationism, according to Morris, peer pressure all but eliminated the conversion of science faculty to the cause. In addition, he concluded, "College professors are so conditioned to intellectualism, to scientism, and to academic prestige and peer pressure, as to be utterly unwilling to pay the price of becoming creationists."[28]

Morris made clear, however, that the creationist movement retained its religious goal, based on traditional evangelical biblical literalism. In addition to representing a campaign supported by democratic, constitutional, and scientific concepts, the drive for equal time was "a spiritual battle, and the battle plans and tactics can only really be understood in spiritual terms. The primeval war against God the Creator still continues," he argued, "and may well be entering its final critical phases." The importance of this campaign emerged forcefully in Morris's concluding chapter, in which he repeated traditional antievolutionist arguments concerning the impact of evolution. He identified evolution as the foundation for all suspect religious and philosophical views, specifically listing atheism, humanism, materialism, Buddhism, Taoism, Hinduism, Confucianism, racism, anarchism, Nazism, and communism. The growing opposition to creationism could also be explained in evangelical terms. Morris observed that "the strength of the anti-creationist opposition is growing (not the strength of the evidence, of course, but the opposition). This is not surprising," he concluded, "in view of the numerous Biblical prophecies concerning the apostasy and growth of organized opposition to God in the last days."[29]

Morris's apocalyptic vision of the late twentieth century did not prevent creationists from continuing their efforts to secure equal time legislation, despite the uncertainties surrounding the judicial fate of such measures. During the 1981-82 legislative sessions, creationist bills appeared in Florida, Georgia, Iowa, Kansas, Maryland, Mississippi, Missouri, South Carolina, South Dakota, and West Virginia. The *McLean* decision and local opposition combined to defeat these measures, most of which died in committee.[30]

The Arizona legislature became involved in a protracted struggle to deal with the creationist controversy beginning in early February 1982. Republican representative Jim Cooper, who chaired the House Education Committee, introduced a bill to prohibit the teaching of evolution "in such a way as to foster a belief in a religion or cause a disbelief in religion." Teachers violating this policy would be subject to a ten-thousand-dollar fine and up to one year in prison. Although the measure floundered for lack of support, a similar bill passed both houses during the spring of 1983. The Senate opposed the creationist legislation, but Representative Cooper held a priority Senate bill in his committee until the upper house agreed to accept the new law. Governor Bruce Babbitt, however, viewed the bill as an attempt to establish religion and limit scientific inquiry. He vetoed the measure on 29 April, less than a week after its passage. His veto was sustained.[31]

Tennessee again expressed its discomfort with evolution during the 1984 and 1985 legislative sessions. Representative Pete Drew, a Democrat from Knoxville, twice introduced "The Balanced Treatment for Creation-Science and Evolution-Science Act," attracting little interest in 1984 but significant attention a year later. Drew's purpose in proposing the legislation was made clear in an interview with Hedy Weinberg, executive director of the state ACLU chapter. He stated, "We are losing children every day to penitentiaries because there is no foundation of values in the schools. We need teaching that puts God back in the classroom." After discussion of the proposed bill before the House Education Committee, Nashville Democrat Steve Cobb moved to defer indefinitely Drew's measure, a motion that passed fifteen to four. Despite his defeat, Drew remained convinced that the bill was appropriate and looked forward to future efforts. "It's not popular politically right now," he told a reporter after the vote, "but as more people learn about the issue, they'll understand that creation is a science." Representative Cobb viewed things from a different perspective. He explained his opposition to a Nashville journalist by emphasizing that the imposition of a religious view was "a misuse of the power of the state."[32]

The Twilight of Creation Science

Despite failures in legislatures and courtrooms, opposition to the teaching of evolution remained evident during the 1980s. As stressed by many observers, creationism represented a grass-roots movement that focused on converting local school boards to the antievolution perspective. Anthropologist Eugenie Scott warned the 1982 meeting of the American Anthropological Association that scientists had no right to be complacent following the *McLean* decision. Not only were local education officials sympathetic to the well-organized creationist campaigns, but individual teachers had many opportunities to introduce their students to creation science, regardless of state or local action. The controversy was far from over.[33]

Opponents of creationism were encouraged, however, by developments in Texas that began in the fall of 1983. Biology texts adopted for state use were still bound by the 1974 rule requiring a statement that evolution was a theory rather than a fact. The rule also mandated that evolution be identified in the texts "as only one of several explanations of the origins of humankind." Opponents of these requirements persuaded state senator Oscar Mauzy, chairman of the Senate Jurisprudence Committee, to request an opinion from the Texas attorney general concerning the constitutionality of the guidelines. After he received this request in October 1983, Attorney General Jim Mattox took nearly five months to develop a comprehensive opinion based on Judge Overton's decision in the *McLean* case. Mattox ruled that the board of education's 1974 rule was unconstitutional. The guidelines represented a clear response to creationist pressure and thus displayed no secular purpose in singling out evolution for special restriction. "The inference is inescapable," he wrote, "that a concern for religious sensibilities, rather than a dedication to scientific truth, was the real motivation for the rules."[34]

Mattox's decision paralleled a growing concern over the inadequacies of public education. Texas had been engaged for several years in a concerted effort to establish itself as an important center for science and technology, upgrading university faculty and investing significant sums in new laboratories. The contradiction between the state's campaign for scientific eminence and the inadequacies of its educational system struck politicians and business leaders forcefully. Governor Mark White's Select Committee on Public Education, chaired by noted industrialist H. Ross Perot, issued a very critical preliminary report in the spring of 1984, blaming the board of education for the state's low academic standards and suggesting that the elected board should be replaced by an appointed body.

The Texas Board of Education responded quickly to this pressure. At its April meeting in El Paso, the board agreed to repeal the 1974 text guidelines. Norma Gabler, who had encouraged the adoption of the original rule, did not think the board's action would make any difference, as she doubted that textbook publishers had ever taken the guidelines seriously. "They still show hunched-over men moving up to man from monkeys and fishes coming out of the water. If you want to believe you came from a monkey," she told a reporter, "that's fine, but I don't." Formal repeal of the guidelines came in June and was followed later in the year by legislation to replace the elected board of education with a body appointed by the governor. Texas officials quickly demanded better coverage of evolution in adopted texts. Publishers met these demands rapidly to secure part of the eighty-million-dollar state textbook budget.[35]

The waning fortunes of creationism were also visible in California. Concerned with inadequate texts, the members of the curriculum commission held hearings on science textbooks in late July 1985. Although creationists repeated their standard charges against evolution, several scientists urged the commission to adopt texts that examined evolution in a more appropriate fashion. After this testimony, the commission rejected all seventh- and eighth-grade science texts submitted for adoption, a decision ratified by the State Board of Education two months later. The board's action pleased superintendent of public instruction Bill Honig, elected in 1982 as a reform candidate, who had long criticized publishers for inadequate texts.[36]

The board asked the publishers of the best texts to revise their publications to improve the discussion of evolution. The subcommittee charged with overseeing the revisions, however, included no biologists and accepted what geneticist Thomas Jukes called "perfunctory and inadequate" revisions that failed to remove many of the most glaring errors. References to evolutionary ideas remained vague because of numerous qualifiers inserted to avoid controversy. Despite objections by scientists and creationists, the latter of whom testified that the texts included too much evolution, the State Board of Education voted seven to two to adopt the ten revised texts. Scientists continued to point out errors, hoping to convince the publishers to correct them before final printing. The likelihood of major changes remained small, however, as publishers emphasized that failure to accept existing revisions would make it impossible to deliver texts for the start of the school year in September.[37]

Although beginning to lose strength because of a growing concern about the quality of science education, creationism remained an effective force in the mid-1980s. A 1984 survey of 2,400 science students at Ohio State University provided little encouragement for science educators. Only 63 percent accepted evolutionary theory, while 80 percent believed that both creation and evolution should be taught in public schools.[38] Creationist sympathies remained at large in the political world as well. Former representative Jim Cooper became education adviser to controversial Arizona governor Evan Mecham after the 1986 election. Testifying in favor of an equal time bill before the House Education Committee, Cooper stressed the traditional fairness arguments. When asked by a committee member to explain what would happen if a student told a geography teacher that his parents said the world was flat, Cooper responded, "The schools don't have any business telling people what to believe." No vote was taken on the bill. In Tennessee, Governor Ned Ray McWherter announced to an office news conference that his administration would "vigorously pursue" the superconducting supercollider project, one of the largest federally funded science programs ever proposed. At the same conference, however, the governor expressed his support for the equal time concept. "I think both theories should be taught," he told the reporters. "That's my own personal opinion. If one's taught, both should be taught."[39] Texas, not Tennessee, was chosen as the supercollider site.

Recognizing the continued support for the creationist outlook, opponents of creation science expanded their efforts. These opponents increasingly investigated the scientific claims of creationists, utilizing accepted methods and techniques. Such investigations led to a dramatic refutation of a major creationist claim in the mid-1980s. Humanlike footprints next to dinosaur tracks near Glen Rose, Texas, had been cited by creationists as evidence that humans and dinosaurs lived at the same time. If true, the contemporary existence of these two organisms would challenge much of evolutionary theory. A closer examination of these tracks, however, disclosed that the supposed human footprints were either "inept carvings" from the 1930s or actual dinosaur tracks that had not been weathered in the same fashion as other tracks. Even creationists accepted these new disclosures, withdrawing their film *Footprints in Stone* from circulation.[40]

Foes of creation science also challenged other aspects of creationist arguments. In 1986 Jesuit priest and geologist James W. Skehan published a carefully written essay in which he examined the origin, background, and purpose of the first part of Genesis. Skehan stressed that Genesis was not history in the modern sense. The authors of Genesis viewed history "as a linear movement of events determined by divine interventions and directed toward a divinely conceived goal," rather than as a careful chronicle of human activity. Equally important, the Genesis creation story followed Babylonian creation myths of which the ancient Israelites were well aware. The purpose of Genesis was to stress the religious aspects of creation that distinguished Israel from its neighbors, making the creation portion of the document a prelude to the more important account of the fall of Adam and Eve and the consequent human estrangement from God. As Skehan concluded, the creation story in Genesis represented the "beginning of salvation history," not a scientific discussion of geologic and biological origins.[41]

Oxford zoologist Richard Dawkins provided an impressive defense of evolution and an effective refutation of the design argument in *The Blind Watchmaker,* published in 1987. Emphasizing the misinterpretations and misrepresentations abundant in creationist literature, Dawkins exposed the flaws in creationists' arguments against evolution. He was particularly effective in refuting the traditional antievolutionist argument that evolution could not lead to observed changes through "blind chance." Dawkins stressed that innumerable intermediate steps took place to transform biological structures. Creationists misrepresented evolution by insisting that such changes took place all at once.[42]

Analyses of the rise of creation science also began to appear in the mid-1980s, leading to intriguing conclusions about American society, thought, and culture in the late twentieth century. Writing in *Nature,* sociologist Michael A. Cavanaugh stressed that contemporary creationists could not be dismissed as marginal members of the current secular society. Their college degrees identified them as participants in America's experiment in mass education. Cavanaugh observed, however, that this mass education effects a mixed blessing, for it "enlarges society's pool of intellectuals, but also confers academic degrees upon people contemptuous of intellect and unfamiliar with the life of the mind." He thus characterized creation science as a "specialized *parascientific* movement" that operated outside professional research channels. "Procedure is disregarded," he wrote, "in favor of direct access to a science-independent, oracular, God's-eye view of nature (literally so)." When combined with the traditional fundamentalist belief that the individual was the unit of knowledge acquisition through rigid inductivism, the creationists' view of the scientific pursuit allowed them to bypass normal research methods. This intellectual base of the creationists' subculture helped to explain the large number of fundamentalists who encouraged their children to enter engineering and other technical fields. By focusing on simple solutions to practical problems, a fundamentalist engineer would not be placed in a position of challenging the subculture's existing order.[43]

Theologian Langdon Gilkey attempted to understand the growth of creation science from a slightly different perspective, focusing on the existence of a scientific culture in America. He accused the scientific community of misusing its cultural dominance by overstating its case. When a biology teacher said that science had disproved Genesis, he or she created a large number of new creationists. Dismissing religion as unimportant went outside the limits of science, a situation that precipitated an understandable reaction on the part of many religionists. Yet these opponents of science did not abandon the scientific culture. Ironically, they based their opposition on a definition of science as "facts," believing that they participated in the accepted scientific culture. Combining this view of science with religion led to the belief—a dangerous one, in Gilkey's view—that all truth, scientific and religious, was defined in the same empirical fashion. Creation science emerged from the fundamentalists' belief that their religious views enjoyed scientific validity. The "facts" of the Bible were as important to creationists of the 1980s as they had been to earlier antievolutionists.[44]

Creationism in the Courts

Despite the criticism and refutation of creation science by scientists, theologians, and others, the immediate fate of the movement remained in the hands of lawyers and judges in Louisiana. After the Louisiana Supreme Court's decision in late 1983, the ACLU case challenging the state's balanced treatment law returned to Judge Duplantier's courtroom. During preparations for the expected trial, the state legislature attempted to repeal the equal time law, but intense lobbying by creationist groups thwarted the effort. Encouraged by the prospect of another full-scale trial, creationist leaders appeared optimistic. Henry Morris observed that the Louisiana case would likely be more important than the *McLean* trial because the state "really *wants* to win the case," a desire shown by the appointment of Wendell Bird as special assistant attorney general. Morris and other defenders of the statute also stressed that the Louisiana law was less vulnerable to the constitutional objections raised against the Arkansas legislation.[45]

Judge Duplantier disagreed with the creationists' evaluation. On 10 January 1985 he granted the plaintiffs' motion for a pretrial summary judgment that the statute was unconstitutional on First Amendment grounds. Reaching the same conclusions about creationism as his Arkansas colleague, Judge Overton, Duplantier argued that the Louisiana balanced treatment law represented an unconstitutional attempt to establish religion. "Because it promotes the beliefs of some theistic sects to the detriment of others," he wrote in his opinion, "the statute violates the fundamental First Amendment principle . . . that a state must be neutral in its treatment of religions."[46]

Not surprisingly, Duplantier's decision troubled creationists. Senator Keith accused the judge of bias, while Bird convinced the state's attorney general to appeal the ruling to the Fifth Circuit Court of Appeals. The three-member panel appointed to consider the case acted quickly on the state's motion to overturn Duplantier's order. On 8 July the appeals court upheld the earlier decision that the Louisiana law violated the separation of church and state. Judge E. Grady Jolly wrote in his opinion that the statute under review continued the 1920s antievolution crusade associated with William Jennings Bryan. "The act's intended effect," he concluded, "is to discredit evolution by counterbalancing its teaching at every turn with the teaching of creationism, a religious belief." Defeated again, Louisiana attorney general William Guste petitioned the entire fifteen-member circuit court for a rehearing of the case. Although the court denied this petition in December, they did so only by an eight-to-seven vote. The minority opinion, written by Judge Thomas G. Gee, criticized the majority for forbidding "a state to require the teaching of truth." Gee stressed that evolution did not represent an "established fact" and cited evidence that the universe and life came about in a different fashion, "one perhaps less inconsistent with religious doctrine." As Attorney General Guste emphasized in his announcement that Louisiana would appeal to the United States Supreme Court, the narrowness of the circuit court's decision indicated significant judicial support for the law. Creationists had made important converts.[47]

The Supreme Court, however, continued to embrace the concept of the wall of separation, a commitment evident in two recent cases concerning Alabama's attempt to return state-sponsored prayers to the public schools. Despite earlier judicial opinions, the Alabama government had composed a prayer for use in the public schools, an action invalidated by the Court in 1984. Undaunted, the legislature passed a new law that created a moment of silence at the beginning of the school day "for meditation or voluntary prayer." In a six-to-three vote in 1985, the Court ruled that this law was an unconstitutional attempt to advance religion. In her concurring opinion, Justice Sandra Day O'Connor emphasized the difference between a moment of silence, which would probably be constitutionally acceptable, and a state-sponsored religious exercise.[48]

On 5 May 1986 the United States Supreme Court announced that it would hear the Louisiana case. The growing opposition to creation science mobilized quickly, filing a dozen *amicus curiae* briefs supporting the lower courts' decisions. The brief filed by the National Academy of Sciences discussed in detail the evidence supporting evolution, while other documents stressed weaknesses in the Louisiana law in particular and creation science in general. Nobel laureate Murray Gell-Mann of the California Institute of Technology coordinated the preparation of a brief bearing the signatures of seventy-two Nobel Prize winners, opposing the law as disguised religion rather than science.[49]

During oral arguments on 10 December, each side repeated its earlier positions. Bird told the Court that Duplantier's summary judgment had been in error and that a full trial was needed to weigh the merits of creation science. Such a trial would prove, Bird stressed, that creation science was indeed science. He also examined the *Lemon* test at some length, stressing that the Louisiana statute passed all three prongs. The law had as its primary purpose the promotion of academic freedom, clearly the required secular purpose. Because creation science did not necessarily assume the existence of a supreme being, it could not be an attempt to establish religion. Finally, Bird argued that teachers' good faith could be assumed, obviating the need for close monitoring of their performance. This eliminated the possibility of excessive entanglement. ACLU attorney Jay Topkis stressed the religious nature of creation science and argued that the Louisiana law had a religious purpose. Despite frequent challenges from Justice Antonin Scalia, Topkis argued persuasively that the statute violated the First Amendment prohibition against an establishment of religion.[50]

The Supreme Court announced its decision in *Edwards v. Aguillard* on 19 June 1987, finding the Louisiana law unconstitutional by a vote of seven to two. In his majority opinion, Justice William J. Brennan made it quite clear that the state's arguments in defense of the statute were unconvincing. The claimed secular purpose of the act could not be justified. "While the Court is normally deferential to a State's articulation of a secular purpose," he observed, "it is required that the statement of such purpose be sincere and not a sham." An analysis of the legislative history of the act left little doubt that Senator Keith's purpose in sponsoring the bill was a narrowing of the science curriculum to protect specific religious sensibilities. The law similarly failed to achieve the stated goal of fairness. The act required curriculum guides for creation science, but not for evolution. Only creationists were to serve on the resource panel, not evolutionists. The act protected those who taught creationism, but not those who taught evolution. Such contradictions made it impossible to take the act's claims seriously.[51]

Equally damaging to the act was its overt religiosity. Placing Louisiana in the tradition of historical antievolutionism, Brennan stressed that the purpose of the legislation could only be the advancement of a specific religious viewpoint. The act's primary goal could not be defined as advancing academic freedom, but only as an attempt to modify the public school science curriculum "to provide persuasive advantage to a particular religious doctrine that rejects the factual basis of evolution in its entirety." Interpreting the law as favorably as possible, Brennan concluded that the purpose remained either to promote creation science, which embodied a particular religious view, or to prohibit the teaching of a scientific theory that offended certain religious groups. In either case, the law violated the establishment clause. The clear religious nature of creation science, as portrayed in Louisiana's statute, could not be constitutionally justified.[52]

Although agreeing with the need to strike down the law, justices Lewis Powell, Jr., and Sandra Day O'Connor contributed a separate opinion. Written by Powell, the concurring opinion emphasized that the law attempted to advance religion. The claim that it promoted academic freedom Powell found "puzzling." The concept of academic freedom, as Powell understood it, did "not encompass the right of a legislature to structure the public school curriculum in order to advance a particular religious belief." Powell and O'Connor wished to stress, however, that the Court's decision should not be seen as outlawing all mention of religion in the public schools. Teaching *about* religion in public schools was both appropriate and constitutional. Indeed, knowledge of religion remained important to an understanding of much of American history, and comparative religion courses had long been judged to be acceptable. The Louisiana law, however, attempted to accomplish a different goal, which clashed with the First Amendment. "The Establishment Clause is properly understood," Powell wrote, "to prohibit the use of the Bible and other religious documents in public school education only when the purpose of the use is to advance a particular religious belief." The Louisiana law failed, not because it had some vague connection with religious concepts, but because it attempted to provide a state sanction to a specific religion.[53]

Chief Justice William Rehnquist and Justice Scalia could not accept their colleagues' arguments. In a blistering dissent, Scalia argued that the majority had made a far broader judgment than necessary. The Louisiana legislature's statement of secular purpose could not be so cavalierly dismissed as a "sham," especially as the state supreme court had never had an opportunity to rule on the law. The absence of a hearing based on evidence further suggested to Scalia that the Court had proceeded too hastily. Faced with affidavits that creation science was science, the Court must conclude that creationism could be taught without religious doctrine, a conclusion probably reached by the Louisiana legislature. "Our task is not to judge the debate about teaching the origins of life," he wrote, "but to ascertain what the members of the Louisiana Legislature believed. The vast majority of them voted to approve a bill which explicitly stated a secular purpose; what is crucial is not their *wisdom* in believing that purpose would be achieved by the bill, but their *sincerity* in believing it would be." Based on the record available to the justices, there existed no reason to reject the scientific legitimacy of creation science. The legislature's purpose should be accepted at face value.[54]

Scalia repeated many of the arguments that had surfaced during the various antievolution campaigns. He argued that creation science was not necessarily religious, observing that "to posit a past creator is not to posit the eternal and personal God who is the object of religious veneration." He accused the majority of misunderstanding the concept of academic freedom, which in this case meant "freedom from indoctrination." The Louisiana legislature believed that creationists were being discriminated against; they acted to correct this situation. By requiring creationist curriculum guides, they had merely attempted to balance the guides already in place that included evolutionary concepts. Scalia also employed the creationist complaint that antievolutionists had assumed the mantle of John Scopes as individuals whose rights had been trampled. The state of Louisiana, he stressed, had as much right to require the teaching of the scientific evidence against evolution as Scopes had to teach the evidence supporting evolution.[55] In the present case, the Court could go no further:

> Perhaps what the Louisiana Legislature has done is unconstitutional because there *is* no such evidence, and the scheme they have established will amount to no more than a presentation of the Book of Genesis. But we cannot say that on the evidence before us in this summary judgment

context, which includes ample uncontradicted testimony that "creation science" is a body of scientific knowledge rather than revealed belief. *Infinitely less* can we say (or should we say) that the scientific evidence for evolution is so conclusive that no one could be gullible enough to believe that there is any real scientific evidence to the contrary, so that the legislation's stated purpose must be a lie. Yet that illiberal judgment, that *Scopes*-in-reverse, is ultimately the basis on which the Court's facile rejection of the Louisiana Legislature's purpose must rest.[56]

Scalia and Rehnquist also embraced the nonpreferentialist view of the establishment clause. Scalia concluded that "it is far from an inevitable reading of the Establishment Clause that it forbids all governmental action intended to advance religion; and if not inevitable, any reading with such untoward consequences must be wrong."[57]

Despite Scalia's dramatic dissent, the Louisiana law had been declared unconstitutional and void. Responses to the decision were mixed, even among creationists. A few hours after the decision was announced, the Reverend Pat Robertson called it an "intellectual scandal." Wendell Bird admitted his disappointment but stressed that the Court had issued a rather narrow decision. The justices had not ruled on the constitutionality of teaching scientific creationism in the classroom; they had only declared unconstitutional a state attempt to require such teaching. Louisiana attorney general Guste picked up on the same hopeful sign, explaining to a New York *Times* reporter that "this decision, while it struck down the Louisiana law, in fact unshackled teachers and enabled them to teach all scientific evidence with regard to the origin of human life, plant life, animal life and the universe." Those who had labored so diligently to overturn the statute, however, viewed the Court's decision as an encouraging sign that they could return to teaching science in a professionally acceptable fashion. Donald Aguillard, the first-named plaintiff in the case, focused on the immediate impact of the decision on his own Acadiana High School, stating: "We just don't have the money now to be spending on bad science. I'm excited, I'm pleased, I'm relieved."[58]

Whether or not the Supreme Court had dealt creationism a fatal blow, the *Aguillard* decision clearly constrained antievolutionists in their efforts to secure legislation to further their cause. Individual teachers could continue to present creationist dogma in their biology classes, and local school boards could remain committed to avoiding the controversy by downplaying evolution in the science curriculum. Textbook publishers, although increasingly aware of the opposition to mediocrity in science education, made no more than incremental changes, to alienate as few text selection committees as possible. The *Aguillard* decision focused only on state legislative action; it made no attempt to go further. At that level at least, the creation science campaign had ground to a halt, facing a barrier in the establishment clause that could be neither broached nor dismantled. ACLU executive director Ira Glasser provided a poignant perspective on this latest chapter in the antievolution controversy shortly after the *Aguillard* decision. "Somewhere in heaven," he told a reporter, "John Scopes is smiling."[59]

Epilogue

Educational reform efforts would have been well served had the *Aguillard* decision eliminated the controversy over evolutionary teaching in American public schools. Despite the Supreme Court's decision, however, the place of evolution in the biology curriculum was only slightly more secure than it had been at the apex of the creationist crusade. Evangelists such as Jerry Falwell, Pat Robertson, and Jimmy Swaggart continued to preach a gospel to their electronic flocks that defined evolution as the foundation of many of the world's problems. Their declining political power—as shown by Robertson's abortive effort to secure the 1988 Republican presidential nomination—and the exposure of questionable moral and financial activities had little impact on the converted, who continued to support their television shepherds through media tribulations and courtroom trials. When Falwell disbanded the Moral Majority in 1989, only the institutional focus faded; the foes of modernism continued their efforts to censor school textbooks and to secure legislative support for their moral and political views.[1] The late 1980s and early 1990s witnessed no high-visibility creationist crusades to be sure, but opponents of evolution remained committed to their cause and continued to enjoy notable success.

Shortly after the *Aguillard* decision, antievolution sentiment attracted the attention of officials in the nation's capital. Despite a growing awareness that American students' knowledge of science was grossly inadequate, National Science Foundation programs in science education remained vulnerable to political pressures. Congressional officials recognized that the so-called Christian Right continued to represent an important political force. In addition, members of Congress and their aides were generally poorly informed about issues in science and technology. When creationists paraded their scientific credentials and employed technical jargon in discussions, their arguments appeared as definitive as those made by scientists from major universities. With no basis for evaluation of the evidence presented, aides frequently recommended political solutions to the problems presented by the creationist-evolutionist clash. The fairness arguments that had formed the keystone of the creationist political campaigns thus proved seductive and curtailed prospects for the improvement of science education through federal action. National Science Foundation officials recognized the situation in Congress and tacitly agreed to sacrifice science education programs to maintain support for their many other endeavors.[2]

The lack of scientific awareness among members of Congress was hardly surprising, as the public they represented was still scientifically illiterate. The dismal quality of Americans' scientific knowledge emerged dramatically from various surveys conducted during the late 1980s. In one poll conducted during the summer of 1988, only 12 percent of the respondents agreed with the statement that astrology was "not at all scientific." A team of researchers from Northern Illinois University surveyed more than two thousand adults and discovered a significant lack of the most basic scientific knowledge. More than a fifth of those interviewed believed that the sun revolved around the earth. Less than half of all respondents knew that the earth revolved around the sun once a year, with an incredible 36 percent answering that they did not have any idea how often the earth revolved around the sun. Scientific illiteracy was not restricted to astronomy. Fewer than half of those interviewed knew that the electron was smaller than the atom, while 37 percent said they did not know.[3]

A survey of public school biology teachers brought equally disturbing results. Researchers from the University of Texas at Arlington polled four hundred biology instructors throughout the nation and found that only a quarter had biology degrees. Not surprisingly, their knowledge of science and its implications remained fundamentally flawed. Half of those interviewed either agreed with the statement "Some races of people are more intelligent than others" or were not sure. Twenty-seven percent said it was possible for the living to communicate with the dead. The Arlington researchers also found that one-third of biology teachers either believed that dinosaurs and humans lived at the same time or were not sure.[4]

The institutional foundation of the creation science movement weathered various storms during the five years following the *Aguillard* decision, with somewhat ambiguous results. The ability of the Institute for Creation Research to function as an educational center was compromised by California's continuing efforts to improve education. The state had become a haven for mail-order colleges, which granted academic credit for "life experiences" and enabled individuals to obtain undergraduate or graduate degrees with very little academic effort. In 1986 the California legislature tightened requirements and review procedures for schools that had taken advantage of the state's policy toward private post-secondary institutions. Among those programs that operated under such approval was the graduate school attached to the Institute for Creation Research.

During the summer of 1988 the ICR graduate school applied for reapproval of its program under the new law. A team of five scientists visited the institution in August to determine whether the program warranted continuation. The panel remained doubtful about the "science" taught at the school but felt uncomfortable with the idea of closing the facility. They thus voted three to two to reapprove the program. Superintendent of public instruction Bill Honig, who had been conducting an active campaign to improve the state's educational system, asked the panel to reconsider its decision. He informed ICR that his office would only approve recertification if the institute stopped calling what it taught "science." Henry Morris and his staff steadfastly refused to accept this ultimatum, maintaining the position that their credentials qualified them as scientists. After further review of the situation, a Stanford geophysicist who had earlier supported recertification switched his vote, providing a majority to revoke the ICR's license. Honig announced on 7 December that the ICR graduate school had been barred from granting graduate degrees in science. Understandably, Morris saw Honig's actions as yet another example of the evolutionary establishment at work. "We think this is a matter of discrimination against creationists," he told a New York *Times* reporter. Repeating standard arguments that creation science included no religion, Morris insisted that the only difference between ICR courses and secular science courses was that creationists "assume that animals were created by God and that they did not evolve."[5]

Despite the apparent chasm between the views of Morris and Honig, discussions continued concerning potential modifications to ICR's program that would prevent decertification. These discussions led Honig to schedule a second review for the summer of 1989, which resulted in a forty-eight-page report filed the following January. The review panel criticized the quality of science education offered by the institute, although it did not specifically focus on creationism in its recommendation to deny reapproval of the graduate program. In March Honig announced that he had accepted this recommendation to revoke the institute's license. The Institute for Creation Research soon filed suits in both federal and state courts on First Amendment and procedural grounds, respectively.

Before arguments could be made in these cases, however, the California legislature intervened. During the summer of 1990 the legislature adopted a statute that removed responsibility for licensing private schools from the Department of Education. A new agency, the Council for Private Post-Secondary and Vocational Education, would begin operating the following January. Honig agreed to restore the ICR license and turn the decision on recertification over to the new agency. The education department abandoned its position in state court in November, citing technical flaws in its earlier procedures and emphasizing that its revocation of the ICR license no longer held.

The attorney for the department hoped that the restoration of the ICR certification would convince the institute to abandon its federal suit as well. Morris and his colleagues, however, remained committed to the goal of establishing their curriculum as legitimate science and continued their preparation throughout 1991. Because the Department of Education no longer had jurisdiction over licensing, the board's attorney decided not to contest the suit and agreed to an out-of-court settlement, announced on 31 January 1992. In this settlement, the state agreed to remove the earlier negative reviews of the ICR program from its files and to prevent Honig from participating in future reviews of the institute. The institute would remain free to teach creation science as a scientific discipline and would receive $225,000 from the state of California. A review of the ICR graduate program would be conducted by the new agency, but the necessity of reviewing more than two thousand private unaccredited institutions in the state made such a review unlikely before 1995. Until then the ICR graduate program could continue to offer graduate degrees in creation science.[6]

The continued strength of the creationist effort also led to ambiguous results in attempts to revitalize science teaching in the public schools. In January 1989 the California Board of Education announced its decision to strengthen the teaching of evolution. Theories based on religious beliefs were described as only appropriate in nonscience courses. Although associate state superintendent Francie Alexander applauded the announcement as a message to textbook publishers to remove unwarranted qualifying statements concerning evolution, others were less pleased. The Reverend Louis Sheldon of Anaheim, president of the Traditional Values Group, criticized the decision and expressed his fear that it would bar students from challenging the teaching of evolution in class.

Implementing the board's new policy required appropriate textbook guidelines. In July the state curriculum commission adopted seven-year guidelines for science texts for grades one through eight. These guidelines, approved after a heated exchange between creationists and evolutionists, excluded biblical teachings from science classrooms. Because the guidelines would have to be approved by the board of education during its meeting in November, intensive lobbying efforts soon began. At their Los Angeles meeting, board members made concessions to the creationist position by deleting a phrase from the document that referred to evolution as a "scientific fact." They also removed discussions of the National Academy of Sciences publication *Science and Creationism* and the United States Supreme Court's decision in *Edwards v. Aguillard.* The ambiguity of the board's position was heightened by its retention of a later statement that described evolution as "both a fact and a theory." Superintendent Honig was pleased with the board's decision, telling a New York *Times* reporter, "The things that stayed in were more powerful than the things that were taken out." Other observers were less satisfied with the compromises. Eugenie Scott, executive director of the National Center for Science Education, expressed her concern that the board's actions would send mixed signals to textbook publishers.[7]

During the fall of 1990 Texas again became the center of attention for those concerned with the teaching of science in public schools. In November the Texas State Board of Education voted eleven to four to approve eight new biology texts for grades one through twelve, all of which gave extensive coverage to evolution. Despite significant lobbying by creationists, the board refused to consider textbooks that discussed creation science. The Texas decision appeared to be a notable defeat for creationists. In March 1989 the board had adopted a last-minute amendment to new science education guidelines that required the inclusion of "other valid scientific theories" in addition to evolution. This decision was now overturned. Even more important, two of the books approved in November were editions of BSCS texts that had been excluded from Texas schools for the past twenty years. The science textbook committee that had reviewed texts ranked the BSCS volumes first and second among the texts under consideration. The return of recognized textbooks of high quality suggested that creationists in Texas had lost significant political power.[8]

Although decisions concerning texts and curricula focused on the local level, America's continuing evolution controversy retained the potential to attract national attention. During the fall of 1990, for example, observers of the controversy learned of science writer Forrest M. Mims III and his clash with the respected periodical *Scientific American.* Mims, who had contributed to such science magazines as *National Geographic World* and *Science Digest,* had applied in May 1988 to take over the "Amateur Scientist" column for *Scientific American.* By the summer of 1989 Mims had emerged as the leading candidate to assume this position, leading editor Jonathan Piel to invite the writer to New York for an interview. During their discussion, Mims described himself as a conservative Christian who accepted the biblical account of creation. When asked by Piel if he accepted evolution, Mims replied that he did not. The writer stressed that he was not part of the creation science movement, but his admission led to considerable discussion among the editors at *Scientific American* and many telephone conversations between Mims and the magazine's staff.

Although several editors accepted Mims's work as "perfectly good" and thought that he should be hired to write the column, Piel proved more concerned with the potential implication of a "creationist" on the staff of one of America's leading scientific periodicals. Even if Mims did not abuse his position to advance the creationist cause, Piel concluded, his connection with *Scientific American* would likely be cited by leaders of the creation science movement in support of their arguments for scientific legitimacy. Piel eventually agreed to print three of Mims's columns, the last of which appeared in the October 1990 issue, but he decided not to hire the writer to oversee the "Amateur Scientist" column.

Piel's decision precipitated widely divergent comments. Suggestions that Mims was a victim of discrimination by the evolutionary establishment were countered by arguments that the magazine's credibility could be compromised with Mims on the staff. Everett Olson, emeritus professor of biology at UCLA, told a New York *Times* reporter, "If it were known that he was a creationist, it would give quite a boost to those pushing creation science." Other biologists were less certain of the threat posed by Mims. Mary Ann Rankin, chair of the division of biological sciences at the University of Texas, admitted that Mims could create a problem for *Scientific American* if he spoke out about creationism. "But," she concluded, "he would have to be making a real fuss about creationism for it to be much of a factor." The Mims controversy had largely evaporated by the spring of 1991, but it had demonstrated that the evolution debate remained a topic of interest.[9]

During the summer of 1991, another chapter in the evolution controversy in America attracted national attention. University of California law professor Phillip Johnson published *Darwin on Trial,* designed to show the weaknesses in evolutionary theory. Stressing that he was not an advocate of creation science, Johnson nonetheless repeated many of the arguments used by creationists and soon won the endorsement of the Institute for Creation Research. *Darwin on Trial* cited disagreements among evolutionists as evidence of the theory's weaknesses, emphasized the irrationality of "chance" leading to complex organs, and stressed the lack of fossil evidence that clearly showed constant progression. Examining evolution from the perspective of his legal training and experience, the Berkeley professor followed a path parallel to that of antievolutionists who insisted on direct observational evidence as the only "proof" of evolution. Failing to find such evidence, Johnson rejected evolution, as had his predecessors. He thus concluded that evolution was only accepted among scientists because it was the secular religion with which they were comfortable.

Johnson's book aroused much interest in both the electronic and print media, which viewed *Darwin on Trial* as an intriguing new evaluation of the evolution controversy. Reviewers of this work tended to follow predictable paths. Author Doug Bandow told readers of the conservative *National Review*, for example, that Johnson had attacked "perhaps the most bloated of sacred cows: evolution." Paleontologist Stephen Jay Gould understandably expressed a rather different perspective in his review for *Scientific American*. Gould's negative review stressed two shortcomings in Johnson's discussion of the supposed weaknesses of evolution. The lawyer attempted to apply legal criteria to the evolution debate without making any effort to understand the criteria biologists used. Even more disappointing, however, was Johnson's obvious lack of knowledge concerning the theory of evolution itself. Gould wrote, "I see no evidence that Johnson has ever visited a scientist's laboratory . . . or has read widely beyond writing for nonspecialists and the most 'newsworthy' of professional claims." The lack of specific knowledge and the inability to comprehend the scientist's craft combined to discredit Johnson's attack. Yet the notoriety Johnson's book achieved during the last few months of 1991 served as another reminder of the continuing controversy.[10]

Creation science emerged again as a potentially important part of the nation's political structure in the early 1990s. Responding to reports and widespread perceptions that the nation's schools were failing in their educational functions, the administration of President George Bush announced a plan to make federal funds available for parents to send their children to any school they wished. The "school choice" proposal was designed to allow parents to send their children to public, private, or parochial schools, using "vouchers" to offset part of the cost. Defended by administration officials and sympathetic observers as returning power to "education's consumers," the proposed program encouraged creationists. Private religious schools, long the principal market for creationist texts and educational material, could now attract larger numbers of students. Families who remained uncomfortable with public education would be able to send their children to "Christian schools" with the financial support of the federal government. Although congressional support proved inadequate to implement the voucher plan, the concept of school choice remained an important issue throughout the 1992 election campaigns.[11]

The defeat of President Bush by Democrat Bill Clinton obscured several important aspects of the November elections. Postelection analyses showed that the Christian Right had, in fact, enjoyed success in presenting its agenda to the public. In San Diego, a meeting of school board candidates elicited various proposals. Among the most noteworthy were calls for organized school prayer, the teaching of creation science, textbook and library censorship, and the public financing of Christian schools. In several states the Republican party machinery came under the control of conservative activists who wrote party platforms that supported their views. In Iowa and Washington, for example, Republican platforms included specific calls for the teaching of creationism in the public schools. Although their support of President Bush had failed to return him to the White House, the religious Right was not completely disappointed at the election of Bill Clinton. Viewing the new president as a proabortion, prohomosexual liberal, these activists quickly began making plans to combat the new administration. The battlefield, however, would be at the local level, where they had been most effective. Their candidates had won approximately 40 percent of the local races they contested, making significant inroads in state legislatures, city councils, and school boards. The Christian Right could thus look ahead to active involvement in monitoring and influencing curricular and textbook decisions.[12]

The decision of the Christian Right to focus on local politics paralleled a similar decision by creationist leaders following the *Aguillard* decision. Failing to convince courts that state-mandated teaching of creation science was constitutionally legitimate, creationists redirected their efforts. They recognized that many educational decisions were made at the local level and believed that they would find there a more sympathetic constituency. Even locally, however, the results of the creation-evolution controversy remained ambiguous. Events in Illinois provided an enlightening case study of the fortunes of contemporary creationism. In the Chicago suburb of New Lenox, junior high school social science teacher Ray Webster regularly taught creation science in his classes. Misinterpreting the Court's *Aguillard* decision as indicating that creationism could not be taught at all, the district superintendent told Webster to end such teaching. Webster filed suit against the New Lenox school district on free speech grounds, which led eventually to a federal appeals court decision in November 1990. The court concluded that the district had acted legitimately in preventing the teaching of religion and had "successfully navigated the narrow channel between impairing intellectual inquiry and propagating a religious creed." As Webster's attorney pointed out, however, the court had not outlawed the teaching of creation science. Its decision concluded only that the district administration had exercised its power appropriately. Local officials were thus given significant discretionary authority over the place of creation science in the school curriculum.[13]

Local authorities frequently provided creationists with opportunities to include their perspectives in Illinois schools. Until challenged by several science education groups, Peoria area schools regularly permitted Institute for Creation Research speakers to address science classes. An elementary school teacher in Collinsville, near St. Louis, told a biologist investigating the teaching of creation science in the state that he regularly taught creationism in his classes. When contacted, the teacher's principal expressed surprise that creation science was not generally regarded as legitimate science and directed all further questions to her school district's curriculum director. This official stated that it was district policy to present all theories when discussing the question of origins. As creation science was as much a scientific theory as was evolution, he said, both would continue to be presented.[14]

In central Illinois similar practices remained visible. During the spring of 1991, the Morton school board decided that science classes were teaching too much evolution and directed staff to develop a creationist curriculum to balance the existing curriculum. The vice president of a nearby school district board took matters into his own hands and wrote a thirty-eight-page document on creationism for teachers' use. Both evolution and creationism were belief systems, he concluded, with proof impossible for either. This document also included the statement that there had to be a "master designer" to explain the order in nature and that children should not be taught as a "fact" that dinosaurs lived millions of years ago. Teachers in the district understood the implications of this semiofficial document. By the spring of 1992 most science teachers simply skipped the textbook chapters discussing evolution and avoided the topic.[15]

Other states witnessed similar ambiguities in their efforts to deal with the evolution controversy at the local level. In Orange County, California, San Juan Capistrano High School biology teacher John Peloza regularly taught creation science in his classes. In the spring of 1991 several parents and students complained to the school district that Peloza was not only teaching creationism but was also proselytizing for conservative Christianity. Receiving a reprimand from the district, which instructed him to cease teaching creationism and to follow state-mandated directives to teach evolution, Peloza filed a suit. The biology teacher argued that the district was violating his freedom of speech and forcing him to teach the religion of evolution in violation of the First Amendment. Federal judge David W. Williams proved unreceptive to Peloza's arguments, dismissing the case in January 1992. Because the district and state required the teaching of evolution, the judge wrote, district officials were acting legitimately in demanding that a teacher follow these guidelines. Specifically stating that he was not deciding whether teaching evolution violated establishment clause provisions, Williams stressed that Peloza could not teach a curriculum of his own choosing that violated established educational guidelines.[16]

Yet the focus on local discretion of the Peloza decision, as well as of the New Lenox case in Illinois, did not dishearten the supporters of creation science. Local authorities could just as easily decide to teach creationism in science classes. The late spring of 1992 witnessed a significant development in the Anoka-Hennepin school district in southeastern Minnesota, the second largest district in the state. Creationists requested the inclusion of material in the curriculum that cast doubt on evolutionary theory but accepted a compromise measure that directed that evolution should be taught as a theory and "not as an absolute scientific principle." The Minnesota campaign displayed a creationist tactic that had recently emerged. No longer were activists seeking the inclusion of creation science in the curriculum. Rather, they petitioned for the inclusion of evidences against evolution. Such evidence, however, came from standard creationist sources and included traditional creationist arguments. This new tactic proved effective. As Dick Clark of the Minnesota Department of Education observed, teachers in some districts were avoiding evolution as much as possible. "They don't even mention evolution in class," he noted, "because they know what's coming and they just don't want to deal with it."[17]

Despite adverse court decisions, legislative failures, and ambiguous results at the local level, creationists retained a realistic hope that they could compromise the teaching of evolution in American public schools. By the early 1990s they had modified their tactics to focus on the local level, where school boards and district administrators possessed the authority to determine the place of evolution and creation in the biology curriculum. As had been the case throughout the evolution controversy in America, however, the deeper meaning of the debate rested not on tactics but on the inability of many Americans to accept the centrality of organic evolution to an understanding of nature. Despite impressive contributions to this understanding, scientists had remained unable to overcome the public's lack of scientific literacy and had failed to ease the long-standing discomfort with the theory of evolution. After more than 130 years, the intellectual revolution begun by Darwin was incomplete—providing an ample forum for antievolutionists' arguments and assuring that the evolution controversy in America would continue.

Notes

Prologue

1. Surveys of the development of Darwin's thought include Loren Eiseley, *Darwin's Century: Evolution and the Men Who Discovered It* (Garden City, N.Y., 1958); John C. Greene, *The Death of Adam: Evolution and Its Impact on Western Thought* (Ames, Iowa, 1959); Peter J. Bowler, *Evolution: The History of an Idea* (Berkeley, Calif., 1984); Michael Ruse, *The Darwinian Revolution: Science Red in Tooth and Claw* (Chicago, 1979); and Ernst Mayr, *One Long Argument: Charles Darwin and the Genesis of Modern Evolutionary Thought* (Cambridge, Mass., 1991).

2. Alexander B. Adams, *Eternal Quest: The Story of the Great Naturalists* (New York, 1969), 389.

3. Ibid.

4. Two insightful discussions of the acceptance of Darwinism in the late nineteenth century are James R. Moore, *The Post-Darwinian Controversies: A Study of the Protestant Struggle to Come to Terms with Darwin in Great Britain and America, 1870-1900* (Cambridge, Eng., 1979), and David N. Livingstone, *Darwin's Forgotten Defenders: The Encounter between Evangelical Theology and Evolutionary Thought* (Grand Rapids, Mich., 1987).

Chapter 1. Origins

1. Asa Gray, *Darwiniana: Essays and Reviews Pertaining to Darwinism*, edited by A. Hunter Dupree (1876; Cambridge, Mass., 1963), 7.

2. For a broader discussion of the Darwinian impact, see Peter J. Bowler, *The Non-Darwinian Revolution: Reinterpreting a Historical Myth* (Baltimore, 1988).

3. A. Hunter Dupree, *Asa Gray, 1810-1888* (Cambridge, Mass., 1959), 246-59, 268-73; Nathan Reingold, ed., *Science in Nineteenth Century America: A Documentary History* (New York, 1964), 195-96.

4. Gray, *Darwiniana*, 10-16.

5. Dupree, *Asa Gray*, 274; Gray, *Darwiniana*, 18-19.

6. Gray, *Darwiniana*, 42-46; Dupree, *Asa Gray*, 266-67, 276.

7. Gray, *Darwiniana*, 46-49; Dupree, *Asa Gray*, 274-76.

8. Reingold, ed., *Science in Nineteenth Century America*, 196-98.

9. Dupree, *Asa Gray*, 284-86; [Francis Bowen], "Darwin on the Origin of Species," *North American Review* 90 (April 1860): 474-506; Charles Darwin, *On the Origin of Species*, facsimile ed. (Cambridge, Mass., 1964), 488.

10. Dupree, *Asa Gray*, 286.

11. Ibid., 287-88.

12. Ibid., 284; David L. Hull, *Darwin and His Critics: The Reception of Darwin's Theory of Evolution by the Scientific Community* (1973; Chicago, 1983), 446-47; Edward Lurie, *Louis Agassiz: A Life in Science*, abridged ed. (Chicago, 1966), 282; "Professor Agassiz on the Origin of Species," in *Darwinism and the American Intellectual: An Anthology*, 2nd ed., ed. R. Jackson Wilson (Chicago, 1989), 17.

13. "Professor Agassiz on the Origin of Species," 11-15.

14. Ibid., 10-11, 16-17; Lurie, *Louis Agassiz*, 283.

15. Dupree, *Asa Gray*, 295-97; Asa Gray, "Darwin and His Reviewers," *Atlantic Monthly* 6 (Oct. 1860): 408-16.

16. Moore, *Post-Darwinian Controversies*, 194; John C. Greene, *Science, Ideology, and World View: Essays in the History of Evolutionary Ideas* (Berkeley, Calif., 1981), 51.

17. Moore, *Post-Darwinian Controversies*, 196; Gray, *Darwiniana*, 19-20, 43.

18. Reingold, ed., *Science in Nineteenth Century America*, 196-97.

19. Ruse, *Darwinian Revolution*, 210-11, 223-29.

20. Moore, *Post-Darwinian Controversies*, 278; Dupree, *Asa Gray*, 358.

21. Lurie, *Louis Agassiz*, 372-74; Louis Agassiz, "Evolution and Permanence of Type," *Atlantic Monthly* 33 (Jan. 1874): 92-101.

22. O.C. Marsh, "Introduction and Succession of Vertebrate Life in America," *Popular Science Monthly* 12 (March 1878): 513.

23. Moore, *Post-Darwinian Controversies*, 14-15, 219; George M. Marsden, *Fundamentalism and American Culture: The Shaping of Twentieth-Century Evangelicalism, 1870-1925* (New York, 1980), 15-16; Paul F. Boller, Jr., *American Thought in Transition: The Impact of Evolutionary Naturalism, 1865-1900* (1969; Lanham, Md., 1981), 26.

24. Marsden, *Fundamentalism*, 14-15, 55-57, 60-61, 112; Theodore Dwight Bozeman, *Protestants in an Age of Science: The Baconian Ideal and Antebellum American Religious Thought* (Chapel Hill, N.C., 1977), 44-48; Moore, *Post-Darwinian Controversies*, 215; Mark A. Noll, "Common Sense Traditions and American Evangelical Thought," *American Quarterly* 37 (Summer 1985): 232-35.

25. Greene, *Science, Ideology, and World View*, 102-6, 114-20; Boller, *American Thought*, 27; Ferenc Morton Szasz, *The Divided Mind of Protestant America, 1880-1930* (University, Ala., 1982), 9-10.

26. Moore, *Post-Darwinian Controversies*, 197-98; Boller, *American Thought*, 23.

27. Moore, *Post-Darwinian Controversies*, 203-4, 212; Cynthia Eagle Russett, *Darwin in America: The Intellectual Response, 1865-1912* (San Francisco, 1976), 22-23, 26-27.

28. Moore, *Post-Darwinian Controversies*, 213-14.

29. "Popularizing Science," *Nation* 4 (10 Jan. 1867): 32-34.

30. Moore, *Post-Darwinian Controversies*, 269-74; [Asa Gray], "Evolution and Theology," *Nation* 18 (15 Jan. 1874): 44-46.

31. [Asa Gray], "What Is Darwinism?" *Nation* 18 (28 May 1874): 348-51; Dupree, *Asa Gray*, 359-60, 363-65; Moore, *Post-Darwinian Controversies*, 329-30, 344-45; Gray, *Darwiniana*, 308-12.

32. Dupree, *Asa Gray*, 367-69; "Gray's *Darwiniana*," *Nation* 23 (14 Dec. 1876): 358-59; Moore, *Post-Darwinian Controversies*, 283.

33. Dupree, *Asa Gray*, 375-77; Moore, *Post-Darwinian Controversies*, 276, 280; "Gray's Religion and Science," *Nation* 30 (22 April 1880): 308-9; "Natural Science and Religion," *Atlantic Monthly* 46 (Aug. 1880): 274-78.

34. Moore, *Post-Darwinian Controversies*, 280-82, 289, 331-36.

35. Moore, *Post-Darwinian Controversies*, 283-86.

36. Moore, *Post-Darwinian Controversies*, 287.

37. Moore, *Post-Darwinian Controversies*, 290-92; review, *Popular Science Monthly* 22 (Nov. 1882): 128-29; Ronald L. Numbers, "George Frederick Wright: From Christian Darwinist to Fundamentalist," *Isis* 79 (Dec. 1988): 624-45.

38. Jon H. Roberts, *Darwinism and the Divine in America: Protestant Intellectuals and Organic Evolution, 1859-1900* (Madison, Wis., 1988).

39. Peter J. Bowler, *The Eclipse of Darwinism: Anti-Darwinian Evolution Theories in the Decades around 1900* (Baltimore, 1983), 13; Moore, *Post-Darwinian Controversies*, 145-46.

40. Edward J. Pfeifer, "The Genesis of American Neo-Lamarckism," *Isis* 56 (March 1965): 156.

41. Moore, *Post-Darwinian Controversies*, 146, 150.

42. Edward Drinker Cope, *The Origin of the Fittest: Essays on Evolution* (New York, 1887), 42-76; Peter J. Bowler, "Edward Drinker Cope and the Changing Structure of Evolutionary Theory," *Isis* 68 (June 1977): 250-57.

43. Cope, *Origin of the Fittest*, 78.

44. Ibid., 122-23.

45. Bowler, *Eclipse of Darwinism*, 123-24; idem, "Edward Drinker Cope," 259-61; Edward Drinker Cope, "The Laws of Organic Development," *American Naturalist* 5 (Sept. 1871): 593-605; idem, *Origin of the Fittest*, 1-16, 173-214.

46. Lester D. Stephens, *Joseph LeConte: Gentle Prophet of Evolution* (Baton Rouge, 1982), 33-40, 81-82, 160-61.

47. Ibid., 125, 160-63; Joseph LeConte, "Modern Biological Inquiry," *Popular Science Monthly* 8 (Jan. 1876): 285-99.

48. Pfeifer, "Genesis of American Neo-Lamarckism," 159-63; Bowler, "Edward Drinker Cope," 262-65.

49. Cope, *Origin of the Fittest*, 410-11, 423; Bowler, "Edward Drinker Cope," 261-63; Moore, *Post-Darwinian Controversies*, 150.

50. Bowler, *Eclipse of Darwinism*, 45, 58-62, 147-48, 218-20.

Chapter 2. Toward the New Century

1. Moore, *Post-Darwinian Controversies*, 219, 334-44; Russett, *Darwin in America*, 11, 29-32.

2. Moore, *Post-Darwinian Controversies*, 245-48; Boller, *American Thought*, 29-31; Marsden, *Fundamentalism*, 18-20. Also see James McCosh, "Is the Development Hypothesis Sufficient?" *Popular Science Monthly* 10 (Nov. 1876): 86-100.

3. Russett, *Darwin in America*, 29; Francis Ellingwood Abbot, "Philosophical Biology," *North American Review* 107 (Oct. 1868): 378-79, 420-22.

4. Paul A. Carter, *The Spiritual Crisis of the Gilded Age* (Dekalb, Ill., 1971), 111, 124-30; Marsden, *Fundamentalism*, 22.

5. Moore, *Post-Darwinian Controversies*, 92; Carter, *Spiritual Crisis*, 113-32; Henry Ward Beecher, "Progress of Thought in the Church," *North American Review* 135 (Aug. 1882): 99-117.

6. "Beecher on Theology and Evolution," *Popular Science Monthly* 21 (Sept. 1882): 697-99; Boller, *American Thought*, 32; Marsden, *Fundamentalism*, 24. See also "Beecher on Evolution," *Popular Science Monthly* 27 (July 1885): 412-13, and "Beecher's Position on Evolution," *Popular Science Monthly* 28 (Feb. 1886): 554-56.

7. Moore, *Post-Darwinian Controversies*, 220; Marsden, *Fundamentalism*, 24.

8. Stephens, *Joseph LeConte*, 173-74; review, *Popular Science Monthly*, 33 (May 1988): 129-31; Moore, *Post-Darwinian Controversies*, 225.

9. Moore, *Post-Darwinian Controversies*, 225.

10. Russett, *Darwin in America*, 27; Moore, *Post-Darwinian Controversies*, 225-36, 248-50.

11. Marsden, *Fundamentalism*, 103-4; Sydney E. Ahlstrom, *A Religious History of the American People* (New Haven, Conn., 1972), 716-17, 726-27.

12. Ahlstrom, *Religious History*, 718; John S. Haller, Jr., *Outcasts from Evolution: Scientific Attitudes of Racial Inferiority, 1859-1900* (Urbana, Ill., 1971), 88-90; F. Gavin Davenport, "Scientific Interests in Kentucky and Tennessee, 1870-1890," *Journal of Southern History* 14 (Nov. 1948): 513-18. Winchell joined the faculty of the University of Michigan after his dismissal.

13. "Religion and Science at Vanderbilt University," *Popular Science Monthly* 13 (Aug. 1878): 492-95.

14. Szasz, *Divided Mind*, 5-6; Clement Eaton, "Professor James Woodrow and Freedom of Teaching in the South," *Journal of Southern History* 28 (Feb. 1962): 4-14; T. Watson Street, "The Evolution Controversy in the Southern Presbyterian Church with Attention to the Theological and Ecclesiastical Issues Raised," *Journal of the Presbyterian Historical Society* 37 (Dec. 1959): 241.

15. For examples of the response to the Woodrow case, see New York *Times*, 2, 4 Nov. 1884; 8 April, 12 Dec. 1885; 10 Dec. 1886. Also see "Notes," *Nation* 39 (21 Aug. 1884): 157-58; "Editors' Table," *American Naturalist* 19 (Jan. 1885): 55-56; "Editors' Table," *American Naturalist* 20 (Aug. 1886): 708-9; Rollo Ogden, "Evolution as Taught in a Theological Seminary," *Popular Science Monthly* 35 (Oct. 1889): 754-59.

16. Moore, *Post-Darwinian Controversies*, 225; review, *Popular Science Monthly* 37 (Aug. 1890): 554-55; "Science, Orthodoxy, and Religion," *Popular Science Monthly* 45 (May 1894): 125-26; Stephens, *Joseph LeConte*, 182-83.

17. Surveys of the broader response to evolution include Russett, *Darwin in America*; Robert C. Bannister, *Social Darwinism: Science and Myth in Anglo-American Social Thought* (Philadelphia, 1979); Richard Hofstadter, *Social Darwinism in American Thought* (1944; Boston, 1955); and Boller, *American Thought*.

18. Greene, *Science, Ideology, and World View*, 71-74.

19. Greene, *Science, Ideology, and World View*, 71-74, 80-81, 132-35; Donald Fleming, "Social Darwinism," in *Paths of American Thought*, ed. A. M. Schlesinger, Jr., and Morton White (1963; Boston, 1970), 123-27; Moore, *Post-Darwinian Controversies*, 174-75; Bowler, *Eclipse of Darwinism*, 71.

20. "The Philosophy of Herbert Spencer," *North American Review* 100 (April 1865): 423-76; Boller, *American Thought*, 48-52; Moore, *Post-Darwinian Controversies*, 162-69; Szasz, *Divided Mind*, 7.

21. Bannister, *Social Darwinism*, 72; E. L. Youmans, "Herbert Spencer and the Doctrine of Evolution," *Popular Science Monthly* 6 (Nov. 1874): 20-48; "The Literature of Evolution," *Popular Science Monthly* 6 (April 1875): 745-48; "The Nation on 'German Darwinism'," *Popular Science Monthly* 8 (Dec. 1875): 235-40; E. L. Youmans, "Spencer's Evolution Philosophy," *North American Review* 129 (Oct. 1879): 389-403.

22. Bannister, *Social Darwinism*, 6-7; "Editors' Table," *American Naturalist* 17 (Feb. 1883): 174-75.

23. Bannister, *Social Darwinism*, 6-7; Robert Green McCloskey, *American Conservatism in the Age of Enterprise, 1865-1910* (1951; New York, 1964), 1-30.

24. McCloskey, American Conservatism, 30-31, 35; Hofstadter, *Social Darwinism*, 51.

25. McCloskey, *American Conservatism*, 30-73; Bannister, *Social Darwinism*, 105-8.

26. McCloskey, *American Conservatism*, 50-51; Fleming, "Social Darwinism," 128-30.

27. Bannister, *Social Darwinism*, 7-15, 33, 126.

28. Ibid., 127; Lester F. Ward, "Cosmic and Organic Evolution," *Popular Science Monthly* 11 (Oct. 1877): 672-82; Fleming, "Social Darwinism," 135-36; Boller, *American Thought*, 66.

29. Boller, *American Thought*, 119-22; Carter, *Spiritual Crisis*, 136-44; Sidney E. Mead, *The Lively Experiment: The Shaping of Christianity in America* (1963; New York, 1976), 173-83.

30. Szasz, *Divided Mind*, 24; Carter, *Spiritual Crisis*, 28, 142-47.

31. Carter, *Spiritual Crisis*, 174.

32. Ibid., 60, 145; Szasz, *Divided Mind*, 45-46, 56-57; Mead, *Lively Experiment*, 179-80.

33. Ruse, *Darwinian Revolution*, 270.

34. O. C. Marsh, "Fossil Horses in America," *American Naturalist* 8 (May 1874): 288-94; idem, "Odontornithes, or Birds with Teeth," *American Naturalist* 9 (Dec. 1875): 625-31; idem, "Introduction and Succession of Vertebrate Life in America," *Popular Science Monthly* 12 (March 1878): 513-27, and 12 (April 1878): 672-97.

35. Bowler, *Eclipse of Darwinism*, 41; Ernst Mayr, *The Growth of Biological Thought: Diversity, Evolution, and Inheritance* (Cambridge, Mass., 1982), 537, 699.

36. Mayr, *Growth of Biological Thought*, 537, 699-706.

37. Bowler, *Eclipse of Darwinism*, 41-42, 59, 75, 78-79, 97.

38. Ibid., 65; Edward Drinker Cope, "On Inheritance in Evolution," *American Naturalist* 23 (Dec. 1889): 1058-71.

39. Edward Drinker Cope, *The Primary Factors of Organic Evolution* (Chicago, 1896), vi-vii, 10-12, 149-50, 173-74, 222.

40. Ibid., 225, 275-85, 288-89.

41. Ibid., 309, 393.

42. Alpheus S. Packard, Jr., "A Half-Century of Evolution, with Special Reference to the Effects of Geological Changes on Animal Life," *American Naturalist* 32 (Sept. 1898): 623-74.

43. Henry S. Williams, "Variation versus Heredity," *American Naturalist* 32 (Nov. 1898): 821-32.

44. Bowler, *Eclipse of Darwinism*, 15.

45. Boller, *American Thought*, 35-37; Bert James Loewenberg, "Darwinism Comes to America, 1859-1900," *Mississippi Valley Historical Review* 28 (Dec. 1941): 360; James Turner, *Without God, Without Creed: The Origins of Unbelief in America* (Baltimore, 1985), 262.

46. Szasz, *Divided Mind*, xi-xii; Marsden, *Fundamentalism*, 102-3.

47. Boller, *American Thought*, 36; Marsden, *Fundamentalism*, 35.

48. Boller, *American Thought*, 36; Marsden, *Fundamentalism*, 33-35.

49. Carter, *Spiritual Crisis*, 10; "Who Are the Propagators of Atheism?" *Popular Science Monthly* 5 (July 1874): 365-67.

50. An Evolutionist, "An Advertisement for a New Religion," *North American Review* 127 (July-Aug. 1878): 44-60.

51. Boller, *American Thought*, 44-46; Turner, *Without God*, 181.

52. Turner, *Without God*, 261.

53. Ibid., 181-87, 204-7.

54. Ibid., 215-17, 237-40.

55. Ibid., 230-33, 257.

56. Ibid., 267.

Chapter 3. Gathering at the River

1. Szasz, *Divided Mind*, 9; Hofstadter, *Social Darwinism*, 120-22.

2. Szasz, *Divided Mind*, 43-64. Good overviews of the period include Martin E. Marty, *Modern American Religion*, vol. 1, *The Irony of It All, 1893-1919* (Chicago, 1986), and Paul A. Carter, *Another Part of the Twenties* (New York, 1977).

3. Marty, *Modern American Religion* 1: 38-43; Marsden, *Fundamentalism*, 105-6; Szasz, *Divided Mind*, 69-71, 94.

4. Szasz, *Divided Mind*, 72-74; Ernest R. Sandeen, *The Roots of Fundamentalism: British and American Millenarianism, 1800-1930* (Chicago, 1970), xiii-xix, 187, 226-29, 240-41, 266-67.

5. Sandeen, *Roots of Fundamentalism*, 188-207; Marsden, *Fundamentalism*, 118-21; Moore, *Post-Darwinian Controversies*, 71-73.

6. Szasz, *Divided Mind*, 81-93; Marsden, *Fundamentalism*, 152-58; Sandeen, *Roots of Fundamentalism*, 233-47.

7. Paul Johnson, *Modern Times: The World from the Twenties to the Eighties* (New York, 1983), 11-14.

8. Marsden, *Fundamentalism*, 141-49; Paul A. Carter, "The Fundamentalist Defense of the Faith," in *Change and Continuity in Twentieth-Century America: The 1920's*, ed. John Braeman et al. (Columbus, Ohio, 1968), 197.

9. Gregg Mitman, "Evolution as Gospel: William Patten, the Language of Democracy, and the Great War," *Isis* 81 (1990): 446-47, 452-57.

10. Marsden, *Fundamentalism*, 148-49.

11. Ibid., 161; Moore, *Post-Darwinian Controversies*, 70-74. For a discussion of another conservative religious response to evolution, see Ronald L. Numbers, "Creation, Evolution, and Holy Ghost Religion: Holiness and Pentecostal Responses to Darwinism," *Religion and American Culture* 2 (1992): 127-58.

12. Marsden, *Fundamentalism*, 7, 60, 212-18.

13. Ibid., 121, 261-62 n. 27.

14. Mayr, *Growth of Biological Thought*, 710, 727-30, 742; "The Progress of Science," *Popular Science Monthly* 57 (1900): 442-48; Hugo de Vries, "On the Origin of Species," *Popular Science Monthly* 62 (1903): 486-87, 490-96; A.A.W. Hubrecht, "Hugo de Vries's Theory of Mutations," *Popular Science Monthly* 65 (1904): 205-23; Bowler, *Eclipse of Darwinism*, 184, 199-201.

15. Mayr, *Growth of Biological Thought*, 745-46, 769-70; Garland E. Allen, "Wilson, Edmund Beecher," *Dictionary of Scientific Biography*, vol. 14 (New York, 1976), 423-36; Alfred H. Sturtevant, *A History of Genetics* (New York, 1965), 33-37; Edwin G. Conklin, "The Mutation Theory from the Standpoint of Cytology," *Science* 21 (1905): 525-29.

16. Mayr, *Growth of Biological Thought*, 746, 751; Garland E. Allen, *Thomas Hunt Morgan: The Man and His Science* (Princeton, 1978), 81, 97, 127-32, 141-43; T. H. Morgan, "Recent Theories in Regard to the Determination of Sex," *Popular Science Monthly* 64 (1903): 97-116; Edmund B. Wilson, "The Chromosomes in Relation to the Determination of Sex in Insects," *Science* 22 (1905): 500-502.

17. Allen, *Thomas Hunt Morgan*, 84, 96-97, 105-8, 120-21; Bowler, *Eclipse of Darwinism*, 202-5.

18. Allen, *Thomas Hunt Morgan*, 108-16, 145-48; Mayr, *Growth of Biological Thought*, 703, 744-45, 754.

19. Allen, *Thomas Hunt Morgan*, 149-50; T. H. Morgan, "Sex Limited Inheritance of *Drosophila*," *Science* 32 (1910): 120-22.

20. Allen, *Thomas Hunt Morgan*, 149-53, 172-73, 179; Mayr, *Growth of Biological Thought*, 753-57, 765-66; T. H. Morgan, "Random Segregation versus Coupling in Mendelian Inheritance," *Science* 34 (1911): 384; Sturtevant, *History of Genetics*, 39, 47.

21. Allen, *Thomas Hunt Morgan*, 164-65, 176-79, 209-13, 234-36, 304-6; Mayr, *Growth of Biological Thought*, 766-67; Sturtevant, *History of Genetics*, 49.

22. Allen, *Thomas Hunt Morgan,* 212-13, 285, 302-13; Bowler, *Eclipse of Darwinism,* 205-6.

23. Allen, *Thomas Hunt Morgan,* 277-78; William Bateson, "Evolutionary Faith and Modern Doubts," *Science* 55 (1922): 55-61.

24. Henry F. Osborn, "William Bateson on Darwinism," *Science* 55 (1922): 194-97.

25. Glenn Gates Cole, "Evolution and Destructive Criticism," *Christian Standard* 54 (1919): 551, 562; Carter, "Fundamentalist Defense of the Faith," 207-10.

26. Edward J. Larson, *Trial and Error: The American Controversy over Creation and Evolution* (New York, 1985), 8-24; O. D. Frank, "Data on Textbooks in the Biological Sciences Used in the Middle West," *School Science and Mathematics* 16 (1916): 354-57; Philip J. Pauly, "The Development of High School Biology: New York City, 1900-1925," *Isis* 82 (1991): 662-88.

27. Larson, *Trial and Error,* 19-20.

28. LeRoy Johnson, "The Evolution Controversy during the 1920's," Ph.D. diss., New York Univ., 1954, p. 56; Willard B. Gatewood, Jr., *Controversy in the Twenties: Fundamentalism, Modernism, and Evolution* (Nashville, Tenn., 1969), 238-41.

29. Szasz, *Divided Mind,* 134; Moore, *Post-Darwinian Controversies,* 73.

30. Stephen Kern, *The Culture of Time and Space, 1880-1918* (Cambridge, Mass., 1983), 34, 88, 114-15, 275-76; Johnson, *Modern Times,* 11; Paul A. Carter, "Science and the Common Man," *American Scholar* 45 (1975-76): 781-91; Szasz, *Divided Mind,* 132-35.

31. Ronald L. Numbers, *The Creationists* (New York, 1992), 54-60, 80; Ronald L. Numbers, "The Creationists," in *God & Nature: Historical Essays on the Encounter between Christianity and Science,* ed. David C. Lindberg and Ronald L. Numbers (Berkeley, Cal, 1986), 400.

32. Numbers, *Creationists,* 72-101; Szasz, *Divided Mind,* 130-31; Henry M. Morris, *A History of Modern Creationism* (San Diego, 1984), 56-59, 79-82.

33. Numbers, *Creationists,* 60-71; Morris, *History of Modern Creationism,* 88-92.

34. Szasz, *Divided Mind,* 92, 126-27.

35. Lawrence W. Levine, *Defender of the Faith: William Jennings Bryan, The Last Decade, 1915-1925* (New York, 1965), 7, 54; Marsden, *Fundamentalism,* 132-35. For a perceptive essay on Bryan, see Stephen Jay Gould, "William Jennings Bryan's Last Campaign," *Natural History* 96, no. 11 (1987): 16-26.

36. Szasz, *Divided Mind,* 108-9; Levine, *Defender of the Faith,* 262-63.

37. Levine, *Defender of the Faith,* 264-73; Szasz, *Divided Mind,* 99, 112-15, 137. Also see Ferenc Morton Szasz, "William Jennings Bryan, Evolution, and the Fundamentalist-Modernist Controversy," *Nebraska History* 56 (1975): 259-78.

38. Johnson, "Evolution Controversy," 93.

39. Levine, *Defender of the Faith,* 264-65, 281.

40. Ibid., 268; Larson, *Trial and Error,* 47.

41. Levine, *Defender of the Faith,* 265.

42. William Jennings Bryan, "Teaching Evolution," *Journal of Education* 158 (1976): 46-47 [reprint].

43. Levine, *Defender of the Faith,* 279; Johnson, "Evolution Controversy," 94.

44. Levine, *Defender of the Faith,* 289; Gatewood, *Controversy in the Twenties,* 137.

45. Szasz, *Divided Mind,* 110-11.

46. Ibid., 107; Larson, *Trial and Error,* 28-30; Marsden, *Fundamentalism,* 169-70.

47. Willard B. Gatewood, Jr., *Preachers, Pedagogues & Politicians: The Evolution Controversy in North Carolina, 1920-1927* (Chapel Hill, N.C., 1966), 16, 30-35, 49. Martin's comments can be found in Gatewood, *Controversy in the Twenties,* 19.

48. Gatewood, *Preachers, Pedagogues*, 50-76.

49. Patsy Ledbetter, "Defense of the Faith: J. Frank Norris and Texas Fundamentalism, 1920-1929," *Arizona and the West* 15 (1973): 48-55; Norman F. Furniss, *The Fundamentalist Controversy, 1918-1931* (New Haven, Conn., 1954), 52-53. On Norris, also see C. Allyn Russell, "J. Frank Norris: Violent Fundamentalist," *Southwestern Historical Quarterly* 75 (1972): 271-302.

50. Levine, *Defender of the Faith*, 277.

51. Furniss, *Fundamentalist Controversy*, 81; Szasz, *Divided Mind*, 111; Johnson, "Evolution Controversy," 104-5.

52. Johnson, "Evolution Controversy," 107-13; Alonzo W. Fortune, "The Kentucky Campaign against the Teaching of Evolution," *Journal of Religion* 2 (1922): 227; Arthur M. Miller, "Kentucky and the Theory of Evolution," *Science* 55 (1922): 178-80.

53. Johnson, "Evolution Controversy," 113-18; William E. Ellis, "Frank LeRond McVey: His Defense of Academic Freedom," *Register of the Kentucky Historical Society* 67 (1969): 40-49; "Proposed Legislation against the Teaching of Evolution," *Science* 55 (1922): 319.

54. New York *Times*, 27 Oct. 1922; Furniss, *Fundamentalist Controversy*, 69; Larson, *Trial and Error*, 49-53; Levine, *Defender of the Faith*, 278; Mary Duncan France, " 'A Year of Monkey War': The Anti-Evolution Campaign and the Florida Legislature," *Florida Historical Quarterly* 54 (1975): 156-59.

55. Ledbetter, "Defense of the Faith," 57-58; Furniss, *Fundamentalist Controversy*, 80, 87-88.

56. Richard David Wilhelm, "A Chronology and Analysis of Regulatory Actions Relating to the Teaching of Evolution in Public Schools," Ph.D. diss., Univ. of Texas at Austin, 1978, pp. 314-15, 352-53.

57. George E. Webb, "Tucson's Evolution Debate, 1924-1927," *Journal of Arizona History* 24 (1983): 2-6.

58. Ibid.

59. Larson, *Trial and Error*, 75; Gatewood, *Controversy in the Twenties*, 249.

60. Pauly, "Development of High School Biology," 685-88; Lloyd C. Douglas, "Mr. Bryan's New Crusade," *Christian Century* 37 (1920): 11-13; New York *Times*, 5 March 1922; Edward L. Rice, "Darwin and Bryan—A Study in Method," *Science* 61 (1925): 249.

61. T. V. Smith, "Bases of Bryanism," *Scientific Monthly* 16 (1923): 505-13.

62. "The Report of the Committee on Freedom of Teaching in Science," *Science* 61 (1925): 276-77; New York *Times*, 16 Nov., 31 Dec. 1924.

63. New York *Times*, 27 Dec. 1922, 27-28 Dec. 1923; "The American Association for the Advancement of Science," *Science* 57 (1923): 103-4; Rice, "Darwin and Bryan," 244-47.

64. Gatewood, *Preachers, Pedagogues*, 14-25, 105-10.

65. Ibid., 38-49, 87-89, 96-100, 230.

66. Ibid., 106; Furniss, *Fundamentalist Controversy*, 85; Edgar W. Knight, "Monkey or Mud in North Carolina," *Independent* 118 (1927): 515.

67. Gatewood, *Preachers, Pedagogues*, 109, 122-26, 140.

68. Ibid., 126-47; New York *Times*, 21 Feb. 1925.

69. Gatewood, *Preachers, Pedagogues*, 149-50.

Chapter 4. The Scopes Trial and Beyond

1. Kenneth K. Bailey, "The Enactment of Tennessee's Antievolution Law," *Journal of Southern History* 16 (1950): 474-76; Levine, *Defender of the Faith*, 325-26; New York *Times*, 23 Oct. 1970.

2. Charles E. Carpenter, "The Constitutionality of the Tennessee Anti-Evolution Law," *Oregon Law Review* 6 (1927): 142; Jeanette Keith, "Missionaries for Progress: Educational Reform and Local Reaction in the Upper Cumberland, 1890-1929," paper presented at the Tennessee Conference of Historians, Cookeville, Tenn., April 1987.

3. Bailey, "Enactment of Tennessee's Antievolution Law," 475-89; Gatewood, *Controversy in the Twenties,* 292, 295.

4. L. Sprague De Camp, *The Great Monkey Trial* (Garden City, N.Y., 1968), 65-67; Johnson, "Evolution Controversy," 184.

5. Orland Kay Armstrong, "Bootleg Science in Tennessee," *North American Review* 227 (1929): 141-42; Sallie H. Peay, comp., *Austin Peay: Governor of Tennessee* (Kingsport, Tenn., 1929), 360-63.

6. Levine, *Defender of the Faith,* 327-28.

7. Larson, *Trial and Error,* 58-60; John T. Scopes and James Presley, *Center of the Storm: Memoirs of John T. Scopes* (New York, 1967), 33, 57-61. Several forests have been denuded for published discussions of the Scopes trial. In addition to Scopes's memoirs and De Camp's journalistic treatment, valuable works include Ray Ginger, *Six Days or Forever? Tennessee v. John Thomas Scopes* (Boston, 1958), and the microfilm transcript of the trial published as *The Scopes Case* (Wilmington, Del., 1978).

8. Larson, *Trial and Error,* 60; De Camp, *Great Monkey Trial,* 84-85, 205-6; Szasz, *Divided Mind,* 116-17.

9. Larson, *Trial and Error,* 61-63; De Camp, *Great Monkey Trial,* 89, 93-95, 130-33, 136-38; Scopes and Presley, *Center of the Storm,* 69-82.

10. New York *Times,* 9 July 1925; De Camp, *Great Monkey Trial,* 141-42; Levine, *Defender of the Faith,* 339.

11. Szasz, *Divided Mind,* 121; De Camp, *Great Monkey Trial,* 246, 294.

12. Scopes and Presley, *Center of the Storm,* 113, 126-27, 131.

13. De Camp, *Great Money Trial,* 131-32, 313.

14. De Camp, *Great Monkey Trial,* 215; Scopes and Presley, *Center of the Storm,* 136-37; Larson, *Trial and Error,* 63-65, 68.

15. Scopes and Presley, *Center of the Storm,* 143-48, 156-58; Larson, *Trial and Error,* 68; De Camp, *Great Monkey Trial,* 349-50.

16. Szasz, *Divided Mind,* 120; De Camp, *Great Monkey Trial,* 221-23.

17. Larson, *Trial and Error,* 68-69; De Camp, *Great Monkey Trial,* 391.

18. De Camp, *Great Monkey Trial,* 381-411; Levine, *Defender of the Faith,* 349-50.

19. De Camp, *Great Monkey Trial,* 417-21; Scopes and Presley, *Center of the Storm,* 186-88.

20. De Camp, *Great Monkey Trial,* 427-28.

21. Joseph Wood Krutch, "Tennessee: Where Cowards Rule," *Nation* 121 (1925): 88-89.

22. "The Dayton Battle May Have Been Bryan's Doom," *Literary Digest* 86 (1925): 42-46; Szasz, *Divided Mind,* 125; Marsden, *Fundamentalism,* 184-89.

23. Ferenc Morton Szasz, "The Scopes Trial in Perspective," *Tennessee Historical Quarterly* 30 (1971): 289-91; Gatewood, *Controversy in the Twenties,* 354.

24. Scopes and Presley, *Center of the Storm,* 206-7, 223, 236-37, 241-66.

25. De Camp, *Great Monkey Trial,* 446-68; Larson, *Trial and Error,* 69-72.

26. *Scopes v. State,* 289 S.W. 363 (1927) at 364-67.

27. Ibid., at 367. During the late 1920s and early 1930s, various attempts to repeal the Butler Act surfaced in Tennessee. None of these efforts gained significant support. Furniss, *Fundamentalist Controversy,* 92. New York *Times,* 14 March 1926; 8, 12, 14, 17 Jan. 1929; 18 March, 11 June 1931; 26 Jan., 16, 20 Feb. 1935.

28. Larson, *Trial and Error*, 72-73; Marsden, *Fundamentalism*, 188; Harbor Allen, "The Anti-Evolution Campaign in America," *Current History* 24 (1926): 893-97.

29. R. Halliburton, Jr., "Mississippi's Contribution to the Anti-Evolution Movement," *Journal of Mississippi History* 35 (1973): 177; Christopher K. Curtis, "Mississippi's Anti-Evolution Law of 1926," *Journal of Mississippi History* 48 (1986): 16-17; Larson, *Trial and Error*, 76.

30. Larson, *Trial and Error*, 77-78; Curtis, "Mississippi's Anti-Evolution Law," 17-23.

31. Halliburton, "Mississippi's Contribution," 179-82; Allen, "Anti-Evolution Campaign," 894.

32. Gatewood, *Preachers, Pedagogues*, 112-13, 152-78, 180-210; B. W. Wells, "Fundamentalism in North Carolina," *Science* 64 (1926): 17-18.

33. Knight, "Monkey or Mud," 516, 523; Gatewood, *Preachers, Pedagogues*, 213-31.

34. France, "Year of Monkey War," 156-69; New York *Times*, 30 April 1927.

35. Los Angeles *Times*, 4 April, 22, 24 July 1925; New York *Times*, 23, 25 July 1925.

36. Miriam Allen de Ford, "After Dayton: A Fundamentalist Survey," *Nation* 122 (1926): 604; Allen, "Anti-Evolution Campaign," 895; Wilhelm, "Chronology," 371-72; New York *Times*, 30 Jan. 1927.

37. "Evolution and Intellectual Freedom," *Nature* 116 (1925): 69; Howard K. Beale, *Are American Teachers Free?* (New York, 1936), 229; Ira D. Cardiff, "Evolution and the Bible," *Science* 62 (1925): 111; R.R. Huestis, "Dr. W.D. [*sic*] Riley on Evolution," *Science* 62 (1925): 220-21.

38. Richard Sherlock, "A Turbulent Spectrum: Mormon Reactions to the Darwinist Legacy," *Journal of Mormon History* 5 (1978): 46-49; Duane E. Jeffrey, "Seers, Savants and Evolution: The Uncomfortable Interface," *Dialogue: A Journal of Mormon Thought* 8(1974): 62-63.

39. Sherlock, "A Turbulent Spectrum" 35-37.

40. *Arizona Daily Star*, 11 Oct. 1927; Webb, "Tucson's Evolution Debate," 12 n 13.

41. *Arizona Daily Star*, 13 Oct. 1927.

42. *Arizona Daily Star*, 13, 16, 17, 19, 21, 22, 23 Oct. 1927; Webb, "Tucson's Evolution Debate," 6-11.

43. R. Halliburton, Jr., "Kentucky's Anti-Evolution Controversy," *Register of the Kentucky Historical Society* 66 (1968): 105-6; Allen, "Anti-Evolution Campaign," 897; "Legislation against the Teaching of Evolution," *Science* 63 (1926): 203-4.

44. Furniss, *Fundamentalist Controversy*, 60-61, 78-80, 83, 93-94. New York *Times*, 3 Oct. 1926; 13, 22 Jan., 26 Feb. 1927; 19 Jan. 1928. Allen, "Anti-Evolution Campaign," 897.

45. Furniss, *Fundamentalist Controversy*, 77-78, 95-98. New York *Times*, 28 May 1925; 14 Oct. 1926; 19 Jan., 9, 10 Feb. 1927. Gatewood, *Controversy in the Twenties*, 39.

46. Furniss, *Fundamentalist Controversy*, 87; Ledbetter, "Defense of the Faith," 47, 59; New York *Times*, 13 July 1926.

47. "Evolution and Intellectual Freedom," 69; John Smith Dexter, "Anti-Evolution Propaganda in Georgia," *Science* 62 (1925): 399. New York *Times*, 31 July 1925; 10 Feb., 13 May 1926. Allen, "Anti-Evolution Campaign," 894.

48. Cal Ledbetter, Jr., "The Antievolution Law: Church and State in Arkansas," *Arkansas Historical Quarterly* 38 (1979): 304-5; C. Bush, "The Teaching of Evolution in Arkansas," *Science* 64 (1926): 356.

49. Ledbetter, "Antievolution Law," 306-8; New York *Times,* 10 Feb. 1927.

50. Ledbetter, "Antievolution Law," 308-10; De Camp, *Great Monkey Trial,* 475; Furniss, *Fundamentalist Controversy,* 94.

51. Ledbetter, "Antievolution Law," 310-12; William Foy Lisenby, "Brough, Baptists, and Bombast: The Election of 1928," *Arkansas Historical Quarterly* 32 (1973): 120-29.

52. Ledbetter, "Antievolution Law," 312; Larson, *Trial and Error,* 80. For an analysis of the initiative voting patterns, see Virginia Gray, "Anti-Evolution Sentiment and Behavior: The Case of Arkansas," *Journal of American History* 57 (1970): 352-66.

53. Ledbetter, "Antievolution Law," 313-14; Arthur O. Lovejoy, "Anti-Evolution Laws and the Principle of Religious Neutrality," *School and Society* 29 (1929): 134-37.

54. New York *Times,* 27 May, 11 Sept. 1925.

55. New York *Times,* 1 Jan., 6 July 1927; 13 April 1928.

56. Kirtley F. Mather, "The Psychology of the Anti-Evolutionist," *Harvard Graduates' Magazine* 25 (Sept. 1926): 8-20; Allen, "Anti-Evolution Campaign," 893.

57. Edward L. Rice, "The Significance of the Scopes Trial: III. From the Standpoint of Science," *Current History* 22 (1926): 889-95.

58. Gatewood, *Controversy in the Twenties,* 176; Maynard Shipley, "A Year of the Monkey War," *Independent* 119 (1927): 326-28, 344-45; idem, "The Forward March of the Anti-Evolutionists," *Current History* 29 (1929): 578-82; idem, "Growth of the Anti-Evolution Movement," *Current History* 32 (1930): 330-32.

59. New York *Times,* 26 Sept. 1925; 30 Jan. 1927; 22 Jan. 1928. Larson, *Trial and Error,* 75.

60. Furniss, *Fundamentalist Controversy,* 54-56. New York *Times,* 9 May 1927; 15 April 1928. Shipley, "Forward March," 581.

61. Larson, *Trial and Error,* 82; Armstrong, "Bootleg Science," 139-41; Orland Kay Armstrong, "Beating the Evolution Laws," *Popular Science Monthly* 115 (1929): 18.

62. Szasz, *Divided Mind,* xii, 137.

Chapter 5. Decline and Revival

1. Arnold B. Grobman, *The Changing Classroom: The Role of the Biological Sciences Curriculum Study* (Garden City, N.Y., 1969), 204; Judith V. Grabiner and Peter D. Miller, "Effects of the Scopes Trial," *Science* 185 (1974): 832-34; Pauly, "Development of High School Biology," 663-64, 685-88.

2. Grabiner and Miller, "Effects of the Scopes Trial," 833-35; Gerald D. Skoog, "The Topic of Evolution in Secondary School Biology Textbooks, 1900-1968," Ed.D. diss., Univ. of Nebraska, 1969, pp. 51-52; Elliott R. Downing, "The Biology Course Outlined in Major Objectives," *School Science and Mathematics* 28 (1928): 501; Pauly, "Development of High School Biology," 672-78.

3. Paul DeHart Hurd, *Biological Education in American Secondary Schools, 1890-1960* (Washington, D.C., 1961), 53-55; Skoog, "Topic of Evolution," 178-95; Norman E. Webb and W.G. Vinal, "Subject Matter Topics in Biology Courses of Study," *School Science and Mathematics* 34 (1934): 829; Otis W. Caldwell and Florence Weller, "High School Biology Content as Judged by Thirty College Biologists," *School Science and Mathematics* 32 (1932): 411-24.

4. Alfred C. Kinsey, "The Content of the Biology Course," *School Science and Mathematics* 30 (1930): 374-84; Skoog, "Topic of Evolution," 130-32.

5. Oscar Riddle, "The Confusion of Tongues," *Science* 83 (1936): 41-45, 69-74.

6. Oscar Riddle, "Educational Darkness and Luminous Research," *Science* 87 (1938): 375-80.

7. Grabiner and Miller, "Effects of the Scopes Trial," 835; Skoog, "Topic of Evolution," 180.

8. Hurd, *Biological Education*, 75-76, 89, 105-6, 183; William V. Mayer, "Biology Education in the United States during the Twentieth Century," *Quarterly Review of Biology* 61 (1986): 497-99; Grobman, *Changing Classroom*, 204.

9. Hurd, *Biological Education*, 90-102; Skoog, "Topic of Evolution," 208.

10. Hurd, *Biological Education*, 106-7; Skoog, "Topic of Evolution," 26-27; Estelle R. Laba and Eugene W. Gross, "Evolution Slighted in High-School Biology," *Clearing House* 24 (1950): 396-99; Adrian N. Gentry, "Teaching of Biological Sciences in the Public High Schools of California," *California Journal of Secondary Education* 26 (1951): 495-501; Sam S. Blanc, "A Comparison of the Biology Interests of Tenth and Eleventh Grade Pupils with a Topical Analysis of High School Biology Textbooks," *Science Education* 40 (1956): 127-32; Burton E. Voss, "Biology—Fact and Future," *American Biology Teacher* 22 (1960): 79-82.

11. Skoog, "Topic of Evolution," 123, 218-19, 234, 272, 306-8; Grabiner and Miller, "Effects of the Scopes Trial," 835-36.

12. Oscar Riddle, "High Schools and Biological Literacy in the United States," *American Biology Teacher* 16 (1954): 179-84.

13. Joel A. Carpenter, "The Renewal of American Fundamentalism, 1930-1945," Ph.D. diss., Johns Hopkins Univ., 1984, pp. 3-7, 137-38; Ahlstrom, *Religious History*, 924.

14. Carpenter, "Renewal of American Fundamentalism," 18-25, 32-33; Ahlstrom, *Religious History*, 913-20.

15. Carpenter, "Renewal of American Fundamentalism," 1-2, 28-29, 93-95, 167-70, 176-78; Joel A. Carpenter, "From Fundamentalism to the New Evangelical Coalition," in *Evangelicalism and Modern America*, ed. George M. Marsden (Grand Rapids, Mich., 1984), 9-10.

16. Carpenter, "Renewal of American Fundamentalism," 4, 38, 85-89; idem, "From Fundamentalism to the New Evangelical Coalition," 5-6.

17. James H. Leuba, "Religious Beliefs of American Scientists," *Harper's Monthly Magazine* 169 (1934): 291-300.

18. Numbers, *Creationists*, 60-71; Carpenter, "Renewal of American Fundamentalism," 73-74, 79, 252; Noll, "Common Sense Traditions," 220-25.

19. Carpenter, "Renewal of American Fundamentalism," 4, 129-30.

20. Carpenter, "Renewal of American Fundamentalism," 137, 184-85, 211-21; Leo P. Ribuffo, *The Old Christian Right: The Protestant Far Right from the Great Depression to the Cold War* (Philadelphia, 1983), 258-59; Carpenter, "From Fundamentalism to the New Evangelical Coalition," 12, 14-15.

21. Carpenter, "Renewal of American Fundamentalism," 222-23; idem, "From Fundamentalism to the New Evangelical Coalition," 15-16; Ahlstrom, *Religious History*, 955.

22. Ahlstrom, *Religious History*, 950-59.

23. Ahlstrom, *Religious History*, 956-58; Ribuffo, *Old Christian Right*, 259; George M. Marsden, "Introduction: The Evangelical Denomination," in *Evangelicalism and Modern America*, ed. Marsden, xiii.

24. Ahlstrom, *Religious History*, 952-62; Carpenter, "Renewal of American Fundamentalism," 229-30.

25. Ernst Mayr, "Prologue: Some Thoughts on the History of the Evolutionary Synthesis," in *The Evolutionary Synthesis: Perspectives on the Unification of Biology*, ed. Ernst Mayr and William B. Provine (Cambridge, Mass., 1980), 3-28; Greene, *Science, Ideology, and World View*, 53.

26. Mayr, "Prologue," 6-36; Bowler, *Eclipse of Darwinism*, 99, 169, 176, 198-99, 209, 213; Bowler, *Evolution*, 293-95.

27. Mayr, *Growth of Biological Thought*, 566-68.

28. Ibid., 553-59; Bowler, *Evolution*, 290-97; Mark B. Adams, "Sergei Chetverikov, the Kol'tsov Institute, and the Evolutionary Synthesis," in *Evolutionary Synthesis*, ed. Mayr and Provine, 242-78.

29. Bowler, *Evolution*, 290-96; William B. Provine, *Sewall Wright and Evolutionary Biology* (Chicago, 1986), 235-37; Mayr, *Growth of Biological Thought*, 555-56.

30. Provine, *Sewall Wright*, 233-36, 277-326; Stephen Jay Gould, "The Ontogeny of Sewall Wright and the Phylogeny of Evolution," *Isis* 79 (1988): 273-81.

31. Mayr, *Growth of Biological Thought*, 561; Provine, *Sewall Wright*, 329-36.

32. Mayr, *Growth of Biological Thought*, 569, 587; Provine, *Sewall Wright*, 327, 342-47, 358-65, 398, 402.

33. Bowler, *Evolution*, 296-99; Mayr, *Growth of Biological Thought*, 565, 601-2; Ernst Mayr, "How I Became a Darwinian," in *Evolutionary Synthesis*, ed. Mayr and Provine, 421.

34. Ernst Mayr, "G. G. Simpson," in *Evolutionary Synthesis*, ed. Mayr and Provine, 452-56.

35. Stephen Jay Gould, "G. G. Simpson, Paleontology, and the Modern Synthesis," in *Evolutionary Synthesis*, ed. Mayr and Provine, 153-72; Bowler, *Evolution*, 299.

36. Provine, *Sewall Wright*, 405; Mayr, *Growth of Biological Thought*, 568-71, 588-89, 768, 793-94; Mayr, "Prologue," 42.

37. Provine, *Sewall Wright*, 344, 362, 404, 410-11, 452-55; Mayr, *Growth of Biological Thought*, 582-83; Bowler, *Evolution*, 300-303; Stanley Miller, "A Production of Amino Acids under Possible Primitive Earth Conditions," *Science* 117 (1953): 528-29.

38. Mayr, *Growth of Biological Thought*, 574, 808-25. Good surveys of the development of molecular biology include Horace Freeland Judson, *The Eighth Day of Creation: The Makers of the Revolution in Biology* (New York, 1979), James D. Watson, *The Double Helix* (New York, 1968), and Robert C. Olby, *The Path to the Double Helix* (Seattle, 1974).

39. Hurd, *Biological Education*, 110-14, 135-36, 157-59, 229-31; Grobman, *Changing Classroom*, 7-9.

40. Larson, *Trial and Error*, 90-91; Hurd, *Biological Education*, 155; Mayer, "Biology Education," 484-85. For a broader discussion of Eisenhower's education policy, see Janet Kerr-Tener, "Eisenhower and Federal Aid to Higher Education," *Presidential Studies Quarterly* 17 (1987): 473-85.

41. W.H. Johnson, "Improving the Teaching of Evolution," *American Biology Teacher* 20 (1958): 121-22; Joan Hunter, "Teaching Evolution to High School Students," *American Biology Teacher* 20 (1958): 283-84; Hermann J. Muller, "One Hundred Years without Darwinism Are Enough," *School Science and Mathematics* 59 (1959): 304-16.

42. John C. Mayfield et al., "Using Modern Knowledge to Teach Evolution in High School," *American Biology Teacher* 22 (1960): 405-13; Cornelius J. Troost, "Evolution in Biological Education prior to 1960," *Science Education* 52 (1968): 301.

43. Grobman, *Changing Classroom*, 10-15, 63-64, 68-76, 204; Mayer, "Biology Education," 485-87.

44. Grobman, *Changing Classroom*, 79-91.

45. Ibid., 18-19, 94-96, 104-5, 109, 112-13, 205; Jack Fishleder, "BSCS: A Happy Partnership," *Science* 144 (1964): 136.

46. Grobman, *Changing Classroom*, 22-24, 31-32, 41-42, 52, 99, 100, 113-16, 138, 165.

47. Ibid., 34-37, 42, 54; John Walsh, "Curriculum Reform: Success Hasn't Spoiled NSF Program, But Biology Study's Status Reflects Problems," *Science* 149

(1965): 280-82; Mayer, "Biology Education," 490, 500-502; Skoog, "Topic of Evolution," 239, 251-52, 267.

48. Skoog, "Topic of Evolution," 30, 33-34, 45-46.

49. Grobman, *Changing Classroom*, 1, 210, 279-80.

Chapter 6. The Passing of the Old Order

1. On the "conservative revolt" of the period, see Theodore H. White, *The Making of the President, 1964* (New York, 1965), 80-122, 123-59, 160-96, 230-65, 351-448; Michael W. Miles, *The Odyssey of the American Right* (New York, 1980), 241-98; and George H. Nash, *The Conservative Intellectual Movement in America, since 1945* (New York, 1976). Goldwater's perspective can be found in Barry M. Goldwater and Jack Casserly, *Goldwater* (New York, 1988), 113-220.

2. Ted R. Vaughan et al., "The Religious Orientations of American Natural Scientists," *Social Forces* 44 (1966): 519-26.

3. Paul L. Murphy, *The Constitution in Crisis Times, 1918-1969* (New York, 1972), 392-94; Larson, *Trial and Error*, 94-95.

4. Grobman, *Changing Classroom*, 210; New York *Times*, 19 Oct. 1964.

5. Lorenzo Lisonbee, "Thwarting the Anti-Evolution Movement in Arizona," *Science Teacher* 32 (1965): 35-37; *Arizona Republic*, 28 Jan. 1962. On the Phoenix controversy, see George E. Webb, "The Evolution Controversy in Arizona and California: From the 1920s to the 1980s," *Journal of the Southwest* 33 (1991): 141-42, 144-46.

6. *Arizona Republic*, 28 Jan. 1962.

7. Grobman, *Changing Classroom*, 205; Phoenix *Gazette*, 18 Dec. 1963; *Arizona Republic*, 7 Nov. 1963.

8. Phoenix *Gazette*, 18 Dec. 1963; New York *Times*, 31 May 1964.

9. *Arizona Daily Star*, 8 Nov. 1963; *Arizona Republic*, 18, 19 Dec. 1963; Phoenix *Gazette*, 18, 21 Dec. 1963; Grobman, *Changing Classroom*, 207.

10. *Arizona Republic*, 19 Dec. 1963; 23 May 1964; Wilhelm, "Chronology," 407; Lisonbee, "Thwarting the Anti-Evolution Movement," 35; New York *Times*, 31 May 1964.

11. New York *Times*, 31 May 1964; Lisonbee, "Thwarting the Anti-Evolution Movement," 36; *Arizona Republic*, 23 May 1964.

12. *Arizona Republic*, 13, 28 June 1964. Wilhelm, "Chronology," 410; Lisonbee, "Thwarting the Anti-Evolution Movement," 337; *Arizona Daily Star*, 12 July 1964.

13. Wilhelm, "Chronology," 116-17, 253; Nicholas Wade, "Creationists and Evolutionists: Confrontation in California," *Science* 178 (1972): 724; Larson, *Trial and Error*, 96-97; Dorothy Nelkin, *The Creation Controversy: Science or Scripture in the Schools* (New York, 1982), 107-8. In 1981 Segraves told a Los Angeles reporter that she had launched her antievolution campaign because "I opposed Bobby Kennedy when he allowed a definite change in the recognition of communism in this country." Los Angeles *Times*, 6 March 1981.

14. Wilhelm, "Chronology," 116-18; New York *Times*, 10 Jan. 1964; Los Angeles *Times*, 10 Jan. 1964; Nelkin, *Creation Controversy*, 108; Webb, "Evolution Controversy in Arizona and California," 142-44.

15. Wilhelm, "Chronology," 98-101; New York *Times*, 2 Aug. 1964.

16. Eliot P. Tucker, "The Anti-Evolutionists of 1964," *Science Education* 51 (1967): 371-76; New York *Times*, 2 Aug. 1964; Grobman, *Changing Classroom*, 207-10.

17. Wilhelm, "Chronology," 101-3; Nelkin, *Creation Controversy*, 63-64.

18. Wilhelm, "Chronology," 103-5; New York *Times*, 11 Nov. 1964.

19. Thomas K. Shotwell, "The Problem of Evolution," *American Biology Teacher* 27 (1965): 766-67; Hermann J. Muller, "Biologists' Statement on Teaching Evolution,"

Bulletin of the Atomic Scientists 23 (1967): 39-40; [Paul Klinge], "Biology Teaching and Controversy," *American Biology Teacher* 29 (1967): 694; Bentley Glass, "The Centrality of Evolution in Biology Teaching," *American Biology Teacher* 29 (1967): 705-15; Addison E. Lee, "Some Suggestions for the Teaching of Evolution in High School Biology," *American Biology Teacher* 29 (1967): 716-20; Claude A. Welch, "Evolution Theory and the Nature of Science," *Science Teacher* 39 (1972): 26-28.

20. Ledbetter, "Antievolution Law," 299-300, 315-16; Larson, *Trial and Error,* 98.

21. Ledbetter, "Antievolution Law," 317-18; *Epperson v. Arkansas,* 393 U.S. 97 (1968) at 100; Larson, *Trial and Error,* 99-100.

22. Larson, *Trial and Error,* 99-101; Ledbetter, "Antievolution Law," 316-22.

23. Larson, *Trial and Error,* 102-3; Ledbetter, "Antievolution Law," 319-22.

24. Ledbetter, "Antievolution Law," 320-21.

25. New York *Times,* 15 Jan., 13 April 1967; Knoxville *News-Sentinel,* 13 Jan. 1967; Martin Southern, Bill for Declaratory Judgment, Knox County Chancery Court, no. 44734. For a discussion of events in Tennessee, see George E. Webb, "The Repeal of the Butler Act," *Journal of the Tennessee Academy of Science* 59 (1984): 14-17.

26. *House Journal of the Eighty-Fifth General Assembly of the State of Tennessee* (Nashville, 1967), 130, 162, 470, 531.

27. New York *Times,* 13 April 1967; Nashville *Tennessean,* 13, 15 April 1967; *House Journal* (1967), 553-55, 566.

28. *Senate Journal of the Eighty-Fifth General Assembly of the State of Tennessee* (Nashville, 1967), 105, 140, 496, 499, 503, 517, 522-23, 546, 557, 577, 579-80, 584; Nashville *Tennessean,* 16, 17, 19, 21 April 1967; *House Journal* (1967), 670, 677, 681, 694, 718, 769; New York *Times,* 21 April 1967.

29. New York *Times,* 15 April 1967; Nashville *Tennessean,* 15 April 1967; Knoxville *News-Sentinel,* 14, 16 April 1967.

30. Knoxville *News-Sentinel,* 16, 19, 20, 28, 30 April, 4, 5, 13 May 1967; Nashville *Tennessean,* 9 May 1967.

31. Knoxville *News-Sentinel,* 12, 15, 16 May 1967; Gary L. Scott, Complainant, Civil Action no. 4761, U.S. District Court, Middle District of Tennessee, Nashville Division, 15 May 1967; New York *Times,* 13 May 1967.

32. *House Journal* (1967), 979-80, 1092, 1103, 1108, 1115, 1200; *Senate Journal* (1967), 862, 896, 912; Knoxville *News-Sentinel,* 17 May 1967; New York *Times,* 17 May 1967.

33. *State v. Epperson,* 242 Ark. 922, 416 S.W. 2d 322 (1967); Ledbetter, "Antievolution Law," 322-23; Larson, *Trial and Error,* 107-8.

34. Larson, *Trial and Error,* 93-94; Leonard W. Levy, *The Establishment Clause: Religion and the First Amendment* (New York, 1986), 122-24.

35. Murphy, *Constitution in Crisis Times,* 392-94; Levy, *Establishment Clause,* 147-48; Philip B. Kurland, "Of Church and State and the Supreme Court," *University of Chicago Law Review* 29 (1961): 1-96; Leo Pfeffer, "Religion-Blind Government," *Stanford Law Review* 15 (1963): 389-406; Donald A. Gianella, "Religious Liberty, Nonestablishment, and Doctrinal Development," *Harvard Law Review* 80 (1967) 1381-431, and 81 (1968): 513-90.

36. Larson, *Trial and Error,* 109-12; Ledbetter, "Antievolution Law," 323.

37. "Opposition to Ban on Teaching Evolution," *School and Society* 96 (1968): 329-30; Larson, *Trial and Error,* 110-13.

38. Larson, *Trial and Error,* 113; *Epperson v. Arkansas,* 393 U.S. 97 (1968) at 102-3, 106-7.

39. Larson, *Trial and Error,* 115; *Epperson v. Arkansas,* 393 U.S. 97 (1968) at 107-9.

40. *Epperson v. Arkansas,* 393 U.S. 97 (1968) at 109-16; Larson, *Trial and Error,* 118-19.

41. Larson, *Trial and Error*, 120; *Smith v. State*, Miss. 242 So. 2d 692 (1970) at 693-94.

42. Larson, *Trial and Error*, 121-22.

43. Ibid., 122; *Smith v. State*, Miss. 242 So. 2d 692 (1970) at 694-98.

Chapter 7. New Directions

1. Numbers, *Creationists*, 57-60, 71, 169-70; Morris, *History of Modern Creationism*, 80-82, 90, 101-2.

2. Morris, *History of Modern Creationism*, 82-83, 92, 101-6; Ronald L. Numbers, "The Dilemma of Evangelical Scientists," in *Evangelicalism and Modern America*, ed. Marsden, 151-55.

3. Morris, *History of Modern Creationism*, 112-13; Numbers, *Creationists*, 104-12.

4. Numbers, *Creationists*, 112-39; Morris, *History of Modern Creationism*, 114-26.

5. Morris, *History of Modern Creationism*, 130-32; Vernon Lee Bates, "Christian Fundamentalism and the Theory of Evolution in Public School Education: A Study of the Creation Science Movement," Ph.D. diss., Univ. of California, Davis, 1976, pp. 33-36; F. Alton Everest, "The American Scientific Affiliation—The First Decade," *Journal of the American Scientific Affiliation* 3 (Sept. 1951): 35.

6. Morris, *History of Modern Creationism*, 135, 141; Bates, "Christian Fundamentalism," 35; Bernard Ramm, "The Scientifico-Logical Structure of the Theory of Evolution," American Scientific Affiliation *Bulletin* 1 (June 1949): 14.

7. P. W. Stoner, "Fifty Years of Development and Its Impact on Scriptural Interpretation," *Journal of the American Scientific Affiliation* 2 (Sept. 1950): 7-8; Delbert N. Eggenberger, "Gamow's Theory of Element-Building," *Journal of the American Scientific Affiliation* 2 (Sept. 1950): 26.

8. "Editorial," *Journal of the American Scientific Affiliation* 2 (Dec. 1950): i.

9. Irving A. Cowperthwaite, "Some Implications of Evolution for A.S.A.," *Journal of the American Scientific Affiliation* 12 (June 1960): 12-13; Numbers, *Creationists*, 158-83.

10. Morris, *History of Modern Creationism*, 93-100.

11. Ibid., 99, 147-49.

12. Ibid., 146-56; Numbers, *Creationists*, 187-208.

13. John C. Whitcomb and Henry M. Morris, *The Genesis Flood: The Biblical Record and Its Scientific Implications* (1961; Grand Rapids, Mich., 1989), 223-24. See also Morris, *History of Modern Creationism*, 146, 169.

14. Morris, *History of Modern Creationism*, 157-78.

15. "Letters to the Editor," *Journal of the American Scientific Affiliation* 14 (Dec. 1962): 126; John W. Klotz, "Theistic Evolution: Some Theological Implications," *Journal of the American Scientific Affiliation* 15 (Sept. 1963): 85; V. Elving Anderson and David O. Moberg, "Christian Commitment and Evolutionary Concepts," *Journal of the American Scientific Affiliation* 15 (Sept. 1963): 69-70.

16. Numbers, *Creationists*, 214-31; Morris, *History of Modern Creationism*, 181-87, 339.

17. "News and Notes," *Journal of the American Scientific Affiliation* 15 (Dec. 1963): 115; Bates, "Christian Fundamentalism," 80-83; Morris, *History of Modern Creationism*, 187-92; Michael Ruse, "Response to Laudan's Commentary: Pro Judice," in *Creationism, Science, and the Law: The Arkansas Case*, edited by Marcel C. LaFollette (Cambridge, Mass., 1983), 170-71.

18. Morris, *History of Modern Creationism*, 213-15; Bates, "Christian Fundamentalism," 57, 61-62, 74, 167.

19. Morris, *History of Modern Creationism*, 143-44, 163-66.

20. Ibid., 197, 224-26, 231-32; Nelkin, *Creation Controversy*, 79-80; Numbers, *Creationists*, 244, 284-85.

21. Duane T. Gish, "A Challenge to Neo-Darwinism," *American Biology Teacher* 32 (Nov. 1970): 495-96.

22. Ibid., 496-97.

23. Morris, *History of Modern Creationism*, 190-95; Bates, "Christian Fundamentalism," 80.

24. John N. Moore and Harold S. Slusher, eds., *Biology: A Search for Order in Complexity* (1970; Grand Rapids, Mich., 1974), xvii, 4, 7-9, 12.

25. Ibid., 98; see also p. 50.

26. Daniel J. Kevles, *The Physicists: The History of a Scientific Community in Modern America* (New York, 1978), 394-403, 410-14; Nelkin, *Creation Controversy*, 165-67.

27. John A. Moore, "Creationism in California," *Daedalus* 103 (Summer 1974): 177-78; Nelkin, *Creation Controversy*, 108; Webb, "Evolution Controversy in Arizona and California," 146-49.

28. New York *Times*, 12 Oct. 1969; Nelkin, *Creation Controversy*, 109.

29. Moore, "Creationism in California," 176-79; Walter G. Peter III, "Fundamentalist Scientists Oppose Darwinian Evolution," *BioScience* 20 (1 Oct. 1970): 1067-69; San Francisco *Chronicle*, 14 Nov. 1969; Nelkin, *Creation Controversy*, 110.

30. Moore, "Creationism in California," 178-80; Peter, "Fundamentalist Scientists," 1069.

31. "The Monkey War Resumes," *Scientific American* 222 (May 1970): 55-56; Bates, "Christian Fundamentalism," 124-35, 140-49; Moore, "Creationism in California," 180-81; Nelkin, *Creation Controversy*, 110-11.

32. Moore, "Creationism in California," 181; "Statements by Scientists in the California Textbook Dispute," *American Biology Teacher* 34 (Oct. 1972): 411-15; Donald H. Layton, "Scientists versus Fundamentalists: The California Compromise," *Phi Delta Kappan* 54 (June 1973): 697; Los Angeles *Times*, 15 Sept., 13, 18 Oct. 1972.

33. William Bevan, "Two Cooks for the Same Kitchen?" *Science* 177 (29 Sept. 1972): 1155; Moore, "Creationism in California," 181; Norman D. Newell, "Evolution under Attack," *Natural History* 83 (April 1974): 39; New York *Times*, 22 Oct. 1972.

34. Bates, "Christian Fundamentalism," 142-45; Los Angeles *Times*, 10 Nov. 1972.

35. Moore, "Creationism in California," 182-83; Los Angeles *Times*, 10 Nov. 1972; New York *Times*, 12 Dec. 1972.

36. Los Angeles *Times*, 17 Nov., 12 Dec. 1972; Moore, "Creationism in California," 184; Nicholas Wade, "Creationists and Evolutionists: Confrontation in California," *Science* 178 (1972): 728.

37. Moore, "Creationism in California," 183; Los Angeles *Times*, 15 Dec. 1972; New York *Times*, 15 Dec. 1972.

38. Moore, "Creationism in California," 182; Nelkin, *Creation Controversy*, 112-13; Los Angeles *Times*, 15 Dec. 1972.

39. Moore, "Creationism in California," 183-84; Nelkin, *Creation Controversy*, 113-17; Los Angeles *Times*, 12, 13, 21 Jan., 9 Feb., 9 March 1973; New York *Times*, 13 Jan., 10 March 1973.

40. Morris, *History of Modern Creationism*, 232-37; Numbers, *Creationists*, 283-86.

41. James W. Skehan, "The Age of the Earth, of Life, and of Mankind: Geology and Biblical Theology versus Creationism," in *Science and Creation: Geological, Theological & Educational Perspectives*, edited by Robert W. Hanson (New York, 1986), 10.

42. John N. Moore, "Evolution, Creation, and the Scientific Method," *American Biology Teacher* 35 (Jan. 1973): 23-26.

43. Duane T. Gish, "Creation, Evolution, and the Historical Evidence," *American Biology Teacher* 35 (March 1973): 132-40.

44. Nelkin, *Creation Controversy*, 156-63; Larson, *Trial and Error*, 130; "Statements by Scientists in the California Textbook Dispute," 411; Ernst Mayr, letter, *American Biology Teacher* 33 (Jan. 1971): 49-50; Los Angeles *Times*, 31 Dec. 1972.

45. Wendell F. McBurney, review of *Biology: A Search for Order in Complexity*, edited by John N. Moore and Harold S. Slusher, in *American Biology Teacher* 33 (Oct. 1971): 441-42; James L. Mariner, review, *American Biology Teacher* 33 (Oct. 1971): 438-41; Richard P. Aulie, "The Doctrine of Special Creation," *American Biology Teacher* 34 (April 1972): 191-200, and 34 (May 1972): 261-68; Ronald D. Simpson and Wyatt W. Anderson, "Same Song, Second Verse," *Science Teacher* 42 (May 1975): 40-42.

46. Larson, *Trial and Error*, 131-33; *Wright v. Houston Independent School District*, 366 F. Supp. 1208 (1972) at 1208-9.

47. *Wright v. Houston Independent School District*, 366 F. Supp. 1208 (1972) at 1210-11.

48. Ibid., 1211; *Wright v. Houston Independent School District*, 486 F. 2d 137 (1973) at 138; New York *Times*, 18 June 1974.

49. Donald C. Orlich et al., "Creationism in the Science Classroom," *Science Teacher* 42 (May 1975): 43-45; Newell, "Evolution under Attack," 32; Wilhelm, "Chronology," 413-25; Nelkin, *Creation Controversy*, 94.

50. William V. Mayer, "Evolution and the Law," *American Biology Teacher* 35 (March 1973): 144-45; Wilhelm, "Chronology," 415-17.

Chapter 8. A Remedy to a Bad Act

1. Wilhelm, "Chronology," 103; Nashville *Tennessean*, 30 April 1973, 10 May 1981. Artist had contributed several sections to the textbook.

2. Nicholas Wade, "Evolution: Tennessee Picks a New Fight with Darwin," *Science* 182 (1973): 696; Larson, *Trial and Error*, 134; *Senate Journal of the Eighty-Eighth General Assembly of the State of Tennessee* (Nashville, 1973), 345, 356; Senate Bill 394 (1973), author's files. For an analysis of the passage of the Genesis Act, see George E. Webb, "Demographic Change and Antievolution Sentiment: Tennessee as a Case Study, 1925-1975," *Creation/Evolution* 8 (Fall 1988): 37-43.

3. *House Journal of the Eighty-Eighth General Assembly of the State of Tennessee* (Nashville, 1973), 533, 567, 844, 1088; *Senate Journal* (1973), 599, 608; Wilhelm, "Chronology," 253-55.

4. Nashville *Tennessean*, 17, 18 April 1973.

5. *Senate Journal* (1973), 742-44, 751; Nashville *Tennessean*, 19 April 1973; transcript dated 18 April 1973, Tennessee Senate, author's files.

6. Larson, *Trial and Error*, 137; Nashville *Tennessean*, 23, 24, 27 April 1973; House Amendments 5, 6, author's files.

7. *House Journal* (1973), 1157-58; Nashville *Tennessean*, 27 April 1973.

8. Nashville *Tennessean*, 30 April, 9 May 1973; *Senate Journal* (1973), 1046-49, 1301, 1527; *House Journal* (1973), 1502, 1574.

9. Plaintiffs' Brief, *Harold Steele et al. v. Hugh Waters et al.*, Davidson County Chancery Court, Nashville, Tennessee, no. A-3407.

10. "Constitutionality of Genesis," *Intellect* 102 (1974): 419; Appellants' Brief, *Joseph C. Daniel et al. v. Hugh Waters et al.*, no. 74-2230, U.S. Court of Appeals, Sixth Circuit, 1974, appendix. A good summary of the plaintiffs' legal perspective is

Frederic S. Le Clercq, "The Monkey Laws and the Public Schools: A Second Consumption?" *Vanderbilt Law Review* 27 (1974): 209-42.

11. Bates, "Christian Fundamentalism," 177-80; Morris, *History of Modern Creationism*, 309.

12. Moore, "Creationism in California," 184; Nelkin, *Creation Controversy*, 118.

13. Larson, *Trial and Error*, 141.

14. Los Angeles *Times*, 11 July 1975.

15. Morris, *History of Modern Creationism*, 246-48; Warren D. Dolphin, "A Brief Critical Analysis of Scientific Creationism," in *Did the Devil Make Darwin Do It?* edited by David B. Wilson (Ames, Iowa, 1983), 25; Henry M. Morris, ed., *Scientific Creationism*, public school ed. (San Diego, 1974), iii-iv.

16. Morris, ed., *Scientific Creationism*, 4-5.

17. Ibid., 99-100, 131, 135, 137, 193.

18. Ibid., 136.

19. Ibid., 200-201.

20. Larson, *Trial and Error*, 139-40, 205 n. 80; Nelkin, *Creation Controversy*, 65, 94.

21. Wilhelm, "Chronology," 255-56, 426-27, 431-32, 434-35, 438-41; Orlich et al., "Creationism in the Science Classroom," 43-45; Seattle *Times*, 17 Feb. 1973.

22. Bates, "Christian Fundamentalism," 173; Nelkin, *Creation Controversy*, 95-96; Edward B. Jenkinson, "Schoolbook Skirmishes," *National Forum* 66 (1986): 44.

23. Nelkin, *Creation Controversy*, 97; Wilhelm, "Chronology," 264, 266.

24. Wilhelm, "Chronology," 94-97, 421-24, 436-37; Nelkin, *Creation Controversy*, 99, 168; Kenneth S. Saladin, "Educational Approaches to Creationist Politics in Georgia," in *Science and Creation*, ed. Hanson, 106.

25. Wilhelm, "Chronology," 96-97; New York *Times*, 23 June 1974.

26. Joseph B. Platt, "NSF and Science Education—Who, Why, and How Did It Work Out?" *Journal of General Education* 27 (1975): 188-98; Gerald D. Skoog, "The Topic of Evolution in Secondary School Biology Textbooks: 1900-1977," *Science Education* 63 (1979): 622; New York *Times*, 10 July 1975.

27. Wilhelm, "Chronology," 432-33, 435; John A. Moore, "On Giving Equal Time to the Teaching of Evolution and Creation," *Perspectives in Biology and Medicine* 18 (1975): 405-9, 411-12, 413-16.

28. Per Curiam Opinion, *Joseph C. Daniel, Jr., et al. v. Hugh Waters et al.*, Civil Action no. 7340, U.S. District Court, Middle District of Tennessee, Nashville Division, 26 Feb. 1974.

29. Memorandum Opinion, *Harold Steele et al. v. Hugh Waters et al.*, Davidson County Chancery Court, Nashville, Tennessee, No. A-3407, 9 Sept. 1974; New York *Times*, 11, 15 Sept. 1974.

30. Appellants' Brief, *Daniel v. Waters*.

31. Appellees' Brief, *Daniel v. Waters*.

32. *Daniel v. Waters*, 515 F. 2d 485 (1975) at 486-89.

33. Ibid., 489, 491-92.

34. *Steele v. Waters*, 527 S.W. 2d 72(1975); New York *Times*, 13 April, 21 August 1975.

35. Larson, *Trial and Error*, 139.

36. Henry M. Morris, *The Troubled Waters of Evolution* (San Diego, 1974), 5.

37. Ibid., 13, 16, 18-19, 123.

38. Robert E. Kofahl and Kelly L. Segraves, *The Creation Explanation: A Scientific Alternative to Evolution* (Wheaton, Ill., 1975), xi-xii.

39. Ibid., xiii.

40. Ibid., 33-45, 50-55, 154-55, 200, 204.

41. Ibid., 11-12, 16.

42. Ibid., 77, 139, 145.

43. Ibid., 218-19.

44. Wilhelm, "Chronology," 243, 442-48; Byron E. Jordan, letter, *Science Teacher* 42 (1975): 38-40; Bates, "Christian Fundamentalism," 174.

45. "Unequal Time," *Scientific American* 236 (1977): 61; Wilhelm, "Chronology," 107-8; New York *Times*, 28 Jan. 1977.

46. Larson, *Trial and Error*, 144-45; Wilhelm, "Chronology," 243.

47. Larson, *Trial and Error*, 145-46; Wilhelm, "Chronology," 111-12, 248-49; New York *Times*, 18 April 1977.

48. New York *Times*, 12 April, 14 Dec. 1978; "Creationists Sue to Ban Museum Evolution Exhibits," *Science* 204 (1979): 925; *Crowley v. Smithsonian Inst.*, 462 F. Supp. 725 (1978) at 726-27.

49. *Crowley v. Smithsonian Inst.*, 462 F. Supp. 725 (1978) at 726-28.

50. New York *Times*, 14 Dec. 1978; 19 May 1979. "Creationists Sue to Ban Museum Evolution Exhibits," 925; Larson, *Trial and Error*, 134.

51. "News Briefs," *Creation/Evolution* 3 (1982): 46-48; Roger Lewin, "A Response to Creationism Evolves," *Science* 214 (1981): 635-38.

Chapter 9. The Creationist Challenge

1. Jenkinson, "Schoolbook Skirmishes," 45.

2. John W. Whitehead and John Conlan, "The Establishment of the Religion of Secular Humanism and Its First Amendment Implications," *Texas Tech Law Review* 10 (1978): 1, 10, 13.

3. Ibid., 18, 42-43, 47-51, 65.

4. Larson, *Trial and Error*, 147-49; Wendell R. Bird, "Freedom of Religion and Science Instruction in Public Schools," *Yale Law Journal* 87 (Jan. 1978): 515-70.

5. Bird, "Freedom of Religion," 518, 523-27, 532-33, 542-43, 547.

6. Ibid., 556-58, 564, 567-70.

7. Wendell R. Bird, "Freedom from Establishment and Unneutrality in Public School Instruction and Religious School Regulation," *Harvard Journal of Law and Public Policy* 2 (1979): 128-29, 139; Whitehead and Conlan, "Establishment of the Religion of Secular Humanism," 3-4.

8. Levy, *Establishment Clause*, 1, 8-10, 25-65, 74-79, 83-84, 108, 114-16.

9. Ibid., 106, 178, 182.

10. Ibid., 130-31, 148-49, 162-67.

11. Larson, *Trial and Error*, 130, 149-50; Roger Lewin, "A Tale with Many Connections," *Science* 215 (1982): 484.

12. Morris, *History of Modern Creationism*, 288; Lewin, "Tale with Many Connections," 484; Larson, *Trial and Error*, 151.

13. Duane T. Gish, *Evolution? The Fossils Say NO!* public school ed. (San Diego, 1978), 7-8.

14. Ibid., 11, 40.

15. Ibid., 24, 26-27, 174.

16. Gerald D. Skoog, "Legal Issues Involved in Evolution vs. Creationism," *Educational Leadership* 38 (1980): 154; New York *Times*, 24 Nov. 1979; Saladin, "Educational Approaches," 107-8; Nelkin, *Creation Controversy*, 99.

17. Jack A. Gerlovich and Stanley L. Weinberg, "The Battle in Iowa: Qualified Success," in *Did the Devil Make Darwin Do It?* ed. Wilson, 189-90; Jack A. Gerlovich et al., "Creationism in Iowa,"*Science* 208 (1980): 1208-11; *Wall Street Journal*, 15 June 1979.

18. New York *Times*, 3 June 1979; Gerlovich and Weinberg, "Battle in Iowa," 194-98; Gerlovich et al., "Creationism in Iowa," 1208, 1210.

19. *Wall Street Journal*, 15 June 1979; Barbara Parker, "Creation vs. Evolution: Teaching the Origin of Man," *American Biology Teacher* 167 (1980): 25-26, 31; Nelkin, *Creation Controversy*, 94.

20. Cheryl M. Fields, "Creationism Debate: Next Round May Be in Local School Boards," *Chronicle of Higher Education* 25 (15 Dec. 1982): 1, 10.

21. Saladin, "Educational Approaches," 110.

22. Stephen G. Brush, "Creationism/Evolution: The Case AGAINST Equal Time," *Science Teacher* 48 (1981): 31 n. 4; Morris, *History of Modern Creationism*, 277-79.

23. Morris, *History of Modern Creationism*, 227, 234, 244-46; Los Angeles *Times*, 6 March 1981; Jenkinson, "Schoolbook Skirmishes," 45.

24. New York *Times*, 7 April 1980; Morris, *History of Modern Creationism*, 239-42, 255, 266-70, 361-65.

25. *Wall Street Journal*, 15 June 1979; New York *Times*, 7 April 1980; James Podgers, "Courts Focus on New Evolution Debate," *American Bar Association Journal* 66 (1980): 551-52; Morris, *History of Modern Creationism*, 308-9, 316-17.

26. Kenneth M. Pierce, "Putting Darwin Back in the Dock," *Time* 117 (16 March 1981): 80; William J. Broad, "Louisiana Puts God into Biology Lessons," *Science* 213 (1981): 628-29; Chris Pipho, "Scientific Creationism: A Case Study," *Education and Urban Society* 13 (1981): 230-32.

27. Roger Lewin, "New Creationism Bill Already Drafted," *Science* 214 (1981): 1224.

28. John Schweinsberg, "The Alabama Creation Battle," *Creation/Evolution* 2 (1981): 31-32.

29. "News Briefs," *Creation/Evolution* 2 (1981): 33-38; William V. Mayer, "Through the Looking-Glass in Colorado," *American Biology Teacher* 43 (1981): 331-32, 340; Lewin, "Response to Creationism Evolves," 635-38.

30. Constance Holden, "Republican Candidate Picks Fight with Darwin," *Science* 209 (1980): 1214; New York *Times*, 7 April 1980; Pierce, "Putting Darwin Back in the Dock," 80; Lewin, "Response to Creationism Evolves," 638; "New Battle over Teaching of Evolution," *U.S. News & World Report* 88 (9 June 1980): 82; Schweinsberg, "Alabama Creation Battle," 31.

31. San Francisco *Chronicle*, 14 March, 5 Dec. 1980; 5 Feb. 1981. New York *Times*, 26 Dec. 1980; Los Angeles *Times*, 6 March 1981.

32. Pierce, "Putting Darwin Back in the Dock," 80; Washington *Post*, 23 July 1981; "News Briefs," *Creation/Evolution* 2 (1981): 2.

33. William M. Thwaites, "A Two-Model Creation versus Evolution Course," in *Science and Creation*, ed. Hanson, 92; Frederick Edwords, "Creation-Evolution Debates: Who's Winning Them Now?" *Creation/Evolution* 3 (1982): 33-34.

34. Washington *Post*, 23 July 1981; "TV Debate on Creationism," *Science* 214 (1981): 37.

35. Stephen W. Tweedie, "Viewing the Bible Belt," *Journal of Popular Culture* 11 (1978): 865-76; Ribuffo, *Old Christian Right*, 262-68. A valuable analysis of this religious movement is Carol Flake, *Redemptorama: Culture, Politics, and the New Evangelicalism* (New York, 1985).

36. Jeffrey L. Brudney and Gary W. Copeland, "Evangelicals as a Political Force: Reagan and the 1980 Religious Vote," *Social Science Quarterly* 65 (1984): 1072-79; Holden, "Republican Candidate Picks Fight with Darwin," 1214; New York *Times*, 24, 27 Aug. 1980; "Carter on Continuous Creation," *Science* 210 (1980): 35.

37. Roger Lewin, "Evolutionary Theory under Fire," *Science* 210 (1980): 883-87; Nicholas Wade, "Dinosaur Battle Erupts in British Museum," *Science* 211 (1981): 35-

36; Roger Lewin, "Lamarck Will Not Lie Down," *Science* 213 (1981): 316-21; G.L. Stebbins and F.J. Ayala, "Is a New Evolutionary Synthesis Necessary?" *Science* 213 (1981): 967-71.

38. John R. Cole, "Misquoted Scientists Respond," *Creation/Evolution* 2 (1981): 34-44; Pierce, "Putting Darwin Back in the Dock," 82; Craig Pearson, "Can Teachers Cope with Creationism?" *Learning* 9 (1981): 33.

39. Nelkin, *Creation Controversy,* 161-63; Pierce, "Putting Darwin Back in the Dock," 82.

40. Morris, *History of Modern Creationism,* 317-18; editorial, *Creation/Evolution* 1 (1980); Wayne A. Moyer, "The Problem Won't Go Away," *American Biology Teacher* 42 (1980): 234; Nicholas Wade, "AAAS in Canada Seeks Peace without Hawks," *Science* 211 (1981): 368-69; Lewin, "Response to Creationism Evolves," 635-36; "The 'Creation-Science' Challenge," *Academe* 67 (Oct. 1981): 298.

41. "New Battle over Teaching of Evolution," 82; Richard A. Walker et al., "Clarifying the Creation-Evolution Issue with Biology Students," *American Biology Teacher* 39 (1977): 49-51; Richard D. Alexander, "Evolution, Creation, and Biology Teaching," *American Biology Teacher* 40 (1978): 91-104, 107; Catherine A. Callaghan, "Evolution and Creationist Arguments," *American Biology Teacher* 42 (1980): 422-25, 427.

42. Harvey Siegel, "Creationism, Evolution, and Education: The California Fiasco," *Phi Delta Kappan* 63 (1981): 97-100.

43. Niles Eldredge, letter, *Science* 212 (1981): 737; "Finding: Let Kids Decide How We Got Here," *American School Board Journal* 167 (1980): 52.

44. Morris, *History of Modern Creationism,* 310; Nashville *Tennessean,* 15 Feb. 1981.

45. James Shymansky, "BSCS Programs: Just How Effective Were They?" *American Biology Teacher* 46 (1984): 54-57.

46. Stuart W. Hughes, "The Fact and the Theory of Evolution," *American Biology Teacher* 44 (1982): 25-32; Arthur Woodward and David L. Elliott, "Evolution and Creationism in High School Textbooks," *American Biology Teacher* 49 (1987): 164-70; Robert Dahlin, "A Tough Time for Textbooks," *Publishers Weekly* 220 (7 Aug. 1981): 28-32.

47. San Francisco *Chronicle,* 28 Feb. 1981; William J. Broad, "Creationists Limit Scope of Evolution Case," *Science* 211 (1981): 1331-32; Siegel, "Creationism, Evolution, and Education," 95-96.

48. San Francisco *Chronicle,* 14 March 1980; 22 Feb., 3 March 1981. Los Angeles *Times,* 4 March 1981; San Diego *Union,* 2 March 1981.

49. San Francisco *Chronicle,* 22, 28 Feb. 1981; Broad, "Creationists Limit Scope," 1332.

50. San Francisco *Chronicle,* 3 March 1981; Larson, *Trial and Error,* 142.

51. San Francisco *Chronicle,* 4 March 1981; Broad, "Creationists Limit Scope," 1331.

52. Los Angeles *Times,* 4 March 1981; New York *Times,* 6 March 1981; San Francisco *Chronicle,* 4 March 1981; Thomas H. Jukes, "Creationists in Court: Sacramento, 1981," *Perspectives in Biology and Medicine* 25 (1982): 211, 217.

53. Jukes, "Creationists in Court," 210-11; San Francisco *Chronicle,* 5 March 1981; Los Angeles *Times,* 6 March 1981.

54. San Francisco *Examiner,* 8 March 1981; Los Angeles *Times,* 7 March 1981; Jukes, "Creationists in Court," 214.

55. Larson, *Trial and Error,* 143; Broad, "Creationists Limit Scope," 1331; New York *Times,* 7 March 1981; San Francisco *Chronicle,* 5 March 1981.

56. Siegel, "Creationism, Evolution, and Education," 101; Los Angeles *Times,* 13 March 1981.

57. Pearson, "Can Teachers Cope," 33; Washington *Post*, 23 July 1981.

58. Broad, "Creationists Limit Scope," 1331-32; Los Angeles *Times*, 15 March 1981; San Francisco *Chronicle*, 18 March 1981.

Chapter 10. Somewhere in Heaven, John Scopes Is Smiling

1. Lewin, "Tale with Many Connections," 484-85.

2. Ibid., 485.

3. Ibid., 485-86.

4. Ibid., 484, 486; *McLean v. Arkansas Board of Education*, 529 F. Supp. 1255 (1982) at 1262.

5. Larson, *Trial and Error*, 151-52; Lewin, "Tale with Many Connections," 486.

6. Larson, *Trial and Error*, 152-53; Lewin, "Tale with Many Connections," 486-87; New York *Times*, 18, 22 March 1981.

7. Larson, *Trial and Error*, 153, 156-57; Lewin, "Tale with Many Connections," 487.

8. Peggy L. Kerr, "The Creation-Science Case and Pro Bono Publico," and Marcel C. LaFollette, "Introduction," both in *Creationism, Science, and the Law*, ed. LaFollette, 114-21, 7; Michael Ruse, "A Philosopher's Day in Court," in *Science and Creationism*, edited by Ashley Montagu (New York, 1984), 320-21, 327. A good overview of the trial, written by one of the plaintiffs' key witnesses, is Langdon Gilkey, *Creationism on Trial: Evolution and God at Little Rock* (San Francisco, 1985).

9. See *McLean v. Arkansas Board of Education*, 529 F. Supp. 1255 (1982) at 1256-57; "The Legal Arguments: Excerpts from the Plaintiffs' Preliminary Outline and Pre-Trial Brief," and "Legal Arguments: Excerpts from the Defendants' Preliminary Outline and Pre-Trial Brief," both in *Creationism, Science, and the Law*, ed. LaFollette, 22-30, 33-41.

10. Roger Lewin, "Creationism Goes on Trial in Arkansas," *Science* 214 (1981): 1104; Lewin, "Tale with Many Connections," 487; Gilkey, *Creationism on Trial*, 83-87, 100-119.

11. Gilkey, *Creationism on Trial*, 87-91, 128-32, 140-44; Ruse, "Philosopher's Day in Court," 330-35.

12. Larson, *Trial and Error*, 159-60; Ruse, "Philosopher's Day in Court," 335-36; Gilkey, *Creationism on Trial*, 76-77; New York *Times*, 12 Dec. 1981.

13. Larson, *Trial and Error*, 161-63; Ruse, "Philosopher's Day in Court," 331; New York *Times*, 10, 12, 16, 18, 24 Dec. 1981.

14. *McLean v. Arkansas Board of Education*, 529 F. Supp. 1255 (1982) at 1257-58, 1263-72.

15. Ibid., 1274; "Darwin Wins," *Time* 119 (18 Jan. 1982): 63; Roger Lewin, "Judge's Ruling Hits Hard at Creationism," *Science* 215 (1982): 381; R. Jeffrey Smith, "Arkansas Declines Appeal of Ruling on Creationism," *Science* 215 (1982): 949.

16. "Creationism in Schools: The Decision in *McLean versus the Arkansas Board of Education*," *Science* 215 (1982): 934-43; Jerry Adler and John Carey, "Enigmas of Evolution," *Newsweek* 99 (29 March 1982): 44-49.

17. Lewin, "Judge's Ruling Hits Hard," 384; Ribuffo, *Old Christian Right*, 268; Jenkinson, "Schoolbook Skirmishes," 45; New York *Times*, 29 Aug. 1982.

18. Broad, "Louisiana Puts God into Biology Lessons," 628-29; Larson, *Trial and Error*, 153-54.

19. Broad, "Louisiana Puts God into Biology Lessons," 629; Larson, *Trial and Error*, 154-55; New York *Times*, 22 July 1981; Thomas H. Jukes, "U.S. Supreme Court to Review Louisiana's Appeal," *Nature* 324 (1986): 423.

20. Broad, "Louisiana Puts God into Biology Lessons," 629; Larson, *Trial and Error*, 163-65; *Keith v. Louisiana Department of Education*, 553 F. Supp. 295 (1982) at

296-300. New York *Times*, 4 Nov. 1982; 20 June 1987. Roger Lewin, "ACLU 2, Creationists 0," *Science* 218 (1982): 1099.

21. New York *Times*, 23 Nov. 1982; Nashville *Tennessean*, 24 Sept. 1982; Larson, *Trial and Error*, 165; Roger Lewin, "Creationists, ACLU to Do Battle Again," *Science* 222 (1983): 488.

22. Frederick Edwords, "Creation-Evolution Debates: Who's Winning Them Now?" *Creation/Evolution* 3 (1982): 30-42; Tucson *Citizen*, 7 Jan. 1982.

23. Karen J. Winkler, "Concerned over Scientific Illiteracy, Scholars Enter Creationist Debate," *Chronicle of Higher Education* 25 (15 Dec. 1982): 33-34; Roland M. Frye, "So-Called 'Creation-Science' and Mainstream Christian Objections," *Proceedings of the American Philosophical Society* 127 (1983): 61-70; Richard P. Aulie, "Evolution and Special Creation: Historical Aspects of the Controversy," *Proceedings of the American Philosophical Society* 127 (1983): 418-62; George M. Marsden, "Creation versus Evolution: No Middle Way," *Nature* 305 (1983): 571-74; Thomas H. Jukes, "The Creationist Challenge to Science," *Nature* 308 (1984): 398-400.

24. Winkler, "Concerned over Scientific Illiteracy," 34; Niles Eldredge, *The Monkey Business: A Scientist Looks at Creationism* (New York, 1982); Norman D. Newell, *Creation and Evolution: Myth or Reality?* (New York, 1982); Douglas J. Futuyma, *Science on Trial: The Case for Evolution* (New York, 1983).

25. Philip Kitcher, *Abusing Science: The Case against Creationism* (Cambridge, Mass., 1982), 4; Michael Ruse, *Darwinism Defended: A Guide to the Evolution Controversies* (Reading, Mass., 1982), 303-19, 327-29.

26. Ruse, *Darwinism Defended*, 315.

27. Ibid., 321.

28. "News Briefs," *Creation/Evolution* 4 (1983): 43; Morris, *History of Modern Creationism*, 105-6, 237, 250-52, 257-66, 292-93, 304, 328-29, 341-47.

29. Morris, *History of Modern Creationism*, 311, 331-32.

30. "News Briefs," *Creation/Evolution* 3 (1982): 43-44; "Legislation Concerning the Teaching of 'Creation-Science' and 'Evolution-Science' in the Public Schools of Maryland: Excerpts from the Opinion of the Attorney General of the State of Maryland," in *Creationism, Science, and the Law*, ed. LaFollette, 221-27; Roger Lewin, "Creationist Bill Fails in Maryland," *Science* 215 (1982): 1378-79.

31. *Arizona Daily Reporter*, 8 Feb. 1982; Tucson *Citizen*, 23 April 1983; "News Briefs," *Creation/Evolution* 4 (1983): 35.

32. "Creationism in the Legislature," *Vigil* (Summer 1985): 1; Nashville *Tennessean*, 28 Feb., 15 April 1985.

33. Fields, "Creationism Debate," 1, 10; Gerlovich and Weinberg, "Battle in Iowa," 198-99.

34. Stephen Budiansky, "Creationism: Still in Evidence in Texas," *Nature* 306 (1983): 529; "The Texas Textbook Censors: Bad for the Image," *Discover* 5 (Jan. 1984): 6; "Texas Drops Requirement of 'Evolution as Theory'," *Publisher's Weekly* 225 (27 April 1984): 19; Roger Lewin, "Antievolution Rules Are Unconstitutional," *Science* 223 (1984): 1373-74; New York *Times*, 14 March 1984.

35. "Texas Textbook Censors," 6; Roger Lewin, "Texas Repeals Antievolution Rules," *Science* 224 (1984): 370; Colin Norman, "A Guide to Biology Texts," *Science* 227 (1985): 731; New York *Times*, 14, 15 April, 3 June 1984.

36. Thomas H. Jukes, "The Fight for Science Textbooks," *Nature* 319 (1986): 367-68; Eliot Marshall, "Science Textbooks Too Bland for California," *Science* 230 (1985): 48; New York *Times*, 14 Sept. 1985.

37. Eliot Marshall, "Dinosaurs Ruffle Some Feathers in California," *Science* 231 (1986): 18-19; Jukes, "Fight for Science Textbooks," 367-68; Tim Beardsley, "California Sells Out on Textbooks," *Nature* 318 (1985): 592; New York *Times*, 14, 15, 17 Sept. 1985.

38. Kim McDonald, "Pervasive Belief in 'Creation Science' Dismays and Perplexes Researchers," *Chronicle of Higher Education* 33 (10 Dec. 1986): 7.

39. *Arizona Republic,* 5 Feb. 1987; Nashville *Tennessean,* 8 April 1987.

40. Eugenie C. Scott and Henry P. Cole, "The Elusive Scientific Basis of Creation 'Science'," *Quarterly Review of Biology* 60 (1985): 26-28; Tony Thulborn, "On the Tracks of Men and Money," *Nature* 320 (1986): 308; Laurie R. Godfrey, "Foot Notes of an Anatomist," *Creation/Evolution* 5 (1985): 16-36; New York *Times,* 17 June 1986.

41. Skehan, "Age of the Earth," 20-29.

42. Richard Dawkins, *The Blind Watchmaker* (New York, 1987).

43. Michael A. Cavanaugh, "Scientific Creationism and Rationality," *Nature* 315 (1985): 185-89.

44. Langdon Gilkey, "The Creationism Issue: A Theologian's View," in *Science and Creation,* ed. Hanson, 174-88.

45. "Creationism Defeated in Louisiana Senate," *Science* 224 (1984): 1079; "Creationism Survives in Louisiana Legislature," *Science* 225 (1984): 36; Morris, *History of Modern Creationism,* 291-92.

46. Roger Lewin, "Louisiana Judge Voids Creationism Law," *Science* 227 (1985): 395; Larson, *Trial and Error,* 165-66.

47. Washington *Post,* 9 July 1985; Roger Lewin, "Creationism Downed Again in Louisiana," *Science* 231 (1986): 112; New York *Times,* 6 May 1986.

48. Levy, *Establishment Clause,* xi-xvi, 92, 154-56, 171-72.

49. New York *Times,* 6 May, 19 Aug. 1986; Jukes, "U.S. Supreme Court to Review," 423-24; Colin Norman, "Nobelists Unite against 'Creation Science'," *Science* 233 (1986): 935.

50. "Creationism Case Argued before Supreme Court," *Science* 235 (1987): 22-23; New York *Times,* 11 Dec. 1986.

51. *Edwards v. Aguillard,* 482 U.S. 578 (1987) at 585-89. Acadiana High School assistant principal Donald Aguillard was one of many plaintiffs in this case. His name appeared first on court documents.

52. Ibid., 587, 591-95, 596-97.

53. Ibid., 599, 605-8.

54. Ibid., 610-13, 619-21, 625-26.

55. Ibid., 626-32, 634.

56. Ibid., 634.

57. Ibid., 639.

58. Ted Gest, "High Court: The Day God and Darwin Collided," *U.S. News & World Report* 102 (29 June 1987): 12; New York *Times,* 20 June 1987.

59. New York *Times,* 20 June 1987.

Epilogue

1. John H. Buchanan, "Religiously Inspired Censorship in Public Schools," *National Forum* 68 (1988): 34-35.

2. Michael Zimmerman, "The Science Budget Must Be Insulated from the Creationist Threat," *Chronicle of Higher Education* 35 (8 Feb. 1989): B2.

3. Barbara J. Culliton, "The Dismal State of Scientific Literacy," *Science* 243 (1989): 600; Jill Rachlin, "Finding the Right Formula," *U.S. News & World Report* 105 (14 Nov. 1988): 59-61.

4. Nashville *Tennessean,* 11 Sept. 1988.

5. New York *Times,* 8 Dec. 1988.

6. Thomas H. Jukes, "More on the ICR-California Settlement," National Center for Science Education [NCSE] *Reports* 12 (Spring 1992): 3, 11; Yvonne Baskin, "Cre-

ationist School Lives On," *Science* 251 (1991): 738; "Creationism Compromise," *Science* 252 (1992): 927.

7. Marcia Baringa, "California Backs Evolution Education," *Science* 246 (1989): 881; Thomas H. Jukes, "California Evolution Guideline," *Science* 246 (1989): 1374; New York *Times*, 14 Jan., 27 July, 14 Nov. 1989.

8. "Darwin Back on the Books," *Science* 250 (1990): 1335; Joseph D. McInerney, "Biology Textbooks," *Science* 251 (1991): 606. New York *Times*, 27 July 1989; 13 Nov. 1990. Washington *Post*, 11 Nov. 1990.

9. New York *Times*, 24 Oct. 1990; "Science's Litmus Test," *Harper's Magazine* 282 (March 1991): 28-32.

10. Phillip Johnson, *Darwin on Trial* (Washington, D.C., 1991); "Johnson vs. Darwin," *Science* 253 (1991): 379; Doug Bandow, "Fossils and Fallacies," *National Review* 43 (29 April 1991): 47-48; Stephen Jay Gould, "Impeaching a Self-Appointed Judge," *Scientific American* 267 (July 1992): 118-21.

11. Ken Sidey, "The Hazards of Choice," *Christianity Today* 35 (24 July 1991): 18; "Choice in Schools," *Congressional Digest* 70 (1991): 290-314; Chester E. Finn, Jr., "Taking Charge," *National Review* 44 (6 July 1992): 42-44; Abigail Thernstrom, "Hobson's Choice," *New Republic* 205 (15, 22 July 1991): 13-16.

12. John R. Cole, "Stealth Politics," NCSE *Reports* 12 (Fall 1992): 1, 3, 15; "Creationism Instruction Mandated by Iowa GOP," NCSE *Reports* 12 (Fall 1992): 5; Nashville *Tennessean*, 6 Dec. 1992.

13. New York *Times*, 27 July 1989; Connie Goddard, "Court Says School May Bar Teaching Creationism," *Publishers Weekly* 237 (23 Nov. 1990): 10.

14. Eugenie C. Scott, "Creationists No Longer Invited to Peoria Public Schools," NCSE *Reports* 12 (Spring 1992): 8; Ransom R. Traxler, "Creationism in Many Illinois Schools," NCSE *Reports* 11 (Summer 1991): 4.

15. Eugenie C. Scott, "Creationists No Longer Invited to Peoria Public Schools," NCSE *Reports* 12 (Spring 1992): 8; Ransom R. Traxler, "Creationism in Many Illinois Schools," NCSE *Reports* 11 (Summer 1991): 4-5.

16. Eugenie C. Scott, "California Creationist Teacher Sues District," NCSE *Reports* 11 (Summer 1991): 1, 6; idem, "Peloza Lawsuit Dismissed by Federal Judge!" NCSE *Reports* 11 (Winter 1991): 1, 17, 22-23.

17. Eugenie C. Scott, "Creationist Cases Blooming," NCSE *Reports* 12 (Summer 1992): 3, 5.

Index

Abbot, Rev. Francis Ellingwood, 30
Abington v. Schempp, 140, 151, 205
acquired characteristics, inheritance of, 2, 14, 23-28, 43-45
Agassiz, Louis, 7-12, 15-16, 19, 22-23; criticisms of Darwinian evolution, 11-12
Aguillard, Donald, 251, 288 n 51
Ahlstrom, Sydney E., 33, 119
Alabama, 74, 100, 213, 247-48
Alaska, 215
Allen, Harbor, 105
American Academy of Arts and Sciences, 9
American Anthropological Association, 242
American Antievolution Association, 102
American Association for the Advancement of Science, 15, 26-27, 46, 61; and challenges to antievolutionism, 77, 105, 111; and challenges to creation science, 190-91, 219
American Association of University Professors, 77, 95, 105, 219
American Biology Teacher, 114, 142, 163-64, 175-76, 219
American Civil Liberties Union, 105, 148, 241, 252; and Scopes Trial, 85, 91; and antievolution legislation, 94-95, 107; and *Epperson v. Arkansas*, 143, 151; and *McLean v. Arkansas*, 230-32, 234; and *Edwards v. Aguillard*, 237, 248
American Council of Christian Churches, 118
American Institute of Biological Sciences, 128-32
American Jewish Congress, 151

American Journal of Science and Arts, 7, 10-11
American Medical Association, 104
American Naturalist, 23-24, 27, 35, 37, 44, 47
American Philosophical Society: *Proceedings*, 238
American Scientific Affiliation, 157-58, 160, 163, 168, 173; *Journal*, 157, 160
Anderson, John B., 217
antievolution crusade (1920s): and fundamentalism, 55-58, 64-66, 70-72, 78-79, 93, 106-8; origins of, 56-57, 62-66; and William Jennings Bryan, 66-70, 73-74, 78, 81-82, 84; legislative efforts, 72-74, 79-80, 82-84, 93-97, 99-103; scientists' challenges to, 76-78, 104-6
Aristotle, 1
Arizona, 75, 98-99, 137-39, 241, 244
Arizona Academy of Sciences, 139
Arizona, University of, 75, 237-38
Arkansas, 81, 142; and antievolution legislation, 101-4, 107; and *Epperson v. Arkansas*, 143-45, 149-53; and "equal time" legislation, 228-30, 247; and *McLean v. Arkansas*, 231-37
Arkansas Congress of Parents and Teachers, 143
Arkansas Education Association, 142-44
Arkansas School Boards Association, 143
Artist, Russell, 141, 180
Atlantic Monthly, 12
Aulie, Richard P., 176, 238
Avery, Oswald T., 127
Awbrey, Frank, 215
Ayala, Francisco, 233

SCIENCE

Florida Creationism Battle

Creationis... ...ing better
teaching o... methods

**Evolution,
creationism
debate slated**

Monkey or Mud in ...

'Creationism'
Back in Schools
As New Science

...na?

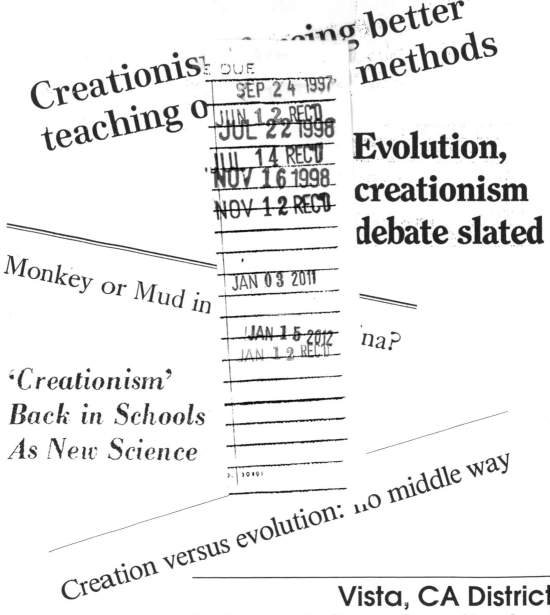

DATE DUE

SEP 2 4 1997
JUN 1 2 RECD
JUL 22 1998
JUL 14 RECD
NOV 16 1998
NOV 1 2 RECD

JAN 03 2011

JAN 1 5 2012
JAN 1 2 RECD

Creation versus evolution: no middle way

Vista, CA District
in Turmoil Over Creationism